Praise for Johanna van Wijk-Bos's
Making Wise the Simple

"While there are several fairly recent fine treatments of the Torah/Pentateuch currently available, Johanna van Wijk-Bos's study achieves a special preeminence. . . . This is a 'must-read' for all who would engage the Torah/Pentateuch for what it has to contribute to our contemporary faith."

— GEORGE M. LANDES
Union Theological Seminary,
New York

"Johanna van Wijk-Bos has written an intelligent and empathetic introduction to the five books of Moses for a Christian readership. Stretching from the story of human hubris in Genesis 11 to the plea for human inclusiveness in Galatians 3, the book offers an open-minded appreciation of Mosaic law and lore that does not dodge unpopular subjects. The argument is rich and thoughtful throughout, sensitive both to 'the limits set by the ancient context' and to 'the urgency of our questions.' It is written in clear and lucid language that, along with the continual scholarly references in the footnotes, makes it pleasant and instructive reading both for students in theology and for interested general readers."

— PETER J. TOMSON
Faculty of Protestant Theology,
Brussels, Belgium

"Leading the charge against an array of popular Christian distortions of the Torah, van Wijk-Bos exposes their perversity with clear biblical evidence. By stripping away the gross misunderstandings that have fed anti-Jewish sentiments for centuries, she also opens up space for the true heart of both the Torah and Christianity."

— ALICE OGDEN BELLIS
Howard University
School of Divinity

D0877602

"Johanna van Wijk-Bos has done Christians, particularly clergy and clergy in training, a great service with her book *Making Wise the Simple*. Her description (borrowing from Jacob Neusner and John the Evangelist) of the Torah as 'God made flesh' illuminates the Torah as God-space and the site of divine disclosure in terms familiar to Christian readers. . . . She does not romanticize the text, recognizing that the deity does indulge in favoritism. Ultimately, she encourages Christians to read not as Jews, but with Jews, to discern the revelation of the Holy One of Sinai in the sacred text."

— WIL GAFNEY
*Lutheran Theological Seminary
at Philadelphia*

"This study demonstrates why a thorough understanding of the Torah is essential for Christian faith. It shows, for example, how texts from the New Testament may enter into conversation with texts from the Hebrew Bible, taking into account the historical circumstances of both biblical and modern times. By doing so, the author does not offer a Jewish reading for Christians, as many have done before her, but paves the way for a fundamental renewal of Christian faith and practice."

— G. J. VENEMA
*pastor of the Protestant Church
in the Netherlands, Leiden*

MAKING WISE THE SIMPLE

The Torah in Christian Faith and Practice

Johanna W. H. van Wijk-Bos

WILLIAM B. EERDMANS PUBLISHING COMPANY
GRAND RAPIDS, MICHIGAN / CAMBRIDGE, U.K.

Wm. B. Eerdmans Publishing Co.
255 Jefferson Ave. S.E., Grand Rapids, Michigan 49503 /
P.O. Box 163, Cambridge CB3 9PU U.K.

Printed in the United States of America

10 09 08 07 06 05   7 6 5 4 3 2 1

Library of Congress Cataloging-in-Publication Data

Van Wijk-Bos, Johanna W. H.
Making wise the simple: the Torah in Christian faith and practice /
Johanna W. H. van Wijk-Bos.
p.   cm.
Includes bibliographical references and index.
ISBN-10: 0-8028-0990-1 (pbk.: alk. paper)
ISBN-13: 978-0-8028-0990-2 (pbk.: alk. paper)
1. Bible. O.T. Pentateuch — Criticism, interpretation, etc.
2. Bible. O.T. Pentateuch — Relation to the New Testament.
3. Bible. N.T. — Relation to the Pentateuch.
I. Title.

BS1225.52.V36   2005
222'.106 — dc22

2005050714

www.eerdmans.com

For Emma Claire Bos

Contents

Acknowledgments   xiii

Introduction   xv

Abbreviations   xxiv

PART I
The Torah in Bible and Tradition

INTRODUCTION: Torah in a Covenant Context   1

1. **The Torah in Judaism and Christianity**   3

   What Is the Torah?   3

   "God Made Flesh" — Jewish Views of the Torah   5

   A Lack of Intimacy — Christian Understandings of the Torah   7

2. **The Bible and the Torah**   15

   A Treasure above All Peoples (Exodus 19:3-6)   15

   God's Own People (1 Peter 2:9-10)   19

   A Conversation between Texts   22

3. **A Way into Torah: The "Stranger in Your Gates"**   25

   The Identity of the Stranger   25

   To Know the Heart of the Stranger (Exodus 23:9)   29

   CONCLUSION: Torah in a Covenant Context   33

CONTENTS

PART II
The World of the Torah

INTRODUCTION: The People of the Tale   35

1. The World of the Tale   40
   Family, Field, and Town   40
   Piety, Practices, and Prescriptions   48
      Worship of the One   48
      Places of Worship   49
      Sacrifice   50
      Prayer   51
      Holy Days and Festivals   52
   Worlds Apart   56

2. The Tale in Historical Context   58
   The Writers of the Tale   58
   The Truth of the Tale   62
   The Boundaries of Truth   66
   A Conversation between the Testaments   69

3. A Tale of One City (Genesis 11:1-9)   71
   "Its Name Is Called Babel"   71
   For the Benefit of the Earth   74
   CONCLUSION: The Tale and Its World   78

PART III
The Story of the Torah:
The Making of a World (Genesis 1:1–11:32)

INTRODUCTION: A Prelude to a Theme   79

1. Motifs of the Theme   81
   The Making of the World   81
   The Marring of the World   83

Contents

World's Mending   84

Instructions   85

A Penchant for What Is Weak   86

Approaches to God   90

    Sacrifice   90

    Prayer   92

    Sabbath   94

The Families of the World   95

    Adam's Descendants (Genesis 4:17–5:32)   96

    From Noah to Joktan (Genesis 10:1-32)   102

    From Shem to Abram (Genesis 11:10-32)   105

2. A Tale of a Garden (Genesis 2:4b–3:24)   109

Of Field, Stream, and Human (Genesis 2:4b-14)   109

A Fit Counterpart (Genesis 2:15-25)   110

The Snake and the Tree (Genesis 3:1-5)   113

With Both Eyes Open (Genesis 3:6-13)   114

Now, Look What You've Done (Genesis 3:14-24)   115

What the Story Is All About   117

Type and Countertype (Romans 5:18-19)   119

In Full Submission (1 Timothy 2:11-15)   121

Ways of Reading   122

CONCLUSION: The Prelude and the Bible   126

PART IV
The Story of the Torah:
The Making of a People (Genesis 12:1–Deuteronomy 34:12)

INTRODUCTION: A People of God's Pasture   129

1. Wandering Arameans My Ancestors (Genesis 12:1–50:26)   133

A Family of Strangers   133

The Presence of the Other (Genesis 16 and 38)   136

Genesis 16   136

Genesis 38   142

Whose Memories Are These?   145

2. **And, There, Became a People (Exodus 1:1–24:18)**   149

Getting Out and Getting On (Exodus 1:1–18:27)   149

The Exodus in History   153

Covenant (Exodus 19–24)   154

   The Announcement of the Covenant (Exodus 19:3-6)   155

   The Ten Words of the Covenant (Exodus 20:1-17)   157

   The Execution of the Covenant (Exodus 24:3-8)   164

   Historical Context of the Covenant Texts   167

3. **"And Brought Us to This Place"**
(Numbers 11:1-15; Deuteronomy 34:5-6)   169

In the Wilderness   169

The Cucumbers and Melons of Egypt (Numbers 11:1-15)   171

The End of the Story (Deuteronomy 34:5-6)   176

4. **Instructions for the Covenant Life**   179

The Book of the Covenant:
Organization and Content of Exodus 20:22–23:19   180

   The Ones Who Cry to God (Exodus 22:21-27)   185

   The Heart of the Stranger (Exodus 23:1-9)   188

The Life of Holiness (Leviticus 19)   192

   The Surplus of the Harvest   193

   Love for the Neighbor   194

   Love for the Stranger   195

Priestly Regulation in Historical Context   197

The Company of Strangers: Deuteronomy   198

The Identity of the Stranger   201

5. **Instructions for Life with God**   203

A Place of Meeting (Exodus 25:1–31:11; 35:1–40:38)   204

Contents

This Is Your God, O Israel (Exodus 32–34)   207

A Way of Meeting (Leviticus)   213

    The Acceptable Sacrifice   215

    Purity and Impurity   218

        Foods   218

        Reprehensible Fluidity: Menstruation   219

        Intimate Relations   223

    Holy Days: Atonement   227

CONCLUSION: A Holy Nation   230

PART V
Living with the Torah

INTRODUCTION: God and People in Covenant   231

1. God in the Torah   233

A God Who Regrets   234

A God Who Appears   242

A God Who Accompanies   246

A God Who Is Prejudiced   251

A God Who Is Passionate   253

Conclusion   262

2. Christ and Torah   263

Jesus and the Torah   264

    Assumptions   264

    The Teachings of Jesus   267

        The Good Samaritan   268

        The Frame   268

        The Story   270

        How Do We Read?   272

Paul and the Torah   275

    Torah and Nomos   276

Context   278

The Teachings of Paul   281

    The Law of Love (Romans 12:9-13; 13:8-10;
        Galatians 5:1, 13-14)   282

    Gender Relations (1 Corinthians 7:17; 11:1-16; 14:33-36;
        Romans 1:26-27)   284

    Post-Pauline Codification of Gender Relations   290

The Gospel of God   292

3. How Then Shall We Live?   **296**

Galatians 3:26-29   296

CONCLUSION: How Do We Read?   300

Bibliography   306

Index of Names and Subjects   316

Index of Biblical References   321

Acknowledgments

My thanks go first of all to the faculty and Board of Trustees of my academic institution, Louisville Presbyterian Theological Seminary, for allowing me an initial sabbatical leave during which the first stages of this book were conceived. To the helpful people at the library of the Seminary, especially Angela Morris, Rick Jones, and Liz van Kleeck: thank you for your patience and help with minutiae. To my friend and colleague, Christopher Elwood, I am indebted for your help with the first part of the book. To my friend and assistant Mary Sue Barnett, I extend my gratitude for your diligent work on the Index of Biblical References.

During my stay in the Netherlands I began writing the outline, and I owe much to enlightening discussions with the ministers of the Amstelkerk and Oude Kerk in Amsterdam, Henk Lensink and Sytze de Vries, as well as to the members of the Monday morning discussion group, "Het Amstelpreekteam." Special gratitude also to Peter Tomson and Karel Deurloo of Amsterdam for responding patiently to my questions, and to René Venema of Leiden for your enthusiasm and encouragement at the early stages of my writing.

To friends and family who hosted me in the Netherlands, Pat Pinedo and Wim Hoedemaker of Amsterdam, Joan van Wijk and Ben Dijkshoorn of Amsterdam, Nadine and François Olivier Manson of Leiden, and especially my sister, Hannah Versteegh-van Wijk and her husband Wouter Hoogland, both of Groningen: thank you as always for feeding my body and spirit.

Not all the people who influenced this writing are living today; these dead are part of a special cloud of witnesses who have surrounded my efforts. I mention here my parents, Gerrit Cornelis van Wijk and Johanna Martina van Wijk-van Dam, who stimulated my imagination and taught me the enjoyment of the well-turned phrase; my earliest mentor and the one who introduced me to the world of the Bible, Pieter Hubrecht de Pree; and, finally, two teachers whom I never met but with whose words and thoughts I have lived for many years, Franz Rosenzweig and Martin Buber. *May the beauty of their lives shine forever more, and may my life always bring honor to their memory.*

To Allen Myers, senior editor of Wm. B. Eerdmans Publishing Company, my thanks for his enthusiasm for the project and patience during its execution.

To my spouse, David Bos, goes my deep appreciation for being a constant source of support and wise counsel. I dedicate this book to our granddaughter, Emma Claire Bos, daughter of Martin Bos and Kim Tatman, bright hope of our future whose delightful presence enlivens our present days.

Johanna W. H. van Wijk-Bos

Introduction

Making wise the simple.[1]

The word "simple," used mostly in Psalms and Proverbs, refers essentially to a naïve person, one who lacks experience and understanding; it carries the connotation of innocence and ignorance. The claim of Psalm 19:7, from which the title of this book is taken, is that the Torah (from a Hebrew word often translated "law" or, more properly, "instruction") clears up this type of simplicity. Innocence may have positive associations, but it can also be understood as an ambiguous word, which in its negative sense can be a quality that keeps intact a status quo of undesirable ignorance and injustice.[2] Ignorance, a more obvious negative condition, may also be seen as ambiguous with both a negative and a positive side.

In the negative sense, simplicity and ignorance manifest themselves in a variety of stances and attitudes toward the Bible. At one extreme end of Christianity is the posture that holds the biblical text to be free of error and literally true, with everything in it of equal authority. According to this perspective, the conviction that all of Scripture is equally authoritative as the word of God overshadows recognition and consideration of the historical circumstances of the text. The fact is that the distance between our world and

---

1. The title of this book is in part a quote from Psalm 19:7 (v. 8 in the Hebrew versions).

2. Allan Boesak defined innocence as a destructive quality that can "block off all awareness and therefore the sense of responsibility necessary to confront the other as a human being"; *Farewell to Innocence: A Socio-Ethical Study on Black Theology and Power* (New York: Orbis, 1977), 4. See also Rita Nakashima Brock's discussion of innocence in a context of Asian American women's need to recognize and overcome conditions of oppression and domination; "Dusting the Bible on the Floor: A Hermeneutics of Wisdom," in *Searching the Scriptures: 1: A Feminist Introduction*, ed. Elisabeth Schüssler Fiorenza (New York: Crossroad, 1993), 66.

the world of the Bible is vast. This distance needs to be carefully established, and the bridge across it can be constructed only when the differences have been laid out and examined. Ignorance of the concerns that gave rise to biblical texts results in a faulty perception of what they may reveal to those who hold them sacred today, and the manner in which they may do so. In addition, every interpretive process is of necessity selective. The stance that all of the Bible is equally authoritative ignores the importance of guiding principles to govern this selectivity. When the selective process goes unacknowledged, it exercises a hidden and therefore dangerous authority of its own.

At the other extreme is a conviction that large parts of Scripture, mostly belonging to the "Old" Testament, are irrelevant to modern concerns and issues of faith. This posture more obviously ignores the biblical text and practices a persistent neglect in regard to the wisdom of the text and its capacity to respond to predicaments of every age — in short, its power to connect the listener to God. Both sides, the one that takes the Bible literally and the one that neglects it, live in ignorance of the Bible. While I recognize that many readers may find themselves somewhere between the two extremes, taking some parts of the Bible literally, some metaphorically, and ignoring others, my concern is especially with the second attitude because it predominates in the sector of the church where I place myself and because I believe there is at least a possibility here for a turn in a different direction, toward the Bible rather than away from it. In any case, no matter where we may place ourselves in regard to the truth of the Bible, I have written for everyone who has a hunger and potential enthusiasm for what the biblical text may convey, who is curious and interested in old words that may bring forth new things and perhaps even make one "wise." Wisdom in biblical terms does not mean some esoteric body of philosophical or theological knowledge. Wisdom means that one knows who one is and how one should live. It is exactly this wisdom that we lack when we lose our footing in the foundational document that informs our faith and practice. It is this wisdom that the Torah of the Holy God may communicate to us, "simple ones."

Simplicity and ignorance may also be virtues that give rise to curiosity and interest: the assumption of a stance of one who does not know, who is willing to begin with questions, move toward learning and return once again to the questions. In terms of the Bible, this is the opposite of already knowing what the text contains. Martin Buber expresses this state of assumed ignorance as one belonging to folks who ". . . take up Scripture as if they had never seen it, had never encountered it in school or afterwards in the light of 'religious' or 'scientific' certainties; as if they had not learned all their lives all sorts of sham concepts and sham propositions claiming to be based on it."[3]

Whatever our perspective on biblical truth may be, it is helpful to begin precisely there, with the insight that there are matters regarding the Bible that we do not know and so want to know more, rather than that we already know it all. The Torah may make us wise if we are willing to ask courageous and persistent questions from the position of our not knowing, and if we are willing to stay with the questions and return to them, rather than seeking a quick response.

For a great part, the root of ignorance of the Bible resides in a Christian inability to take seriously the importance of the Hebrew Bible, or Old Testament, for its faith and practice. The custom of relegating the Old Testament to second place has a long history in Christianity and is still powerfully present both in the classroom and the church. The use of the so-called Ecumenical Lectionary in many congregations illustrates this customary devaluing of the largest part of the Bible.[4] Old Testament passages are served up in a fragmented fashion, subordinated to the agenda of the Christian year, and either trumped by New Testament selections or interpreted as merely a prelude to them. Within the framework of this skewed Christian reading of the Bible, again illustrated by the Ecumenical Lectionary, a second and related problem is the privilege accorded to certain Old Testament material, with an attendant ignoring of other texts, sometimes of entire books. An emphasis on the Prophets, for example, has made the Torah, the first five Books of the Bible, unknown territory for many Christian believers. Hence, few will recognize the emphatic concern for social justice, so prevalent in the prophetic literature, as an issue central to the ethics of the Torah.

Having lost their moorings in the Torah, churchgoers at best assume the central tenets of faith and practice, as love of God and neighbor, to belong mainly to the prophetic critique of biblical Israel's shortcomings, or to have been invented by Jesus and his followers. In losing the connection with and foundation in Old Testament teaching, Christianity is in danger of failing to

---

3. Martin Buber, "People Today and the Jewish Bible: From a Lecture Series" (originally delivered in November 1926), in Buber and Franz Rosenzweig, *Scripture and Translation*, ed. and trans. Lawrence Rosenwald and Everett Fox (Bloomington: Indiana University Press, 1994), 7.

4. For a solid critique of this and other lectionaries, see James A. Sanders, "Canon and Calendar: An Alternative Lectionary Proposal," in *Social Themes of the Christian Year: A Commentary on the Lectionary*, ed. Dieter T. Hessel (Philadelphia: Geneva, 1983), 257-63. According to Sanders, all the lectionaries he has seen "perpetuate a Christocentric reading of the Bible as a whole." Also: "Lectionaries support the Christian bias that Christ revealed God" (259). My experience in Amsterdam during Fall 2001 taught me that a lectionary can indeed be formed responsibly with a view toward the entire Christian canon, when I witnessed its construction by the ministers of the Oude Kerk and Amstel Kerk congregations.

comprehend its own identity or what it means to live as a community that views itself as being in covenant with God. In addition, a mistaken understanding of the place and meaning of divine guidance, as a set of rules, the law — to be followed mechanically, set in false opposition to the gospel, the good news of God's love for the world — has created a deep uncertainty in regard to the practice of faith. How life should be lived within the Christian communion and in the world is left to hazy principles of goodwill, and it is not clear why Christians should follow one path and not another, where the dictates of faith come from or what they consist of.[5]

If my first concern resides in current experience within the context of the Christian church, a second concern is rooted in my personal history as a child of the Second World War and in the intellectual framework into which I later put this experience. Born under Nazi occupation in the Netherlands, I lived the first part of my life in the shadow of that existence and its aftermath. I have described the formative influence of these years elsewhere, and here point only to the conviction that after the attempt at the total annihilation of the Jews during the Hitler years, it cannot be business as usual for Christianity.[6] "After Auschwitz" Christian teaching and preaching must take place in the light of what was perpetrated in Christian lands by Christian hands, and must take account of the ultimate consequences of Christian "teaching of contempt" for Judaism and the Jews. Where it fails to do so, its right to speak of Christian love or consider itself as "the people of God" is called into question.

As a teacher of Old Testament in a mainline denominational seminary for more than 25 years, I have become deeply concerned about the inability of Christian interpreters of both Testaments to reflect on the biblical text in light of the Holocaust/Shoah.[7] It is hard to find reading material on the Bible that takes seriously the failure of Christianity to live up to its calling, which be-

5. I do not mean to imply that in this respect Christianity has "lost" something it once had, for the relationship of Christianity to the Old Testament has for a long time been fraught with difficulties.

6. For a description and an analysis of the war years and my personal experience, see Johanna W. H. van Wijk-Bos, *Reformed and Feminist: A Challenge to the Church* (Louisville: Westminster John Knox, 1991), esp. ch. 1.

7. Interestingly enough, *exceptions* to this failure of scholars to incorporate into their scholarship consideration of the almost successful eradication of Judaism and the Jews by Christianity for the most part take place in Germany, where Christian self-reflection has perhaps taken a more serious tone because of the immediacy of the experience. Such exceptions will be noted in the course of the discussion. I am here speaking of biblical scholarship in general available in the English-speaking world and not of the rapprochement that has taken place especially in the United States between Christians and Jews with a more overtly ecumenical agenda.

came apparent through the events of the Holocaust. Christian anti-Judaism and anti-Jewish attitudes are thus allowed to flourish unchallenged, often covertly and therefore all the more dangerously. Lack of acquaintance with the Bible, our own foundational document, combined with ignorance of a history of discrimination against and persecution of our Jewish sisters and brothers, thus continues to set Christians on a path fraught with uncertainty and potential violence against our neighbor. Today, the existence of the State of Israel, as much as policies of the current government must be held to critique and even disapproval, has unfortunately given rise to a renewed flourishing of hatred of the Jews, this time not only but also and again in Christian lands. As Jonathan Rosen points out, Arab anti-Israel propaganda has "joined hands" with European anti-Semitism, and "something terrible has been born." Rosen, who grew up resisting his father's "refugee sense of the world," came to the sense that he thought he "was living in the post-Holocaust world" and found "it sounds more and more like a pre-Holocaust world as well."[8]

This book then addresses above all the Christian need to engage the entire Bible for its own sake, as a rich source for Christian faith and practice, as well as for the sake of "the other," for the sake of restoring just relations with those we have considered to be estranged from their own inheritance — the Jews, for whom the Christian Old Testament counts as the Bible. I focus on the Torah as a part that is both essential and at the same time more underused and misunderstood in Christian circles than the rest of the Bible. Interpretation of Scripture is always selective, as the questions and issues of the time press upon the text and emphasize the importance of one biblical passage over another. Yet, criteria for the interpretive task may be constructed to serve as a guide at any time, and I have laid these out in some detail in chapter 2 of part II. Where possible, New Testament texts are brought into conversation with texts of the Torah in order to let each text shed light on the other, rather than letting one text determine the meaning of the other.

I have written, as always, as a feminist, as someone who is dedicated to the establishing and maintaining of equal and just relations between women and men, as they are equally created in God's image. My feminist analysis and interpretation of the Bible take place within a confessional arena, in the trust that Scripture when seriously engaged by the believing community reveals God and God's intentions to the faithful. I do not think this happens automatically or mechanically or without a great deal of application on the part of

---

8. Jonathan Rosen, "The Uncomfortable Question of Anti-Semitism," *New York Times,* 4 November 2001.

those who take the Bible seriously. I write as a 21st-century Christian, a white woman of the Western industrialized world who grew up in Europe and made her home in the United States, who is deeply concerned about all that fractures and hurts relations between human beings, between humanity and the earth, and between humans and God. To the healing of this wounding the biblical text speaks strongly and convincingly. It does so especially in the attention given to the treatment of the stranger, an issue I consider to be central to the ethics that infuse the teachings of the Torah.[9]

The first part of the book takes up understandings of the Torah in Judaism and Christianity, and considers next biblical designations assigned to a community that understands itself as living in covenant with its God, both in ancient Israel and early Christianity. Recognizing that instruction for the faith community can be understood only from within the covenant bond, and at the same time aware of the difficulty of connecting ethical demands from the ancient past to today's world, I suggest seeking access to covenant requirements via an initial understanding of the treatment of the stranger demanded from the ancient Israelite community. In order to become reacquainted and reengaged with the Bible, it is important to establish and evaluate the distance between us and the text, between our world and that world. I have therefore presented the world of the Bible in its cultural, social, and economic aspects as well as its religious practices with a good bit of detail in Part II. Following the setting of this context within which the texts of the first five books of the Bible took shape, we read through the Torah, beginning with the first 11 chapters of Genesis, which form both prelude and backdrop for what follows (Part III). I continue with the consolidation of the ancient Israelites into a people by the covenant at Sinai, with all that this entailed, in Part IV. In the last part of the book I take up the manner in which God is depicted in the Torah, to then move to a review of the teachings of Jesus and Paul in the light of their being on a possible continuum with Torah teaching.

The discussion is oriented to a close examination of specific texts that illustrate the line of argument. The choice of passages is perforce selective; much had to be left out, not because of its lack of significance but because of the limitations of space or because I wanted to bring to attention material that I hoped would surprise, intrigue, and above all engage the reader. In my

---

9. The importance of the stranger in the laws of the Torah first came to my attention through the work of Thomas W. Ogletree, to whom I am indebted for an introduction to a topic that has become central to much of my work on the Bible since I first read his book *Hospitality to the Stranger* (1985; repr. Louisville: Westminster John Knox, 2003).

choices I have been guided by the story of the Torah itself and what I consider to be its main theme, and by a desire to highlight what is often ignored because it does not obviously or immediately speak directly into a Christian context. The book of Leviticus is therefore treated more thoroughly than some other material, although without doubt it still is not treated here with the depth it deserves. So-called law codes in their covenant framework are taken seriously and considered on their merit both for the ancient community and for modern-day Christian believers. Torah means "instruction" rather than "law," but moral and ritual legislation is very much a part of the Torah.

It should be clear that in terms of the Bible I do not hold the text to be without error. It should be equally clear that I write as one who is focused on the biblical text, on its capacity to invite us into a different world that yet speaks to our own world and existence, on the intricate and alluring ways it tells its stories, presents its ethics, and displays its commitments. I write for those who similarly are not literalists but who have a desire to take the Bible seriously, who have a sense of their lack of acquaintance with it, who believe there is a redemptive word from God to be found here, and who have the courage to ask disturbing questions of the text.

With only an occasional exception, all the biblical citations in the book are in my own translations. In translating I have followed the principles of Martin Buber and Franz Rosenzweig, who together translated the Hebrew Bible into German in the 1920s.[10] Buber and Rosenzweig followed the principle of hewing as closely as possible to Hebrew language rhythm and word choice rather than adapting the text as smoothly as possible to the language of the translator.[11] The occasional awkwardness that may result is judged to have the advantage of more clearly evoking for the modern hearer the distinctive quality of the world and language of the Bible. In addition, Buber and Rosenzweig were convinced of the need for the listener to be aware of the essential spoken quality of the biblical text, what they called its "orality" — hence, the rendering of the Hebrew text into short lines in the target lan-

10. The first edition of this work, completed by Buber alone after the death of Rosenzweig, appeared in 1936 in what was already a Nazified Germany.

11. For an illuminating review of different principles of translation, see Lawrence Rosenwald, "Buber and Rosenzweig's Challenge to Translation Theory," in Buber and Franz Rosenzweig, *Scripture and Translation*, xxix-liv. Rosenwald and Everett Fox, who edited and translated the English-language edition of *Scripture and Translation*, are to be given great credit for making available the exchanges between Buber and Rosenzweig that took place in the process of their work on the translation of the original German text (*Die Schrift und ihre Verdeutschung* [Berlin: Schocken, 1936]). See also Everett Fox, *The Five Books of Moses* (New York: Schocken, 1995), esp. the Preface, ix-xxvi.

guage, following a natural breathing rhythm. My indebtedness to Martin Buber is of long standing and will be evident in many places other than the translations.

In the context of translation efforts I note my reading of the name of God as *"the Holy One."* It is in my view inappropriate to spell out the four-letter Name of God, the so-called Tetragrammaton, by inserting vowels between the consonants. For a long time unsure as to how to render this word in English, and unhappy with the title Lord, the customary rendition in our English translations, I settled some time ago for a number of reasons on "the Holy One." The reader may assume that everywhere this appellation occurs in the translations the Tetragram underlies the reading.[12]

A further word on terminology: For the Christian Old Testament, the Jewish Tanakh or Miqra', I chose sometimes the term *"Hebrew Bible."* Together with others, I am aware of the shortcomings of this term, of which the most important are that it does not have currency in the faith communities that confess this collection as Sacred Scripture and therefore carries a certain artificiality, and that not all Christians confess the Hebrew canon. Yet, I write as a child of the Protestant Reformation for whom the Old Testament coincides almost in its entirety to the canon composed in Hebrew, with the exception of a few passages in Aramaic. Hebrew Bible is a term coined out of respect for the faith that recognizes this book as its Bible, Judaism, and with all its failings does not suffer the negative connotations that are in Western industrialized cultures assigned to the word "old." I have alternatively also used Old Testament because of the familiarity and long tradition of this designation in Christianity and because it was itself not intended to convey negative associations.

"Ancient Israel," or *"biblical Israel,"* or at times the more biblical term *"the children of Israel,"* is used for the community for whom and by whom the literature of the Hebrew Bible was composed. The still commonly used appellation "Israel" for this group is confusing in light of the current existence of the State of Israel. It constitutes either an inaccurate conflation of the two or, more dangerously, an erasure of the latter, thus playing into Christian anti-Jewish tendencies. I chose *"anti-Judaism"* and *"anti-Jewishness"* over the more common "anti-Semitism." Anti-Judaism indicates a **denigration** of Jewish *religion*, prevalent in Christian scholarship, teaching, and preaching, while anti-

---

12. For those who would like to be acquainted with my arguments for this choice, I refer to my essay, "Writing on the Water: The Ineffable Name of God," in *Jews, Christians, and the Theology of the Hebrew Scriptures,* ed. Alice Ogden Bellis and Joel S. Kaminsky (Atlanta: Society of Biblical Literature, 2000), 45-59. In citations containing the full spelling of the divine name, I have substituted dots for vowels. Thus: Y·hw·h.

Jewishness names the attendant Christian attitudes and practices of hostility and discrimination toward *the people* associated with this religion, and it does so more sharply than anti-Semitism. I recognize that in some circles the word *Shoah* is preferred over the term Holocaust. Elie Wiesel, for example, remarks that the word Holocaust has become difficult for him for it is used and abused without reason and "it no longer burns the lips that utter it."[13] Where a reference occurs to the genocide against the Jews that took place during the Second World War, I have sometimes maintained the traditional word "*Holocaust*," or used both words together, "*Holocaust/Shoah*."

Finally, while I have written this book out of a sense of urgent needs that exist for the Christian family, I have done my work with profound respect for Judaism and the Jewish people. Although I briefly survey Jewish understandings of Torah, and apologize for any inadequacies this section contains, it has not been my aim to teach Christians a Jewish appreciation for this part of the Bible. Such an effort would entail at best the grasp of a vast literature that is outside the reach of most Christians and at worst might constitute a renewed Christian colonization of what belongs properly to Jewish religion and its adherents. My goal has been, above all, to encourage a renewed Christian understanding and appropriation of the Torah as also a part of the Christian Bible, essential to the faith and practice of Christian believers.

> The Torah of the Holy God is perfect,
> restoring the soul;
> the statutes of God are reliable,
> making wise the simple.   (Psalm 19:7)

---

13. Elie Wiesel, in *Jews and Christians After the Holocaust*, ed. Abraham J. Peck (Philadelphia: Fortress, 1982), ix.

Abbreviations

ANET	*Ancient Near Eastern Texts*
BETL	Bibliotheca Ephemeridum theologicarum Lovaniensium
BHS	Biblia Hebraica Stuttgartensia
BZAW	Beihefte zur Zeitschrift für die alttestamentliche Wissenschaft
HAL	*The Hebrew and Aramaic Lexicon of the Old Testament*
HSM	Harvard Semitic Monographs
HTR	*Harvard Theological Review*
JBL	*Journal of Biblical Literature*
JPS	Jewish Publication Society
JSNT	*Journal for the Study of the New Testament*
JSNTSup	*Journal for the Study of the New Testament:* Supplement Series
JSOTSup	*Journal for the Study of the Old Testament:* Supplement Series
KJV	King James Version
MT	Masoretic Text
NRSV	New Revised Standard Version
NTS	*New Testament Studies*
SNTSMS	Society for New Testament Studies Monograph Series
WMANT	Wissenschaftliche Monographien zum Alten und Neuen Testament

PART I

The Torah in Bible and Tradition

Introduction: Torah in a Covenant Context

Torah is a word that indicates both a document and a religious concept and thus can be both narrowly as well as more broadly conceived. We first explore torah and its ramifications in a Jewish context, to then move to Christian understandings and misunderstandings. It is significant for our discussion to consider the biblical context of the reception of torah and its attendant language of chosenness and belonging to the covenant circle. Torah, in my view, can be understood only from within the experience of covenant. Both the Hebrew Bible and the New Testament have preserved important statements in regard to communities whose self-perception reflects the understanding of being God's people. We will explore two texts that speak to this issue in profound ways, Exodus 19:3-6 and 1 Peter 2:9-10. These two articulations of what it means to be God's own are engaged in conversation with each other, in order to arrive at a deeper understanding of their importance and meaning for a community that sees itself as living in a covenant with its God. Because specific instructions as a part of the Torah may not always appear applicable to present-day experience and concerns, we will seek a way into Torah regulations via an initial consideration of the posture and practice required of the covenant community toward the stranger.

The Torah in Judaism and Christianity

What Is the Torah?

A simple question may not always elicit a simple answer. First, as a *document* the Torah is equivalent to the first five books of the Jewish Bible, the Christian Old Testament. One word for the Jewish Bible is TaNaKh, an acronym of which the consonants indicate the three main parts of Scripture. The "T" of this word indicates the *Torah*, the first part of the Bible. Others may call this section of the Bible the Pentateuch, a Greek word meaning "five scrolls."

The Bible itself, both in Old and New Testament, contains references to a document identified by the Hebrew word *torah*. One passage describes the finding of a "scroll of the torah" during a temple renovation in Jerusalem in the last quarter of the 7th century B.C.E.: "And Hilkiah the high priest said to Shafan the scribe: A scroll of the torah I have found in the house of the Holy One, and Hilkiah gave the scroll to Shafan and he read it" (2 Kgs. 22:8). After the Babylonian exile and subsequent return to Jerusalem, sometime after the last quarter of the 6th century, the book of Nehemiah reports that the people gathered in a square where Ezra read to them from "the scroll of the torah of Moses that the Holy One had given to Israel" (Neh. 8:1-3). In both cases the reading of the scroll has a powerful impact on the listeners. Repentance and pledges for renewed dedication to the way of life required by this text follow the reading of this *torah* (cf. 2 Kgs. 22:11; 23:2-3; Neh. 8:9). Yet, neither for the time of King Josiah nor for Ezra and Nehemiah's time is it entirely clear what portion or portions of the books Genesis — Deuteronomy are being indicated, and we cannot be sure of the contents of the documents to which these biblical passages refer.[1]

---

1. Other references to a "scroll of the torah" or "a scroll of the torah of Moses" occur in

3

New Testament use of the words "the law" in reference to the "law of Moses" (e.g., Luke 24:27, 44 NRSV) or to "the law and the prophets" (e.g., Matt. 5:17; Acts 13:15; Rom. 3:21 NRSV) points most likely to the first five books of the Bible in their entirety. Other New Testament usage of "the law" more clearly refers to legal requirements binding on the Jewish community (e.g., Paul's letter to the Romans *passim*).

As a *concept, torah* is a Hebrew word meaning "instruction," or "teaching," a word that in Christian English translation often appears as "law," to a great extent because the Greek translation of the Hebrew word is *nomos* and much of biblical tradition is delivered to us via the medium of Greek language and concepts.[2] The Torah could then be "the law" as an integral part of the Bible. Yet, even the least biblically informed among us know that there is more than law in the first five books of the Bible. If we peer behind the curtain of Greek perceptions on the Torah, a more complex landscape may come into view than simply that of a legalistic desert. With some exceptions demanded by the context, I will use the designation the Torah for the first five books of the Bible: Genesis, Exodus, Leviticus, Numbers, and Deuteronomy.[3] Insofar as *torah* with a small *t* points to the regulations, the law, the instructions for living given by God to the people through Moses, these may be found inside the first five books; understood in that way, you might say that the Torah contains *torah*. Understood more broadly, however, all of the Torah is for *torah*, instruction, and similarly it could be said that all of Scripture is for *torah*.

We may need to maintain a degree of flexibility and ambiguity in regard to the question that heads this section until we find clearer outlines for both the word and the reality to which it points. Even if we assume the Torah to be the first five books of the Bible, we have arrived only at a partial answer. What these books are, how they should be read and understood, how they are received and interpreted differs according to the different faith traditions in which they have their place.

Deut. 28:61; 30:10; 31:26; Josh. 1:8; 8:31, 34; 23:6; 24:26; 2 Kgs. 14:6; 22:8, 11; Neh. 9:3. For an extensive analysis of the phrase in all of these passages see G. J. Venema, *Reading Scripture in the Old Testament* (Leiden: Brill, 2004).

2. Compare the NRSV translation "book of the law" in 2 Kgs. 22:8; Neh. 8:9.

3. In view of the uncertainties about the identity and extent of the document referred to in 2 Kgs. 22:8, 11; Neh. 9:3, I have, therefore, not capitalized the word *torah* in my translation of these verses. But compare with "a scroll of the Teaching" in *TANAKH: The New JPS Translation According to the Traditional Hebrew Text* (Philadelphia: Jewish Publication Society, 5748/1988).

"God Made Flesh" — Jewish Views of the Torah[4]

Blessed are you, Adonai, our God, Ruler of the universe, who selected us from all the peoples and gave us the Torah. Blessed are you, Adonai, giver of the Torah.[5]

A reflection on the meaning and significance of the Torah must at least take up the question of how this document lived, and lives, in the communities that are the direct inheritors of those for whom and by whom the Torah was composed. Some time ago, on a Friday, I attended the synagogue of the Liberal Jewish Congregation of Amsterdam to celebrate the beginning of the Sabbath.[6] This is a liberal congregation; hence, women and men sit together and the cantor for the service is female; this is a synagogue and the service is mostly sung and prayed in Hebrew. At one point during the service the curtains that shield the Torah in the Ark are opened to reveal the brilliantly lit Torah scroll with its decorative coverings. They glitter in their sudden illumined state, and the congregation stands and bows in worship. I think of a synagogue service I attended in my hometown in the United States during which I witnessed the Torah scroll being carried through the midst of the congregation, where it received visible homage and reverence from the worshippers. I think of the heap of damaged, torn, and desecrated Torahs on view in the Holocaust Museum in Washington, mute witnesses to a torn and desecrated people. In considering the question "what is the Torah" from the point of view of the Jews, it may be helpful to keep these images in mind. The Torah is not "five books." The Torah is a scroll, a written ancient testimony to the

---

4. I take the imagery from Jacob Neusner's statement that the framers of Judaism conceived of the Torah as the image of God, as Christians "saw in Christ God made flesh"; *Torah: From Scroll to Symbol in Formative Judaism* (Philadelphia: Fortress, 1985), 8. I undertake a discussion of this subject with a degree of hesitancy as an outsider to Jewish beliefs and practices. As Neusner observes elsewhere, writing about religion is a bit like learning a foreign language; *Fortress Introduction to American Judaism: What the Books Say, What the People Do* (Minneapolis: Fortress, 1994), 16. In my case, the difficulty is compounded by past and present prejudice toward and misunderstanding of Judaism from the Christian side.

5. Traditional Jewish Torah blessing, recited after the reading of the Torah, as cited in, e.g., *Sha'are tefilah/Gates of Prayer: The New Union Prayerbook: Weekdays, Sabbaths, and Festivals: Services and Prayers for Synagogue and Home* (New York: Central Conference of American Rabbis, 5735/1975), 419, 426, 432, 438, 444.

6. Liberal congregations in the Netherlands are roughly equivalent to Reform congregations in the United States. The service that I attended was, however, except for the explication of the text, conducted entirely in Hebrew and made few accommodations to those with no familiarity with that language.

faith of Ancient Israel and Judaism through the ages, a sacred and revered entity that is central to the liturgy of the synagogue, a text that stands in the center of Jewish faith.

In Jewish practice, the Torah as a document is read during the liturgy in the synagogue through the year in its entirety in 54 sections, ending on the feast day of *Simhat Torah,* the Joy of Torah, after which the cycle is begun anew. Only a trained reader may read from the scroll, which is handwritten with meticulous care by an authorized scribe.[7] Every Jew has the sacred obligation to study Torah, and such study lies within the reach of everyone.[8]

What I have described here points to the reality that the Torah as a document is considered the holiest object in Jewish life. But for Jewish understandings the Torah is more than only a document, holy though it may be, more than just the first part of the Bible. The entire Bible is understood to be Torah since all of it is for teaching. In addition, the rabbinic books contained in the Talmud are a part of the Torah also, originating as they did in the oral *torah* that accompanied the written one given to Moses. Yet even more, the Torah "supersedes the boundaries of these rabbinic books and includes the Jewish religious thinking and writing of our generation."[9] The concept of *torah* is far broader than that of *law.* Torah is considered to be God's special and exclusive gift to the Jewish people and is thought of as the source of its life. One blessing expresses this thought as follows: "Blessed is our God, who has . . . separated us from them that go astray, and has given us the Torah and thus planted everlasting life in our midst."[10] Judaism is the religion of the Torah which is at the center of belief and practice, originating in the special relationship between God and the Jewish people.[11]

---

7. Torah scrolls read in the synagogue must be written by hand. It usually takes an experienced scribe about a year to complete the writing of a Torah scroll, which may cost from $25-50 thousand. Great care is extended to the appropriate handling of a scroll that may weigh 20 or more pounds. Joseph Telushkin, *Jewish Literacy: The Most Important Things to Know about the Jewish Religion, Its People, and Its History* (New York: Morrow, 1991); Norman J. Cohen, *The Way into Torah* (Woodstock, VT: Jewish Lights, 2000), 49.

8. Even though traditionally "everyone" did not include women, today women in liberal Jewish communities are under the same obligation as men toward the Torah, while in more orthodox circles they are "permitted" to study the written Torah; Cohen, 49.

9. Cohen, 11.

10. *The Oxford Dictionary of the Jewish Religion,* ed. R. J. Zwi Werblowsky and Geoffrey Wigoder (New York: Oxford University Press, 1997), 696.

11. Thus Jacob Neusner observes: "Knowledge of the Torah promised not merely information about what people were supposed to do, but ultimate redemption or salvation"; *The Encyclopedia of Judaism,* ed. Neusner, Alan J. Avery-Peck, and William Scott Green (Leiden: Brill, 2000), 3:1448.

A Lack of Intimacy — Christian Understandings of the Torah

Such a rich multilayered understanding of the Torah is alien to most of Christianity. Indeed, the most appropriate analogue may well be that the Torah is for Judaism what Christ is for Christianity.[12] If it is correctly observed by John Calvin that the face of God is a labyrinth outside of Christ, then Judaism can perhaps make the same statement about God's incomprehensibility outside of the Torah, for it reveals to the Jewish community the presence of God.

In most Protestant resource works that survey Christian theology there are few entries under the heading *law,* or *Moses,* or *Torah.* The latter two may be considered under the heading *Judaism,* but they are rarely discussed as topics with an important place in a Protestant Christian framework.[13] Christian attitudes toward *torah* and the Torah are, however, more complex than a simple absence of attention. From early on the relationship between Christianity and Judaism, between Christians and Jews, was fraught with tension, a tension that in the centuries after the birth of Christianity resulted in Christian persecution of the Jews, especially in Western Europe. Within Christianity there arose a "teaching of contempt" toward the Jews and their beliefs and practices.[14] Such contempt focused especially on the issue of so-called Jewish "legalism." There is in Christianity a conviction with deep historical roots that Jews are believers in and practitioners of a legalistic, basically dead, religion. According to this Christian conviction, the tendency toward the worship of rules rather than of God had already arisen in the period after the great prophets had spoken in biblical Israel, following the Babylonian exile, and it was very much around at the time of Jesus, personified in the figures of the "scribes and Pharisees" in the Gospels. When the Jews were offered yet another chance at a different way of life and faith in the person of Jesus, they missed the boat entirely and persisted in their stubborn rule-oriented ways, so the thinking went. Christianity became henceforth the true inheritor of ancient Israel and of the promises made to the children of Israel in the Bible.[15] The first Bible of Chris-

---

12. Neusner, *Torah,* 8.

13. Naturally, the case is different for the Roman Catholic Church with its strong tradition of canon law, "an integrated system of legal concepts, principles, rules, procedures and institutions, covering virtually all branches of law"; Harold J. Berman, "Law and Theology," in *The Westminster Dictionary of Christian Theology,* ed. Alan Richardson and John S. Bowden (Philadelphia: Westminster, 1983), 322.

14. For a survey of anti-Jewish traditions in the church fathers, see Rosemary Radford Ruether, *Faith and Fratricide: The Theological Roots of Anti-Semitism* (New York: Seabury, 1974), ch. 3.

15. So, e.g., Augustine, who in his *Tractate Against the Jews* wrote: "Because of unbelief

tians, the "Old Testament," was interpreted insofar as the texts spoke of God's relationship to the church and as it reflected the promised future that found fulfillment in Jesus Christ. Although officially both Testaments were viewed as equally revealing of God, and the open rejection of the Old Testament called *Marcionism* was declared a heresy, popular opinion placed the value of the Old Testament and its revelation, often seen as that of a wrathful God, on a lower level than that of the New Testament and its focus on Jesus Christ and a God of love.[16]

Not only popular opinion but also scholarship participated in the perpetuation of this distorted view of Judaism and the relationship between Judaism and Christianity, between Jews and Christians. No less a thinker than Julius Wellhausen, the famous 19th-century German Old Testament scholar who dominated the field of biblical scholarship in his time and for at least a century after, wrote scholarly works in which the "legalistic" character of Judaism was taken to task. More influential than his academic works on the Old Testament, because it addressed a much wider public, was Wellhausen's article "Israel" in the 1881 edition of the *Encyclopaedia Britannica,* in which he stated that in Judaism

> monotheism is worked out to its furthest consequences, and at the same time is enlisted in the service of the narrowest selfishness. . . . The Creator of heaven and earth becomes the manager of a petty scheme of salvation; the living descends from His throne to make way for the law. The law thrusts itself in everywhere; it commands and blocks up access to heaven; it regulates and sets limits to the understanding of the divine

the Jews are now cut off from the root to which the Patriarchs belong, and . . . Gentiles have been grafted in by the humble faith instead. . . ." On observing the prescriptions of the Old Testament on the part of Christians: ". . . we do keep and observe all these things in a way that goes deeper than carnal observance. For we keep them all in their spiritual significance. Thus the Old Testament belongs in truth more to us Christians than to Jews." On the claim of the Jews that they are the people of God: "If indeed you do claim to be the people, then acknowledge that it was by your iniquities that He was led to death (Isa. III,8); that you in the persons of your ancestors led Christ to death." *Tractatus Adversus Judaeos* I.1; II.3 and VII.10, in Lukyn Williams, *Adversus Judaeos: A Bird's-Eye View of Christian Apologiae until the Renaissance* (Cambridge: Cambridge University Press, 1935), 312-17. In this introduction to the review of this treatise, Williams calls it a "delightful little sermon" (312).

16. Marcion was a Christian scholar of the 2nd century who openly rejected the Old Testament and its God as incompatible with the God of love revealed in Christ. He also condemned the Jewish religion as one of worship of the law. In Marcion's thought, law and gospel stand in complete contrast to one another. Marcion himself was excommunicated, but he established a large following that lasted for centuries, and his views persist until today.

working on earth. As far as it can, it takes the soul out of religion and spoils morality.[17]

It is perhaps not such a long step from declaring the religion "immoral" to considering the people who hold these beliefs to be immoral. In any case, this step was taken many times and at no time more so than during the Second World War. On my visit to the Amsterdam synagogue, it was clear to my eyes that this synagogue was built during the postwar years in Amsterdam, a city that held a large concentration of the Jewish population of the Netherlands during the Second World War, a city from which most of this population was deported to be exterminated during the war years. As I looked around me, I saw a number of people my age or older, and I know that they are survivors. In Amsterdam one does not have to ask Jews of a certain age whether they survived; it is only a question of *how* they survived. After the service my friend and I were welcomed by a member of the synagogue, a woman who made us feel at home. Later, I heard that she is the adoptive child of a Christian family who sheltered her during the war period and that only her brother survived with her. In the Netherlands there lived approximately 150,000 Jews at the beginning of the war. Of this number, about 45,000 survived.[18]

17. Julius Wellhausen, *Prolegomena to the History of Ancient Israel: With a Reprint of the Article "Israel" from the Encyclopaedia Britannica* (Cleveland: World, 1957), 509. It is telling that the article which originally appeared in the early 1880s again saw light of day in 1957, more than a decade after the ending of the Second World War, without any qualifying comments or critique from the editors.

18. A large number of these survivors either emigrated to the United States or to Israel, so the actual size of the Jewish community in the Netherlands after the war was somewhere around 20,000. The most thorough analysis of the destruction of the Jews in the Netherlands during the war was done by J. Presser, whose book *Ondergang: De Vervolging en Verdelging van het Nederlandse Jodendom 1940-1945*, was published by the Dutch Institute for War Documentation/Rijksinstituut voor Oorlogsdocumentatie (The Hague: Martinus Nijhoff, 1965). This book was a landmark, not only in that it meticulously tracked the process followed by Nazi Germany in its systematic destruction of the Jews, but also in its honest questioning of Dutch cooperation with or passivity in the face of the events that happened. Presser's book is translated into English as *The Destruction of the Dutch Jews* (New York: Dutton, 1969). Unfortunately, the translation is in fact an inadequate abridgement of the original.

At the end of his book, Presser remarks on the fact that the Jews were more severely affected in the Netherlands than in any other Western European country and gives voice to his fear that the Germans may have created the actual possibility of a country without Jews in the future of the Netherlands (*Ondergang*, 510-11). Fortunately, these fears, all too understandable in the immediate aftermath of the war, were not borne out by the subsequent decades. Today, the Jews in the Netherlands number around 43,000. A recent demographic, cultural, and religious profile of Dutch Jews and Jewish communities bears out a steady growth in numbers during the

While it has been stated, perhaps correctly, that Hitler's hatred of the Jews was not motivated by Christian impulses, Christians must also admit that the deliberate, systematic extermination of Jewish people during the Nazi period took place in Christian lands, was perpetrated for the most part by baptized Christians, and was, if not created by, certainly fed by Christian anti-Judaism, Christian anti-Semitism, and Christian anti-Jewish tendencies that had existed for most of the centuries of Christianity's existence. The Holocaust/Shoah uncovered the true face of those prejudices. Consequently, after the Second World War, after Auschwitz, it cannot be simply business as usual for Christian relations to the Jews, for a Christian appraisal of Judaism and for a Christian approach to the Hebrew Bible, the Christian Old Testament. While some headway has been made, especially in the United States in the first two areas of concern, and new conversations have opened up between Jews and Christians, much is still lacking in terms of a Christian reappraisal of its approach to the Old Testament in view of the reality that this is also and foremost the Hebrew Bible. To begin such a reappraisal with the first five books of the Bible is especially appropriate since there is perhaps no other part of Scripture shared by Christians and Jews on the study of which turn so many issues of Christian misunderstanding of both Judaism and the Bible.

We are, then, about to engage in a Christian reappraisal of the Torah in the face of past and present prejudice and hatred of the Jews. But there is yet more at stake than a mending of torn and shattered relations insofar as it lies within our capacity, as important as this attempt may be. The loss of the Torah is also a serious loss for Christianity itself, for its faith and practice. The Bible in its entirety speaks about God and God's concern for the creation and all creatures, including human creatures; it speaks of God's involvement with the creation for the benefit and the healing of it. The premise of all of Scripture is that without this involvement on God's part, the creation would perish in an abyss of violence. We will look closely at how Scripture expresses these concerns in the first 11 chapters of Genesis. The Old Testament speaks to God's engagement with the creation and in particular with God's people, biblical Israel, in a many-voiced testimony.[19] A crucial part of this testimony is the Torah, because in it are described the beginnings of "it all," both in terms of the creation and the ancient covenant people, Israel. As Christians we are surely oriented to this same God, to whom we have access through Jesus the

---

past 20 years. See *De Joden in Nederland anno 2000: Demografisch Profiel en Binding aan het Jodendom*, ed. Hanna van Solinge and Marlene de Vries (Amsterdam: Aksant, 2001).

19. For an extended use of the term "testimony" for the biblical witness, see Walter Brueggemann, *Theology of the Old Testament: Testimony, Dispute, Advocacy* (Minneapolis: Fortress, 1997).

Christ. As Christians, how can we understand God's gracious gift in Christ, if we pay so little attention to how God acted in the creation "in the beginning," and with God's people in the wilderness? How can we understand ourselves as children of God's creation, as creatures taken up also, belatedly, into the covenant, as children in need of instruction, of *torah,* without a careful and consistent consideration of the text we confess to be God's word also in its aspect of *torah?* It is our task, also on our own behalf, to study the Torah. We will not do this as Jews; we do not aim to equate our understanding or our approach with theirs, even if we could gain such an understanding. We study the Torah as Christians, having come to believe in the same God who called ancient Israel, who still calls the Jews, who also calls Gentiles into relationship with this God for the healing of the creation.

In her essay "Losing a Friend: The Loss of the Old Testament to the Church," Ellen F. Davis observes that the loss of the Old Testament in Christian circles is due to a "loss of intimacy."[20] Davis then sets out certain conditions that may create new possibilities for cultivating friendship with the Old Testament. I propose that we consider a *closer acquaintance* a necessary condition for intimacy. In this study of the Torah, therefore, we aim first of all for increased acquaintance with the text in order to create possibility of friendship, of intimacy. If it leads to intimacy, this renewed acquaintance may then in turn have a profound influence on the understanding of our faith and practices and of ourselves as a community of faith.

There is yet more to be said about a Christian need for reappraisal of the Torah. I have said that all of the Torah is for *torah,* that is, for instruction. In Scripture it is assumed that the people taken into covenant by God are in need of divine instruction, that left to their own devices they would not know how to live a life that is reconciled both to God and the neighbor.[21] It is noteworthy that the word often translated "obey" in Hebrew primarily means "listen." In a number of key texts that reflect on the desired posture of the ancient commu-

---

20. In *Jews, Christians, and the Theology of the Hebrew Scriptures,* ed. Alice Ogden Bellis and Joel S. Kaminsky (Atlanta: Scholars, 2000), 83-94. Davis argues that it is not so much a case of a loss of authority but a loss of intimacy that is at stake in Christian dealings with the Old Testament. Thus she states: "For many Christians profound friendship with the Old Testament is no longer a live possibility" (83).

21. In an article on the subject of the Dutch Bible society Tanakh and Gospel, Dutch theologian G. H. ter Schegget reflects on the essential work of this group and its presuppositions. In the course of his review he remarks that, biblically speaking, reconciliation with God always includes reconciliation with the neighbor but that Christianity split these two apart; "Veertig Jaar Bijbelsocieteit," in *Veertig Jaar "Tenach en Evangelie,"* ed. René Venema and Ranfar Kouwijzer (Delft: Eburon, 1998), 15.

nity in relation to torah, the emphasis is on listening as a crucial requirement for those who consider themselves allied with God in covenant. There may be no lines that express this concept as eloquently as these from Deuteronomy:

Deuteronomy 31:11-13

11. When all Israel comes to appear
    in the presence of the Holy One, your God,
    in the place of God's preference,
    you will read aloud this instruction (torah)
    in front of all Israel, in their hearing.
12. Assemble the people, men, women and babes,
    and your stranger who is in your gates,
    so they may listen, so they may learn,
    and be in awe of the Holy One, your God,
    and will be careful to do all the words of this instruction (torah).
13. Even your children who have no knowledge
    will listen and will learn
    to be in awe of the Holy One, your God,
    all the days that you live on the soil
    that by crossing the Jordan you will possess.

The people are required to "listen" so they may "learn" and "do." A word that connotes listening occurs in each verse of this brief section, an indicator of its significance for a proper understanding of the content. The focus for the people's attention, for their listening, is "this instruction/torah." In Exodus 24, where the making of the covenant between God and the crowd in the wilderness at Sinai is described as brokered by their leader, Moses, the people promise to listen, to be attentive, to have an open ear, since the covenant represents the living presence of God with them: "And he took the scroll of the covenant and read it in their hearing and the people said: All that the Holy One has spoken we will do and we will listen" (Exod. 24:7).[22] Nothing Jesus taught or did changes the biblical perception that human creatures, including those

22. We note that the order of "listen" and "do" is the reverse in Exodus 24 from that in Deuteronomy 31, which has the effect of drawing more attention to the importance of listening. Standard translations such as the NRSV read "obey" for the Hebrew *shama* used here. Thus: "All that the Lord has spoken we will do, and we will be obedient" (Exod. 24:7 NRSV). Cf. also Exod. 19:5, where the NRSV reads "if you obey my voice." Certainly the connotation of obedience is embedded in the very *shama*, since listening without action would be seen as meaningless. Yet something essential is lost when the notion of attentiveness is no longer present so that the translation "listen" for *shama* is to be preferred.

who view themselves as reconciled to God in Christ, need instruction as to how to conduct their lives with God, with each other, and with the creation.[23]

A renewed acquaintance and intimacy may lead to the kind of listening required of those who consider themselves living in covenant relations with God and the neighbor, thus taking seriously the instruction that is embedded in the Torah. We will listen attentively as a Christian community, removed in time and space from the covenant community by whom and for whom the Torah was given shape and form. This remoteness means that understanding must be worked at; we will have to listen closely to the text because most of the time it will not be immediately obvious how we should read and interpret the directives, the stories, and the myths that are part of the Torah.[24]

If we really intend to listen to a person, it may mean that we must set aside some of the prejudices we held about the person previously. In terms of the biblical text, the same principle is valid: as Christians we must set aside certain prejudices if we intend to listen with the seriousness that the Torah itself requires. We need to set aside a Christian understanding of the Old Testament that views the Old Testament to be lower on the scale of revelatory value than the New Testament, either because it speaks of a different God, thus being set aside by the New Testament, or because it speaks of promises that are fulfilled in Christ alone, serving only a *preparatory* value, thus being superseded by the New Testament. We need to set aside Christian prejudice that views the Christian faith as the appropriate successor to the faith of ancient Israel and Christian believers as the inheritors of the traditions of ancient Israel, with Christians a new chosen people, a choice that cancelled the election of the Jews and the promises made to them.[25] Finally,

---

23. For insightful and critical discussion of the relationship of Jesus to the Torah, as well as of Paul's views of "covenantal nomism," see the following works of E. P. Sanders: *Paul and Palestinian Judaism: A Comparison of Patterns of Religion* (Philadelphia: Fortress, 1977); *Paul, the Law, and the Jewish People* (Philadelphia: Fortress, 1983); and *Jesus and Judaism* (Philadelphia: Fortress, 1985). For a detailed discussion of Christian anti-Judaism in a New Testament context, see *Paul and Palestinian Judaism*, 33-75.

24. As Sanders observes: "The relevance of the ancient world for understanding the present world is . . . always oblique. Looking back enables one to look around with fresh perspectives, but usually not with ready-made solutions to current problems of law and ethics." E. P. Sanders, "When Is a Law a Law? The Case of Jesus and Paul," in *Religion and Law: Biblical-Judaic and Islamic Perspectives*, ed. Edwin Brown Firmage, Bernard G. Weiss, and John Woodland Welch (Winona Lake: Eisenbrauns, 1990), 158.

25. It goes without saying that New Testament texts that ostensibly aid such perspectives need to be reevaluated also. See, e.g., Peter J. Tomson, *"If This Be from Heaven . . .": Jesus and the New Testament Authors in Their Relationship to Judaism* (Sheffield: Sheffield Academic, 2001). For an example of how this might be done, see further in this chapter.

we need to set aside Christian views of Christ as obviating human need for instruction and of a Christian community as no longer in need of divine guidance for its life.

CHAPTER 2

The Bible and the Torah

But you are a chosen race, a royal priesthood, a holy nation, God's own people.[1]

A Treasure above All Peoples (Exodus 19:3-6)

We cannot speak of the Torah or of *torah* and make any sense without speaking of the covenant God formed with ancient Israel. This covenant is described in the Torah and is intimately connected with torah/instruction and with law giving. Much ink has been spilled and could still be spilled in attempting to define the covenant concluded between God and people at Sinai. We will look at its contours and implications again when we visit the books of the Torah in a later chapter.[2] There is no doubt that ancient Israel understood itself as a people liberated by God. Two definitive liberations provide the markers for this self-understanding: the first and determinative liberation was the one from Egypt, the "house of bondage"; the second, patterned after it in the text in terms of language and imagery, was the liberation from the Babylonian exile. The author of this liberation is understood to be God. God is thus the one who "brought the people out."[3]

The liberating act of God constitutes freedom from socio-economical, physical, and psychological oppression and has as its goal life in the land of the promise. On a more profound level, the people are liberated from a life of

1. 1 Pet. 2:9 NRSV.
2. Relevant historical critical issues will be raised at a later point in the discussion. For the moment, we will regard the covenant made between God and people at Mount Sinai at face value in a wilderness setting before there was a settled people in a land.
3. See, e.g., Exod. 20:2; Deut. 26:8; Josh. 24:5, 6; Isa. 43:5-6.

15

bondage in order to live a life in God's presence: "And you I carried on wings of eagles and brought you to myself" (Exod. 19:4). The intimate bond between God and people already existed before Sinai. The covenant made at Sinai does not so much create a bond as formalize an already existing one. It is by the covenant that the people are constituted as a community and are given the task to conduct their life as a community marked by its belonging to God. With the gift of the covenant, the ancient Israelites are also given a promise of what sort of community they may become. Once the people are freed from Egypt, and are encamped at the foot of Mount Sinai, Moses is commanded to make the following announcement:

Exodus 19:3-6

3. And Moses went up to God;
   and to him called the Holy One from the mountain:
   thus you shall say to the house of Jacob
   and tell the house of Israel:
4. You yourselves have seen how I dealt with Egypt
   and carried you on wings of eagles
   and brought you to myself.
5. And now, listen, yes listen to my voice
   and keep my covenant;
   and you will be for me a treasure above all peoples.
   For mine is all the earth,
6. and you yourselves shall be for me
   a royal realm of priests
   and a holy nation.
   These are the words you shall speak
   To the children of Israel.

The designations applied to the "children of Israel" of "treasure," "realm of priests," and "holy" or "dedicated nation" must be allowed to illumine each other; specifically, the second and third designations fill in the content of the first and focus its meaning. The first label, of "treasure," indicates that these are "God's own people," that they belong especially to God. Yet, in the same breath, the biblical text asserts that the entire earth belongs to God; the phrase "for mine is all the earth" certainly points to the understanding that God's concerns are larger than those having to do with Israel alone and that God's interests exceed the limits of the liberated crowd at the foot of the mountain. Israel belongs to God in a special way: as a "realm of priests" and a "holy/dedicated nation."

The phrase "a royal realm of priests" indicates that ideally there is no hierarchy among the members of the community in term of their relationship to God, who is their ruler. In a "realm of priests" all have equal access to God. As "priests" they will also make access to God possible for others, for the rest of the world that belongs to God, for people who are not explicitly taken into covenant with this God. Priests, after all, mediate access to God on behalf of others. As priests, the people are also set apart, other, holy.

The concept of a "holy" or a "dedicated nation" anticipates the demand made elsewhere that the people shall be holy because God is holy (e.g., Lev. 19:2). The people's holiness will consist in their modeling themselves on God. God's "holiness" can be understood, of course, as God's otherness, a contemplation of which causes human awe and adoration.[4] We may think in this connection of the proclamation of the Seraphim: "Holy, holy, holy, Holy One of hosts/filled is the earth with his glory!" (Isa. 6:3). Isaiah, who contemplates the vision of God, is faced with his own imperfection in view of the perfection of God and therefore cries out that he is unclean and that his people are unclean (Isa. 6:5). On the other hand, the Bible also states that God is in the midst of the people as the Holy One: "For I am God and not a man/in your midst the Holy One;/I will not come in anger" (Hos. 11:9). It is precisely as "the other" that God is declared to be "in the midst" of the people. Furthermore, it is God's forgiveness ("not in anger") that constitutes God's otherness at this point. According to biblical scholar Baruch Levine, God's holiness is not intended to describe God's essential nature but rather how God is manifest. In Hosea 11 God's holiness is made manifest by God's forgiveness. Levine observes: "The statement that God is holy means . . . that He acts in holy ways; He is just and righteous." For ancient Israel "the way to holiness. . . was . . . to emulate God's attributes.[5] If we follow both these insights, it means that the ancient covenant community's holiness will manifest itself insofar as it emulates God's passion for justice.

The word "treasure," as filled in by the terms that follow it, thus takes on a particular meaning. This people belongs to God as a "realm of priests" and a "holy nation." What seems at first to indicate a special status has turned into a charge, so that even the word treasure takes on the character of a charge. Ancient Israel belongs to God in a certain way, closer to God than anyone and closer to the neighbor than anyone. As Martin Buber observed: "The . . .

---

4. See Johanna W. H. van Wijk-Bos, *Reimagining God: The Case for Scriptural Diversity* (Louisville: Westminster John Knox, 1995), 31-33.

5. Baruch Levine, *Leviticus* ויקרא. JPS Torah Commentary (Philadelphia: Jewish Publication Society, 5749/1989), 256.

Speech itself opposes the haughty stressing of the choice by the subsequent message that the choice means a charge imposed on them and nothing more; and that therefore the choice, so to say, exists only negatively unless the charge is also fulfilled.[6]

Turning to the opening lines of this speech, the initial description has its focus on God, and on what God has done for the people as they themselves have witnessed. All three actions undertaken by God, "how I dealt with Egypt, I carried you. . ., and brought . . . ," point to the people as passive recipients of God's activity. Now is the time for the people to grow up, to "become," as the eagle's young grow up.[7] The movement from the state of passivity to one of active participation turns on the requirement to listen: "and now listen, yes listen to my voice" (Exod. 19:5).[8] The possibility for an active and adult partaking in the covenant relationship is thus created by attentiveness to God's voice. In fact, this listening is on a par with keeping the covenant. Logically, then, the people's promise at the execution of the covenant includes a commitment to listen (Exod. 24:7; see below, 164ff.).[9] *Torah*/instruction is the primary expression of God's voice for the covenant community. By means of it the way to becoming God's people is clarified, for above all torah addresses how the people should live together as a community in covenant with its God.

6. I owe much to Buber's discussion of this passage in the chapter "'Upon Eagles' Wings' (The Eagle Speech)," in *Moses: The Revelation and the Covenant* (New York: Harper, 1958), 105.

7. Indeed, it is possible to translate the verbs of vv. 5 and 6 *(heyitem* and *tihyu)* with a form of "becoming," to bring out clearly the idea that here a process is spoken of rather than a completed task.

8. I have translated the opening phrase of v. 5 with "and now listen, yes listen" rather than the customary "if you listen," on the basis of the Hebrew, which warrants such a translation if the initial *'im* is read emphatically rather than conditionally as, e.g., in Judg. 5:8, where the conjunction emphasizes the absence of shield and lance. See also Buber's translation of Exod. 19:5: "Und jetzt hört ihr, hört auf meine Stimme"; *Die Fünf Bücher der Weisung: Verdeutscht von Martin Buber gemeinsam mit Franz Rosenzweig,* 3rd ed. (Cologne: Jakob Hegner, 1968), 203. Everett Fox, who follows Buber/Rosenzweig in many particulars, reinserts the "if"; *The Five Books of Moses* (New York: Schocken, 1995), 365. The idea of a process that involves "listening" and "becoming" is much weakened if one translates "if you obey my voice" as does the NRSV together with other standard translations.

9. For an insightful contemporary discussion of the Hebrew verb *shama,* see Daniel J. Elazar, *Covenant and Polity in Biblical Israel: Biblical Foundations and Jewish Expressions.* The Covenant Tradition in Politics 1 (New Brunswick: Transaction, 1995), 70: ". . . *shamoaʿ* is sometimes translated as 'obey' in more modern English versions of Scripture. But they are not the same at all, and . . . represents the abandonment of a critical biblical concept so as to change the whole meaning of the text and the whole biblical understanding of how humans act." The translation Elazar proposes is "to hearken."

God's liberating activity assures ancient Israel of God's loving protective care and of God's desire that the people should be in God's presence. God's covenant, as delineated in Exodus, assures ancient Israel of God's ongoing presence and of the people's special place with God in an ongoing covenantal relationship. God's torah guides and instructs the covenant community as to how it should conduct its life within this relationship so that it will be indeed a full participant with God. Nothing is said here, or anywhere in the Bible, about the possibility of God canceling divine participation in this relationship.

Biblical scholar James A. Sanders has argued that the nature of the canon of Scripture is to be "a mirror for the identity of the believing community which in any era turns to it to ask who it is and what it is to do, even today."[10] Within this framework, the covenant bond addresses the question of identity, while torah responds to the question of how the community should conduct its life. The two responses are as inextricably related as are the questions: without the covenant bond, God's torah would lack grounding in the people's sense of identity as "God's own people" and in the mutual promises God and the community make to one another; without torah, the people would be at a loss as to how they should live as God's people, how they should respond to God's presence. Torah is the guidance that is God's gracious gift to the covenant community so it may know how to conduct life as it should be lived in covenant with God. The guidance includes rules, regulations, prescriptions — the law as it pertains to all areas of life, the social, the religious, and the economical; but it also includes stories, songs, and prayers, as these too are intended to guide the people in their life together and in their life with God.

God's Own People (1 Peter 2:9-10)

The foregoing review of the relationship between covenant and torah should establish these basic points: the covenant without torah is meaningless and torah without covenant is hopeless. The two together stand at the heart of what it means to be God's "own people," as the verse from 1 Peter has it. The

---

10. James A. Sanders, *Torah and Canon* (Philadelphia: Fortress, 1972): xv-xvi. Sanders argues the same point in a subsequent book: "As history changed and the fortunes of the people, even their habitats and customs changed, they needed to know ever anew *who they were and what they should do*"; *Canon and Community: A Guide to Canonical Criticism* (Philadelphia: Fortress, 1984), 28.

passage that includes this phrase, based in part on Exodus 19:3-6, reads as follows:

1 Peter 2:9-10

9. But you are a chosen race,
   a royal realm of priests,
   a holy nation, a people of God's acquiring,
   so that you may tell of the goodness of the One
   who called you out of darkness into God's marvelous light.
10. Once, not a people,
    now, a people of God;
    once, not pitied,
    now you are pitied.

This text forms an amalgam of lines borrowed from Exodus 19:5-6 and Isaiah 43:20-21, with allusions to Hosea 1:9; 2:23.[11] We note that the words "chosen race," derived from Isaiah 43, are added to the three designations of the covenant community borrowed from Exodus 19. 1 Peter 2:9-10 in this way clearly places itself on the ground of the community's chosenness, its election. This election is grounded in the acceptance of Christ, called "a living stone" in verse 4. The covenant language, borrowed from the Exodus text, is applied to a new community taken up into a relationship with God through Jesus Christ. Thus, they are called "out of darkness into God's marvelous light" (another allusion to a prophetic text, Isa. 9:2). Although the idea that the community with whom God is in covenant is one *chosen* by God is not alien to the thought world of ancient Israel and belongs to certain descriptions of the God-Israel covenant, it does not stand in the foreground in Exodus 19, and the word itself is missing. In fact, the notion of God's choosing the people does not occur until Deuteronomy, where the word and the concept take on some significance.[12] An important question in regard to 1 Peter 2:9-10

---

11. For a discussion of this "collation of epithets," see John H. Elliott, *The Elect and the Holy: An Exegetical Examination of 1 Peter 2:4-10 and the Phrase* Basileion hierateuma. Supplements to Novum Testamentum 12 (Leiden: Brill, 1966).

12. Of the 98 times that the verb *bahar* occurs in the Hebrew Bible with God as subject, the preponderance is in Deuteronomy or in Deuteronomistic literature, esp. 1 Kings and 1 and 2 Chronicles. In particular, God chooses: a place for the divine name to dwell, i.e., Jerusalem (Deut. 12:18, 26; 14:25; 15:20; 16:7; 17:8, 10; 18:6; 31:11); David and his dynasty (Deut. 17:15; 2 Sam. 6:21); and the people for God's own possession (Deut. 4:37; 7:6ff; 10:15; 14:2; 1 Kgs. 3:8). Horst Seebass argues that the election of the people must be seen as a separation in service of the world: "The horizon of the election of the people of Israel is the peoples of the world, in rela-

is whether the writer intended to have his proclamation of a "chosen race" as a *de facto* rejection of the previous chosen race, namely, ancient Israel and by extension the Jews of his day. Was this community, now taken into a relationship with God, "called out of darkness into light," intended as a replacement of the old covenant community?

It is certain that, regardless of the intentions of the writer of 1 Peter, subsequent Christian interpretations of this text took up the theme of the rejection of the Jews in favor of Christians. A traditional Christian way of reading this passage considers it to be a testimony to the faithlessness and unbelief of the Jews, and to their rejection as God's "own people." In commentary after commentary from ancient times to the modern day, one can find this understanding.[13] We may take as representative the remarks of William Barclay in his immensely popular and influential series on the Bible. In his comments on the first chapter of 1 Peter, he remarks: "But the nation of Israel failed in the purposes of God, for. when he sent his Son into the world, they rejected and crucified him. When Jesus spoke the Parable of the Wicked Husbandmen, he said that the inheritance of Israel was to be taken from them and given to others (*Matthew* 21:41; *Mark* 12:9; *Luke* 20:16). That is the basis of the great New Testament conception of the Christian Church as the true Israel, the new Israel, the Israel of God (cp. *Galatians* 6:16). All the privileges which had once belonged to Israel now belonged to

---

tionship to which as a whole the 'individual' Israel was chosen. *bahar* as a technical term for the election of the people of Israel stands under the symbol of universalism"; *Theological Dictionary of the Old Testament*, ed. G. Johannes Botterweck and Helmer Ringgren (Grand Rapids: Wm. B. Eerdmans, 1977) 2:83.

13. A representative sample of such readings includes, from the 16th century: "The meaning then is, as though he had said, 'Moses called formerly your fathers a holy nation, a priestly kingdom, and God's peculiar people: all these high titles do now far more justly belong to you; therefore you ought to beware lest your unbelief should rob you of them"; John Calvin, *Commentaries on the Catholic Epistles*, trans. and ed. John Owen (Grand Rapids: Baker, 1981), 73. From the 19th century: "They (i.e. the Christians addressed in 1 Peter) are the family of God in a far higher sense than ancient Israel . . ."; John Brown, *Expository Discourses on the First Epistle of the Apostle Peter* (Evansville: Jay Green, 1868), 281; and "The oft-repeated promise of God was that obedient Israel should be to Him in this sense a peculiar people — a special treasure above all people. . . . Now, this prerogative also has passed over. . . from the rebellious Jew to the Christian Church"; John Lillie, *Lectures on the First and Second Epistles of Peter* (1869; repr. Minneapolis: Klock & Klock, 1978), 122. From a time closer to our own: "This assumption that the Church is the new Israel, the appointed heir of both the revelation and the promise made to the old, is a NT commonplace . . . which goes back to our Lord's interpretation of His person and mission in the light of key ideas of the OT"; "Israel after the flesh, on which God's choice originally fell, has been supplanted because it was found wanting in faith"; J. N. D. Kelly, *A Commentary on the Epistles of Peter and Jude* (1969; repr. Grand Rapids: Baker, 1981), 40, 96.

the Christian Church."[14] Barclay thus reads in 1 Peter 2:9-10 a direct rejection of God's former people, Israel, and their replacement by the new community of those who believe in Christ: "The great promises which God made to his people Israel are being fulfilled to the Church, the new Israel."[15]

Recently, many commentators do not explain the passage in such crass terms. A more common approach in contemporary commentaries is to deny that a problem exists.[16] Representing this position is the following observation presented by the German scholar Wolfgang Schrage in the highly respected series *Das Neue Testament Deutsch,* where he comments on 1 Peter 2:9: "The writer transfers to the church traditional sayings and epithets which originally applied to Israel and emphasizes thereby the continuity of the church with the covenant people of the Old Testament. This happens so naturally and without controversy that, unlike in Paul, 'Israel after the flesh' is no longer a problem."[17] It is well known that it was Hitler's intention to create a German empire that was free of Jews, a situation for which the German word is *Judenrein.* Schrage by his analysis, together with other scholars, appears to have created a *Judenrein* 1 Peter!

A Conversation between Texts

Neither direction, either declaring the Jews to be a community rejected by God and replaced by the church, or declaring the text to be "free" of the problem of the Jews, is one which a Christian interpretation may take in dealing responsi-

14. William Barclay, *The Letters of James and Peter,* rev. ed. (Philadelphia: Westminster, 1976), 166.

15. Barclay, 198.

16. The following observations are typical for this perspective. After remarking on the prolific use of Old Testament texts in 1 Peter, Peter H. Davids comments: ". . . there is absolutely no sense of an Israel-church tension in the use of these texts"; *The First Epistle of Peter.* New International Commentary on the New Testament (Grand Rapids: Wm. B. Eerdmans, 1990), 25. From David Bartlett: "Unlike such New Testament writings as Romans and the Gospel of Matthew, 1 Peter does not attend to the relationship between Christians and Jews as possible heirs to Israel. The epistle simply takes over images and phrases that the Old Testament applies to Israel and applies them to the church. Christians are now the people who were once no people. . . . For 1 Peter, the OT was not written to point to Israel but to point to Christ and through Christ to point ahead to the life of the church"; *The First Letter of Peter: Introduction, Commentary and Reflections.* New Interpreter's Bible 12 (Nashville: Abingdon, 1998), 236, 237. Pheme Perkins writes: ". . . 1 Peter does not refer to Jews"; *First and Second Peter, James and Jude.* Interpretation (Louisville: Westminster John Knox, 1995).

17. Horst Balz und Wolfgang Schrage, *Die "Katholischen" Briefe: Die Briefe des Jakobus, Petrus, Johannes und Judas* (Gottingen: Vandenhoeck & Ruprecht, 1993), 85.

bly with this text. Such a path takes us directly or indirectly to old and harmful prejudices. How then are we to interpret? First, we need to openly recognize that the transfer of "sayings and epithets" that originally belonged to ancient Israel, and therefore also to the Jews who are the direct inheritors of such promises, creates a problem for a Christian understanding of the text if we intend to interpret in a way that is not harmful to others, whether the writer of the passage intended it or not. Furthermore, in order to find a solution to our dilemma, and in view of our concern with a Christian appropriation of the Torah that enhances our understanding of God and ourselves without doing harm to the Jewish neighbor, we turn once more to a consideration of Exodus 19:3-6 and let it enter into conversation with 1 Peter 2:9-10.

The opening lines of the Exodus passage point to the protective care God has exercised toward the community. It is by God's action that the community has received liberation from bondage. Thus, to God belongs the credit, and to God should go the gratitude. 1 Peter 2:9 points in a similar direction. The desired result of the new identity of the community is that it should "tell of the goodness of God." The proclamation of God's goodness is the first marker set up in 1 Peter 2 to orient the community first of all to the loving merciful care of God rather than to its own outstanding qualities or to the shortcomings of others. In the Exodus text, this orientation is expressed in verse 4: "You yourselves have seen how I dealt with Egypt/and carried you on wings of eagles/and brought you to myself."

In addition, the Exodus text contains a promise of "becoming," of growing up into a full covenant relationship with God (see above, 18). As a Christian community, we need to consider what it may mean to embrace this process of becoming adults. Are we set to contemplate seriously, in the words of Exodus 19 and 1 Peter 2, what it might portend for us to become a "holy nation," "a realm of priests," "a people of God's acquiring"? A beginning point for this process may be the understanding that we are not the only ones to whom God's loving care is extended. There is all the world which is under God's care ("for all the world is mine," Exod. 19:5). There is, above all, the first community with which God entered into a covenant relationship, ancient Israel and its direct inheritors, the Jews. John Calvin interpreted Paul in the letter to the Romans as stating that Christians are children of Abraham by *adoption*.[18] As adoptive children we are not invited to extend condemnation and judgment to the rest of the world, especially not to the household of Israel, the first-born of God's love. As adoptive children, we need to look to our own

18. John Calvin, *The Institutes of the Christian Religion*, trans. Ford Lewis Battles (Philadelphia: Westminster, 1960), 1336.

household and consider how we have responded and are responding to God's torah in the process of our growing up into a people that emulates God's passion for justice.

Covenant and torah go together, also in 1 Peter. God's choice involves a charge rather than a special status. The community taken up into covenant is in need of instruction, of torah, for its life, in order that it may indeed live as "God's own people." 1 Peter 2 opens with directives for relationships with the neighbor and follows verse 10 with a string of instructions for appropriate conduct. Indeed, after 2:10 the rest of the letter is taken up almost entirely by such instructions. Some of these sound quaint, because they are outdated, as the requirement to "accept the authority of the emperor" (2:13). Some need a lot of thought and interpretation because they are off-putting, as the requirement for slaves to "accept the authority" of their masters (2:18) and for women to "accept the authority" of their husbands "in the same way" (3:1). Rules and regulations that arrived in the wake of the early Christian movement can appear as outdated as those coming from ancient Israel, and sometimes more so. Specific rules for the common life of a community can be understood only out of their context, and such rules are at times also limited to a specific context. There may yet be something to be gleaned from such torah, but the lesson is not immediately obvious. In searching for understanding of regulations that no longer fit our context, a deeper acquaintance with the original context may provide an opening into the forest of rules.

CHAPTER 3

A Way into Torah:
The "Stranger in Your Gates"[1]

*The esteem for and love of the stranger is a reflection of our love of
God. In the alien we are first and foremost bidden to discover the
presence of the redeeming God and thereby to reinforce the bonds
with all humanity.*[2]

The Identity of the Stranger

The audience of 1 Peter is specified in the opening address of the letter as "exiles" (1:1 NRSV). Immediately following the proclamation of 2:9-10, the same
identification occurs, this time supported by the word "alien." ("Beloved, I
urge you as aliens and exiles . . ."; 2:11 NRSV).[3] Those who lack the rights and
privileges of citizens, because they are classified as outsiders in their societies,
are the very ones who are "God's people." Yet, in the concreteness of their existence, these people are "aliens," outsiders, marginals. Thus they have to live

---

1. I have taken this heading in part from the title of Norman Cohen's book *The Way into
Torah.*

2. תורה *The Torah: A Modern Commentary,* ed. W. Gunther Plaut (New York: Union of
American Hebrew Congregations, 1981), 1410.

3. For an analysis of the Greek terms used here, see John H. Elliott, *A Home for the Homeless: A Social-Scientific Criticism of 1 Peter, Its Situation and Strategy* (Minneapolis: Fortress,
1990). The pertinent words are *paroikos* and *parepidēmos.* It is certain that with these terms are
meant those who were somewhat on the outside of the social arena, who lacked the privileges
and rights of those who belonged by birthright. Elliott: ". . . these people lacked the security of
the citizen. . . . The fundamental distinction . . . between the rights, privileges and rewards of full
citizenship and those of all others remained clear and binding" (33).

according to torah that is congruent with their life as God's own people while not putting further at risk their lives as "aliens and exiles." The identity of this community resides both in belonging to God and in not quite belonging to their context.

Marginal existence characterized the people who meet their God in the wilderness at Sinai. This rag-tag horde of escaped slaves has been liberated from a context in which they were oppressed aliens into one of living as "God's own people." Now, they are ready to receive a new identity, as a people that belong. If, however, in the process of becoming partners with God in a covenant relationship, the liberated community loses sight of the charge that is imposed on it by God's choice, if this choice becomes the guarantee of a special status rather than a charge, then those outside of the covenant community are easily considered outsiders and aliens who have no right of belonging. To safeguard against this particular misunderstanding, the "children of Israel" are required to establish their treatment of aliens or strangers on the basis of their own identity as "strangers in the land of Egypt," thus keeping one foot planted, as it were, in their existence as oppressed aliens even as they find the place of their belonging with God.

Outsiders are present in the Torah and the rest of the Hebrew Bible in various ways.[4] "Foreigners" are those who have come to stay for a limited period of time. "Aliens" are those who pose a threat to the community. "Resident aliens" or "immigrants" are those who live together with the community, sometimes having joined with it in religious affiliation. Finally, there is a large category of "strangers," those from elsewhere who have come to stay. The latter group is the one most frequently mentioned in the Torah and is indicated with the Hebrew word *ger*.[5] Basically, the *ger* has come from outside the fam-

---

4. We will revisit the subject of the strangers as they occur in the different law codes within different possible historical contexts at a subsequent point in the discussion. At this point, I want to highlight the depth and extent of the regulations concerning the stranger as guided by the torah of Exod. 23:9, within the framework of ancient Israel's historical existence but apart from a specific historical period.

5. The words I have translated with "foreigner," "alien," and "immigrant," are indicated respectively by Hebrew *nokhri, zar,* and *toshav,* while the "stranger" is the *ger.* Unfortunately, the differentiations are lost in English translations, which generally choose a rendering of any of these words that fits the contemporary context rather than the ancient one, thus providing a handful of different translations for all four categories without much consistency. In this context, it is worth noting that the Septuagint almost always translates the word *ger* with *prosēlytos,* i.e., "proselyte" or convert to the faith of ancient Israel, when it refers to a person not originally a member of the tribes; when the term is used for ancient Israel itself, or e.g. one of the ancestors, the Greek word is usually *paroikos.* The choice of *prosēlytos* could only come out of a period when the concept and practice of conversion took on significance, i.e., after the Jewish di-

ily, the clan, the tribe, or the entire people to stay with the community. Eventually, the reality of the *ger* began to coincide more with our concept of "resident alien" as ancient Israel became more settled as a people. Initially, anyone who from origin did not belong to the immediate community circle was considered a *ger*. Thus an Ephraimite would be a *ger*, a stranger, in the tribe of Benjamin (Judg. 19:16).[6]

In the small-town European context of my youth, anyone not from the village was essentially considered an outsider, a stranger.[7] When I spent a year teaching in southern France in the early 1990s, I found a similar understanding of the identity of strangers among the inhabitants of the small town where we lived. Anyone from another town was considered a stranger, and people from Paris were certainly viewed as strangers. Moreover, strangers were regarded with suspicion and mistrust, if not outright hostility. The same social outlook is probably found wherever small-scale communities with their own histories still exist across the world. In other words, the primary circle in relation to which individuals stand in a posture of strangers can be quite contained, even today.[8]

Certainly, today as in the past, strangers lead an uncertain existence, since they lack the rights and privileges automatically afforded to the dominant group. Strangers exist on the margins of the group or society. Economically and politically, their lives are uncertain, depending on the legal and

---

aspora was well established in the 3rd century B.C.E. and afterwards; it obscures the original inclusivity of the category of *ger*, as well as the importance of the requirements laid on the ancient community in terms of its behavior toward outsiders who were not necessarily of the same religious convictions.

6. The translation "stranger" for *ger* thus seems the most appropriate, since it carries both the connotation of "otherness" and the ambiguity in terms of its exact social location that the Hebrew term includes. This contra Christiana van Houten, *The Alien in Israelite Law.* JSOTSup 107 (Sheffield: JSOT, 1991), *passim.* The term "alien" fits a contemporary socio-political context that does not coincide with the ancient one, and it does not cover biblical usage. The word "stranger" is flexible enough and vague enough to fit a category that was not clearly defined until perhaps the time after the Babylonian exile.

7. In my hometown the word used for such people was *vreemde* or, in our dialect, *vremde*, obviously related to the German *fremd*.

8. In considering the social location of the *ger* it is important to keep in mind that in terms of ancient Israel one is quite far removed from the industrial/technological, large-scale societies of the contemporary world. See *Man in Society: Patterns of Human Organization*, ed. Mary Douglas, Gerald Barry, J. Bronowski, James Fisher, and Julian Huxley, rev. ed. (Englewood Cliffs: REC, 1968). In this volume see esp. Douglas, "Scale of Organization," 46-63. If, at least for a part of its existence, ancient Israel consisted of self-contained, small-scale societies or "bands," anyone from outside a given "band" could be considered a *ger*.

economic rights the group is willing to grant them.[9] Socially and psychologically, their lives are vulnerable as long as they are not accepted fully by the dominant group. Socially, they are viewed as "other" and therefore inferior. Psychologically, they are destabilized because the manner in which they are perceived as outsiders causes persistent psychological stress. Moreover, disorientation and depression many times follow being uprooted from a familiar place and people, even if that familiarity was an oppressive situation. Frequently, strangers are abused and violence breaks out against them. Such is the experience of many ethnic minorities in the world today. Such was the experience of the people that escaped from Egypt; there they had to endure violence in all its forms, social, economical, physical, and psychological. Such was the experience of most Jewish communities in Western Europe during the centuries of their existence.

The passage in Deuteronomy considered in chapter 1 refers to "your stranger who is in your gates" (Deut. 31:12; see above, 12). By this statement, the text includes strangers as being called to the same requirements of listening to torah and acting upon it as the rest of the community. There are other examples of the inclusion of the stranger in the religious practices of ancient Israel, and we will review the full scope of regulations pertaining to the stranger at a subsequent stage of our study of the Torah. For now, I note that the regulations that apply to the stranger are unique to ancient Israel in its cultural and geographical context, and that they count as the most frequently stated law in the Torah; that they occur in every major law code; that their articulation covers a wide area, from the prohibition to oppress, to specific behavior in term of care-giving, to the requirement to love the stranger. Such provisions point to an ongoing concern with the welfare of the stranger throughout the history of ancient Israel, as well as to the possibility of development and adaptation of laws pertaining to the stranger.

Here we will take a closer look at the essential posture required of ancient Israel toward the stranger by considering Exodus 23:9.[10]

9. It is, e.g., noteworthy that even today in the United States "resident aliens" are deprived of the right to vote and that they may be seriously damaged economically by inheritance laws that disadvantage them. Clearly, also, the status of aliens in the U.S. became more unstable after the Sept. 11, 2001, attacks on New York City and Washington. Especially, certain parts of the world are experiencing prejudice and discrimination in terms of visa extensions, etc. Hundreds of "suspected" aliens were arrested during the months after the attacks and were held without representation or counsel, without being formally charged, and even at the time of this writing many are still held in custody.

10. Stipulations regarding the stranger occur three times within the framework of the Book of the Covenant (Exod. 20:22–23:33). In Exod. 22:21 the prohibition to oppress is stated as follows:

To Know the Heart of the Stranger (Exodus 23:9)

Exodus 23:1-9 concerns itself with a variety of appropriate and inappropriate behaviors toward certain groups. The first three verses articulate which groups should not receive support in legal disputes: justice should not be based on size, power, or status. The last four verses provide protection for the poor, the innocent, the righteous, and the stranger (vv. 6-9). The style of the text is prohibitive, "you shall not," except in the two central verses (4-5) which function as a bridge between the two sections. These bridge-verses are in a more leisurely descriptive style, and they depart from the prohibitive absolute style to present case law, followed by positive demands in the absolute form. These laws essentially move the concern for one's neighbor to a different place: not only vulnerable people, but unlikely groups such as one's enemies must be within the full range of concern of the covenant community. Such then is the context for the demand made in verse 9: "A stranger you must not oppress; you yourselves know the heart of the stranger, for strangers you were in the land of Egypt."

The word "stranger" comes first in the Hebrew sentence, a sign of the weight it carries here. It is repeated at the end of the second phrase, and then once again at the beginning of the third phrase. The threefold repetition alternating with three verbs in the second person clearly positions the community toward the stranger: this requirement concerns the "stranger" and "you"; it concerns "you" and your knowledge of the "stranger"; it concerns "you" and your own experience of being "strangers."

The verb "to oppress" literally means "to press," or "squeeze," and has connotations of physical and psychological violence. The recipient of this violence in the Hebrew Bible is most often ancient Israel, as it experienced oppression consisting of cruel treatment by hostile powers.[11] Such treatment as it received then, the community must not in its turn practice toward others. The prohibition is followed by a double motivation, the last of which, "for strangers you were in the land of Egypt," is the common expression of motivation for the proper treatment of strangers. Israel's own suffering during the time it was a stranger in a strange land typically provides the basis for a prohi-

---

"A stranger you must not abuse and you must not oppress him, for strangers you were in the land of Egypt." Following 23:9, v. 12 in the same chapter reads: "Six days you will do your work and on the seventh day you will rest, in order that your ox may rest, and also your donkey, and so that your servant and the stranger may take a breath." This repetition of concern for the stranger is all the more remarkable in view of the relative lack of repetition of laws in the Book of the Covenant.

11. See the use of the verb *lahats* in Exod. 3:9; Judg. 4:3; 10:12; and Isa. 19:20. For a literal use, see Num. 22:25, where Balaam's donkey "squeezes" itself and thus Balaam's foot against the wall in terror at the sight of God's messenger.

bition of the same type of suffering on the part of others with a similar position in their midst as had once been their own in Egypt.[12]

In a literal sense, this basis for behavior would function only for the generation of those who had experienced the oppression in Egypt. Afterwards,
this suffering existed only in the memory of the people. We observe, then, that
the community is called to its task of preventing suffering of strangers through
a recall of its own painful history. That they were once "strangers in the land of
Egypt" is a strong part of their identity, and through the recall of this identity
the covenant community has access to past experience as if it were their own.
Much of the history of ancient Israel as a settled people involved subsequent
suffering and oppression, so that ongoing experience provided a ready access
to memory. It is remarkable that the appeal to personal experience of past suffering from hostile behavior of host to stranger became a motivation not for
revenge but for avoiding the same behavior.[13]

Whereas the motivation of a recall of the past of Exodus 23:9 is a common feature of regulations that pertain to the stranger, the phrase that pre-
cedes it is unique in the Bible: "You yourselves know the heart of the
stranger." The verb has changed to a plural form from the second singular in
the first phrase, to underscore the significance of the involvement of the entire community. The community has a personal involvement with the
stranger and "knows its heart." The verb "to know" in Hebrew always carries
connotations of intimate acquaintance and also here points to thorough and
intimate knowledge. The word translated with "heart" is the Hebrew word
nefesh, many times rendered as "soul" in English translations. It is difficult to
find an adequate equivalent for this word. *Nefesh* indicates the "self" or entire
being, and can be used to refer to animal as well as to human life in the Bible.
One does not *have* a *nefesh;* one *is* a *nefesh.* The verb "to know" together with
its object *nefesh* signifies that ancient Israel has intimate acquaintance with
the *self* or the *being* of the stranger. Taken together with the last phrase, this
statement becomes true insofar as the community can locate and identify its
Egypt-experience.

Covenant and torah go together. The covenant community knows it be-

12. See, e.g., Exod. 22:21: Deut. 5:15; 10:19; 24:17.

13. Rabbi Jonathan Sacks observes that this text does not base itself on reason or emotion
but rather speaks of history: "You know what it is like to be different, because there was a time
when you, too, were persecuted for being different. Indeed, that is what the Israelites are commanded never to forget about their shared experience of exile and slavery. They have to learn
from the inside and always remember what it feels like to be an outsider, an alien, a stranger";
The Dignity of Difference: How to Avoid the Clash of Civilizations (New York: Continuum, 2002),
59.

longs to God and is thereby called to live a life that emulates God's concern for the creation. It also recognizes itself in the experience of suffering, as "aliens and exiles," "strangers in the land of Egypt," and the exercise of its call depends to a great extent on its ability to name and recognize its suffering. The stranger will not be excluded from the community insofar as the community is able to name its own experience of exclusion. Rather than pushing this experience away, the call of the text is to acknowledge it as a mark of identification, and by implication the text calls the community to *become* strangers in the land of Egypt. And as the community is called to name and embrace the Egypt experience in past and present, so it is also exhorted by implication to gain intimate knowledge of the stranger's existence. Without such knowledge, after all, the required posture toward the stranger would not be possible.

This is a rich text, with much torah, also for the Christian community. We shall return to the concern for the stranger that is expressed here as it occurs in all the significant law codes of the Bible. The implication of Exodus 23:9 is that the beloved community, the community of the chosen ones, the ones close to God's presence, is able to conduct itself appropriately toward the stranger as it has access to the experience of suffering and deprivation and at the same time denounces the practices of the oppressor.

The experience in Egypt was foundational for ancient Israel for its experience both of oppression and of liberation. The Egypt-experience may be seen as a metaphor for a type of oppressive existence, where the lowly and downtrodden are not cared for, but rather crushed, where strangers are squeezed even further to the margins. Biblical Egypt is a symbol for a society that has no standard but a bent sense of its own importance, no values but those of profit, no understanding of strength unless it is violent. Egypt is a place where, in the words of the poet Audre Lorde, "Decisions to cut aid for the terminally ill, for the elderly, for dependent children. . . are being made by men with full stomachs who live in comfortable houses with two cars and umpteen tax shelters. None of them go hungry to bed at night."[14] Vis-à-vis this existence, the covenant community is called to live as a stranger.

In his *Theology of the Old Testament: Testimony, Dispute, Advocacy,* biblical scholar Walter Brueggemann draws attention to the centrality of claims of justice in the Bible. He observes that the kind of justice we find there is not so much *retributive* as *distributive.* This type of justice means that God has a burning love for those on the underside of the society, for those who are "down and out," who do not share in the benefits of the dominant groups.

---

14. Audre Lorde, *Sister Outsider* (Trumansburg, NY: Crossing, 1984), 140.

This type of justice, Brueggemann remarks, "is inherently destabilizing of the status quo, for redistribution means to place established interests in jeopardy."[15] Following Brueggemann, I propose that this understanding of justice underlies the concern expressed for the stranger and that it is, moreover, at the heart of the Torah and of all torah, as a claim laid on the community that is charged with modeling itself and its concerns on God and God's concerns. By studying its demands, we hold the key to interpreting and practicing torah for our day. Its standard will be the one to which we hold other rules and regulations that come to us from the ancient teaching of the Bible.

15. Walter Brueggemann, *Theology of the Old Testament: Testimony, Dispute, Advocacy* (Minneapolis: Fortress, 1997), 738.

Torah in a Covenant Context

What is the Torah? It is both a document and a concept, a principle of faith and a set of biblical texts. For Judaism, the Torah is at the center of belief and practice, and its perimeters can be extremely wide, beginning with the Bible, including rabbinic writings, and extending to include all Jewish religious thinking and writing. Within a Christian framework, the Torah, often called the Pentateuch, consists of the first five books of the Bible, which as a part of the Christian Old Testament suffer from neglect and misunderstanding in a Christian context. The purpose of the Torah is for *torah*, "instruction" or "teaching" for the community that has been taken into covenant with God. Torah, which speaks to the task of how the covenant community should conduct its life, can be properly understood only within the Sinai covenant, to which it is called by God and which speaks to its identity. With the covenant given at Sinai God promises presence, and the people make a promise to be attentive to this presence, to "listen to God's voice." The community that views itself in covenant with God through its faith in Jesus Christ would benefit from a similar attentiveness. Listening requires paying close attention and setting aside prejudice. Early followers of Jesus saw themselves also as a called community with a special charge, as exemplified by 1 Peter 2:1ff. In words that lean heavily on epithets applied to ancient Israel in Exodus 19, the writer assures the addressees that they are "God's own people." Exhortations to live a life that accords with their high calling surround the declarations of 1 Peter 2:9-10; many of these instructions cannot be taken out of the ancient context to make them functional today.

Traditionally, Christians have interpreted the words of 1 Peter to mean that the Jews are excluded from the gifts and promises of God, to be replaced by those who confess faith in Jesus Christ. Letting the text of 1 Peter enter into conversation with the text of Exodus 19 enables us to see that the calling to be a "holy nation" is not intended to create a superior in-group compared to whom all other religious alliances, especially those of the Jews, are inferior. Rather, the covenant community both at the time of the Exodus and at the time of 1 Peter is called to a life that mirrors God's passion for justice in the world. Such emulation is exemplified especially by the required posture and practices toward the stranger. The regulations that cover the behavior and attitude toward the stranger include an assumption of intimate acquaintance with the being of the stranger on the part of the covenant community and a prohibition against meting out to the stranger the same oppressive treatment it once received itself, as illustrated by Exodus 23:9. While rules for a given group both in the Old and the New Testament are often context-specific, a community that responds to the stranger in appropriate ways as guided by torah may learn to interpret for its own day guidance specific to the ancient context.

PART II

The World of the Torah

Introduction: The People of the Tale

Telling, and hearing, came first, and the process was marvelous, metaphoric, meant. We were beguiled by, and brought together upon, narratives which in their recounting allowed for — indeed, which compelled — all kinds of speculation as to their outcome and as to their ongoing likelihood.[1]

Jews, as well as Christians, are sometimes called "the people of the Book." In his essay on Esther, Richard Howard suggests that the Jews should instead be called "the people of the Tale."[2] For the story came first and the hearing of it, rather than the text and the reading of it.[3] The Bible tells a story; the Torah tells a story. The story of the Torah is complex and weaves an intricate tapestry of tales within the larger tale, but it has an overarching theme: the books of the Torah

---

1. Richard Howard, "Esther — Apart: Hearing Secret Harmonies," in *Congregation: Contemporary Writers Read the Jewish Bible,* ed. David Rosenberg (San Diego: Harcourt Brace Jovanovich, 1987), 407.

2. Howard, 407.

3. With this observation I do not intend to address the issue of the process of text formation, as if there were a linear progression from an articulation of the text in oral form to a written one. I will take up the issue of this process later in the chapter. Here I point rather to the character of the Bible as *spoken word,* to its essential orality. Franz Rosenzweig observed that the Bible "must remain word" ("Scripture and Word: On the New Bible Translation," 41), while Martin Buber said, "We had . . . in mind the Bible 'aloud'. . . .We proceed from the notion that the Bible is a product of living recitation, and is intended for living recitation: that speech is its nature, and the written text only a form for preserving it" ("A Translation of the Bible," 170); in Buber and Franz Rosenzweig, *Scripture and Translation* (Bloomington: Indiana University Press, 1994).

tell of the creation of Israel, God's covenant people, in the context of the creation of the world, God's covenant world.[4] A good story contains tension, introduces complexities and difficulties into the theme, and the story told in the Torah is no exception. The desired outcome, both for the world and for God's covenant people, is not a sure thing. Many times, the situation seems so fragile and uncertain that everything hangs by a thread. Sometimes, there is a long pause in the action, and nothing much seems to be happening at all. Other times, there is so much human waywardness that only destruction seems a possible outcome. Yet, the story moves on through all the ups and downs, until at the end the crowd of God's choosing, the covenant people ancient Israel, are on the verge of entering the land promised to them and their ancestors.

In speculating on the content of the first books of the Bible, some scholars have proposed adding Joshua to the Torah as the continuation of the history of ancient Israel, thus creating a Hexateuch, or a unit consisting of six rather than five books.[5] Apart from the questionable wisdom of extending the traditional bounds of the Torah, in terms of the story it may be unwise, theologically speaking, to end it with the occupation of the promised land. At the end of the story of the Torah the covenant people are still outside of the land God promised to them, on the verge of entering but no further than that. Their leader, Moses, has died and the gift of the land still awaits them, so the ending of the story is left open, full of possibilities rather than closed off. The story line of the Torah does not come to a grand conclusion with the sounds of trumpets and clash of weaponry that accompany the conquest of Canaan. Rather it ends in a pause, an almost breathless waiting to see what will happen next. Instead of a "happy ending" there are tension and anticipation.[6]

It is significant that the story of the covenant people begins with the origin of the world, and with God's involvement both with its making and its

4. The covenant with Noah as described in Gen. 9:8-17 is in truth a covenant between God and the entire creation. The composers of the Torah thus framed the Sinai covenant against the backdrop of the covenant God had established with "all flesh," both human beings and animals, and even with the entire earth since this is a covenant between God and "the earth."

5. See, e.g., Gerhard von Rad, *The Problem of the Hexateuch and Other Essays* (Edinburgh: Oliver and Boyd, 1966).

6. Cf. the following observation by Terence E. Fretheim: "The ending defers the fulfillment of the promise; it gives to the Pentateuch the character of an unfinished symphony. The promise is left suspended and the people are dispirited and fearful ([Deut.] 31:6). The future is not simply filled with delights; it is fraught with danger"; *The Pentateuch* (Nashville: Abingdon, 1996), 54. Also: "The Pentateuch does not end with an arrival, but with a suspension of the moment before departure"; Thomas W. Mann, *The Book of the Torah: The Narrative Integrity of the Pentateuch* (Atlanta: John Knox, 1988), 159. See also David J. A. Clines, *The Theme of the Pentateuch,* 2nd ed., JSOTSup 10 (Sheffield: JSOT, 1997), 26.

continuation. The first 11 chapters of Genesis paint on a wide canvas as the entire earth and its inhabitants come into view. Regularly, the focus of the story narrows from the large to the small, from all the world's citizens to individuals. Lists of genealogies enter the text to widen the scope, and individuals come forth from these lists to illustrate the encounter of God with the world and to narrow the focus once more, until the searchlight finally picks out the family of Terah and a beginning is made with the ancestral tales of ancient Israel.[7] The telling of the origins of God's covenant people Israel is thus set into the large framework of God's concern for the whole world. Logically, then, God's promise to Abram includes a blessing for "all the families of the earth" (Gen. 12:3). Human ambitions and occupations are woven into these chapters. Smiths and farmers, tent-dwellers and herders, vintners, builders, and musicians appear. Movements of peoples across the land are noted until the migration of Abram, which follows a specific command from God.

From Genesis 12 on until the end of the book, other groups and people will come into view only as they relate to the patriarchs and matriarchs of ancient Israel. As the stories commence that tell of ancient Israel's ancestral beginnings, a family emigrates out of its native land and culture (Gen. 11:31-32). One part of this family, in the person of Abram, is called by God to locate in a specific place with the promise of multiple descendants (Gen. 12:1-3). Eventually, the promise of permanent occupancy of the land of Canaan is added (Gen. 15:18-21). Much of the tension in the subsequent narrative revolves around the difficulty of securing sufficient progeny to warrant populating the land. Ironically, at the end of the tale the ancestral families find themselves with some certainty in terms of their number but far from the land of the promise, leaving the full completion of God's double promise still in doubt.

This ambiguous conclusion to Genesis opens up into the somber beginning of the book of Exodus with the offspring of the ancestors enduring harsh servitude in the Egypt to which their forebears had fled. A land of plenty has become a place of suffering and forced labor (Exod. 1–2). From this unendurable situation the people are freed by God through the agency of Moses (Exod. 3–15), and in the wilderness they are forged into a people in covenant with their God (Exod. 19–24). In order to live as a covenant people

7. It is common to begin the ancestor narratives with the "call" to Abram in Gen. 12:1-3. The transitions to this section are actually quite fluid. Gen. 11:10ff. describes the descendants of Shem issuing in the parentage of Abram, and it is possible to understand this listing as the opening of the Abram cycle. Another possible beginning of the ancestor cycle can be seen in 11:27 with the listing of the descendants of Terah, or in 11:31 with the departure of Terah and his extended family from Ur.

they receive instructions, torah, a compendium of how to conduct their life as a community with each other and with God (Exod. 20–24) The book of Exodus contains both the story of the liberation and the constitution of a people, called "the children of Israel."[8] The story of this people-making proceeds far from smoothly. Many bumps in the road provide doubts as to the successful outcome of the adventure (see esp. Exod. 16–17; 32–33). A pause in the narrative is taken up by elaborate instructions for the construction of a mobile sanctuary (Exod. 26–31).

An even longer pause occurs with Leviticus, a book that concentrates on worship and ritual, the maintenance of its apparatus, and conduct of its personnel. Rules are laid down for the maintenance of purity and holiness both for the specialists and the people as a whole. In Leviticus the story of the people's trek through the wilderness on their way to the land of the promise halts to project images of what it entails for the people and their appointed cultic officials to be a people so closely related to God. These images come to us veiled in ancient custom and ritual, foreign to much contemporary Christian religious sensibility. With Leviticus it becomes especially important to listen as attentively as we can and set aside the Christian prejudice that there is nothing to be found here of religious value and direction for our lives.

In Numbers the story of the people's trek under the leadership of Moses continues, preceded by a census and lists of different tribal groups with their specific tasks and prescriptions for specific religious ritual (Num. 1–10). Numerous incidents take place in the wilderness while the newly minted covenant people make their way to the land of the promise, until finally, after an initial exploration of what awaits them in Canaan, the mistrust and lack of confidence on the part of the "children of Israel" so inflame God's anger that the period of their wilderness wanderings is extended by 40 years (Num. 12–14). In the last chapters of Numbers the people find themselves across the Jordan busy divvying up allotments of land for different kin-groups. Generally, the story in Numbers is darker in tone than in Exodus, God is more easily angered, the people more resentful and rebellious. However, some of the most vibrant and detailed episodes occur in this text, and the parade of different characters is rich and varied. Here we meet not only the familiar figures of Moses, Aaron, and Miriam but also Caleb and Joshua (Num. 13ff.), Balaam, the reluctant prophet (Num. 22–24), and the daughters of Zelophehad (Num.

8. In this context, Buber's observation still rings true: "YHVH and Israel enter into a new relation to one another by making the Covenant, a relation which had not previously been in existence; and further could not have been in existence because Israel as a nation . . . had been constituted only in that hour"; *Moses: the Revelation and the Covenant* (New York: Harper, 1958), 104.

27–36), among others. Numbers moves the story along until the people tread "the verge of Jordan."

Now the story comes mostly to a halt, as Deuteronomy contains for the greatest part recollections of the way the people have come to this moment just before entry into Canaan, with commentary on the relationship that has been established between God and people and torah requirements for their existence in the land they are about to enter. The form of the book is almost entirely cast as a speech from the mouth of Moses. A brief concluding section describes the demise of Moses, a prophet the like of which was never again to rise in Israel (Deut. 34:10). Deuteronomy contains some material that is particularly difficult to interpret for a contemporary context, such as the sections that command the utmost destructive violence toward the populace of Canaan in the process of inhabiting it (Deut. 7:1-26) or the curses attached to potential violations of covenant obligations (28:15-68). Here, the covenant between God and the people stands in the foreground as also a potentially endangered reality, and Deuteronomy offers a particular perspective on the covenant relationship and what it entails for the people who have entered into covenant with God. Profound statements about the community's required love for God and neighbor and about God's bias toward deprived groups can be found here also (e.g., Deut. 6:5; 10:12-22).

CHAPTER 1

The World of the Tale

*The unity of Israel depends on kinship, the community of soul aris-
ing out of a common character and a common history, and it is expressed by dating the people back to a common ancestor.*[1]

Family, Field, and Town

As I have described the story line of the Torah in broad strokes, we ask about
the world that formed the context of the tale. Out of what sort of world did
this story arise, and to what specific concerns of this world does it address itself? When faced with the texts of Holy Scripture we are not confronted with
one world, of course, but with many worlds. The Bible is also a written record that reflects a history of more than a thousand years, a period that naturally saw great change on all levels of the society, social, political, and religious. Were we to describe in rough outline the story of the people that gave
birth to the Bible from the time of their beginnings up until the time of Jesus, it would look as follows according to the biblical record: A kin-group of
herders and tent-dwellers migrated from Mesopotamia to the small habit-
able area on the Mediterranean coast that the stories called Canaan. This
group expanded slowly and finally was forced by famine to migrate to Egypt
for their survival. In another period, after the kin-group in Egypt had expanded considerably and their members were put to work at forced labor,
the group escaped and trekked through the Sinai Peninsula back to Canaan,
where they eventually settled. The kin-groups lived in a loose federation in

1. Johannes Pedersen, *Israel, Its Life and Culture* (London: Oxford University Press, 1926),
1:57.

the land of Canaan until the needs of the times required a more centralized manner of government.

The loose federation of groups became a more centrally organized nation some time during the 10th century B.C.E. The coalition, thus forged, fell apart by the end of the century and two realms came into existence, one in the south and one in the north, each with its own central administration. Both kingdoms were vulnerable to outside attack, beset by powerful and expansive empires to the southwest (Egypt) and the northeast (Mesopotamia). At times the kingdoms themselves were also at war with each other; thus, peaceful times were rare for ancient Israel. In the last quarter of the 8th century the northern kingdom succumbed to the Assyrian Empire. About 150 years later, around 590, the same fate overcame Judah in the south and Jerusalem fell to Babylon. Persia followed Babylon as the reigning power in the area, and after 50 years of exile a decree from the Persian king made it possible for those from Judah who wished to do so to return "home." Then followed two centuries of rebuilding and restoration, but Judah remained a province of the large empire of which it had become a part, first Persia, then Greece, and finally, in the days of the New Testament, Rome. This reality colored the lives of people until the days of Jesus and afterwards. Dependence, heavy taxation, hard labor, and frequently a presence of foreign armed forces were all part of the normal routine. Instability and oppression provided much of the context for the texts that comprise the Bible, especially the Old Testament.

In such an unstable world, how did families and communities live together, and what social and cultural norms governed human relations? The mode of social and economic life of the loosely organized tribal federation during the early periods was that of a small-scale agricultural, self-sustaining society. Historically, we are speaking of the Late Bronze and the Early Iron age (1600-1000), when survival of groups depended on their ability to produce enough healthy offspring to guarantee an ongoing population.[2] Threats of war, famine, epidemic, and endemic parasitic diseases were a constant threat. For most women, bearing enough children to insure a surviving population left them weak and more vulnerable than men to such threats.[3] The obsession

2. Population figures for these as well as later periods in the region of our concern are extremely hard to come by. Norman K. Gottwald laments that all the figures arrived at are "crude estimates based on sparse data and using virtually none of the techniques and controls of modern demographic studies, so that the question of the population of ancient Palestine cries out for fresh examination"; *The Tribes of [Y·hw·h]: A Sociology of the Religion of Liberated Israel, 1250-1050 B.C.E.* (Maryknoll: Orbis, 1979), 742-43 n. 186.

3. Where men's life expectancy was somewhere around 40 years at this time, for women this could be put more realistically at 30. Childbirth itself weakened a physical system that had

with biological productivity is clear from many biblical narratives and should be understood from within this context. Regulations of sexual relations should be viewed likewise.

During the period of the monarchies, agriculture continued to secure sustenance and well-being for extended families or kin-groups outside of the two main cities, Jerusalem and Samaria, neither of which probably ever exceeded 30,000 people in population.[4] The type of agriculture practiced is called intensive, with women spending as much as five hours in the field next to their men. Daily life was centered on what can be called the "family household," an economic as well as a biological unit. The household produced most of what it needed to sustain itself for survival, and the family household was the determinative location for most women, men, and children. The more urban culture of city life was characterized by a governing male bureaucracy and a more market-oriented economy.[5] From the vantage point of people in the Western industrialized world, especially the United States, we need to scale down our perspective when considering the world of the biblical tale. Everything was smaller than we consider normal for towns

to sustain many threats. See Carol L. Meyers, "The Roots of Restriction: Women in Early Israel," in *The Bible and Liberation: Political and Social Hermeneutics,* ed. Norman K. Gottwald (Maryknoll: Orbis, 1983), 289-306. Athalya Brenner, in analyzing reports from burial grounds dating back to the early Roman periods, more than a thousand years after those researched by Meyers, puts the average age of mortality for women at 20-25 years; *The Intercourse of Knowledge: On Gendering Desire and "Sexuality" in the Hebrew Bible* (Leiden: Brill, 1997), 65.

4. Together with other scholars, Roland de Vaux estimates the total population of Israel and Judah at the time of the monarchies to have been around one million. There would have been some variation depending on the social and economic circumstances. "Even so," de Vaux observes, "at the height of this prosperity, in the first half of the eighth century B.C., the total population of Israel and Judah cannot have been much more than one million"; *Ancient Israel* (1961; repr. Grand Rapids: Wm. B. Eerdmans and Livonia: Dove, 1997), 67. More recent estimates have created even greater uncertainty. According to B. S. J. Isserlin, it is possible that the total population in the northern and southern kingdoms of the 8th century B.C.E. amounted to roughly 500,000, only half of the earlier estimates. Although Isserlin remarks that such estimates may "err on the side of caution," he provides no correctives to the figures; *The Israelites* (Minneapolis: Fortress, 2001), 95.

5. According to Meyers, this change of agricultural to urban life occasioned a change in the status of women: ". . . the former socioeconomically *functional* significance of women's restricted roles was perpetuated and hardened into fixed practice based on *ideological subordination of women* to men. This theologized endorsement of an older functional necessity was passed along later to Jews and Christians as normative tradition and behavior"; "The Roots of Restriction," 289. See also Carol Meyers, *Discovering Eve: Ancient Israelite Women in Context* (New York: Oxford University Press, 1988), esp. 189-96; "Everyday Life: Women in the Period of the Hebrew Bible," in *The Women's Bible Commentary,* ed. Carol A. Newsom and Sharon H. Ringe, rev. ed. (Louisville: Westminster John Knox, 1998), 258.

and cities, regions and country. Life for a large part was hardscrabble. Early settlement especially took place in rather inhospitable environments where adequate water supply proved a perennial problem. A preoccupation with this essential commodity, whether coming from springs, wells, or rain, is evident from biblical narratives.[6]

Outside of the cities, life was lived in villages and small, fortified towns.[7] Climate and poor locations in terms of agricultural productivity insured mutual dependence within the community as well as a sense of urgency about providing sufficient offspring to guarantee a sufficient workforce.[8] Within this mostly agricultural society, organized on lines of kinship, class divisions were initially not large but tended to grow as a central administration took over and a degree of urbanization took place. From the many regulations in the Torah, as well as prophetic concerns, we conclude that the poor must have been, in any case, an ongoing presence in ancient Israel, with perhaps some fluctuations depending on the circumstances, some of which were not within human control. The rather harsh climate of biblical lands, with hot, dry summers, presented a fairly constant danger of drought, since rain could not be counted on to arrive as necessary, with the accompanying threat of famine — hence, the many accounts of drought and famine in biblical narrative.

The smallest unit of significance for ancient Israelite society was the "house," or the "father's house" (Hebrew *beth av*), with members living together in a family compound of several dwellings. Such an extended family would comprise a man with his wife or wives, their sons and their children, unmarried daughters, and servants or slaves.[9] All lived together with their

6. For an extensive description of the agricultural scene of ancient Israel, esp. in the days of the early settlements, see Meyers, *Discovering Eve*, ch. 3.

7. Population of villages may have ranged between 100 and 300, while fortified towns could have accommodated as many as 1500 people. For an extensive discussion of towns and villages in ancient Israel as well as cities, see Isserlin, ch. 5. Also Ferdinand E. Deist, *The Material Culture of the Bible: An Introduction* (Sheffield: Sheffield Academic, 2000), 197ff.

8. Thus Deist, 233-34: "One of the ways of ensuring survival in subsistence economies is securing enough hands to carry out the necessary tasks and, in view of a high infant mortality rate in such communities, a large enough offspring to take care of parents in their old age."

9. Families were patrilineal and patrilocal. The line of succession was counted through the father, and brides moved into their in-laws' housing compound. For descriptions of family life, see Philip J. King and Lawrence E. Stager, *Life in Biblical Israel* (Louisville: Westminster John Kox, 2001); Isserlin; Deist. The size of the *bet av* is not easy to determine and would depend somewhat on social and economic circumstances. In view of the average life expectancy, mentioned above, and of the high mortality rate of children, which would affect poorer classes more severely, the number of people in a compound may have been between 10 and 15, servants in-

cattle under one roof, with most family activity such as eating and sleeping taking place in one room.[10] The family was organized under the authority of the oldest male, hence it was patriarchal, with women under the stewardship of their husband or other responsible males.[11] Although a woman's contribution to the household productivity would have been essential, her rights were limited, even if within the "father's house" her authority may have been considerable. As observed by one scholar, ". . . women were under perpetual wardship — first of their father's and then their husband's or another responsible male's. They could be divorced by their husbands but not divorce them. . . . it is also doubtful whether they could testify in courts, and their religious activities were restricted."[12] Given this social structure, it is understandable that outside of the family unit a woman's life was tenuous in the extreme. It is thus for good reason that widows, together with their children (who as fatherless offspring were named "orphans"), occur frequently in legal material in the Torah as a class of people to be protected.[13] The laws of the Torah address the community mostly via its male members, while issues pertaining to women were dealt with under separate rubrics[14] (see for example Lev. 12-15). In Deuteronomy, however, women, together with other groups such as children and strangers, are explicitly included in the covenant and hence in the covenant obligations (Deut. 29:11; 31:12).

Regulations that governed sexual relations in the biblical world were primarily intended to further biological productivity in all biblical periods, in view of the scarcity of population, demands created by the agricultural life-

---

cluded, in a family of what today we might consider the middle class. See the difference in estimates of numbers per family between King and Stager (15ff.) and Isserlin (101).

10. For good depictions of the so-called "pillared house," see King and Stager; also Isserlin.

11. Polygyny, the custom of more than one wife to a husband, was certainly considered normal, although it may have been somewhat restricted in terms of affordability. See Deist, 264.

12. Isserlin, 102ff. Cf. Deist, 266.

13. Deist, 266: "Given the legal status of women in 'biblical' society, the death of a husband leaves his wife defenceless; she does not have the rights of property or inheritance, nor any means of sustaining herself. Even if her parents would still be alive, she could hardly return to them, . . . for her husband's household would have paid a bride-price for her. She is practically in the hands of the inheritor of her husband's property, who is not necessarily her own son. If she also has children to support, her position is worse, but if she has none, her position, especially in her old age, is critical."

14. Thus Phyllis A. Bird: "The basic presupposition of all the laws, though modified to some extent in the later period, is a society in which full membership is limited to males, in which only a male is judged a responsible person"; "Images of Women in the Old Testament," in Religion and Sexism: Images of Woman in the Jewish and Christian Traditions, ed. Rosemary Radford Ruether (New York: Simon and Schuster, 1974), 49.

style, and the high mortality rate of women and children (see 41-42, note 3). Boundaries around sexual relations arose generally speaking from concerns about orderly family relations and the greatest biological productivity possible. Intimacies that threatened order and procuring of progeny — such as adultery, incest, prostitution, and homosexual relations — were forbidden.[15] Sexual arrangements that would be frowned upon in contemporary Western Christianity are found without sanction in the Bible, as polygyny, brother-sister marriage, and concubinage.

The centrality of the family is evident from narratives in the Torah that center on the family and family relationships as, for example, all the ancestral stories in Genesis, a characteristic continued in the opening chapters of Exodus. Also in Numbers family matters receive close attention as in the chapters on Aaron and Miriam's dispute with Moses (Num. 12) and the property grant to the daughters of Zelophehad (Num. 27; 36). Even when the scope of the narrative widens to include the entire people, the frame of reference is often that of family, with the entire community depicted as a brood of, often unruly, children who relate to their leader, Moses, as a family to its *pater familias*. The word "house" is thus frequently applied to the entire people, for whom the most frequently used appellation is "children of Israel" (cf. Exod. 19:3).

The next unit of significance is the extended family or clan (Hebrew *mishpahah*), which is the entity that provides for a larger community of responsibility and protection. It is within this circle that the role of the *go'el*, the redeemer, could take on significance. For modern readers of the Bible in Western lands, this type of unit may seem vague, and the lines between it and the father's house may appear blurry. The best analogy today may be with populations that still count their lineage by clans and recite the names of their ancestors within these clans. It sounds confusing only to the outsider.[16] It was probably customary to marry within the clan in order to prevent the loss of property to the clan, although many exceptions may have occurred.[17]

The tribe (Hebrew *shevet* or *matteh*) is well attested to in the biblical literature and indicates the social unit consisting of a number of clans who may have inhabited the same region and traced their lineage back to a common

---

15. For various prohibitions, see Lev. 18; 20; also Deut. 27:20-23.

16. I have found in teaching students from a nonindustrialized part of the world such as Western Africa, e.g., that they were able to recite long lists of their ancestors and had a clear sense of clan identity.

17. Meyers, *Discovering Eve*, 183. For examples of both, see Gen. 38; Exod. 34:11-16; Num. 25:1-8; 31:9-18; Deut. 7:3-4.

ancestor. Thus the census in Numbers 1 takes account of the "congregation of the children of Israel," according to their clans *(mishpehot)* by ancestral house *(bet avotam)*, and the ones heading the registration are the "leaders of the ancestral tribes" (*mattot avotam;* Num. 1:2-16). Scholars generally agree that the 12-tribe system depicted in the Bible is an artificial construction, but this does not make the tribe itself an insignificant phenomenon. In a hostile environment tribal allegiance may have afforded a sense of community and protection, but how such protection was organized beyond the raising of military force in time of need is not clear, for we know little about the tribes in terms of social organization or constitution.[18]

With the rise of the state and monarchy the concept of a "people" united under one administration took on more concreteness, but for the most part the immediate communities of family and clan would have the most significant function in the life of the ancient Israelite. In the literature, the people are thus spoken of as a family, one community with one common ancestor. Although the statement from Johannes Pedersen at the start of this section may strike us today as somewhat romantic, it is not alien to the spirit of the writing that speaks of and addresses the people as a "congregation," a "house," and as "children." It is probably a mistake to assume too great a homogeneity among the people until after the Babylonian exile. Following Isserlin, we may assume that "ancient Israelite society . . . was never purely Israelite, for intermixed with free Israelites there were descendants of Canaanite and other Bronze Age town and country folk, landless alien labourers in the countryside, as well as a scattering of foreign craftsmen and traders."[19] In addition, the country afforded the major trade route between Mesopotamia and Egypt, so that a good deal of traffic must have taken place with a consequent intermingling of different populations. Last, frequent warfare would have caused sizeable numbers of displaced persons and refugees from neighboring peoples that ended up in ancient Israel. The frequent mention of the stranger, the *ger,* in the Torah points to a situation where people who were not from the family, the clan, or the tribe would have to be dealt with on a regular basis (see 25-28 above).

After the Babylonian exile, the return and the restructuring of Judah in

---

18. Cf. Isserlin, 100: "About the tribes we know least. Their boundaries, claimed or real, as described in the Bible (as well as their kinship groups) may reflect pre-Israelite regional divisions. . . . We are, however, ignorant of what kind of tribal government there may have been, especially in peacetime." King and Stager provide no particulars about the tribe at all. Roland de Vaux spends a number of pages on the tribe, but the actual information gathered from his discussion is minimal.

19. Isserlin, 93.

postexilic times, renewed anxiety about biological productivity came to the fore. With greatly reduced numbers, and chances of survival once again at an extremely low point, the emphasis on reproduction occurred with renewed vigor.[20] Further, land claims and inheritance drove an interest in descendance and appropriate genealogical lists. Central authority, in preexilic times located in the royal administration and cultic apparatus, was destabilized for a long period. For all these reasons, family took on an even greater importance than it had before, filling in also as the locus of piety and faith practice.[21] In addition, and most likely for the first time in its history, concerns arose for the ethnic purity of the community, a concern that caused internal conflict as well as conflict with the outside world. Finally, with class divisions exacerbated, heavy taxation brought about specific economic hardships weighing especially heavy on the poor.[22]

A preoccupation with reproduction, both in the human and the vegetative world, is clearly present in the material that makes up the tale of the Torah. It is equally apparent that the world is viewed from the perspective of the family. The presence of those who are not a part of the family or clan causes numerous regulations for dealing with the constant presence of strangers *(gerim)*. In addition, divisions between those who are not well-off and the more well-to-do provoke interest in the welfare of those who are not able to provide for themselves. Arrangements that fit an agricultural environment — concerning the theft of cattle, accidents caused by the same, and the growing of crops — are regulated in the oldest of the laws of the Torah. Concern with the land itself and its productivity is a strand that runs through the first five books of the Bible. In the opening chapters of Genesis, the entire earth and its

20. Once again, population figures for the postexilic period are not easily garnered. John Bright estimates the number of people in Judah after the return of the first exiles to be 20,000; *A History of Israel*, 3rd ed. (Philadelphia: Westminster, 1981), 644. See also Johanna W. H. van Wijk Bos, *Ezra, Nehemiah, and Esther* (Louisville: Westminster John Knox, 1998), 11.

21. On the role of the family in exilic and postexilic times, see Claudia Camp, *Wisdom and the Feminine in the Book of Proverbs* (Sheffield: Almond, 1985), 261ff. Also Rainer Albertz, *A History of Israelite Religion in the Old Testament Period* (Louisville: Westminster John Knox, 1994), 2:407: "Not only did family piety become significant for all of society, but for the first time the family itself joined the ranks of those who handed on official religion."

22. As Albertz observes (2:495-96): "All the groups were caught in the mill of the harsh ancient law of credit, which allowed the creditor to seize the property and the family of the debtor. . . if they were unable to pay. . . . The poorer strata of the population were driven into increasing poverty and had to hand over their children, i.e. their workforce, to their creditors as slaves; they had to give them the lion's share of the produce of their fields and vineyards and themselves worked only as leaseholders or as slaves on their former property — that is, if they and their children were not driven out and sold into slavery abroad."

well-being are of central interest to the tellers of the tale. Gradually, the spotlight falls on the land of Canaan, the land of the promise, often called "a land flowing with milk and honey,"[23] given to Israel by God as an "inheritance to possess" and, according to Deuteronomy, held by the people on the condition of their faithfulness to their God.[24]

Piety, Practices, and Prescriptions

Worship of the One

What went on in the life of religious experience in ancient Israel, and what should have gone on according to the sacred text? In the realm of religious piety and practice, which imbued all of life rather than being experienced as a separate sphere, a major concern in the Torah is with loyalty to the God who has entered into covenant with this people. One of the most common ways this concern is expressed is in the prohibitions against idol worship. The first three commandments of the Decalogue focus on the issue of idolatry, and other ancient laws of the Torah contain many proscriptions of idol-making and worship.[25] Where there exists an ongoing articulation of a concern, we may assume an abundance of practices that need to be addressed. Indeed, from archaeological testimony it appears that veneration of local Canaanite deities was common, probably until the Babylonian exile.[26] Such artifacts as have been found that witness to the significance of female deities, related to concerns of fertility for family and field, make clear that in "popular religion" the female element of the divine was highly significant to ordinary people's lives.[27]

---

23. Exod. 3:8, 17; 13:5; 33:3; Lev. 20:24; Num. 13:27; 14:8; 16:13, 14; Deut. 6:3; 11:9; 26:9, 15; 27:3; 31:20.

24. Deut. 4:39-40; 28–30 *passim*.

25. Exod. 20:3-7, 22-23; Deut. 4:15-24; 5:8-11; 6:14-15; 7:25-26; 9:12-21; 11:16-17; 12:29-32; 13:1-18; 31:16-21; 32:15-18.

26. William G. Dever mentions more than 2000 mold-made terra-cotta female figurines dating to the days of the divided monarchy which, according to him, had obvious "cultic connotations." In addition, "dozens of terra-cotta offering-stands" have been found dating to the 12th–7th centuries, miniature four-horned altars, ranging from 10th–6th centuries, as well as various "vessels and implements" and figurines with possible cultic application; *What Did the Biblical Writers Know and When Did They Know It? What Archaeology Can Tell Us about the Reality of Ancient Israel* (Grand Rapids: Wm B. Eerdmans, 2001), 174-98.

27. "It would not be surprising if [Y•hw•h] — portrayed almost exclusively as a male deity, involved in the 'political history' of the nation — seemed remote, unconcerned with women's needs, or even hostile. Thus one-half of the population of ancient Israel, women, may

In the biblical text the involvement with this aspect of piety is present for the greatest part in a negative way.[28] For the composers of the Torah, loyalty to the God whom alone the people should worship and serve is an absolute requirement, as expressed most clearly in the first three commandments of the Decalogue. The requirements not to have other gods before God (lit., "before my face"; Exod. 20:3), not to make idols (i.e., representations of anything that could be used for a worshipful purpose; Exod. 20:4-6), and not to put the name of God to wrongful use (lit., "lift it up for an illusory purpose"; Exod. 20:7) all testify to the demand for "the exclusive recognition of the exclusive rule of the divine lord, the exclusive leadership of the divine leader."[29]

Places of Worship

The impulse to connect divine manifestations with a place is probably universal and was not absent in ancient Israel from its earliest days. A number of such places are mentioned in the ancestral stories in Genesis and again in Exodus, where the place of the burning bush (Exod. 3–4) and Mount Sinai (19–24) are locations where God becomes manifest in a special way. A good deal of the material in Exodus is devoted to the description of what one might call a mobile sanctuary (Exod. 25–31:11; 35–40). The tabernacle described here, housing a powerful symbol of God's presence in the ark, is most likely a later version of what had originally been a tent where the religious leader conferred with God, a sort of oracular vehicle, rather than a representation of God's permanent presence.[30]

As long as there were many possible places at which to worship and sac-

---

have felt closer to a female deity, identified more easily with her"; Dever, 193. Dever defines popular religion as "an alternate, nonorthodox, nonconformist mode of religious expression. . . . it appeals especially to minorities and to the disenfranchised (in the case of ancient Israel, most women) . . ." (196). So also Karel van der Toorn, *From Her Cradle to Her Grave: The Role of Religion in the Life of the Israelite and the Babylonian Woman* (Sheffield: JSOT, 1994), 37: "Female piety flourishes primarily outside the official cult, behind closed doors, so to speak." See also Erhard S. Gerstenberger, in whose opinion "the household cult was women's business"; *Theologies in the Old Testament* (Minneapolis: Fortress, 2002), 42. Also Phyllis Bird, who remarks that "women's religious activities — and needs — tend to center in the domestic realm and relate to women's sexually determined work"; "The Place of Women in the Israelite Cultus," in *Community, Identity, and Ideology: Social Science Approaches to the Hebrew Bible*, ed. Charles E. Carter and Carol L. Meyers (Winona Lake: Eisenbrauns, 1996), 521.

28. The narrative in Genesis that describes Rachel's theft of the "household gods" relates their presence matter-of-factly and without condemnation (Gen. 31:19-46). See also Judg. 17:5; 18:4, 17, 20; 1 Sam. 19:13-16.

29. Martin Buber, *Moses*, 132.

30. See Albertz, 57ff.; de Vaux, 294-302.

rifice in ancient Israel, a strict control over practices of piety was hard to achieve, so that an eventual movement toward centralization of worship practices was essential. Before the Babylonian exile such centralization, in Jerusalem and Samaria, did not guarantee the purity of worship, however, and syncretistic elements were no doubt present in both places, necessitating periodic "cleansings" as the one under King Josiah described in 2 Kings 23.[31] Indeed, centralized worship in the form of a state-supported cult brought with it tensions of its own since it required the transformation of a number of concepts originally attached to the perceptions of the God who had liberated the people from Egypt.[32] Suffice it to say that unification of sacred practices into one location did not take place until codification of sacred texts was well under way some time after the exile in the early period of the restoration, at the time of the second temple in Jerusalem.

Sacrifice

One of the major ways to establish connection between the human and the divine was through sacrifice. One part of Leviticus, the book of the Torah most concerned with ritual, is devoted to the different types of sacrifices and the appropriate way to execute them (Lev. 1–7). While the descriptions of sacrifices are elaborate, there exists in the Bible no rationale for the bringing of sacrifice, which is natural enough if there existed a common understanding of its raison d'être. Scholars are divided on the meaning and the purpose of sacrifice, and it may be helpful to consider sacrifice in the context of the broader perspective of the meaning and purpose of worship, since sacrifice was an essential part of worship for ancient religion.[33] Worship, according to

31. As Dever points out (195), rather than a picture of "Deuteronomistic propaganda," 2 Kings 23 provides a realistic appraisal of an actual religious situation: ". . . every single religious object and/or practice that is proscribed in 2 Kgs. 23 can readily be illustrated by archaeological discoveries."

32. As Albertz points out (1:136): "Whereas [Y•hw•h]'s bond with a particular group had been a characteristic of the earlier [Y•hw•h] religion, the Jerusalem theologians substituted for it his close connection with a place." For a detailed discussion of the state cult in the south and the north of the divided monarchy, see Albertz, 1:126-56. For a discussion of the tension between a theologoumenon of presence through space and one of presence through time, see Samuel Terrien, *The Elusive Presence: Toward a New Biblical Theology* (San Francisco: Harper & Row: 1978), 165 and *passim*.

33. The literature on the subject is too vast to provide more than a partial overview. I have found the most helpful discussions in de Vaux, 271-517; Mann, 113-24; Fretheim, 127-31; Rolf Rendtorff, *The Old Testament: An Introduction* (Philadelphia: Fortress, 1986), 96ff.; Baruch A. Levine, *Leviticus* (Philadelphia: Jewish Publication Society, 1989), esp. 215-20.

Baruch A. Levine, has as its main objective ". . . to create an environment conducive to establishing a relationship that allows humans, individually and collectively, to bring their needs to the attention of God, the source of power and blessings."[34] Sacrifice is the means to the end of "creating this environment" in which the encounter with God is made possible, and in ancient Israel it was the major means if not the only one.[35] If in popular religion encounter with a number of deities was sought to find help with the prospering of home and hearth, of field and cattle, the texts of the Torah, especially in Leviticus, provide the prescriptions of how the God of Israel should be approached appropriately and by what manner of sacrifice.

Prayer

Establishing connection between God and humanity takes place also through prayer. Technical terms for prayer, the Hebrew verb *hithpalel* and the noun *tefillah*, occur rarely in the Torah, and are used only for Abraham and Moses in connection with intercessory requests. Noteworthy is the comment at the conclusion of the first chapters of Genesis that "they began to call on the name of the Holy One" (Gen. 4:26b), which indicates the beginning of a worship practice. Prayer in ancient as well as in modern times counts on the capacity and will of the godhead to intervene in the state of affairs. Prayer in the Bible is no different in this regard. Prayer to God in the Bible counts on the fact that God is involved with the creation and can intervene.[36] In addition and most importantly, prayer counts on God's willingness to have a change of heart and turn God's anger to compassion. This trust is evident in the prayers of especially Abraham in regard to Sodom and Gomorrah and of Moses in regard to the covenant people (Gen. 18:22; Num. 11:2; 21:7; Deut. 9:20, 26).

Most often in the Genesis narratives, people speak to God and God speaks to them in turn outside of the confines of liturgical times and places. More formal prayer, in the form of seeking God's guidance, is uttered by Moses during the desert wandering in a special designated tent, but even there it

---

34. Levine, 216. Levine observes also that "in God-centered religions, the operative theory holds that a 'present' God may be expected to be more responsive to human needs, more approachable than a deity perceived to be distant, in the far heavens."

35. Prayer was another common device to approach God, as witnessed by the biblical text. The majority of the Psalms are prayers, and besides the psalms many other prayers are recorded in the Bible.

36. "The mind and heart of God are vulnerable to the pleas *and the arguments* of human creatures"; Patrick D. Miller, *They Cried to the Lord: The Form and Theology of Biblical Prayer* (Minneapolis: Fortress, 1994), 126.

is not the apparatus of sacrificial liturgy that legitimates prayer. Most likely, ancient Israel always retained the notion that God could be called on by the believer, any believer, in prayer (cf. the story of Hannah's prayer in 1 Sam. 1:1–2:10). Directness and bold speech marked in the Bible the imprecations directed to God.

Holy Days and Festivals

Besides places and actions of worship, every religion sets aside special times, holy days and festivals, as expressions of religious experience. Ancient Israel was no exception. The foundational feast day was the Sabbath, "a cornerstone of Israelite religious practice from earliest times."[37] Scholars generally agree that the Sabbath was original to ancient Israel and that it is of high antiquity. According to Gunther Plaut, the Sabbath ". . . illustrates a genial marriage of social and cultic legislation, for it enjoins rest from labor in a cultic framework. Other ancient societies had rest days, some of them of fixed number and frequency, but none at unvarying, religiously demanded intervals."[38] Sabbath requirements occur in all the law codes of the Torah, besides being the only stipulation related to the religious calendar that is included in the Decalogue (Exod. 20:8-11; Deut. 5:12-15). The Sabbath is a feast day of which the meaning stretches back to the creation (Exod. 20:11), outward to the social context (Exod. 23:12; Deut. 5:14), and into the history of the people as a liberated people (Exod. 31:12-17; Deut. 5:15). In addition, as a time of rest, it is brought to bear on the agricultural environment in terms of the year of Shabbat, when the fields must lie fallow (Exod. 23:10-11; Lev. 25:1-7; Deut. 15), a requirement which in effect benefits the use of the land itself and was also designed to be of social benefit (Deut. 15).

In the Decalogue, the section on the Sabbath reads:

Exodus 20:8-11

8. Remember the day of Shabbat,
   To hallow it.
9. Six days you shall serve
   And make all your work;
10. And the seventh day
    Is Shabbat for the Holy One, your God.

---

37. David A. Glatt and Jeffrey H. Tigay, "Sabbath," *Harper's Bible Dictionary,* ed. Paul J. Achtemeier (San Francisco: Harper & Row, 1985), 888.

38. W. Gunther Plaut, ed., *The Torah* (New York: Union of American Hebrew Congregations, 1981), 548.

You shall not make any work;
Not you, nor your son, daughter,
Male or female servant,
Your cattle,
Nor your stranger who is in your gates.

11. For in six days the Holy One made
The sky and the land,
The sea, and all that is in them;
And God rested on the seventh day.
Therefore the Holy God blessed the seventh day
And hallowed it.

For the first time in the Decalogue a stipulation is articulated in a positive way: "Remember the day of Shabbat, to hallow it." The next lines unfold the implications of the commandment. "To remember" in Hebrew always has a more active connotation than that of a mere mental exercise. In what follows, it is made clear that the remembrance of the day first of all consists in refraining from work, the verb and noun *Shabbat* indicating "cessation." Holiness here consists first of all in separation, apartness. By determining the seventh day as a breather, a cessation from work, the community sets this day apart. Verbs that occur in the opening lines of the Decalogue, "making" and "serving," in a negative context, here are drawn into the positive sphere. "Serving" and "making" work belong to the first six days of the week. On the seventh day, Shabbat, the community is "not to make work," and in so doing the people copy the Creator God who rested from the work God made.[39]

Sabbath requirements call for a general cessation from work and leave the details to be worked out for different generations. Naturally, questions

---

39. The creation text reads:

1. Thus they were finished, sky and land
   and all their host.
2. God was finished on the seventh day
   with all the work he had made,
   and God rested on the seventh day
   from all the work he had made.
3. And God blessed the seventh day
   and hallowed it,
   for on it God rested from his work
   which God created by making. (Gen. 2:1-3)

The verb used for "rested" in these verses is *yishbot,* from the root *shabat,* whereas the Exodus text employs the root *nuh.*

arose as to what constitutes "work"; hence, two tractates of the Talmud deal with the Sabbath laws.[40] Rather than regarding such regulations as the inhibiting and limiting preoccupations of those who idolize rules, we should view them as a natural response to a need to know concretely what is involved in stopping with work, especially since the penalty for breaking the Sabbath was severe (Exod. 31:12-17). Motivations for Sabbath observance may consist of a combination of the social, practical-agricultural, and the religious. It is no longer possible to determine which came first, nor is it perhaps that important. It is for certain that a regular lying fallow of the fields benefits the ultimate productivity of such ground as it has had a rest, just as human beings derive benefit from a regular break in the rhythm of work.

In the Deuteronomic version of the Sabbath law in the Decalogue (Deut. 5:12-15), the benefits of the day of rest expressly include "servants." An expansion of the day of Sabbath into a year of rest may be found in Leviticus, where the seventh-year yield expressly benefits those without resources — servants and bound laborers, as well as animals (Lev. 25:2b-7).[41] Sabbath laws occur in all the law codes of the Torah, which points both to the importance of the day as well as to difficulties with the maintaining of strict Sabbath practices.[42] Without a doubt, the celebration of Sabbath gained in significance in exilic times, when it served as a mark of identity both for the community in exile and for the one left behind in Judah, with holy time replacing holy space as long as the temple lay in ruins.

Regularly held festivals are part of most liturgical calendars: besides the Sabbath, there were three major religious festivals in ancient Israel: unleavened bread (April), reaping the barley harvest (May), and ingathering (September). These three evolved into the Passover, the Feast of Weeks, and the Feast of Booths, as originally agricultural occasions were gradually reshaped to fit into the people's historical-theological understanding of themselves as God's liberated people. The oldest laws in Exodus mention these three simply as *ḥag*, pilgrimage festival:

---

40. *Tractates* Shabbat *and* Erubin, *The Babylonian Talmud* (London: Soncino, 1938). In addition, the Tractate *Shebi'it* in the *Seder Zera'im* concerns the laws of the sabbatical years. For a more detailed presentation, including analysis, see Jacob Neusner, *The Halakhah: An Encyclopædia of the Law of Judaism* (Leiden: Brill, 2000).

41. "Sabbath rest sends all alike back to symbolic egalitarianism. It is a regular stay against the activity that engenders inequality on the other days of the week"; John Dominic Crossan, *The Birth of Christianity: Discovering What Happened in the Years Immediately After the Execution of Jesus* (San Francisco: Harper Collins, 1998), 189.

42. Exod. 16:23-29; 20:8-11; 31:12-17; Lev. 23; 25:2-6; Deut. 5:12-15.

Exodus 23:14-17

14. Three times you shall make me festival in the year:
15. The feast of Matzot you shall keep;
    for seven days you shall eat Matzot
    as I commanded you at the appointed time of the month Abib,
    for in it you went out of Egypt —
    no one shall be seen empty-handed before me — ;
16. and the feast of harvesting
    of the first fruits of your work
    of what you sow in the field;
    and the feast of ingathering
    at the year's ending
    when you gather your harvest from the field.
17. Three times in the year
    all your males shall be seen before
    the Lord the Holy One.

In a mostly agricultural environment, the great marking periods are set by the harvests, which are from days immemorial times of celebration in predominantly rural areas. Hence, in mostly agricultural ancient Israel, harvest spelled feast. According to many scholars, there is no doubt that the liturgical calendar of the three main festivals goes back to ancient times, perhaps even to days before the religion of ancient Israel took shape, but gradually ancient Israel historicized these festivals. We may thus agree with Albertz when he observes: "The three festivals were originally agricultural festivals: they were ritual accompaniments to the harvest and served primarily to secure the powers of blessing for the land and to express joy and gratitude for the produce that had grown and been gathered in." The theological meaning of liberation then put its stamp on the main festivals "and added a new level of meaning." In this way "The festivals were successively historicized, i.e. in addition to safeguarding the blessing they took on the function of commemorating the history of the foundation of Israel and presenting it cultically."[43] Since festival time traditionally draws a large number of people, it is very likely that almost all of the community participated in some way, even though only the males of the community were officially approved as having a role in the cultus (Exod. 23:17). To what degree the theological meaning of the celebrations had an impact is difficult to discern. Again, the Babylonian exile and subsequent period of the restoration drew into the center of attention what set the community

43. Albertz, 1:89-91.

apart from its neighbors. Hence, it may well be at that time that the three main feasts became solidly anchored in the history of the Judah community as a liberated people.

A liturgical event that is not linked to ancient Israel's history is the Day of Atonement, the rituals for which are described in Leviticus 16. Since it is mentioned in only one book of the Torah, opinions differ on the ancestry of this occasion. Whether the ritual of *Yom Kippur* goes back to preexilic times or not, it is certain that the collapse of the nation during the Babylonian exile and afterwards brought a sense of guilt and need for expiation in its wake, which firmly established the Day of Atonement as one of the central events of the liturgical calendar.[44] Because of a deep sense of failure on the part of the community and self-blame in view of the loss of the promised land, which was by many received as a punishment from God's hand, postexilic times saw a rise in the frequency of and emphasis on expiatory ritual.[45]

Worlds Apart

From this overview, it is clear that much of the world of the Bible is disjunctive with contemporary experience. In terms of social, cultural, and economic life, the size of the population, concerns with biological reproduction, a predominantly agricultural environment, and family arrangements speak to vast differences in experience and outlook. Today, the entire population of ancient Israel would fit into a sizeable city in the United States. We live in a world where overpopulation rather than the threat of depopulation is a concern of global proportions. Increased urbanization is a feature of the global landscape, where the global market rather than local agriculture drives the economies of the world. Family arrangements, at least in the Western industrialized world, no longer bear the marks of the extended family or clan, nor do we live in a culture where concubinage and polygyny are accepted practices. In considering the world of the text in search of guidance, torah, for our life, we need first to become aware of the differences before we can find points of

44. Thus Walter C. Kaiser, Jr. in his commentary on Leviticus remarks that this "is the single most important day, and most characteristic ritual, in all of the legislation of the Pentateuch"; *New Interpreter's Bible* (Nashville: Abingdon, 1994), 1109. Today Judaism observes *Yom Kippur* as the last of the 10-day period that begins with *Rosh Hashanah*.

45. So Albertz (2:377): "As far as we can see, the main cult of the exilic period was predominantly lamentation. . . . This occasional form of worship, which even in the pre-exilic period was not necessarily tied to a holy place, became the element which supported the regular main cult in the exilic period."

convergence. In a sense, we must increase the distance between ourselves and the text and familiarize ourselves with its alien features before we can discern where and how we may connect with the world that gave birth to the Scripture. A process of careful listening may thus lead to renewed acquaintance and intimacy.

In terms of the world of piety and religious practice, there is great distance between ourselves and the text as well. As Christian and Jewish communities we no longer practice sacrifice, even though that reality may have different contours in the two faiths. Sabbath is still a concept that guides at least Christian public piety, but Christian Sabbath practice is a far cry from the Shabbat required in the Bible or that celebrated by Judaism today. It is perhaps nowhere so clear as in texts that prescribe religious practice how, for Christianity, a part of Scripture has entirely lost discernible relevance. Tempting as it may be to try to cross the distance, build connections, we remain for the moment in the awareness of what separates us from the text, and return to a possible bridging of the gap between our world and the biblical world in a subsequent chapter.

CHAPTER 2

The Tale in Historical Context

The Writers of the Tale

We too translate the Torah as one book.[1]

Who wrote the Torah and when was it written? Unfortunately, we do not know the answer to this straightforward question. For a long period, both in Judaism and Christianity, it was simply assumed and only rarely questioned that the writer was Moses. Finally, the occasional voice raised periodically against Mosaic authorship was joined by many others, and a theory was developed about the process of composition of the books that make up the Torah. This theory, called the Documentary Hypothesis, was articulated first by Julius Wellhausen in Germany in the 1870s and subsequently adopted by the world of biblical scholarship.[2] The theory claimed four sources for the Torah: the oldest was J, so named after the name of God, which in German begins with a J. Then came E, using the more generic name *Elohim* for God. Both were active during the monarchies, one in Judah and one in the northern kingdom. J worked as early as the 10th century B.C.E. according to some scholars and no later than the first half of the 8th, according to others. E was active between the years 922 and 722, the centuries of the existence of the

---

1. Franz Rosenzweig, "The Unity of the Bible: A Position Paper vis-à-vis Orthodoxy and Liberalism" (1927), in Martin Buber and Rosenzweig, *Scripture and Translation,* 23.

2. For a presentation of the hypothesis in its classical form, see Richard Elliott Friedman, *Who Wrote the Bible?* (Englewood Cliffs: Prentice-Hall, 1987). For an overview of the source theory together with the most recent developments, see R. N. Whybray, *The Making of the Pentateuch: A Methodological Study.* JSOTSup 53 (Sheffield: JSOT, 1987); Joseph Blenkinsopp, *The Pentateuch: An Introduction to the First Five Books of the Bible* (New York: Doubleday, 1992), esp. ch. 1.

northern kingdom. Eventually, these two sources were combined into one, after the fall of Samaria in 722.

Next in chronological order comes D, a source roughly equal to Deuteronomy which was a scroll that either originated in the northern kingdom, to be discovered eventually during the temple restoration under King Josiah of Judah in 622, or that was constructed at the time of this king for the purpose of liturgical renewal and reformation. Deuteronomy may thus be dated to the early 8th or late 7th century. If Deuteronomy as a document did not originate at the time of Josiah, it was certainly edited at that time, and from this editing process a school of editors/scribes arose called the Deuteronomists. These editors and theologians were active in the process of composing and compiling until well after the exile, and their hand can be seen in texts of the Torah outside of Deuteronomy. Thus, one might conceive of the editorial process of the texts that comprise the Torah as going from J and E to the editor or compiler of these two sources, then to the writers or editors of Deuteronomy (D), who added no new material to J/E but "tweaked" the text here and there into a Deuteronomistic direction. D conceives of the promise of the land as conditioned by the covenant obedience shown by God's people. If they "walk in God's ways," God will preserve them and the land and make them prosper. If they are disobedient, a disobedience that consists especially in worshipping other gods, the land will be taken from them. Deuteronomy and the Deuteronomists worked from the perspective of the loss of the land, either because it had already happened or was about to happen. The tone of these writers is one of warning against infractions of the covenant regulations, lest what happened once will happen again and even the little they have regained after the exile will be lost to them.

The last group of writers are designated with P for priests, and they produced texts that either directly pertained to ritual, the cult, and its apparatus, as does all of Leviticus, or that exhibit an interest in sacred places and times and designations of purity and impurity. Thus P is evident in all the books of the Torah except Deuteronomy. P is also concerned with ancestry, the showing of an orderly descent from one male to the next, and genealogical lists are usually assigned to this source. P is dated either to shortly before or during a period after the exile, but in either case a final redactor of the priestly school laid the last hand on the documents that comprise the Torah. Sometimes this last redactor is equated with Ezra, which would place the time of finalizing the text of the Torah no earlier than the 5th century.[3]

---

3. Most scholarship took for granted that all four sources could and did incorporate materials older than those assigned to the sources themselves.

With this theory — which underwent some revisions and adaptations but basically stayed intact for about a hundred years — it is possible to assign a given passage to a given source and thus provide for it a historical context, even if the margins of the historical period remained rather unstable, as well as a geographical location. The final redactor was not to be underestimated in terms of skill. In the words of Richard Elliott Friedman, "The redactor was as much an artist, in his own way, as the authors of J, E, P, and D were in theirs. His contribution was certainly as significant as theirs. His task was not merely difficult, it was creative. It called for wisdom and literary sensitivity at each step, as well as a skill that is no less an art than storytelling. In the end, he was the one who created the work that we have read all these years."[4] In this extremely positive evaluation of the redactor, Friedman echoes the opinion of Franz Rosenzweig, who suggested that "R," the symbol for the redactor, should be understood to indicate *rabbenu*, "our teacher," since ultimately the Scriptures come from this writer's hands.[5]

This hypothesis ruled virtually unchallenged in scholarly circles during almost the entire 20th century, and students were taught to dissect passages of the Torah according to the principles of this source theory. It had much to recommend it. Apparent contradictions, anachronisms, stylistic differences, and emphases were reconciled by it. A more or less solid chronological framework was erected for it that rooted the different texts more certainly in the history of ancient Israel. There were also problems. The Wellhausian premise had a built-in prejudice against Judaism (see above, 8-9), and the priestly writers are therefore of little account, mired as they were in ritualistic and legalist prejudice according to the Wellhausian view. Circular reasoning was ever present in decoding the different sources. That is, the text was used simultaneously to posit that four different sources existed and to prove the existence of the sources.

It comes perhaps as no surprise that today the situation in biblical

---

4. Friedman, 232. The certainty with which Friedmann presents the Documentary Hypothesis as fact is astonishing in view of the questions that have been put to the theory during the past decade. It was always easy for scholars to lose sight of the fact that the hypothesis was just that, a theory rather than historical fact.

5. Rosenzweig, as cited in John Barton, *Reading the Old Testament: Method in Biblical Study*, 2nd ed. (Philadelphia: Westminster, 1984), 47. See also Rosenzweig, "The Unity of the Bible": "We name that mind among ourselves by the abbreviation with which the Higher Criticism of the Bible indicates its presumed final redactor of the text: R. We, however, take this R to stand not for redactor but for *rabbenu*" (23). For one-author theories as the source of the Torah, see Whybray, 221ff.; also John Van Seters, *The Pentateuch: A Social-Science Commentary* (Sheffield: Sheffield Academic, 1999); *The Life of Moses: The Yahwist as Historian in Exodus-Numbers* (Louisville: Westminster John Knox, 1994).

scholarship is changing and the source theory or Documentary Hypothesis is called into question by a number of scholars. This move away from J, E, D, and P and a clear assignment of historical periods makes matters more complicated if we want to speak with some clarity about the ones who wrote the Torah. Out of the different proposals, there is one strand that bears looking at more closely. It is the theory that the Torah in its entirety comes from two hands, or two schools of thought, that were not always in agreement. One of the two is clearly the priestly tradition. If anything, this latest analysis views P as more important and more influential in the composition of the Torah than did earlier scholarship. The other group or school comes from the tradition of D, also postexilic.[6] Rainer Albertz, for example, proposes that the Torah is a "compromise text" dating from the end of the 6th to the beginning of the 5th century, and as such a result of the work of two groups — a group of lay theologians, whom he identifies with D because of theology and general outlook, on the one hand, and priestly composers on the other, who wrote, compiled, and edited partly in response to the first group.[7] Both theological schools incorporated much material that predated them. Whichever theory will win out in the end, the movement seems to be toward a reduction rather than a multiplying of sources, and so we are perhaps on the way toward a perception of one writer, although not one who wrote at the time of Moses.

If we maintain the notion that much in the Torah comes from a time long before the exilic periods, so that all the history of the communities that preceded the exile is reflected in them, without presenting an eyewitness account, it seems that the more recent theories have much to be said for them.[8] In fact, the notion of one writer may not be so far-fetched any more. More importantly, the perspective from which the writer wrote and with which the lis-

6. To my knowledge, this alternative has been worked out most convincingly by Joseph Blenkinsopp in the United States and by Rainer Albertz in Germany. Although the two scholars do not present identical theories, there is similarity in bringing the four sources back to two, both postexilic, each with some tension toward the other. I am here not entertaining the recent suggestions made by biblical scholars that the Torah was a product of the Hellenistic age in Judah and that the history of a people called ancient Israel is largely fiction. The motivations for this theory are suspect, in arguing for the erasure of the history of the direct ancestors of the Jews and thus implicitly for the illegitimacy of the claim of modern Israel to the land. Renewed anti-Jewish impulses, an ever-present danger in Christianity, also in Christian scholarship, seem clearly at work.

7. Albertz, 2:466-93.

8. See e.g., the care with which Rainer Albertz outlines a possible history of ancient Israel, beginning with the ancestors. Although Albertz assigns the Torah to writing schools that were active after the exile, he does not consider the history described in the Torah to be fiction; vol. 1: *From the Beginnings to the End of the Monarchy.*

tener is intended to hear the tale of the Torah is a postexilic one, which incorporates the experience of the loss of land, city, and temple. Those who tell the story of the wonderful escape from Egypt, and recite the trek to the land of the promise, dwell in a small section of that land on sufferance, by the grace not of God but of the Persian overlord. The bitter prayer of Nehemiah 9 makes clear that the community considers itself once more in slavery: "Here we are, slaves to this day . . ." (Neh. 9:36).[9] A time of great insecurity and need in all respects, social, religious, and economic, produced the need to anchor the identity of the community and its relationship to God firmly in its history, beginning with the ancestors who come forth from the backdrop of the creation. In addition, the experience of loss during the exile had caused wrenching reflections on the contribution of the community toward this tragedy. The book of Lamentations testifies, for example, to the depth of the feelings of guilt and responsibility regarding the events that had overcome Jerusalem. The tale of liberation from bondage in Egypt and its aftermath therefore includes an emphasis on the responsibility of the members of the community to live the life God calls them to and the consequences that overcome them through God's wrath as they fail to do so. In Deuteronomy this responsibility becomes the guarantor of the continuation of the covenant community in the land.

Finally, with the rebuilding of the temple, the failure to reestablish kingship, and the rise of the priesthood to the center of political as well as religious power, a highlighting of all that bound the community especially to its God, through religious ritual and cultic apparatus, was to be expected. In such distinct activity, at least one answer was found to the quest for identity and unity. If the land was no longer theirs, there was the ritual of feast and temple to provide a sense of security and continuity. Ironically, it was not the apparatus of the priests or the central sanctuary that in the end safeguarded the survival of this community but rather the tale itself in its written form, so that eventually they came to be called "the people of the book."

The Truth of the Tale

What people do not want to be told is what so many biblical scholars and theologians now believe, that is, that it is quite wrong to ask the question, "What really happened?"[10]

9. See Johanna W. H. van Wijk-Bos, *Ezra, Nehemiah, and Esther,* 79ff.

10. James Barr, *History and Ideology in the Old Testament: Biblical Studies at the End of a Millennium* (Oxford: Oxford University Press, 2000), 9-10.

I have said that "the Bible is also a written record that reflects a history of more than a thousand years" (see above, 40). It would, however, not be accurate to equate the story in the Torah with history as we understand it today. The difference between our perception of history and that of the ancient world lies above all in a different understanding of what constitutes a true story. In her book *The Battle for God,* Karen Armstrong speaks of the different ways of perceiving reality that existed in premodern times, roughly up until the 18th century, as compared to people's perceptions in the modern world. She argues that for people of the past the category of *mythos* was primary and that of *logos* secondary, while for modern people the reverse is the case. According to Armstrong, myth, as a primary category of perception and gaining knowledge, was not so much concerned with practical and factual matters but with meaning: "The mythos of a society provided people with a context that made sense of their day-to-day lives."[11] Furthermore: "To ask whether the Exodus from Egypt took place exactly as recounted in the Bible or to demand historical and scientific evidence to prove that it is factually true is to mistake the nature and purpose of this story. It is to confuse *mythos* with *logos*."[12] For the modern world, a story is not true unless it happened as it is told, more or less exactly. For the people who composed the Torah, truth is not primarily located in a sequential relating of the facts but in the meaning the story can lend to people's lives.

The world of *logos* relates to facts and factual truth. In the world of *myth*, the world of *logos* is not absent. Just so, myth is not absent in our contemporary modern world. The question that James Barr surmises as inadmissible by biblical scholars — "what really happened?" — is not a wrong question, of course. But it comes out of a different mindset than the one that produced the biblical text, so that we will most likely not receive a satisfactory answer if we ask whether the story told in the Torah really happened just as it is told.

I will use a personal example to illustrate how today we may have access to mythological story and its function. I was a young child during the five years of the Second World War when Germany occupied my native country, the Netherlands.[13] Details of this experience were for me provided by the intense story-telling that went on in my extended family circle following the war. I remember how no gathering of family members would pass, no birth-

---

11. Karen Armstrong, *The Battle for God* (New York: Knopf, 2000), xiii.

12. Armstrong, xiv.

13. For a detailed account of my war experience and its subsequent influence on my life, see Johanna W. H. van Wijk-Bos, *Reformed and Feminist* (Louisville: Westminster John Knox, 1991), ch. 1: "Dutch, Reformed and Feminist."

day party nor anniversary, without blow-by-blow accounts of numerous incidents that had occurred during the war years. We lived in a small rural community, and the characters that peopled the stories were well known to all those present. Often the central character in the tale played a role that showed up the German enemy for a fool.

One such story concerned my father, and it was always someone else who was the raconteur for this episode. My father was known as mildly eccentric and prone to somewhat reckless behavior, flouting the rules of convention when he could. It was told that at one time during the war a German convoy was coming by in our village to round up laborers who would be forced to work in some German enterprise or other. Forced labor and forced labor camps were not concentration camps, but they constituted at the same time a dangerous and life-threatening reality in the war, causing hardship not only among the laborers themselves but in the families they perforce left behind. At the time of the incident, our family had been required to leave our house for temporary quarters with another family on their farm in the region. Word had gone out and reached my parents that a roundup was taking place, and my father took refuge behind one of the huge haystacks on the property where he planned to hide until the danger was past.[14] As he was peering out at the open truck coming by, already filled with men who had been unlucky enough to be caught unawares, or who had reported themselves out of fear for reprisals, my father suddenly detected a close acquaintance of his among the soon-to-be-deported men. At this sight, he is said to have dashed from his hiding place, shouting loud greetings and hallooing to his friend, forgetting all danger, running after the slowly-moving vehicle, gesticulating wildly. Meanwhile, my mother inside could only look on in petrified horror.

The German truck rode on. My father was known everywhere because of his noticeable speech handicap since he was born with a cleft palate. Either the German soldiers never noticed my father, or — and this was the clear implication put out by the storyteller — they were under the impression that some Dutch maniac had been let loose whom they would do well to leave alone. The strange sounds my father produced under the best of circumstances would have enhanced this impression, since stressful occasions usually created a stutter to aggravate his already serious speech problem. In any case, my father was left alone, a fact which afforded the listeners to the story great satisfaction and amusement.

---

14. Such roundups generally did not involve intensive house searches of the kind that would take place in cases of suspected hiding places for Jews, members of the underground, or other victims of the Nazi regime.

It did not occur to us to ask whether this was a true story. Of course it was true! Such roundups took place all the time in our towns, especially during the last years of the war when the workforce in Germany lacked able-bodied men. One such roundup must have taken place during which my father was able to hide and so got out of a hazardous and potential life-threatening situation. But there are also parts of the story that may not be true. Would even my somewhat eccentric father have been foolish enough to leave his hiding place on the mere sighting of an acquaintance on the truck? Would he have so endangered himself, not to speak of his wife and three young children? Even had he left the haystack, would he have gone so far as running after the truck? The story is also a kind of myth, and as a myth it speaks of a number of truths. The context for the story is factual, verifiable in history: the situation of oppression and danger in which the war engulfed us at the time and of the mortal fear that was an essential part of it. It speaks of that truth in a particular way: by highlighting the daredevil character of my father's action, the story also points up that there were always those who, foolhardy perhaps, managed to escape and show the enemy for the obtuse fools they really were. In the end it was not my father but the Germans who were the fools, since they missed catching my father. My father's speech impediment added piquancy to the story. Our environment did not deal kindly with his handicap, and he was the butt of mockery many times. But in the story, it is not my father who is at the receiving end of mockery. The story told truths about context and about persons in their context. It told also a truth about my father and others like him who, even in the face of grave danger, refused to ignore ties of community and friendship. Such ties become tenuous and frayed in times of danger, and their upholding, in for example the utterance of a simple greeting, is of far greater value than simply the maintenance of the manners of daily intercourse.

The Germans were, of course, far from foolish, but for the myth it was necessary to show them that way since we were still busy taming the beast that had us in its grip for so long. Our communities in those years after the war were occupied with coming to terms with many aspects of the horrors that had overcome us.[15] One way of coming to terms was by means of the stories. Perhaps my father in truth only *peered* from his hiding place, only *thought* of hailing his acquaintance, only took *one step* from behind that haystack, where the story has him brazenly appearing, running, and loudly shouting in full view of everyone. With myth we need to take facts into account and look beyond them to what truths the story addresses and to what end it is telling

---

15. For one example of such horrors, see van Wijk-Bos, *Reformed and Feminist*, 13-15.

these truths. Myth-making goes on not only on account of war times, of course, and many of us may be able to think of parallel examples to the one I have provided here.

The Boundaries of Truth

To return to the biblical text and the story of the Torah, the truths that are told there are more important than a mere recording of historical fact. At the same time, the historical context of the story is important, for it may provide at least a partial answer to the question of why the story was told just in this way. In addition, the historical setting of a story helps to understand the concerns of the text in this setting. Automatic and direct connections made from the text to the contemporary world rarely provide useful guidance for today's predicaments. I have therefore outlined the historical context in as much detail as possible, insofar as we can know it, in order that a careful bridge between our concerns and the concerns of the text may be constructed.

In the case of the Bible, our knowledge of the context in which the text came into being is partial, but with care and imagination we may achieve a fair picture of the lives of people as I have done in the preceding pages. We draw in this effort not only on the information provided by the Bible and on biblical scholarship, but also on other fields, such as sociology, anthropology, and archaeology. Without any information about the history of the people that produced the Bible, it is extremely difficult, if not impossible, to gain access to the truths that the text may have to convey. If one had, for example, no knowledge of war in general, or of the Second World War in particular, or of the German occupation of countries in Europe, the story of the German roundup of forced laborers might be understood entirely differently. The word "roundup" receives its threatening connotation precisely from that context. Already, a few generations and a continent removed from those events, I felt it necessary to explain the activity of the German occupier in some detail. Without this information, the story might be interpreted simply as a friendly endeavor to provide transportation for vehicle-less poor farmers. Without some information about my father, his character and speech impediment, the story might still be understood but would not reach its potential as a subversive story, in which role reversals take place and the weak triumph over the strong. Many biblical stories partake of this characteristic, as the tale of Tamar in Genesis 38, the narratives of Joseph, the story of the exodus proper, some of the David stories, and especially the book of Esther.

Knowledge about the historical context also sets appropriate boundaries around the interpretation of a story, including the biblical story.[16] Not *every* construal is valid. Information about historical context limits the truths embedded in the text. I use the word "truths" advisedly here to avoid the notion that there is one great truth to be found in a given text for the discovery of which we do our listening, our reading, our interpreting. More appropriately, we recognize that there are multiple levels of truth in the biblical text and that we may never come to the end of these in our understanding. As we read and interpret, the different levels make for a rich tapestry of meaning that provides a number of possible connections to the truths of our lives.[17]

A second factor that is crucial in terms of the gathering of information, as well as establishing limits of interpretation, is that of language. Grammar and the conventions of language provide information on the meaning of a text and also set limits as to what is possible in regard to our reading of the tale. In addition, literary style, word choice, sentence structure, literary genre, structure of the text, stylistic features such as word and phrase repetition must be taken into account. Naturally, in this area imagination and educated speculation are added to formal knowledge of the Hebrew language and skill in translation.[18] In other words, in the realm of language we are no more

16. In the words of biblical scholar Blenkinsopp (142): ". . . the historical-critical reading of texts at least acts as a constraint on the tendency for the text to be subjugated to the self-understanding and agenda of the interpreter."

17. I thus subscribe to a modified postmodernism. The case for postmodernist interpretation of the Bible is most cogently made by Walter Brueggemann in his *Texts Under Negotiation: The Bible and Postmodern Imagination* (Minneapolis: Fortress, 1993). In arguing that all knowledge is contextual, local, and pluralistic, Brueggemann observes that "there is no answer in the back of the book to which there is assent, no final arbiter who will finally adjudicate rival claims" (10). While I allow for the multiple claims, or what Brueggeman terms the "cacophony of voices," I propose that the historical context sets limits to what may or may not be claimed as truth. The second limiting factor is the information that we arrive at via language and grammar, word choice, etc. See further on this below.

18. I have adopted here a combination of critical-historical reading and a literary-critical reading. The latter has come to the fore especially in the last few decades of the 20th century. Literary-critical readings received new impetus with the publication of *The Art of Biblical Narrative* by Robert Alter (New York: Basic Books, 1981). Since then the body of works that approach the biblical text from a literary-critical perspective without taking the historical context into account has become too voluminous than can be described here. Much excellent work has been done and is still being done in the realm of literary analyses of the biblical text. It seems clear that the greatest benefit of all the work done in the previous century and a half would be achieved if literary readings were always read in a historical context. For an overview of the two approaches, see *To Each Their Own Meaning: An Introduction to Biblical Criticisms and Their Application,* ed. Steven L. McKenzie and Stephen R. Haynes, rev. ed. (Louisville: Westminster John Knox, 1999).

dealing with hard facts than we are in the realm of history. There is much we do not know, and there is much we can only guess at. Moreover, the language in which the greatest part of the Bible was written, Hebrew, is for most Christians a territory with which they become familiar only if they have an interest in pursuing a field of biblical study. Familiarity with Hebrew is not embedded in the religious life and experience of the Christian, as it is in Judaism, and to an extent Hebrew remains always a somewhat alien branch on the family tree of languages for the Westerner. Furthermore, we are no longer familiar with literary conventions that governed the telling of the tale in biblical times. Alternating the story line with long lists of names, sets of laws and prescriptions for liturgical activity, and census counts would not be the way we would tell a story. Within the narratives themselves, patterns of story-telling that once were important vectors of meaning and tension may no longer be clear. In all respects, regarding the language as well as the composition of the text, a posture of humility in view of the lack of our knowledge is appropriate, as well as an openness to new information.[19]

A third factor that enters into our evaluation of the text as to its truth is related to content. In order for the story of the Torah to speak truthfully to a contemporary situation, there needs to be what I will call thematic consistency. Thematic consistency sets up a third limit to the range of legitimate interpretations of the biblical text. To give an obvious example: In the Torah, and in the entire Bible, including the New Testament, God is described as consistently on the side of the poor, the weak, the vulnerable. In the words of Psalm 146, God is the one who "watches over the strangers, and upholds the orphan and the widow" (Ps. 146:9). If we found a text in which God expresses preference for the rich, the strong, and the powerful and sides with them, it would be thematically inconsistent with the rest of the Bible, and we would need an evaluation of such a text on a different level than the one immediately apparent.

Finally, the last boundary is set by current concerns, problems, and questions. These texts of the past, out of a very different social, economic, and religious context than our own, told in a language that is foreign to us, speak

---

19. As I pointed out, a great deal of work has been done in the past three decades, especially on literary analysis of different texts. Even before this period, there were always those who were alert to features of literary composition. See, e.g., Martin Buber and Franz Rosenzweig in their exchange of thought on translating the Bible in *Scripture and Translation*. Buber was one of the first writers on biblical literature to emphasize the importance of "key words" in the text, by which he meant "a word or word root that is meaningfully repeated within a text or sequence of texts or complex of texts"; "Leitwort Style in Pentateuch Narrative" from a Lecture, January 1927, 114; cf. Rosenzweig, "The Secret of Biblical Narrative Today," 129-42; Buber, "Leitwort and Discourse Type: An Example," 143-50.

into our context if we but dare to ask the questions that arise from our contemporary situation. All the truths that the biblical story has to tell would stay on a merely informative level if it did not engage us at the point of our own questioning. This last boundary takes into account the pressing predicaments of our day as they engage with the story. In the years following the Second World War, my small community wrestled with questions of identity, of moral guidance, of the presence of evil, all of which had become sharpened for us during the war. Our stories attempted to engage these questions by the way they were told and their portrayal of characters. Our context presses us to come to the biblical text with our most urgent questions so we may engage the text at the level of deepest truth.

A Conversation between the Testaments

In reviewing the criteria for establishing the limits of interpretation of a given biblical text, where and how does the relationship between the two Testaments enter into the process? What boundaries and guidelines to the "truth" of biblical interpretation are provided by the fact that we as Christians approach the Old Testament from a Christian perspective?

First, while we acknowledge this fact as a given and thus are not able to read the biblical text as we find it in the Old Testament apart from Christian convictions, it must be said that Old Testament texts do not stand in need of a text from the New Testament for their interpretation. The Torah does not depend on the New Testament for an exploration of its theological importance and relevance for the Christian life today. This conviction flies in the face of much worship practice in Christian congregations, where New Testament readings are frequently presented without an accompanying reading from the Old Testament but the Old Testament is rarely read without the New. When passages from both Testaments are read in worship, it is not rare to find them set in contrast to one another, while in the sermon that follows, the New Testament passage regularly overrules the one from the Old. An implied rule is that the New Testament provides a standard by which to judge the material of the Old.[20] As James A. Sanders has pointed out, "The Old Testament is usu-

---

20. The current Ecumenical Lectionary used in many mainline denominations in the U.S. as well as on the European continent contributes to this problem by the selection of texts as guided by the Christian liturgical year in which New Testament texts dominate, are set in contrast with texts from the Old Testament, or are linked to the Old Testament without apparent connections. Moreover, the Old Testament is presented in a disjointed fashion with entire books hardly represented or altogether absent. See van Wijk-Bos, *Reformed and Feminist*, 40ff. For a

ally gutted and sacrificed on the altar of the Christian need to believe it has superseded Judaism."[21]

If as Christians we are to become reacquainted with the Old Testament, if we are to regain intimacy with this part of the Bible, we must orient ourselves differently. We must read the Old Testament as revealing of God, the God of ancient Israel, bound in eternal covenant relationship with the ancestors of the Jews and the Jews themselves — the same God to whom Gentiles receive access in Jesus the Christ, in whom they are received into eternal covenant relationship with God. The good news, the gospel, is always that of God's grace-filled involvement with the creation. The particular expressions of this involvement we find in the Old and the New Testaments, but not in one more than in the other.

Thus, certain texts will call out for an engagement with each other, as the Exodus and 1 Peter passages I reviewed in a previous chapter. Other texts more naturally stand on their own. In principle: a text from the Old Testament does not need a text from the New Testament to complement it or reveal its full gospel potential. When texts from both Testaments are brought into conversation with each other, usually because of quotations or thematic representation of the Old in the New, this process needs to be one of mutual illumination whereby one passage is allowed to enter into dialogue with the other and the two may shed light on each other.[22]

---

more detailed critique of the standard lectionary, see James A. Sanders, "Canon and Calendar: An Alternative Lectionary Proposal," in *Social Themes of the Christian Year,* ed. Dieter T. Hessel (Philadelphia: Geneva, 1983), 257-63. As Sanders observes: "Lectionaries as usually conceived destroy the Bible as God-spell, or God's story. God is the principal actor throughout the Bible, but Christian lectionaries leave the impression for the most part that the whole truth is told in the New Testament and that the Old Testament merely points to it" (259). See above, xiii.

21. Sanders, 258.

22. In contemporary biblical scholarship, the awareness of the need for a new perspective on the relationship of the two Testaments in a postholocaust world is best represented by the work of Erich Zenger. Zenger writes that the books of the Bible lack conceptual unity and yet, in their polyphonic character, present a unity that is best articulated as coherence (see the discussion on the need for thematic consistency above, 68). He observes that the coherence of the Bible resides in the conviction that all the traditions of Scripture relate to the one and only God of Israel who is the Creator of the world and the Parent of Jesus Christ. See Erich Zenger, "Heilige Schrift der Juden und der Christen," in *Einleitung in das Alte Testament,* ed. Zenger, Georg Braulik, and Heinz-Josef Fabry (Stuttgart: Kohlhammer, 1998), 12-36. This perspective on the coherence of the entire Christian Bible contradicts Barr, who argues for separate theologies of Old and New Testament because ". . . the synthetic, holistic shape of the one is very different from the other"; *The Concept of Biblical Theology: An Old Testament Perspective* (Minneapolis: Fortress, 1999), 186.

CHAPTER 3

A Tale of One City (Genesis 11:1-9)

"Its Name Is Called Babel"

Myth as a primary category of truth understood in a historical context, together with language and the rules of grammar, thematic consistency, and the contemporary context, sets up four seedbeds for interpretation and at the same time creates the limits of the range of the hermeneutical endeavor.[1] One example will suffice to illustrate how such criteria can be brought to bear on a text. This story, Genesis 11:1-9, is a part of the first 11 chapters of Genesis and forms the direct prelude to the list of names of the ancestors of Terah, the father of Abram, who was called by God to emigrate.

Genesis 11:1-9
1. And all the land was one of tongue
    and one speech.
2. When they migrated from the east,
    they found a valley in the land of Shinar
    and they settled there.
3. They said to one another:
    Come, let us build bricks,
    and let us burn them well.
    And brick was their stone,
    and bitumen was their mortar.
4. They said:
    Come, let us build a city

---

1. For a discussion of constraints on possible meanings of text with some similarity to my approach, see Terence E. Fretheim, *The Pentateuch*, 35-36.

and a tower with its top in the sky,
and make for ourselves a name;
lest we be scattered on the face of the land.

5. Then the Holy One came down to see
the city and the tower
which the children of humanity built.
6. And the Holy One said:
Look, one people, and one tongue for all;
this is the beginning of their making;
and now there will be no stopping them
in all that they plan to make.
7. Come, let us go down
and let us make their tongue into a babble there,
so that no one will understand
the tongue of their neighbor.
8. Then the Holy One scattered them from there
on the face of all the land,
and they ceased building the city.
9. Therefore, its name is called Babel,
for there the Holy One made into a babble
the tongues of all the land
and from there the Holy One scattered them
on the face of all the land.

Wedged between two genealogies, one for the line of Noah (10:1-32) and the other for the descendants of Shem (11:10-26), this story interrupts the flow of the generations that leads to Terah, the father of Abram. Its opening line about the unity of language contradicts statements made already about varieties of languages among the peoples (10:5, 20, 31). If we were telling the story, it would precede the genealogy that comes before it, but for the biblical storyteller linear sequencing is not the overriding motivation for the placement of a narrative. For example in the creation stories, Genesis 2:4b begins the myth at a new starting point, with the lack of rain, while it all seemed finished already with the conclusion of the creation in the first half of this verse. Source theory explains such weaving together of narratives by assigning them to different sources. In both cases, Genesis 2–3 as well as Genesis 10–11, the text before us appears to be a combination of priestly and J material. In the combination of the material we see the hand of R, the final redactor, or *rabbenu*.[2]

2. For three insightful analyses of the pericope, see Joseph Blenkinsopp, *The Pentateuch,*

We assume the ordering of the material in just this way to be the result of deliberate choice rather than mere coincidence. On the surface, the narrative of the city and the tower of Babel explains the variety of languages. On another level, it tells of far more profound truths some of which we explore here.

The passage is filled with irony and wordplay. In Hebrew the most obvious of these is the play on the name of the city, Babel, and the confusion of tongues which draws on a verbal root similar in sound to Babel. Babylon, a place introduced in the story with the reference to Shinar (see 10:10), literally means "the gate of the gods." Precisely this place turns out to be a place of confusion, or as I have translated it, "babble." The Hebrew word *safah*, "lip" or "language" or "tongue," is pivotal. The oneness of the people can be maintained only through their having one "language" or "tongue." This crucial unity is expressed both by the narrator and by God: "one tongue" (11:1), "one people, one tongue" (v. 6). Another wordplay, difficult to detect in the translation, occurs with the word for "there" and the word for "name," *sham* and *shem* in Hebrew. These folk want a name (a *shem*) there (*sham*; vv. 2, 4), which is where God causes a babble to break out, and from where God scatters them (vv. 7, 8) and subsequently called "its name" *(shemah)* Babel. The opening lines in verse 1 correspond in a contrasting manner to the last line: what was once "one" in "all the land" has become many and varied "on the face of all the land." "All the land . . . one of tongue . . . one speech" (11:1) becomes "a babble . . . tongues of all the land . . . scattered them . . . face of all the land" (v. 9). Exactly what the folks with their building projects do not want to happen, does happen: they are scattered. The intervention that brings the undesirable result about is undertaken by God, and the passage turns on verse 5, a descriptive line which has God coming down and viewing the construction site. The "come, let us . . ." from God's side echoes the same expression uttered by humanity (v. 3). This humanity goes curiously unnamed in the text. Where the surrounding genealogies convey precision by the recital of exact names, this passage refers in the opening lines to a vague "they". Both humanity and the Holy God use the self-reference "us" and "we."

"All the land" is clearly a key expression, occurring in four of the nine verses and twice in verse 9. We will return to the importance of these repetitions for the interpretation of the passage. In terms of human activity, "making" and "building" are key-words, together with the objects of their activity, bricks, a city, and a tower. The word for brick and the words used in combination for bricks, stone, and mortar in verse 3 are elsewhere in the Torah used

---

90-93; Ellen van Wolde, *Stories of the Beginning: Genesis 1–11 and Other Creation Stories* (London: SCM, 1996), 162-69; and Martin Buber, "Leitwort Style in Pentateuch Narrative."

only in connection with the oppressed descendants of Jacob in Egypt and their building on behalf of Pharaoh (Exod. 1:14; 5 *passim*). The storyteller hints here by word choice that nothing good is taking place. The city-building and brick construction that preceded the exodus were a part of the oppressive universe of the Pharaoh and were used to demoralize and abuse the slaves. Here nothing so overtly wicked is taking place, but the word choice suggests connections that hint at contexts in which humanity and the land that depends on them do not thrive. Twice God is said to "come down." As Martin Buber observes: God "answers humans in human fashion, but a superior human fashion."[3] The divine echo of the human word may thus be called a "come-down" indeed.

The specific place where the opposite of what is intended happens is Babylon, a name that in postexilic times reverberated with echoes of wickedness. In the words of Psalm 137, Babylon was viewed as a predator (Ps. 137:8). It was by Babylon's power and might that nothing they planned to do or make seemed beyond them (Genesis 11:6), and what they did and made was destruction for Jerusalem and its inhabitants. Delicious irony then has confusion breaking out just there, a confusion which results in the thwarting of all wicked Babylonian plans. The story most likely dates back to preexilic times, but the historical context would have been for hundreds of years that of a threatening power in Mesopotamia, whether from Babylon or earlier from Assyria. This is one people in one place, and their name became odious to ancient Israel. In Buber's words: ". . . a name arises for this work; the name of the world-city opposed to God, the name deriving from the accumulation and confusion of languages: 'jumble,' 'babble,' 'Babel'. . . . Human perversion is itself reversed."[4]

For the Benefit of the Earth

Traditionally, interpreters view this passage as concerned with human pride: these are folk who reach to heaven with their "tower with its top in the sky" (v. 4). The people depicted in this story are presumptuous in wanting to make for themselves a name, and God punishes them accordingly. On a certain level, it is probably true that pride and arrogance, specifically as personified

---

3. Buber, "Leitwort Style in Pentateuch Narrative," 117.
4. Buber, "Leitwort Style in Pentateuch Narrative," 117. See also Blenkinsopp, 91: "This little story may plausibly be read as satire directed against the Neo-Babylonian empire, comparable in intent if not in form, therefore, to certain passages in Second Isaiah."

in Babylon, are here thwarted by divine intervention. Although we should be careful not to insert concepts that do not infuse the passage and there is no mention here of either God's anger or of punishment, the reality is that the people of the story end up in just the position they were trying to avoid. Human pride and overreaching, especially as it was witnessed at the time shortly before, during and after the Babylonian exile, are taken down a few notches in this story. An additional insight, when the story is understood thus, could be that with the image of the tower, mostly likely pictured on the model of the Babylonian *ziggurat,* a tower/shrine, the story also undermines the power of Babylonian worship.[5]

Most recently, some commentators conclude that the issue with which the passage is most concerned is the earth. The tower, seen as so central by many interpreters, actually disappears in the story to be replaced by the city. There is a problem depicted here and it is perhaps not the problem of human pride, but that of remaining in one place and building/making constructions that do not directly benefit the earth, whereas the intent of the Creator had been to have humanity "fill the earth" (Gen. 1:28). As Terence Fretheim observes: "Only by spreading abroad can human beings fulfill their charge to be caretakers of the earth. . . . For the builders to concentrate their efforts narrowly on the future of the (only) human community places the future of the rest of creation in jeopardy."[6] Unity and the preservation of one community is a goal that is not an ultimate good in this story. Ellen van Wolde puts it more strongly: "Gen. 11.1-9 is not about the upward striving of human beings but about their horizontal striving: these people did not want to get to heaven or to God, but to remain on earth in one place." In van Wolde's opinion, the dispersion that happens is not a punishment for a sin, but it is "a necessity."[7] Van Wolde views the story as putting the earth in the center of the attention, by means of the key phrase "all the earth/land": "People think that it is about them and their building of a city and a tower, whereas God only puts emphasis on the earth and the dispersion of human beings."[8] It is, according to van Wolde, the cultivation of the earth which is at stake. If we understand the story in this way, historical concerns for unity and community, as described in the preceding pages, might be laid open to a critique in this passage. Being at one as community is a good, but it may not

5. So, e.g., Blenkinsopp, 91: "The satire would be taking aim at the imperial cult as legitimating the political aspirations of the city."

6. Terence E. Fretheim, "The Book of Genesis: Introduction, Commentary and Reflections," *New Interpreter's Bible* 1 (Nashville: Abingdon, 1994), 412.

7. Van Wolde, 168.

8. Van Wolde, 169.

be the highest good and does not come before the task of maintaining and looking after the land.

What is the truth of the tale? Truth may be told here on many levels. Human pride and powerful overreaching are indeed reviewed here as being brought to a poor end by divine intervention. Specifically, Babylonian power is thwarted. The ironic tone would provide satisfaction for the listeners in their context who had suffered from the great power to the north and east of Judah. Historically, nothing good had come from that "one place," and the dispersal depicted here promises also a diminution of power and oppression. As in the story of my father and the Germans, the powerful group comes off as foolish. Such a story would help reestablish the identity of the ones who had suffered at the hands of the oppressive power, in the case of the tale of the city of Babel because in the end their cleverness is no match for God's cleverness.

On another level, the importance of community and unity among the different members was indisputable in ancient Israel, whether before or after the exile. The story may also sound a warning note, that such emphasis on human unity may not benefit the greater good that God has in mind for the creation. It does this in subtle ways, by referring to bricks and brick-building and mortar that holds it all together, all of which would bring to mind the painful oppression suffered in Egypt, none of which benefited the community that eventually was taken into covenant with God. In the end, the earth — or as I have translated it, the "land" (the same word in Hebrew) — is just lying there while people are busy building and constructing, and that is not at all what God had in mind for it. Only if humanity is spread out can cultivation happen. Cultivation was of primary importance in the agricultural context of ancient Israel, and everything in this story points to the notion that the earth is at the center of God's attention and thus should be at the center of human attention. If this one people with one language gets what it wants, the earth will eventually be one huge parking lot! On this level, the truth of the story speaks clearly to a contemporary context. For us today, no matter where we live on the globe, the health of the earth is vital to our own well-being and our future is tied to its future. The story on this level resonates with meaning that we might not have seen there at first blush. In addition, we may today recognize that not all land benefits from cultivation, something that might be outside the scope of the ancient storyteller. Some parts of the earth may be best left alone, without any interference from human hands. We will see whether the theme of concern for the earth and its well-being is part of a theme that is consistent in the Torah.

Other more traditional interpretations are not to be ruled as irrelevant and may also speak meaningfully into a particular context today. So Rabbi

Jonathan Sacks views the story as paradigmatic for a "supreme act of hubris, committed time and again in history." In Sacks' opinion, the Babel construction is *"the attempt to impose an artificial unity on divinely created diversity."*[9] Sacks connects this diversity directly with biblical ethics concerning the stranger, for "the human other is a trace of the Divine."[10]

9. Jonathan Sacks, *The Dignity of Difference* (New York: Continuum, 2002), 52 (emphasis original).

10. Sacks, 59-60.

CONCLUSION

The Tale and Its World

In the introduction to Part II I explored the significance of the category of *story* or *tale* for the self-understanding of the community that constructed the story about its antecedents and its history with its God. There I reviewed the story that the Torah tells of God's way with the world, with the ancestors of ancient Israel, and with the group that escaped from Egypt on its way to the land of the promise. Subsequently, in Chapter 1 I presented a close look at the world of the people described in this story, their economic and social circumstances, and their religious practices. This exploration in part made clear the great distance between the Western industrialized world and the world of the Bible. Chapter 2 on the authors of the documents that make up the Torah reviewed the classic Documentary Hypothesis, with its four strands each dating to different time periods, as losing its hegemony in biblical scholarship. Today the theories that challenge the four-part documentary theory pose a postexilic two-part editorship, perhaps Deuteronomic and Priestly, and the day may not be far off that a single authorship, albeit a postexilic one, will be more generally assumed.

A scrutiny of the category of story for purposes of interpretation led to an examination of the importance of the understanding of *myth* as the primary way to understand the world in biblical times. In view of the presence of multiple levels of truth in a text, I outlined four criteria that set boundaries around the possibilities of "true" interpretation. The historical context, grammar and language, thematic consistency, and the contemporary context together set a framework around the legitimacy of textual interpretation. Because it is often assumed otherwise, "A Conversation between the Testaments" raised the possibility of a New Testament passage setting limitations to the interpretation of an Old Testament text; this possibility was rejected. Finally, a detailed interpretation of Genesis 11:1-9, the story of Babel's city builders, provided an illustration of the stated criteria.

PART III

The Story of the Torah: The Making of a World
(Genesis 1:1–11:32)

Introduction: A Prelude to a Theme — God's Covenant World as a Setting for the Creation of God's Covenant People

Unity of theme is a function of the unity of the literary work.[1]

If we assume that the story of the Torah has "an overarching theme" and that the books of the Torah tell of "the creation of Israel, God's covenant people, in the context of the creation of the world, God's covenant world" (see above, 35-36), the outlines of this theme are discernible in the first 11 chapters of Genesis. It is here that the framework for and the starting point of God's involvement with ancient Israel is articulated as being the entire creation. That the whole creation is the setting for the theme of the Torah was a perception never quite lost from the horizon of the writers. Thus, Exodus 19:5 declares the context of the special vocation of the "house of Israel" to be God's relationship to the entire world, "for mine is all the earth" (see above, 16).[2] In a similar vein, the call to Abram includes a blessing for "all the families of the earth" (Gen. 12:3; 18:18; 22:18; 26:4; 28:14). Thus, the creation and preservation of Israel is for the end of the saving of the world, not for the end of the saving of itself.[3]

---

1. David J. A. Clines, *The Theme of the Pentateuch* (Sheffield: JSOT, 1997), 23.

2. According to Norbert Lohfink, S.J., and Erich Zenger, covenant is an "open" category, and in the enlistment of Israel into service by its God this service had "from the beginning . . . the nations of the world in mind"; *The God of Israel and the Nations: Studies in Isaiah and the Psalms* (Collegeville: Liturgical, 2000), 192.

3. "God's promises and salvific acts must finally be seen as serving all of creation. God

While it is possible to define the theme of the Torah in more than one way, I would argue that, however one defines it, the theme is anticipated and sketched out in the 11 opening chapters of Genesis. The rest of the first five books of the Bible articulates details and motifs of the theme as they are first laid out in Genesis 1–11.[4]

---

acts to free people, indeed the entire world, to be what they were created to be"; Fretheim, "The Book of Genesis," *New Interpreter's Bible* 1 (Nashville: Abingdon, 1994), 329.

4. Commenting on the first edition of his work, *The Theme of the Pentateuch,* written in 1978, David Clines declares it inappropriate to find "one theme" in the literature of the Bible, since the text does not have a "determinate meaning," in which case the search for "just one theme" is fruitless; 2nd ed. (1997), 132. I myself have argued in these pages that the text allows for "multiple levels of truth" (see above, 67). Yet, such an understanding in itself does not prevent the articulation of a theme, but only the perception that one theme would be true to the exclusion of others. Certainly I agree with Clines that "there is more than one way of saying 'what the Pentateuch is all about'" (132). We may consider, e.g., the attractive proposal made by Martin Buber that the fundamental theme of the Bible is "the encounter of a group of people with the Nameless Being whom they . . . ventured to name"; "People Today and the Jewish Bible," in Buber and Franz Rosenzweig, *Scripture and Translation* (Bloomington: Indiana University Press, 1994), 4.

Motifs of the Theme

Every biblical scene will be laden — artistically, theologically, psychologically, spiritually — with all that has come before.[1]

The Making of the World

Genesis 1–3 contain, it is generally agreed, two creation stories — two stories that light up the making of the world from different angles, with distinct perspectives on God, the earth, and humanity. The first narrative, Genesis 1–2:4a, is tightly structured, depicting eight acts of creation in six days, ending with a day of rest on God's part. The style of the story is rhythmic, punctuated by the repeated phrases of the counting of the days: "It was evening, it was morning, day" (Gen. 1:5, 8, 13, 19, 23, 31), and the contemplation by God of what comes into being: "and God saw that it was good" (vv. 10, 12, 18, 21, 25), with two variations in verses 4 and 31 (v. 4: "God saw that the light was good"; v. 31: "and God saw all that he had made and see it was very good").[2] It ends in the Sabbath rest of the seventh day. God in the story is not engaged with the world apart from its making and is portrayed as an all-powerful creator whose word brings into being and sets fertility in motion. Separation and appropriate divisions, "after their kind," are a mark of God's creative work.

The reoccurring pronouncement that what God sees is "good" may also

---

1. Richard Elliott Friedman, *A Commentary on the Torah: With a New English Translation* (San Francisco: HarperSanFrancisco, 2001), 3.

2. For an insightful analysis of the structure of Gen. 1:1–2:4a, see Joseph Blenkinsopp, *The Pentateuch* (New York: Doubleday, 1992), 60-63.

be translated "beautiful." The conviction that permeates the narrative is not necessarily connected with a moral "good," but rather with what is fitting and with what works. Everything God makes goes together and is set in motion to continue the heavenly and the earthly bodies. As Ellen van Wolde points out, Genesis 1 "is not just about the creation of the beginning, but about creation and procreation, about the beginning of all things and the continuation of all things. . . . This is the story of the beginning of the beginning . . . and of the beginning of the continuation of the beginning."[3]

Humanity is created as the last work of God to represent God to the creation (vv. 26-28). Unlike the rest of God's created work, human beings exist not just for the sake of themselves but they relate at once to God ("in God's image"), to one another ("male and female"), and to the earth ("fill the land, . . . subdue . . . and govern"). To one another they do not stand in a hierarchical relation — both male and female are created in the image of God. There is thus no theo-mythical foundation to be found here for the subordination of women in patriarchal ancient Israel. Besides the instruction to reproduce and continue, which also the animals receive (v. 22), human beings alone receive instructions, torah, on their relationship to the world in which they are to exist. In relation to the earth and its creatures, male and female are to stand in a relation of governance. They are by implication to exercise this governance in accordance with being created in the image of God. Their food will therefore not be animal but vegetable matter (v. 29).[4]

In fact, now that all has been set in motion, a true story can begin, as it does in Genesis 2:4b. In the second creation story, God creates one human being, before plants and animals, with the specific purpose of "serving and keeping" the garden God has planted (2:15). Eventually, God creates another human being to complement the first one, and so male and female ensue in a relationship, not of ruling and subservience, but of belonging and partnership.[5]

All is well in this garden it seems, but all does not end well. The harmonious relationships designed by God are disturbed by the act of eating from the tree of knowledge of good and bad, and humanity must face the conse-

3. Ellen van Wolde, *Stories of the Beginning* (London: SCM, 1996), 19.

4. "It is for human beings to fulfill their instructions towards the earth and animals in a way which accords with their being in the image of God"; van Wolde, 31.

5. Much work has been done on this text in contemporary scholarship to rectify the traditional view that the woman was created inferior to the man in this story. Traditional views of the relationship of the two, and of the woman as the instigator in the act of disobedience, including those of New Testament writers, should be corrected to conform with the pattern established by Gen. 1:27ff. and by contemporary insights into the equality between the two sexes established there. See below, 123.

quences of its transgression of the boundary set by God. The first story seemingly left a set of unanswered questions to which the second story responds. Anyone who is observant, either in ancient Israel or today, would ask where all the trouble in the world comes from if it was all created so "good" by God.

The Marring of the World

In whatever way we define what is described in Genesis 1–3, it is clear that the first 11 chapters of Genesis describe a humanity that is on its own not able to foster its own well-being nor that of the rest of creation. Much of this material relates an ever-increasing rift between human and human, between human and creation, and between the human creature and God. Deep flaws are running through these relationships, flaws that are described in general in Genesis 3:14-19 and in detail in Genesis 4. Sin is directly connected with violence in the story of Cain and Abel (Gen. 4:7). Thus a motif is begun that will find countless repetitions in the Torah, where strife will often mark the relation between siblings. Isaac and Ishmael, Jacob and Esau, Joseph and his brothers, Moses with Aaron and Miriam portray family links fraught with uneasiness, rivalry, and open hostility. As told in Genesis 1–11, human violence threatens to undo all God's designs. This violence becomes so overwhelming that God begins to view humanity and the earth with revulsion:

Genesis 6:5-7
5. And the Holy One saw
   that the evil of humanity was great in the land
   and that all the imagination of the deliberations of their heart
   was only evil, all the day.
6. Then the Holy One rued
   having made humanity on the land,
   and God had pain in his heart.
7. The Holy One said:
   I will destroy humanity that I created
   from the face of the ground,
   from human to beast
   to crawling creature and bird of the sky,
   for I rue having made them.

God wishes earth's preservation rather than its destruction. However, human violence has become so pervasive that even God is affected, so much that the Holy One must become involved in destructive action. The pain that was announced to be the lot of male and female in procuring for themselves offspring and fertility (Gen. 3:16-17) is now God's. God rues having engaged in the enterprise of making and will embark on unmaking. Yet, just at this point a note of hope sounds, wedged between two sections that describe earth's devastation, Gen. 6:5-7 and 11-13: "And Noah had found favor in the eyes of the Holy One" (6:8). With this note begins a motif that will recur in the Torah: one individual or one group arises to thwart destructive tendencies and activities and to become a means of healing and restoration.

World's Mending

By God's initiative, the process which seals the preservation of creation is the making of a covenant. Covenant, although not present at the beginning of creation, is central to the new start God makes with the earth after the flood (Gen. 9:1-17) and is equally pivotal to the creation of the people after the liberation experience as described in Exodus.[6] Covenant-making between God and the earth, and between God and the "children of Israel," takes place in the midst of the brokenness of the creation, and it assumes this brokenness. It is not the creation itself which necessitates covenant, but the brokenness of the creation.

Genesis 9:8-11
8. And God said to Noah,
   and to his sons with him:
9. As for me, look I establish
   my covenant with you
   and with your seed after you;
10. and with all living beings
    that are with you:
    with the birds, the beasts
    and with all life of the land with you,
    from all that came out of the Ark
    to all life of the land.

---

6. The notion of covenant as a key concept by which to read the Bible has been somewhat discredited in biblical scholarship in the past two decades. It is, however, difficult to see how a concept that occurs in all the books of the Torah would somehow not be key to our understanding of this material.

11. I establish my covenant with you all,
    and all flesh will never again be cut off
    by the waters of the flood,
    and not again will there be a flood
    to ruin the land.

This covenant is binding on God alone. It is a covenant of self-obligation. Only God is required to abide by its torah, never again to bring "ruin" on the land — no matter how ruined by human violence it may become. Constant repetition of words for "all life" and of the word *erets*/"land" underscores the centrality of the entire creation for this covenant, not just of human creatures.

Covenant will find many-sided expression in the rest of the Torah, from the covenant of promise of God to an individual (Gen. 15), to one of mutual obligation between God and individual (Gen. 17), to a covenant of mutual obligation between God and people (Exod. 24).

Instructions

From the start, creatures receive direction, guidance, *torah* from God for their conduct. In the first creation story, human beings, once created in the image of God, receive the tasks to "be fruitful and be many," to "fill the land and to subdue it," and to "govern" over the earth. Humanity is responsible for biological productivity and for being God's agent on earth (Gen. 1:28). Immediately following, a rule is given for food which is clearly of the vegetarian sort: "the green stuff, self-seeding . . . it shall be to you for food" (Gen. 1:29).

In the second creation story, the human creature is directed to "till and serve" the garden. At the same time God "commands" it "not to eat" (Gen. 2:15-17). A task and a commandment were there at the beginning. Humanity has the purpose of maintaining the garden God has created, while a negative rule sets a boundary around its existence.

Once God has decided on destruction of humanity and at the same time on the preservation of it (Gen. 6:5-8, 11-22), Noah receives detailed instructions on the construction of the means of survival, instructions which resound with the word "to make" (6:14-16). In the context of the covenant God makes after the flood, Noah receives the command to "be fruitful and be many" and to "fill the land" (9:1), in a deliberate echo of the first creation command in 1:28. Here, as there, follows God's "blessing." To underline its importance, this particular requirement is repeated in 9:7: "And you, be fruitful and be many, swarm on the land and be many on it."[7] A new beginning is made with the creation, with former instructions emphatically repeated.

As in the creation accounts, provisions for food receive attention, and they receive both an expansion and a limitation. Whereas heretofore only vegetable matter served as food, now every living thing that moves (lit., "crawls/teems") will be available for consumption, although it may not be eaten with its blood in it (Gen. 9:3-4), a restriction which will be repeated in the Torah (Lev. 17:10-14; Deut. 12:15-27). The mention of blood brings up the issue of the possibility of human bloodshed and human responsibility:

Genesis 9:6
Who sheds the blood of humanity,
by humanity will their blood be shed;
for in the image of God
God made humanity.

Unlike the first creation story, the new beginning takes place in a marred world. Shedding of blood is taken for granted. New instruction is therefore given, and boundaries are set in place.

In the aftermath of the flood, God makes a repeated promise never again to seek the earth's destruction and thus assumes *torah* for Godself, for which the bow in the clouds will be the reminder (Gen. 9:11-17). In the covenant with Noah and "with all flesh," God sets up binding promises and restrictions for God's own relationship to the creation.

A Penchant for What Is Weak

In the choice of a covenant people, those who represent God to the rest of the world, God chose a group that, according to the Torah, was not attractive on the face of it: "Not because you were more numerous than any other people did the Holy One desire you and choose you but because you were littler than all nations. For out of love for you and out of keeping the oath God swore to your ancestors the Holy One brought you out by a strong hand and rescued you from the house of slavery from the hand of Pharaoh

7. The word "swarm" (Heb. *sharats*) is used only rarely for human beings and occurs only here and in Exod. 1:7. Elsewhere it indicates animal life.

the king of Egypt" (Deut. 7:7-8). This penchant of God for what is not highly regarded is present, mostly by inference, already in the story of Cain and Abel: "And the Holy One had regard for *Hevel* and his offering; and for *Cayin* and his offering God had no regard" (Gen. 4:4b-5a). Abel (Hebrew *hevel*) is a name, as Ellen van Wolde has observed, that points to what is of a "transitory nature" and lacking in worth.[8] On the other hand, Cain (from the Hebrew root *qanah*, "create" or "acquire") is connected with productivity, with creation and acquisition (Gen. 4:1). It is the one whose name is "worthless," Abel, whom the Holy One favors, a bias which is not to the liking of the one whose name connotes the power of acquisition and fertility, Cain. Van Wolde maintains that the entire Bible shows a God who is on the side of the *hevels.*[9]

In the Torah, this penchant of God is laid on the community as an obligation to protect and care for the weak and vulnerable members of the society. One category of people for whom this protection is most frequently called into effect is that of the stranger (see above, 25-32). Many times we find next to the stranger the listing of "the orphan and the widow," fatherless children and mateless women having a very small chance for survival in the ancient society that is reflected in the biblical texts.[10]

God's cherishing of the earth may be viewed on a continuum with God's preference for what is weak and not able to protect itself. Because the human creature represents God's image on earth and God cherishes the earth, the human creature is called on to reflect this cherishing. Specifically for ancient Israel, the earth and the concern for the earth are made concrete in the promise of a particular "land." The word for both "land" and "earth" is the same in Hebrew, *erets,* and the significance of the entire *erets* finds its focus in the *erets Kena'an,* the "land of Canaan." This land was to be viewed by the ancient Israelites as a gift from God. Their possession of it was fragile and tentative; they entered it in the midst of great struggle, and in the end they no longer possess it. If we agree with David J. A. Clines that the primal travel story of Israel is "the story of an *escape* from a home that was not a home in order to make for a home that had never been a home," we must also say that

---

8. Van Wolde, 77.

9. "It is not just a matter of a covenant with the elect people: everyone is chosen who belongs to the weaker group, the group which is denied. Together they form the people of the *hevels.* God makes a covenant with them. God looks on them, since they urgently need it. Alas, only a few people look with him"; van Wolde, 86.

10. In the book of Deuteronomy the occurrence of the stranger is most often combined with that of the orphan and the widow. Elsewhere we might find them listed separately (e.g., Exod. 22:21-23).

it was a home that they lost, regained only partially and lost again, in the devastation of the Babylonian exile and its aftermath and the subsequent destruction of Jerusalem under the Romans in 70 C.E.[11]

God's penchant for what is weak and "worthless" must be imitated by the ones who walk in God's ways. Hence the insistence in the Torah on the care for those who have not the means to take care of themselves. In both creation stories, the human creature is created explicitly in relation to the earth and life upon it:

Genesis 1:28
God blessed them and said to them:
be fruitful and be many,
and fill the land and subdue it,
and govern the fish of the sea
and the birds of the sky,
and all animal life that crawls on the land.

Genesis 2:15
Then the Holy God took the human being
and led it to the garden of Eden
to serve it and keep it.[12]

Perhaps because of this close relationship to the earth, the earth participates in the brokenness of the creation, and its fertility will come only after hard human labor, in response to which it may still not render what is useful for life (Gen. 3:18-19). In the account of the murder of Abel by Cain, blood takes on a voice and the ground gets a mouth:

Genesis 4:10-11
10. God said: What have you done?
    The voice of your brother's blood
    is crying to me from the ground.

11. Clines, *The Theme of the Pentateuch*, 118.
12. In the first creation story, Gen. 1–2:4a, only plants and trees are brought forth by the earth itself. All other earth life is created by God. In the sequence of the creation narratives, this natural productivity of the earth is interrupted by the act of eating of the fruit of the tree of the knowledge of good and bad. For the ancient Israelite, land was dependent on human hands and labor for fertility and productivity. That and the regular supply of water guaranteed a thriving earth that bore fruit. Not surprisingly, these two issues, water and human labor, receive attention at the opening of the narratives in Gen. 2:4b-ff.

11. Now, cursed are you from the ground
which opened its mouth
to take the blood of your brother from your hand.

When in the prelude to the flood story God contemplates what has become of the creation, the text expresses the state of the earth as follows:

Genesis 6:11-12
11. The land was gone to ruin before God,
the land was filled with violence.
12. God saw the land
and look, it was gone to ruin
for all flesh ruined its way upon the land.[13]

Clearly, the *erets*/"land" and its "ruin," from a Hebrew root *shahat*, "to spoil," are central to these verses. Yet the land's ruin is the result of the ruination that "all flesh" brings upon it. In itself the land does not have the capacity for evil. Immediately following the events of the flood and its aftermath, God decides not ever again "to curse the ground on behalf of humanity" (Gen. 8:21). Logically then, God establishes a covenant not only with human creatures but explicitly with the entire earth.[14]

In the story of the city-builders of Babel and its aftermath (Gen. 11:1-9), a narrative discussed at the conclusion of the previous chapter of this book, God intervenes on behalf of the land. The divine soliloquy of Genesis 11:7 ("Come, let us go down") echoes the creating activity of God in 1:26 ("Let us make humanity") in its choice of plural pronouns for the godhead. There, God made one humanity in two entities for the benefit of the earth; here, God will undo a oneness of humanity that will not benefit the earth. In addition, the soliloquy echoes two divine self-consultations: the one that led to the flood (Gen. 6:6-7) and the one that preceded the covenant made after the flood which established God's promise never again to include the earth in divine intervention for ill (8:21-22). Henceforth, any "ruin" that befalls the land will come from human hands alone. God is bound by God's own promise

13. These verses are a parallel to 6:5-6, where the evil of humanity is at the center of God's attention.

14. "In the cosmology of the ancient Israelites, nature has a 'value of its own,' a value that does not derive from nature's significance to human society. The fact that the God of the Hebrew Bible makes a covenant with the animals and blesses them is unique"; Jan J. Boersema, *The Torah and the Stoics on Humankind and Nature: A Contribution to the Debate on Sustainability and Quality* (Leiden: Brill, 2001), 246.

both to earth and humanity, and the intervention toward the city-builders is a corrective rather than a destructive one.

Approaches to God

Sacrifice

If covenant is the bridge constructed by God to mend the breach between God and the creation, human beings in these stories reach out to God. Like covenant, human worship assumes alienation between God and the creature and arises out of this alienation. A number of worship practices are mentioned in these first 11 chapters of Genesis, practices that will find elaboration in the remainder of the Torah. First, while much of the intercourse between divine and human in Genesis 1–11 is direct, there is also mention of sacrifice at an early point in the narratives. Both Cain and Abel bring an offering:

> **Genesis 4:3-5**
> 3. After some time
>   *Cayin* brought from the fruit of the ground,
>   a gift-offering to the Holy One.
> 4. *Hevel* also brought
>   from the first-born of his flock and their fat.
>   And the Holy One had regard for *Hevel* and his offering;
> 5. And for *Cayin* and his offering
>   God had no regard.[15]

Two brothers bring the same offering; out of God's regard for the one and disregard for the other mayhem ensues. There are different ways of interpreting the Cain and Abel story, and I have already offered one perspective on this narrative. Although we may find one or another interpretation more satisfying, very likely a nagging question as to God's preference persists: why did God have regard for the one offering and not for the other? Could it be that this text, which reflects the common way people of that time and place approached the godhead, intends also to sound a note of warning that sacrifice in itself may not accomplish the desired outcome?[16] Sacrifice in this story be-

---

15. The type of sacrifice mentioned is that of *minhah,* a kind of generic offering meaning "present" or "gift."

16. This line of thought is of course common in prophetic literature, where the emphasis

comes the springboard that leads to murder rather than to greater harmony between human and human and between human and God.

Not sacrifice alone but actions that benefit the weakest brother are required in order to bring about encounters that lead to well-being of the different parties.

Genesis 4:6-7

6. The Holy One said to *Cayin:*
   why are you angry
   and why is your face fallen?
7. Is it not so that if you *do good,* it will be lifted?
   And if you do not *do good,*
   at the door sin is crouching,
   and to you is its desire
   and you will rule over it.[17]

Cain's refusal to recognize that the action of "doing good" is an essential element of the God-human and human-human relation leads to the unwitting participation of the ground in the disturbance brought about by his violence.

One could speculate that although Abel's offering was regarded by God, neither his nor Cain's sacrifice was effective in accomplishing a healed connection between God and human. In counterpoint to this failure, the sacrifice brought by Noah after the flood has a favorable outcome:

Genesis 8:20-22

20. Noah built an altar to the Holy One
    and took of every clean beast
    and every clean bird
    and brought burnt sacrifices on the altar.
21. And the Holy One smelled the pleasant odor
    and said in his heart:
    I will not again account as cursed the ground

---

falls on the connection between right relations among neighbors and a relationship with God. See, e.g., Jer. 22:13-17; Mic. 6:6-8; cf. Ps. 50:7ff.

17. We may think here of the famous speech by Jeremiah, the so-called "temple speech" in which the worshipers in Jerusalem are exhorted that just actions, i.e. protection of the weak, combined with appropriate worship are the only guarantee of God's presence with them: *"Rather, make good your ways and doings/make, yes make, justice . . ."* (Jer. 7:5). The verb *make good* used here is identical to the form employed in Genesis 4:7, the Hif'il of the Hebrew root *yatav.*

because of humanity,
for the imagination of its heart
is evil from its youth;
and not again will I strike all life
as I have done.
22. From now on all the days of the land,
seed-time and harvest,
cold and heat,
summer and winter,
day and night,
they will not cease.

The "pleasant odor" indicates the positive reception of the sacrifice on God's part. God responds with a soliloquy on the divine intent to preserve the future of the land henceforth, an intention which finds outward expression in the covenant that follows. We note that in this passage there is mention of "an altar" and of the proper victims for burnt sacrifices (v. 20). This may imply that some ways of bringing sacrifice are more in line with the requirements of worship than others and therefore more likely to bring success. Sacrifice abounds in the rest of the Torah, often taking place on altars built for the purpose. It is only gradually that the lines of what is appropriate sacrifice and where it is appropriately brought are more finely drawn. There may be a hint in the account of the sacrifice brought by Noah that it is wise to follow the rules in order to achieve effectiveness by this means of approaching God. However, there may also be hints in this episode that worship may be acceptable without the benefit of clergy, or special hallowed places, and also outside of the boundaries of the people of God's covenant. As Terence E. Fretheim observes: "We must recognize that God's saving act occurs in the world outside Israel. God as *Creator* acts in *saving* ways on behalf of creational goals. Such actions are not confined to Israel and need not be mediated by the community of faith."[18]

Prayer

Increasing violence marks the sequel to the story of Cain, until, five generations later, his descendant Lamech utters a speech that is filled with words associated with violence:

18. Fretheim, "The Book of Genesis," 395.

Genesis 4:23-24

23. And Lamech said to his wives:
    Ada and Zillah,
    listen to my voice;
    wives of Lamech,
    lend your ear to my speech;
    for a man I slew for my wound,
    and a boy for my slash.
24. For seven times will *Cayin* be avenged
    and Lamech seventy-seven times.

Yet, in the midst of what appears to be a tale of human relations going downhill, notes sound that mark the future of civilization and of life. Cities are founded; herders, tentdwellers, musicians, and smiths appear on the scene (Gen. 4:17).[19] Also in, what sounds to a contemporary ear, an abrupt switch back to the generation of Adam and Eve, a new birth announcement heralds the birth of a son to replace Abel: Seth, who in turn becomes the founder of the line out of which Noah will be born (Gen. 4:25-26; 5:1-32). In addition, one sentence marks a practice of worship said to begin at this time: "Then they began to call on the name of the Holy One" (4:26b). To call on the name of the God of Israel certainly indicates a reference to worship, specifically the practice of prayer. Like sacrifice, prayer is done in the awareness of the need to bridge the distance between God and human, and with it the need for propitiation. At the end of Genesis 4 there are burgeoning of life, the hope for a future with new life, but also the burgeoning of violence. In the midst of thriving human life, the sound of hammer and anvil, the noise of construction, the music of harp and flute, the lowing of cattle, two voices are heard: one (4:23-24) is full of braggadocio and hatred; it announces the endless and hopeless cycle of violence that begets violence in arrogant self-reliance. The other (4:26b) can be raised only once it recognizes that for humanity and creation hope lies in the ongoing presence of God, and in reaching out for this presence through prayer in the midst of the abyss of violence it has created for itself.

Genesis 1–11 depicts more often direct communication initiated by God from God to human rather than the human-initiated approach to God through prayer. In the remainder of the Torah, direct communication will be

19. I agree with Fretheim that the description of Gen. 4:17-22 should be viewed positively rather than negatively. "Just as one may marvel at the great diversity of God's creation, so also human creativity mirrors God's in producing numerous gifts and interests"; "The Book of Genesis," 375.

the rule, with occasional mention of the practice of prayer.[20] Prayer was never subject to formal rules in ancient Israel, or at least such rules are absent from the Old Testament. Speech to God, whether formally identified as prayer or not, is often bold in the Torah, bordering on the insolent (e.g., Gen. 17:17; Exod. 3:1–4:17; Num. 11:11ff.). The replies of Cain to God in Genesis 4 fit this pattern of speech that responds to God as a real conversation partner rather than an overwhelming superior presence.

Sabbath

It should not be overlooked that the holy day foundational to all other festivals in ancient Israel is established in the creation story:

> **Genesis 2:1-3**
> 1. Thus they were finished, sky and land
>   and all their host.
> 2. God was finished on the seventh day
>   with all the work he had made,
>   and God rested on the seventh day
>   from all the work he had made.
> 3. And God blessed the seventh day
>   and made it holy,
>   for on it God rested from his work
>   which God created by making.

Although it is sometimes assumed that the high point of the creation is the arrival of humankind as described in Gen. 1:26-28, in truth the crowning moment of the making of the world does not arrive until the seventh day on which God "rested." In this way the Sabbath is connected with and rooted in the creation of the world.[21] The required observance of the Sabbath as stipulated in the Decalogue of Exodus 20 (v. 11) is thus logically based on this ces-

---

20. The phrase "to call on the name of the Holy One" may also be translated "to invoke/call out the name." It occurs also in Gen. 12:8; 13:4; 26:25. The most common verb used for prayer (Heb. *hitpalel*) and its accompanying noun *(tefillah)* are rare in the Torah, used only of Abraham and Moses (Gen. 20:7; Num. 11:2; 21:7; Deut. 9:20, 26).

21. Blenkinsopp, 61ff. As Blenkinsopp observes (62), the Sabbath as terminus of the creation in Gen. 1:1–2:4a parallels the way in which it "crowns the work of constructing the wilderness sanctuary (Ex 31:12-17)" and "is one of several indications of a parallelism between world-building and sanctuary-building. The point is being made that Sabbath is rooted in the created order of things."

sation of God's making. Of the significance of the Sabbath in terms of the life of ancient Israel I have spoken already (see above, 52-54). Here, we may add that by concluding the work of God's creating with the Sabbath the narrators include the entire world within the framework of sacred time.[22]

The Families of the World

The material of Genesis 1–11 does not fit together in a random way. As a whole, it has momentum that drives toward the emigration of Abram and his family from Mesopotamia to Canaan on instruction from God. The means used to structure the movement of the text in this direction is the insertion of genealogies. Regularly the progression of the story of the world's beginnings is punctuated by lists of names, names which shift the scenery from one person or one group to the next, from Adam and Eve to Noah, and from Noah to Terah's family, including Sarai and Abram. Such lists are generally not favorite reading material for most contemporary readers. They seem to interrupt the text more than add information to it. With their long recital of unpronounceable names, they present stumbling blocks rather than a means of access. Yet, the genealogies of these chapters not only fill a crucial role and are integral to the tales told here, but they tell a story of their own and are worth contemplating in their own right.[23]

First, lists of ancestral families provide a kind of ordering of the past. They impose structure on what may seem random and chaotic. The storytellers were careful, therefore, to fit the life spans of the pre-Israelite ancestors into a chronological schema.[24] Second, anchoring present generations firmly in the past provides a group with identity: this is where we come from; these are the ones to whom we belong. We may note that the ancient Israelite com-

---

22. Blenkinsopp notes that such connections in principle are not peculiar to Israel. "Just as the P narrator traces a line from creation to the construction of the sanctuary and the establishment of the cult, so in the *enuma elish* the creation of the world concludes with the building of a temple for the praise of the creator-deity"; 63. While in such matters ancient Israel certainly shared perspectives with its neighboring cultures, the "spin" given to the connection between creation and sacred rest must also be allowed to be ancient Israel's own.

23. For general remarks about the importance of genealogies, see Johanna W. H. van Wijk-Bos, *Ezra, Nehemiah, and Esther* (Louisville: Westminster John Knox, 1998), 22, 68. For an illuminating discussion of the genealogies in Genesis 1–11 in particular, see van Wolde, 103-4, 151-62, 169-71. For insight into the structure of the genealogical lists found here, see Blenkinsopp, 71-97.

24. Cf. van Wolde's observation that genealogies are "the most convincing reflection of the continuity in life and death. Thus they bear witness to a certain determinism: they put the past in an irrevocable order"; 103.

munity was careful to locate its roots in the context of the peoples of the entire world and that these peoples in themselves were also of interest to the ancient believer. The lists of ancestors are not strictly linear. They take detours into different territory, and so they tell of more than the linear descendance of one man to the next. Finally, specific names are often significant. In many cases, this significance is lost to us today, but at times we may still receive a glimpse of what were once references to a more profound truth than the merely obvious. In the end, ancestor lists belong also to myth. They do not primarily pass on information, but in their own way they tell the truth of the tale to those who come after.[25]

Besides their role of moving the story purposefully forward, the lists of names in the first 11 chapters of Genesis fulfill the functions I have mentioned. Here we will also take into consideration that the lists may have a truth of their own to tell. I propose that we briefly consider three main lists, with their subdivisions. They are: (1) Genesis 4:17–5:32, Adam's descendants through the lines of Cain and Seth; (2) 10:1-20, Noah's descendants through his sons Japheth and Ham; (3) 10:21-31; 11:10-32, Noah's descendants through his son Shem, ending with Terah and his offspring.[26]

Adam's Descendants (Genesis 4:17–5:32)

We may divide this section in two, with the first, Genesis 4:17-26, pursuing initially the line of Cain, to conclude with murdered Abel's replacement, Seth, and his offspring. The second part of the list, Genesis 5:1-32, opening with a new announcement of family history ("This is the scroll of the family history of Adam") subsequently reviews the descendancy of the ancestors from Seth to Noah. As it is, the record of family lines begins with a detour, for it is not Cain's line which will lead up to Abram but Seth's. At the end of the Cain/Abel episode, the future does not look particularly promising for Cain, who is now destined to be a fugitive and wanderer. He is, on the other hand, the only surviving child of Adam and Eve and, true to a name that connotes acquisition and creativity, produces offspring. The short genealogy mentioned in 4:17-22 is of interest for a number of reasons. First, here are mentioned not

25. So Blenkinsopp would have genealogies carrying "their own distinctive 'message'"; 58. Yet, Blenkinsopp seems to have in mind what he calls "narrative expansions of genealogies," whereas my suggestion is that the list itself tells a story, albeit in a form of code.

26. Blenkinsopp's argument that Gen. 1–11 renders a five-part structure, with the flood story as central panel, an arrangement which in itself is an important "vector of meaning" (59), is certainly worth noting. In the final analysis, it is not altogether clear, however, whether this five-part structure is one organic to the material itself or one imposed by the biblical scholar.

only men's names but also their occupations. From city-builder, to herdsman, to musician and metal-worker, a parade of professions files by. Finally, the review ends with Lamech and his song of vengeance. In Genesis 4 two streams issue from Cain, one of violence and one of productive contribution to culture and society. The addition of Cain's family line indicates complex characterization. There is more to a person than just his or her crime, and the sequel to 4:1-16 certainly introduces ambiguity into the Cain history.

Herdsmen, smiths, and flautists come from super-violent Lamech and his two wives, Ada and Zillah, names meaning perhaps Dawn and Dusk. Remarkably, three women's names occur in this family history. Mostly, the family line goes straight from father to son, as it will in Genesis 5. Genesis 4:19 mentions Lamech's two wives by name, and then a daughter born to Zillah (v. 22) called Na'amah, a name which connotes pleasure, delight, or charm. Lamech's boasting song is given in the presence of his wives, whose names occur once more in his speech (vv. 23-24).[27] Why did Lamech not call on his sons to listen? Is there a special meaning in displaying his desire for violence in front of his wives? Is this the male primate beating his chest and bellowing belligerently before his cowering females? From such a perspective, Lamech appears slightly ridiculous. It is certain that the mention of the women's names, so unusual in this particular context, causes a wrinkle to appear in the smooth transition from one generation to the next.[28]

Following this detour into Cainite territory, the text returns to the issue of descendants of Adam through the Abel/Hevel line, the original second son, the line that will issue eventually in Abram. At this point, God's role in the birth process is acknowledged by Eve, here referred to as Adam's wife without mention of her proper name. The fourth woman to be present in the family history at this stage, she contributes to the family productivity by bearing and naming. The name of her son is explained in a word association as related to appointing or granting. God, so Eve maintains, has "appointed" or "granted" her seed in place of Abel/Hevel, who was killed by Cain.

---

27. It is certainly of interest to note that one traditional Jewish interpretation of Lamech's words sees them as words of regret and confession. In that tradition, Lamech who was blind had inadvertently killed two people on account of his blindness, referred to as "his wound" and "his blow" in a passage which expresses bewilderment about his action and assurance of God's revenge even on someone so innocent. See van Wolde, who takes this tradition into account in her interpretation; 96-98. I am more inclined to take Lamech's words at face value as those of someone more violent than Cain and intentionally so.

28. Cf. van Wolde's observation (95) that "women appear on the stage when something special is about to happen. They form a kind of crossroads on the otherwise straight highways of male genealogies."

Genesis 4:25-26

25. And Adam knew his wife
    and she gave birth to a son
    and called his name *Shet*
    for (she said) God has granted me another seed
    in place of Abel
    for Cain slew him.
26. Then to *Shet* also was born a son
    and he called his name Enosh.
    Then they began to call on the name of the Holy One.

God's "granting" is thus set in opposition to human violence. This pronouncement is followed by the mention of Enosh, the son of Seth/*Shet*, who will reappear with his offspring in the list of chapter 5. For now, the section ends with the observation on the practice of calling on God's name that is begun at this point. Within the literary structure of these verses it is striking that the verb "to call" (Hebrew *qara*), used here for the invocation of God's name, echoes the naming done by humanity of its offspring: "she called," "he called," "they began to call." The names of humanity are thus set in relation to the name of the Holy One. Looking at the same passage in another light we may read as follows:

Genesis 4:25-26

25. Then Human again knew his woman
    and she bore a son
    and called his name Grant
    for (she said): God granted me another seed
    in the place of Mist
    for Increase killed him.
26. And to Grant also a son was born
    and he called his name People.
    — Then they began to call on the name of the Holy One.

I have here translated all the names to give a sense of the direction in which the process of lineage is driving. Eve's name, not mentioned, yet resonates through the verses. Adam and *Hawwa*/Eve, or Humankind and Life, issue forth in People, for that is what the word *Enosh* means. Fertility of life and offspring are hope-giving, even in the midst of ambiguity and violence brought on the earth by humankind. For the story of humanity to go on, it is not enough to have individuals; *people* are needed. It is telling that God's role in the process of birthing is recognized by one of the women in the text. Only in this first section, Genesis 4:17-26, is the verb "to give birth" (the Hebrew root *yalad*) used with female subjects. Once the text focuses on the male fathering of male, females are no longer the subject of the birth-giving process and God's role is equally ignored. In van Wolde's words: "In the list of fatherings in Gen. 5, by contrast, only the male capacity for procreation is mentioned. None of these men recognizes God's contribution to their fertility in so many words."[29]

Before we go on with the next listing of ancestral lineage, I invite us to review the entire passage of Gen. 4:17-26 in translation. Such recitals may be especially difficult because of the alien form of the names embedded in them. I have here translated all the names. All of the translated names are speculative, but all have some basis in associations with root meanings. The Hebrew storyteller freely associated meanings of names with same-sounding verbal roots, as the name *Shet* with a verb that means "to appoint, to put." Solid etymology was not a first concern here but rather a play on sound and meaning.[30]

Genesis 4:17-26

17. Increase knew his wife
    and she conceived and bore Pursuit
    and he became a city-builder
    and Increase called the name of the city
    like the name of his son "Pursuit."
18. Then was born to Pursuit Resolve
    and Resolve produced Godson
    and Godson produced Godman
    and Godman produced Strongfellow.

19. Then Strongfellow took two wives,
    the name of the one was Dawn
    and the name of the second was Dusk.
20. And Dawn gave birth to Waterman;
    he became the ancestor of tent-dweller and cattleherder.
21. The name of his brother was Brooks,
    he became the ancestor of players of lyre and flute.
22. And Dusk also gave birth,

29. Van Wolde, 100.

30. For an interesting exploration of the play with names in the literature of Genesis, see Herbert Marks, "Biblical Naming and Poetic Etymology," *JBL* 114 (1995): 21-42.

to Irons, worker of implements of bronze and iron.
And the sister of Irons was Delight.

23. Then Strongfellow said to his wives:
Dawn and Dusk, listen to my voice;
wives of Strongfellow,
hear my speech:
For a man I slew for my wound
and a boy for my slash.
24. For seven times will vengeance be done for Increase
and for Strongfellow seventy-seven times.

25. Then Human knew his wife
and she bore a son
and called his name Grant
for she said: God granted me seed
in the place of Mist
for Increase killed him.
26. And to Grant also a son was born
and he called his name People.
Then they began to call on the name of the Holy One.

From here on, the list, beginning again with Seth, will move from father to son relentlessly without mentioning either women's roles or their names, following the same pattern of listing a father's age at the birth of his son, then the years of his total life span and finally his death, until Noah, the son of a second Lamech. In this rather monotonous recital, a few narrative comments stand out. First, the entire list is introduced by a reference to the likeness of God in which male and female are created:

Genesis 5:1-3
1. This is the scroll of the family history of humanity
on the day that God created humanity;
in the likeness of God he created it.
2. Male and female he created them
and he blessed them
and called their name "humanity"
on the day they were created.
3. And Adam was thirty and a hundred years
when he produced one in his likeness
and called his name *Shet.*

Before the actual recital of names, we find here a reaffirmation of God's likeness in humanity which is thus to be passed on through the generations. That is, the likeness did not begin and end with the first creatures. Also, the inclusion of "female" precisely at this point when the likeness of God is mentioned both highlights and counteracts the absence of females in the list that follows. It highlights, for by all rights there should have been names of women in the ancestor list. That they are not there is an outcome of a distorted perspective by which males are the only ones that count. This perspective is a result of the disharmony, the disturbance between male and female that has become a part of the created world. The reference to "male and female" in the likeness of God also counteracts, for the explicit mention of "female" in the "likeness of God" once again lays down the principle of equality between male and female and makes clear the lack of a theo-mythical foundation for inequality between the sexes and domination of one sex by the other. Almost perversely, then, verse 3 draws only the male human being to the fore. He does the producing; he does the naming; his offspring is in his likeness. Both God and female have disappeared from the process.

Enoch (Hebrew *Hanokh*) in Genesis 5:18ff. is a different man than the son of Cain mentioned in 4:17. Although one may remember Methushelach rather than Enoch because of his long life span, it is Enoch who receives the following comment:

Genesis 5:22-24
22. *Hanokh* walked with God
    after he produced Metushelach three hundred years
    and he produced sons and daughters.
23. And all the days of *Hanokh*
    were three hundred and sixty-five years.
24. And *Hanokh* walked with God
    and he was no more
    for God took him.

Enoch/*Hanokh*'s walk with God is stated twice, the second time taking the place of the formula "and he died" that closes the life span of the other ancestors. The statement about walking with God anticipates Noah, about whom it will also be said that he walked with God (Gen. 6:9). Enoch is so close to God that his ending differs from that of his entire family line. Whatever the enigmatic "he was no more for God took him" means, it definitely indicates closeness to God.

Finally, there is Noah, son of another Lamech, who together with his three sons closes the list and who receives promising statements from his progenitor:

Genesis 5:28-29

28. Lamech was one hundred and eighty-two years old
   and he produced a son.
29. And he called his name Noah, saying:
   This one will comfort us in our work
   and the pain of our hands from the ground
   which the Holy One cursed.

Noah, in Hebrew more closely connected with the word "rest," is freely associated with another verbal root meaning "to comfort."[31] It is by the person of Noah that the human race will be preserved through the destruction of the flood. The pronouncements about Noah take the place of a recital of his life span and demise. Instead, the names of his three sons end the family history recorded in this chapter.

The immediate sequel to the list of ancestors in Genesis 5 is the story of sexual intercourse between human and divine beings, which causes God to set a limit to human life spans (Gen. 6:1-4). Once stories of procreation are begun, they are apparently hard to stop.[32] The bulk of the material subsequent to the first genealogy is the story of the flood and its aftermath. The next list occurs after the episode where Noah's nakedness is discovered by his son Ham (Gen. 9:18-28).

From Noah to Joktan (Genesis 10:1-32)[33]

Genesis 6–9 is for the most part taken up by the story of the flood, with its prelude and aftermath. Chapter 10 then takes up the continuation of the family line of Noah, bringing into view all the peoples familiar to ancient times

31. On the significance of Noah's name, see Marks, 25-29.

32. Van Wolde calls this story a "mini-myth" and sees it fitting into its context of God's concern for earth and how humans relate to the earth, to God, and to each other effectively. Other ancient Near Eastern myths deal with the issue of over-population of the earth, as e.g. the Atrahasis and Gilgamesh myths. It is, as van Wolde observes, not, however, the issue of over-population that brings about the flood but rather the unethical behavior of humanity. The overpopulation issue is dealt with by limiting the human life span. Van Wolde, 112-19.

33. For an analysis of the structure of the genealogies in this chapter, see Blenkinsopp, 87-90: "The descendants will form a macrocosm of seventy peoples corresponding to the microcosm of Israel, also originally seventy in number (Gen. 46:27; Ex. 1:5)" (88).

— unlike the list of Genesis 5, which moves from individual to individual. Noah's sons were mentioned already at the end of the list in Genesis 5. Here, their existence and descendance are unfolded. Shem, whose name means "name," from whose line will come Abram and from whose name all the "names" of the ancestors of Israel's children will come forth, is in some ways the one who counts. But it is not his lineage leading up to Terah and then Abram that is listed first.

Genesis 10:1-5

1. This is the family history of the sons of Noah,
   Shem, Ham, and Japhet;
   and there were born to them sons after the flood.
   . . . .
5. From these were spread out the coastlands of the peoples,
   according to their lands, their tongue,
   their clans of their peoples.

The sons of Noah and their lineage are taken up in reversed order from their mention in both Genesis 5:32 and 10:1. Shem does occur in the list, but appears last, and his lineage is given only in part. Subsequently, Genesis 11:10ff. will return to the descendants of Shem, in the pattern of individual father to individual son familiar from Genesis 5. The end of the list of peoples in Genesis 10 echoes its beginning:

Genesis 10:31-32

31. These are the sons of Shem
    according to their clans,
    and their tongues, in their lands by their peoples.
32. These are the clans of the sons of Noah,
    by their families in their peoples;
    and from these were spread out
    the peoples of the land after the flood.

Peoples and their subdivisions, clans and families, are clearly in the foreground both in opening and closing statement of this chapter, and the emphasis throughout is on the peoples of the ancient world in their geographical regions. The entire known world of that day is reviewed in this listing by naming a father and then a number of sons rather than the one father/one son listing of chapters 5 and 11. The sons, moreover, represent distinct population groups. Some of the geographical and ethnic references are still clear today, while others must remain obscure. Whatever clarity there is for our understanding, the list testifies to an enduring interest in naming the world and its peoples with their lineages, an interest that is broader than the lineage of the Israelite ancestor group alone.

The longest section in this list is devoted to Ham, the son cursed by Noah in the short story immediately preceding chapter 10. While the nature of Ham's sin is not self-evident from that episode, Noah's judgment on Ham is abundantly clear. Each pronouncement in Genesis 9:25-27 highlights the character of Ham's relationship to his brothers as that of servitude.[34]

Genesis 9:25-27
25. He said: "Cursed be Canaan;
     servant of servants
     he will be to his brothers.
26. He said: Blessed be the Holy One,
     the God of Shem;
     let Canaan be a servant to him.
27. May God make Japheth great,
     and he will dwell in the tents of Shem
     and may Canaan be his servant."

The reference to Ham by the name of his son Canaan highlights the eponymic quality of this material as it declares Canaan "cursed" and refers three times to his posture of servitude in relation to his brothers. Hostility between ancient Israel and Canaan is often taken for granted by the reader of the biblical text, and indeed some of the literature of the Bible reflects a deep aversion to anything that is Canaanite and a destructive posture toward this group.[35] Yet, in the peoples' ancestor list Canaan is mentioned without negative reverberations and prominent peoples are his descendants.[36] The posture toward Canaan was probably ambiguous, with positive or neutral and negative evaluations existing side by side, and only at a later date became one of hostility only, notably at a time when Canaanites no longer inhabit the land. Here, Noah's words to and about Canaan clearly weigh in on the negative

34. The references are clearly intended to highlight hostilities between different ethnic groups of the region, hence the use of "Canaan" rather than "Ham" in the curse and blessing words of Noah (Gen. 9:25-27).

35. See Gen. 24:3, 37; 28:1, 6, 8; Deut. 7:1-3; 20:17.

36. See Gen. 10:6, where Ethiopia, Egypt, Libya, and Canaan are the ethnic and geographical entities of reference. A great many references to Canaan and to Canaanites are clustered in Genesis where the references are only rarely negative.

side, while the lineage of Ham as recounted in Genesis 10:6ff. counts on the neutral or even positive side. We will return to the issue of Canaan and its historical reality in a subsequent chapter.

The biblical testimony is, in any case, not univocal on the relationship of ancient Israel with Canaan. Such cannot be said of subsequent readings of this material, especially those from a Christian perspective, which used the "curse on Ham" as justification for slavery, the politics of apartheid, and the dehumanization of races other than the white. Van Wolde's observation is particularly relevant here: "What had first begun as the interpretation of a story to explain a people's position in the world had far-reaching consequences. . . . Thus a view of the world seems to be attached to the story of Noah and his three sons, which has also contributed towards the world becoming as it now is."[37] A seemingly harmless listing of peoples casts a long and sinister shadow into the future. Genealogies are neither alien nor powerless travelers in the world of the tale, it appears.

Van Wolde claims that this list not only presents "an exercise in world cartography" but provides also a "socio-cultural description of the then known world."[38] In other words, not only the peoples and their geographical locations but their cultures and occupations come into view. While some are seafarers, others build cities, hunt game, live in an urban culture, or go from place to place as the name "'Eber" (Hebrew "pass through") seems to indicate. In sound, at least, this last name is connected with what is transitory and passes by, and may well connote a more nomadic lifestyle than that of urban or even agricultural life.[39] Eber is thus the direct ancestor of Terah, the father of Abram. This list in Genesis 10 develops the "social aspect of human beings: a human being is a social being living in a people and a land, in a particular social group with its own language."[40]

From Shem to Abram (Genesis 11:10-32)

After the tale of the city of Babel (Gen. 11:1-9), which we have already considered in some detail (see above, 71-77), the genealogical listing is continued. The list begins once more with Shem, whose lineage was reviewed also in the previous chapter (10:21-31). Hence Arpachshad, Shelah, Eber, and Peleg have

---

37. Van Wolde, 152-53.

38. Van Wolde, 158-59.

39. According to van Wolde (160), we find in Gen. 10 a "sociographic description" of groups in which Japheth is the ancestor of seafaring nations, Ham the ancestors of sedentary and urban peoples, and Shem the ancestor of nomads.

40. Van Wolde, 161.

already received mention. The present listing is, however, much like the one in chapter 5, one of father to son in a straight line, rather than the one of multiple offspring indicating the spread of different population groups in their regions. Elam, Asshur, Lud, and Aram, present in the earlier genealogy as descendants of Shem (10:22), have dropped out in favor of Arpachshad, of whom subsequently only one son is mentioned and so on, down the list to Terah (vv. 24-27).[41] The pattern of recording is identical up until that point: the age of the father is provided at the time the son is produced, followed by the number of years the father lived afterwards. The recital ends with the mention of "other sons and daughters" rather than the death of the ancestor which ended the individual listing in chapter 5. It is not so much the end of life but its continuation which receives emphasis here.

A shift occurs at the end of the list. In verse 24 Nahor is registered as the father of Terah, who in turn is named as the father not of one but of three sons: Abram, Nahor, and Haran (Gen. 11:26). The list resumes in verse 27 with a renewed mention of these three sons together with the offspring of Haran, Lot.[42] Let us take a closer look at the section that ends our "prelude."

Genesis 11:27-32

27. And this is the family history of Terah:
     Terah produced Abram and Nahor and Haran;
     and Haran produced Lot.
28. Then died Haran,[43]

---

41. Van Wolde (170): "In Gen. 5 and 11 only the firstborn sons are given a name; here everything turns on the individuals, fathers, and oldest sons, whereas Gen. 10 is above all focused on human beings as part of a people or a population group."

42. I am at this point adhering to the traditional division of allocating Gen. 11:10-32 to the previous rather than the following chapters. There are, however, a number of different possibilities. The dividing line between the primeval stories and subsequent material with a focus on the direct ancestors of ancient Israel may be drawn at Gen. 11:10, e.g. (so Joel W. Rosenberg in the *Harper Collins Study Bible* [New York: HarperCollins, 1993], 5), in which case the genealogy from Shem to Abram heads the narratives to follow to form an inclusion with the genealogical listing in 25:1-18). It would also be possible to commence the narratives of the patriarchs and matriarchs with 11:27 since it repeats the genealogical introduction ("this is the family history of . . .") and picks up a narrative strand. Yet we have seen that such narrative comments are not alien to genealogies. Also, one could begin the Abram/Sarai story with 11:31, the first mention of migration of this family. Naomi A. Steinberg makes a cogent and convincing argument for allocating 11:10-26 as the genealogical prologue to the narratives that follow; *Kinship and Marriage in Genesis: A Household Economics Perspective* (Minneapolis: Fortress, 1993), 41.

43. I am leaving the word order of the Hebrew in place, in spite of the awkward phrasing this causes in English, to bring out the emphatic use of the verb "died" in the first part of the sentence.

       in the presence of Terah his father,
       in the land of his family, in Ur-Kasdim.
29. And Abram and Nahor took for themselves wives;
       the name of the wife of Abram was Sarai,
       and the name of the wife of Nahor was Milcah
       daughter of Haran,
       father of Milcah and Iscah.
30. And Sarai was barren;
       she had no child.

31. Then Terah took Abram his son
       and Lot, the son of Haran,
       the son of his son,
       and Sarai and Milcah,
       his daughters-in-law,
       wives of Abram and Nahor, his sons;[44]
       and they went together from Ur-Kasdim
       to go to the land of Canaan.
       They came as far as Haran
       and lived there.
32. And the days of Terah
       were five and two hundred years
       and Terah died in Haran.

The first death to be mentioned in the genealogy of chapter 11 is that of Haran, a son who dies before his father, literally, "in the presence of his father." An unnatural and tragic event opens the account of the immediate family of ancestor Abram.

Yet, Haran has left offspring, Lot. Perhaps the one mention of death does not outweigh the repeated "produced" of Terah and Haran. To continue the optimistic tone, the record next cites the "taking" of wives by Abram and Nahor, the two other sons of Terah. At this point, as in Genesis 4:17-24, and as unexpectedly, the names of women occur; both Milcah, the wife of Nahor, and Sarai, the wife of Abram, receive mention by name. Milcah and Nahor will figure subsequently in the family narratives (Gen. 22:20-24; 24:1-67). Sarai will not only be a name in the stories but will become a presence to be reckoned with. Such a complete mention of family life, with the names of

44. Adopting the reading of the Samaritan Pentateuch rather than the MT for the persons who accompanied Terah.

daughters-in-law included with those of the sons, surely bodes well for the future of this family. Precisely here a negative note is sounded: "And Sarai was barren/she had no child" (11:30). The double mention of Sarai and Abram's lack of children is dire indeed. Fecundity and proliferation abounded even when death occurred, but now the whole enterprise might well come to a standstill. The tension, introduced by Haran's untimely death, is here continued and increased. This is the first time that a threat to continued progeny is introduced into the story, and it will not be the last.

Verse 31 picks up the thread of the story with Terah, the family patriarch, as the subject of a migration from the homeland to "the land of Canaan." Yet, they do not arrive in Canaan but rather in Haran, where they reside and where Terah eventually dies. A glance at the geography of the region in the ancient world makes clear that Haran is not exactly on a direct route from Ur to Canaan. Did the family make a detour, and did they find Haran an attractive place to settle, at least temporarily, and did Abram complete a journey already begun by his father? Or are different pieces of the story woven together here, and are the seams showing?[45] Whatever the case may be, Genesis 12:5 has Abram ending up in Canaan on a directive issued by God, as if it had not been the original destination of his family.

The prelude is completed with the death of Terah, recorded in verse 32. From now on it will be the descendants of Terah who will be in the center of the story of God's involvement with the world and its peoples.

---

45. Additional uncertainty is created by Terah's age at his death, which cannot have been more than 145 if Abram left Haran after his father's death, which seems to be assumed in Acts 7:4, and by a combined reading of Gen. 11:26 and 12:4.

CHAPTER 2

A Tale of a Garden (Genesis 2:4b–3:24)[1]

Before we turn to the material that makes up the main part of the Torah, it will be helpful to consider how at least a part of the text of Genesis 1–11 has fared in Christian interpretation. For reasons of space, only a small part of this rich tapestry can be explored here, but the text selected for closer analysis is one that exerted, and continues to exert, enormous influence in both a Jewish and a Christian context. Different understandings of Genesis 2:4b–3:24 determine how groups and communities conceive of the relations of humans to God, to the earth, and to one another. Most of us are familiar with this text, and we probably have it in mind as the story of the creation of humanity and its subsequent "fall." For our purposes here, we begin by dividing the passage into smaller units and looking briefly at each in turn.

Of Field, Stream, and Human (Genesis 2:4b-14)

Genesis 2:4b-14 contains a good deal of information about the created world. Words such as "field," "land," and "ground" occur frequently. These terms are

1. In part because of renewed interest in relations between male and female, the creation myth in these chapters has seen a great deal of interpretation in the past three decades of Old Testament scholarship. One analysis of far-reaching influence was that of Phyllis Trible, who published *God and the Rhetoric of Sexuality* in 1978 (Overtures to Biblical Theology 2 [Philadelphia: Fortress]), although some of the work on Gen. 2–3 that came to represent chapter 4, "A Love Story Gone Awry," had been originally published in 1973. Trible's analysis, although eventually challenged by some biblical scholars, provided a landmark in terms of feminist scholarship of the Bible, and many of her insights have stood the test of time. The discussion presented here is most indebted to the following works, besides that of Trible: Robert B. Coote and David Robert Ord, *The Bible's First History* (Philadelphia: Fortress, 1989); Carol L. Meyers, *Discovering Eve* (New York: Oxford University Press, 1988); and Ellen J. van Wolde, *Stories of the Beginning*.

amplified by words including "produce," "plants," "garden," "trees," and "rivers" with their specific names.[2] Such repetitions at least represent an interest in and emphasis on the land and its fecundity. We note also the attention given to water as a necessary source of fruitfulness. The lack of "rain" necessitates a substitute, "dew," and four "rivers" are mentioned elaborately with specific geographical locations. The creation of the human being is integrated into the description of field, garden, and stream and itself partakes of created matter, "dust from the ground" (in English, we might say "human" from "humus"). The human being is a part of all that grows and blooms and bursts with life in the creation God has fashioned:

Genesis 2:7-9

7. And the Holy God fashioned the human being
   with dust from the ground
   and blew into its nostrils the breath of life,
   and the human one became a living being.
8. And the Holy One planted a garden in Eden, in the East,
   and put there the human God had fashioned.
9. Then the Holy One caused to sprout from the land
   all the trees that are pleasant to see
   and good to eat
   and the tree of life,
   in the midst of the garden,
   and the tree of the knowledge of good and bad.

A Fit Counterpart (Genesis 2:15-25)

In the next unit, the human being receives a purpose and companions, of whom the woman (Hebrew *isha*) is the one most fitting for it as a counterpart. The animals, who seem to be the first candidates for companionship (vv.

---

2. While the Tigris and Euphrates are rivers familiar to the biblical landscape, the Pishon and Gihon are today unknown, although theories abound. The source of the four rivers, if Tigris and Euphrates are included, would be northern Mesopotamia. Most likely, the story intends to include both known and unknown regions, since it is in essence myth. Alternatively, the names of the rivers may have been known once and lost to us. They could indicate the Indus, the Ganges, and/or the Nile. Van Wolde observes (41): "Whereas the earth outside the garden is watered by an undefined flood, the garden itself is watered by a river. This is so richly provided with water that, just outside Eden, all the great rivers of the then known world flow out of it; the Pishon, the Gihon, the Tigris, and the Euphrates."

19-20), figure importantly in the scenery of abundance and life that is being painted here. The human being first receives a purpose of "tilling" and "serving" the garden God has made (v. 15), a task that shifts the responsibility of subduing and governance given in Genesis 1:28 into a direction of faithful attentive activity (tilling) with a posture of humility (serving). While it receives this task, the human also receives a command from God in the first words that God speaks in the narrative, not to "eat" from the tree of the "knowledge of good and bad," although all other fruit is there for the "eating" (v. 17). God thus sets a limit for the human being and warns that transgression of this limit will bring about death. Directly following this directive, God ruminates that "it is not good" for the human to be alone and that it needs a counterpart. God, who knows "good and bad" (see 3:22), makes a decision based on this divine discernment, perhaps in the belief that two will be able to withstand more easily the temptation to transgress the limits set by God.

Genesis 2:18, 21-25

18. The Holy God said:
    It is not good for the human to be by itself;
    I will make for it a helper as its counterpart.

    . . . .

21. The Holy God caused a deep sleep to fall
    on the human and it slept;
    and he took one of its ribs
    and closed the flesh beneath it.
22. And the Holy God built the rib
    which he took from the human into a woman
    and brought her to the human being.

23. The human said:
    This is finally it!³
    bone of my bones
    and flesh of my flesh.
    This one will be called woman *(ishshah)*
    for from man *(ish)*
    was taken this one.

24. Therefore a man will leave
    his father and mother

---

3. This translation is close to that of Everett Fox: "This-time, she-is-it!"; *The Five Books of Moses* (New York: Schocken, 1995), 20.

and cling to his woman,
and they will be one flesh.

25. And the two of them were naked,
the human and his woman,
and they were not ashamed.

With the goal of finding a fit counterpart, God seems first to try the animals (vv. 19-20), who are named by the human being but among whom no fitting companion is to be found. So rather than dust, which furnished material for both human and beast, human flesh itself becomes the vehicle of God's fashioning. In verse 23, the human being, now a male distinguishable from his female counterpart, speaks his first words in exultation over the one "who is it." The narrator then adds two comments about the male-female relationship (vv. 24-25). It will cause separation from parental ties, specifically here for the man. Next, there is no shame between male and female; their nakedness causes no insight into their vulnerability.[4]

It is clear that here we do not find the perfect/beautiful/good creation of Genesis 1. From a certain perspective, the text describes certain aspects missing, certain lacks and how these are addressed and solved in the creation process. First is the lack of "rain," a foreboding issue in arid climates. Lack of rain can spell death. This lack is made up for by dew and abundant rivers that provide moisture for earth's thriving. Next the creature made from "dust" lacks "life," which is provided by God's breath. The earth, specifically the garden, lacks a worker, a "tiller," to make it flourish, and the human creature fits the bill. Humanity lacks "knowledge of good and bad," a lack expressed both in the command from God (v. 17) and in the statement from the narrator about the absence of shame (v. 25). This lack is supposedly beneficial for the human being, but it will nevertheless be provided for in the next episode. One human being alone lacks a "companion," lacks differentiation, and God makes good the lack by a new fashioning, this time from bone and flesh.

4. Trible deduces on the basis of v. 24 that here "only the man is identified with father and mother; the woman continues to stand alone. Her uniqueness and independence as a human creature remain intact, and her prominence in the design of the story persists. . . . The man does not control her; he moves toward her for union." Trible also connects this "oneness" that the narrator observes with the original twoness that resulted from the creation of woman in v. 22: "From one comes two; from wholeness comes differentiation. Now, at the conclusion of the episode, this differentiation returns to wholeness; from two come the one flesh of communion between female and male"; 104.

The Snake and the Tree (Genesis 3:1-5)

A new character enters in the third episode. The snake, who is in its own way naked, traditionally is associated with wisdom and cleverness. In Hebrew the words for "naked" *(arom)* and "clever" *(arum)* are quite close, and the transition to the presence of the snake in the story is made natural by this word association.

Genesis 3:1-5
1. The snake was clever
   above all the animals of the field
   that the Holy God had made.
   And it said to the woman:
   Even though God said
   not to eat from all the trees of the garden. . . .[5]
2. The woman said to the snake:
   From the fruit of the trees in the garden we may eat.
3. And from the fruit of the tree
   that is in the midst of the garden
   we may not eat
   and we may not touch it,
   lest we die.
4. The snake said to the woman:
   Die! You will not die!
5. For God knows
   that on the day you eat from it
   your eyes will be opened
   and you will be like God,
   knowing good and bad.[6]

In the traditions, the snake is made out to be more of a negative presence than is perhaps warranted by the text, since the word used here for its cleverness is more often used in a positive context than not.[7] Of course, cleverness can be used for a negative end, and there is certainly some ambiguity here. The snake utters an incomplete sentence (3:2), because it states so obvious an un-

---

5. So Fox, 21.

6. The verb forms and personal pronouns in this sentence are all plural, indicating that the snake is addressing both the man and the woman.

7. See, e.g., Prov. 13:16; 14:8, 15-18; 22:3; 27:12.

truth that the woman with whom it is conversing jumps in to correct and contradict. In contradicting she overstates her case and adds the limitation of "touch" to that of "eating." If not an outright lie, at least a bending of the truth takes place and a deceptive statement has received a deceptive response.[8] The snake is having a good time setting everyone straight and makes God out to be the liar. Not death but knowledge will be the part of humanity after eating, and this will make them "like God, knowing good and bad." In the end the snake is both wrong and right. They do become like God, knowing good and bad (see 3:22), but death will be their part, even though not at the instant of eating. A limited life span will be their protection against living forever with the knowledge of good and bad, and God intervenes to keep it so (3:23).

With Both Eyes Open (Genesis 3:6-13)

The act of eating, described in the next episode (3:6-7), indeed opens the eyes of the human couple. But instead of this knowledge bringing them closer to God, it separates, creature from creature and creature from God.[9] Their nakedness is now clear to them, and they take pains to find a covering for it. In the episode that follows (3:9-13), God addresses each character separately, again emphasizing the separation between what should have been one.

Genesis 3:9-13
9. The Holy One called to the human
   and said: Where are you?
10. And he said: The sound of you I heard in the garden
    and I was afraid for I am naked,
    and I hid.
11. He said: Who told you
    that you are naked?
    From the tree about which I commanded you
    not to eat from it, did you eat?
12. The human said:
    The woman that you gave to be with me,

---

8. This contra van Wolde (51), who maintains that the problem with the snake is not that it "tells untruths," but that it does not tell the whole truth. In terms of the degree of the snake's deceptiveness, much depends on how one reads 3:1.

9. To my view, Trible was one of the first biblical scholars to emphasize the man's presence throughout the episodes, during the conversation with the snake (see above, n. 6) and during the act of eating; 113.

she gave to me from the fruit of the tree, and I ate.
13. The Holy One said to the woman:
What is this you have done?
The woman said:
The snake tricked me and I ate.

There is no oneness between God and the human creatures, for they are hiding from God, and no oneness with each other, for they exist now in a context of accusation. God asks questions only at this point, questions which find their point in the "did you eat?" of verse 11. To this both male and female respond "I ate" (vv. 12-13), although both point the finger at someone else who is more to blame than they are themselves. Again, their new knowledge has not produced oneness but rather separation, not only from God and each other but also from the animals as they are represented by the snake.

Now, Look What You've Done (Genesis 3:14-24)

The rest of chapter 3 contains the recital of the consequences of what snake and human couple have done (vv. 14-19), with a brief narrative conclusion to close out the entire creation myth (vv. 20-24). The divine speech does not prescribe so much as describe: this is what you have done, and therefore this is the way it will henceforth be.[10] The way things will be are marked by separation and alienation. First, God points to the alienation between animal and woman (vv. 14-15). Next, a woman's desire for her man will be responded to with dominance, and the link with the next generation will be established in pain (v. 16). Finally, the ground from which the human came will give up its riches grudgingly (17-19). Fertility of human and field will happen in the midst of "pain" (vv. 16-17). Immediately following God's words, a narrative comment introduces a note of hope into the dire prognosis:

Genesis 3:20-24
20. And the human being called the name of his woman Eve/*Hawwa*
for she became the mother of all life *(Hay)*.
21. The Holy God made for the human and his woman
tunics of skins and clothed them.

10. Cf. Trible: "The divine speeches to the serpent, the woman, and the man are not commands for structuring life. To the contrary, they show how intolerable existence has become as it stands between creation and redemption"; 123.

22. The Holy God said:
    Look, humanity has become like one of us
    in knowing good and bad;
    now, lest it stretches out its hand
    and takes also from the tree of life
    and eats and lives forever!
23. And the Holy One sent it from the garden of Eden,
    to till the ground
    from which it was taken.
24. God drove the human out
    and made dwell east of the garden of Eden the Cherubs
    and the flaming sword
    turning back and forth to guard
    the road to the tree of life.

Words for "life" bracket these verses. The woman's name Eve/*Hawwa* is associated with "life," and at the end the "tree of life" is safe inside the garden with humanity henceforth existing outside of it. The lack of knowledge that characterized humanity has been made up, but it has come at a cost. Alienation, domination, and pain will from now on be a part of created life. Yet life has not stopped. In fact, it has only just begun, and God does not abandon the created world. God, in this text, acts protectively, first, in turning tailor and making clothes for the human pair (3:21) and, second, in protecting both humans and garden by barring the place from humanity and preventing a nightmare of an everlasting duration of alienated existence (v. 24). The banishment from the garden is in a way required by the existence of the earth. The mandate of the first story to fill the earth and govern it (Gen. 1:28) is not fulfilled as long as humanity exists in a garden.[11] The earth is "out there." It lies waiting for the human hand to "till and serve it" (cf. 2:15). We note also that God is not shut in the garden but has barred the divine self from the garden's protected existence. We will speak more of this when we consider the nature of God in the Torah in a following chapter.

11. Van Wolde makes this point when she observes: "From the perspective of the earth, it is thus a positive development for the human being to be driven out of the garden, less so for the human being." Furthermore, she wonders whether the story is set up in such a way that the human creatures were bound to leave the garden: "Might one conclude . . . that it was God's intention for the human being (after a first phase in the garden) to have to go out of the garden to cultivate the earth?" (43-44).

What the Story Is All About

This is the story to this point. What is it all about? What were the storytellers trying to get across to the ancient believer? The story is so complex that surely there is not just *one truth* the reader is meant to derive from it. Rather, here is told of a web of meanings relating to existence in the presence of God. It is clear that certain preoccupations of the ancient world with food and fertility, for example, are strongly present in the story.[12] Another element is the importance of the earth itself, which partly resides in the linkage between the word for "human" (Hebrew *adam*) and the word for "ground" *(adamah)*. As van Wolde points out: "Human beings and earth resemble each other; they are bound to each other; the human being is an 'earth-being' and the earth is dependent on the human being. . . . Origin and name, name and surname, all this binds human beings to the earth."[13] Van Wolde is arguing strongly to understand these beginning stories in an "earth-centered" way.

Especially intriguing are the references to the "tree of knowledge of good and bad." Does this tree indicate the knowledge of what is ethically good and what is evil? Or does it simply mean "everything," as van Wolde would have it?[14] Is the process of eating a necessary one to symbolize maturation, or does it constitute the break, the beginning of the flaw of alienated existence? Whether the knowledge the tree imparts is of "everything" or of that which is

---

12. Meyers draws attention to the frequency with which the root of the verb "to eat" occurs in these chapters: "This striking repetition and placement carries its own message; it tells us that the beginning of human existence coincides with the concern for food"; *Discovering Eve*, 89.

13. Van Wolde, 44.

14. This conviction motivates van Wolde to choose the translation "good and bad" rather than "good and evil." She states that "'good and bad' stand for 'everything'; that is why the phrase is not translated with the ethically colored 'good and evil' here"; 46. For van Wolde, "knowledge of good and bad" indicates general discernment, and she quotes 2 Sam. 19:36(35) and Deut. 1:39 in support. In an earlier interpretation, Martin Buber argues against such an understanding and wants the tree to be about "adequate awareness of the opposites latent in creation." God in Buber's argument encompasses the opposites and is untouched by them. Not so humanity who "knows oppositeness only by his (sic!) situation within it." By this understanding a human being knows "evil" only by taking part in an evil deed or being part of an evil situation. This understanding also explains the recognition of nakedness as a consequence of the eating from the tree, since the two recognize their differentiation; Martin Buber, *Good and Evil: Two Interpretations* (New York: Scribner, 1953), 70-78. Buber's interpretation is the most acceptable in my view, even though I follow van Wolde in the translation. Although I agree that there is no question here of "sin" and "a fall," her generally positive reading of the events in the garden do not entirely jibe with tone and language use in the story. Van Wolde is not alone, of course, in her interpretation, which is shared by a number of interpreters.

morally good and evil, surely the storytellers mean to relate that this knowledge sets humans on the wrong path. In my reading, it seems clear that the story intends to explain what went wrong in God's good creation and that the act of eating from the tree symbolizes the beginning of this situation.

Placing the garden story in the appropriate historical context may help us to get closer to a valid reading of the narrative and to an understanding of what the original storytellers had in mind. The quest for a historical setting is in this case, however, not a simple one. Since many cultures share a story of origins, the garden story could be very old and its original context may be lost in the mists of time. If one follows traditional source analysis, the narrative is a part of the J strand, which would determine its original context some time during the 10th century B.C.E. (see above, 58). Biblical scholars Robert Coote and David Ord would thus have the main point of the story in Genesis 2–3 be a defense of the Davidic monarchy in comparing it to "sweatless" labor in the garden.[15] Yet, traditional source analysis has come under serious attack in recent decades (see above, 61-62) and an interpretation that grounds itself solidly in a theory that has become more and more tenuous would seem to lack the credibility it might have had in an earlier stage of biblical scholarship. A postexilic context, the surest ground to stand on when considering the final shape and context of the story, has been taken into account in my reading at many points. That was a time when a need for identity, a desire for order, and a perspective on the world as "filled with violence," would dictate an emphasis on many of the concerns found in these chapters. Historical contexts, on multiple levels, may be the best we can assign for stories of the world's beginnings in ancient Israel. Perennial concerns of the ancient Israelite context are also evident, such as those of fruitfulness, of people and earth, and of providing for the necessities of life such as food and clothing.[16] To focus on one agenda with which the writers constructed their story may be taking too narrow a perspective on the text.

Throughout my reading of the garden story, language, the way in which

---

15. Coote and Ord place the J strand in the earlier part of the 10th century during the establishment of the Davidic monarchy. "The immediate occasion for the composition of J was the necessity of validating the establishment of the Davidic royal house, which replaced a much less centralized political arrangement in the highlands of Palestine"; 6. And further: "The very character of the god of the Davidic state is that of deliverer of the Israelites from precisely that work for which in Mesopotamian tradition human beings were created. . . . In J's history, sweaty labor is not inherent in the created order. The human in the garden is a sweatless figure"; 50.

16. Thus Meyers highlights the concerns around "work" and "food" in Gen. 2–3: "The tale, and in particular the oracles [i.e., Gen. 3:14-19], must not be lifted from their social and literary context. They must be seen primarily as helping highland settlers cope with life's demands, difficult as they may be"; *Discovering Eve*, 93-94.

writers emphasized certain words, has been a predominant concern. From the perspective of language use, it seems clear that in general the outcome of the events as described in Genesis 2–3 was not viewed as positive. Animal and woman, woman and man, man and nature are henceforth at cross-purposes with one another. Seen in this way, Genesis 4 with its tale of kin-strife and kin-murder is a direct and logical outcome of the garden story, as is much else that happens in the first eleven chapters of Genesis. From now on, good outcomes for the world will have to be struggled for, and they are by no means guaranteed. There exists in this way thematic consistency between the garden narrative and the rest of the Torah. God has the good of the world in mind and to this end engages with humanity to redeem what has gone "awry," using Phyllis Trible's word. Life is not as it should be or could have been, but in the good purposes of God the mending of the world is on its way.[17]

Type and Countertype (Romans 5:18-19)

That things have gone wrong and that the world needs reparation is also the view of Paul, who had his own take on the garden story and who wrote about it in his letter to the Romans as follows:

Romans 5:18-19
18. Now then, just as through one person's wrongdoing condemnation extended to all, in the same way through one person's righteous deed acquittal for life extends to all. 19. For, as by the disobedience of one man the many were made sinners, so by the obedience of one man will the many be made righteous.

The argument that Paul builds in Romans 5:12-21 is that one person, Adam, sinned and through his sin dragged everyone else into sinfulness. The direct consequence of Adam's sin was death, to which the entire human race is subjected. Adam is called in verse 14 "a type of the one who was coming." Verses 18-19 sum up the argument by which Adam and Christ are set up as type and countertype: One man (Adam) sinned and thus brought condemnation (i.e., death) to all; one man (Christ) was obedient and thus brought acquittal (i.e.,

---

17. Cf. Nahum M. Sarna, who views Gen. 2–3 as an explanation of all the situations and relations that have gone wrong in the world, since what is observed in the world of human experience is so strikingly different from the "vision of God's ideal world" as it is depicted in Gen. 1:1–2:4a; *Genesis* בראשית. JPS Torah Commentary (Philadelphia: Jewish Publication Society, 5749/1989), 16.

life) to all. The section concludes by Paul's observation that in this context under the law sin proliferates. Sin is everywhere and everyone sins, but where there is law there is specification of wrongdoing. He will then go on to explain how the dominion of sin is overcome (Rom. 6:1ff.).[18]

Paul was a child of his time and understood the garden story out of his own religious and literary context as a story of sin and death. The "idea that death was the punishment for Adam and Eve's sin is widespread in rabbinic sources."[19] In addition, the idea that all humanity was affected by sinfulness because of Adam's sin was also expressed in Judaism, although this concept took on far greater prominence and significance in later Christian thought than in Judaism.[20] More importantly, Paul's overarching concern in the Letter to the Romans is with the entrance of Gentiles into the community of faith, into the grace of the God of Israel, into salvation and everlasting life which is made possible by Christ rather than by becoming Jewish, with the attendant prescriptions of circumcision and keeping the food and Sabbath laws. Jewish believers already knew that laws such as these had no salvific power but that salvation resides in God's saving activity. This had to be made clear to the Gentiles who were invited into the circle of those who believe in the God of Israel. God had engaged in a final act of salvation in Jesus Christ. In Christ God's saving activity takes a new turn, and Christ is thus the perfect counterimage of the imperfect Adam.

To make his argument work, Paul has to ignore the fact that the garden story presents two human beings rather than one and that one of these is the initiator in the act of disobedience. That one was, after all, the woman, and to

18. Paul's argument is intricate, and many have labored to interpret his words in great detail. It is not possible here to give an adequate overview of all the important works produced in the Christian world on Paul's letter to the Romans. The core of his message in this section of chapter 5 is, however, rather easily captured. As Paul J. Achtemeier observes, according to Paul in Romans 5: "Christ got us out of the mess Adam got us into. What Adam did, Christ undid; where Adam failed, Christ succeeded"; *Romans.* Interpretation (Atlanta: John Knox, 1985), 97. Paul's argument is much the same in 1 Cor. 15:21-22: "For since death came through a human being, the resurrection of the dead has also come through a human being; for as all die in Adam, so all will be made alive in Christ" (NRSV). The interpretative schema is consistent in both the Romans and the Corinthians passage.

19. For an overview, see James L. Kugel, *Traditions of the Bible: A Guide to the Bible As It Was at the Start of the Common Era* (Cambridge, MA: Harvard University Press, 1998), 127, where he refers to *Genesis Rabbah* and two of the Sanhedrin tractates.

20. For an expression of this thought dating from the 1st century B.C.E., see 2 Esdr. 3:21-22: "For the first Adam, burdened with an evil heart, transgressed and was overcome, as were also all who were descended from him. Thus the disease became permanent; the law was in the hearts of the people along with the evil root; but what was good departed, and the evil remained" (NRSV).

set up the woman as the type to which Christ was the countertype would not have worked unless Christ had been a woman. It is clear, then, that Paul makes his reading of Genesis 2 and 3 subservient to his agenda of making believers out of Gentiles. It is also clear that his understanding is much indebted to the understanding of the Genesis 2–3 story that was predominant in his day. Paul's own context and concerns thus interact with the text to produce a reading of the text. In fact, Paul was probably very little concerned with what the story was trying to convey in its own time.

In Full Submission (1 Timothy 2:11-15)

When the presence of the woman does receive attention in the New Testament, it is to paint her as the real culprit in the garden and the first one to sin.

1 Timothy 2:11-15
11. Let a woman learn in silence in full submission.
12. Teaching for a woman I do not permit, nor to have authority over a man, but to be in silence.
13. For Adam was first formed, then Eve.
14. And Adam was not deceived, but the woman fell into transgression by being deceived.
15. But she will be saved through childbearing; provided they remain in faith, love and holiness, with modesty.[21]

The context of 1 Timothy was very likely that of the early church in the first part of the 2nd century c.e., when it was incumbent on the burgeoning Christian community to regulate itself in such a way that it would be least vulnerable to the authorities. Hence, it was a high priority of the writer of this letter for the congregations not to appear outlandish, different from surrounding cultures in terms of gender roles.[22] In order to get his point across, the writer employs the text of Genesis 2 to bolster his argument that women should be silent, not teach or have authority over a man. Twice he uses the word "silence" to underscore the importance of this womanly posture. The woman's silence surrounds the proscription of her giving voice to the benefits

---

21. Cf. 1 Cor. 14:34-36, where women are also charged to be silent, albeit in a more clearly defined location (i.e., the churches).

22. It is generally assumed that 1 Timothy is not from the hand of Paul and dates from the first part of the 2nd century.

of her "learning" in verses 11-12. Moreover, the word "silence" is underlined by the attached directive of "full submission."[23] The author could hardly make it more clear that a good woman is a silent woman.[24] In verses 13-14, two proofs from the Hebrew Bible are used to support the directive. One is that Adam came first, and what comes second must be viewed as inferior. In addition, it was Eve who was deceived and fell into transgression.

The writer of this letter was a child of his time and adopted current religious opinion in painting Eve as the one having primary responsibility for sin. In view of this reasoning, her silence and her submission are a kind of punishment. That this is the direction of his thought is borne out by the last phrase, which speaks of a woman's salvation. Underlying this pronouncement is surely the idea that a woman is not saved in the same way that a man is. The opinion that it was the woman who caused "it all" can be found as early as the 2nd century B.C.E. in the deuterocanonical writings of Jesus ben Sirach: "From a woman sin had its beginning/and because of her we all die."[25] 1 Timothy may have been composed for a particular context, but like the curse of Ham in Genesis 10, the declaration of Eve's culpability and that of all her daughters after her cast a long shadow forward into the Christian religious world. It still has power in numerous contexts, as in the many parts of the Christian family where woman's equality is not recognized and her role in submissine obedience vis-à-vis her husband is reaffirmed.

Ways of Reading

The garden story in Genesis 2–3 is read in the New Testament in two ways, one in which the man is the primary sinner and another in which the woman

23. The word "submission" (Greek *hypotagē*) is used also of children in relation to their parent in 1 Tim. 3:4.

24. Some scholars see the point of "learning," which was according to them against Jewish custom, as progress. One wonders, however, to what advantage learning may be if one cannot ask questions or discuss the results of one's learning. See Thomas C. Oden, *First and Second Timothy and Titus.* Interpretation (Louisville: John Knox, 1989), 96-98.

25. Sir. 25:24. For similar conclusions about who was to blame for sin in the context of Judaism, see Philo, *Creation* 151-52; Josephus, *Jewish Antiquities* 1:49; 2 En. 31:6; *Yebamoth* 103b. In the context of the Christian world this conviction was taken up vigorously by, among others Tertullian and Augustine. Tertullian in *De cultu feminarum (The Apparel of Women)* addressed Eve and Everywoman thus: "You are the devil's gateway. . . . On account of your desert, that is death, even the Son of God had to die." (Tertullian may not have had time for the notion that Eve may have been the "type of the one who was coming," as it should have been if one follows Paul's logic in Rom. 5).

takes the starring role in terms of sin. These two ways of reading proceed from very different agendas. One agenda is to convince Gentiles of the possibility of their being *included* in the community of the redeemed. The other agenda aims to contain and limit, to set strictures and to conform to the norm in terms of gender roles. Whatever we think about either reading in itself, it should be clear how much the context and the agenda of the writers determined how they interpreted the myth of Genesis 2–3. It should also be clear that there is nothing wrong with this in itself. In my reading of the garden story, our own context and agendas were brought to bear wherever possible. Contemporary interpretation may be driven by an agenda in which interest in the earth and its well-being, for example, receives central emphasis. This emphasis coheres with word use in the text itself. Concerns for proper care in taking of the earth/land and for the provision of adequate food distribution are not peripheral to Genesis 2–3. In addition, relationships between different parts of the creation and between them and God are of central concern, and these include relations between male and female. A world where male and female are set at odds with one another and where the one sex dominates the other is depicted as a direct consequence of the act of eating from the tree of knowledge of good and bad, rather than as a part of the design for God's good creation. In the first creation myth, Genesis 1:1–2:4a, male and female are equally created in the image of God. In the second myth, Genesis 2–3, the woman is created as a fit counterpart to the man without a hint of subordination on her part. Both are present during the conversation with the snake and both eat from the tree. Alienation between the two and between them and God is described as a result of the eating and manifests itself in their acts of hiding, from each other in clothing and from God in the garden, and of blaming, the man blaming the woman and the woman the snake.

In considering all three texts, Genesis 2–3, Romans 5:18-19, and 1 Timothy 2:11-15, and bringing them into conversation with each other, how do we evaluate the significance of each for Christians today? A dominant strain in Christian tradition almost automatically relegates an Old Testament text to secondary status when it is paired with one from the New Testament, even where official doctrine would demand otherwise.[26] One of the concerns in my reading of texts is to set them in a different relation to one another. We have seen how words, applied to the early Christian community in 1 Peter, gained in significance and were illumined and enriched by an investigation into the application of the same appellations as they were used to describe the

---

26. So, e.g., in congregations in the U.S., even those with a Calvinist heritage, where this habit is reinforced by the use of the so-called Ecumenical Lectionary. See above, xiii and 69ff.

initial covenant community at Sinai in Exodus 19 (see above, 22-24). Further, we discovered significant insights and guidance for our own world in the ancient story of the tower and city of Babel without having to augment its relevance with a text from the New Testament (see above, 71-74). At this point, we are faced with three texts that show serious tensions with each other when they are read side by side. How are we to interpret and evaluate in that case?

Rehearsing the main points made by each passage, we arrive at the following: Genesis 2–3 tells of God's world as it was affected in all its relationships by a human act of disobedience. The text depicts a world that is deeply wounded by alienated relations. It also depicts a God who remains engaged with this world. Paul, in the Letter to the Romans, seems to be thinking along these same lines. For Paul, the entire world was affected and wounded by human disobedience; and now, in Christ, the whole world is invited into the healing of the broken relationship between God and humanity. Christ's act of obedience cancels the first human's act of disobedience, and in Christ a healed relationship between God and the world may now be embraced by those who were not a party to the Sinai covenant but who from the beginning were a part of the circle of God's love which went out to the whole world. As Christians, we may still gratefully accept this invitation today.

Where Paul's reasoning falls short is in not taking into account that there were *two* human beings involved in the act of disobedience and that a first result of this act was alienation between these two.[27] Taking Paul's logic of God's redemptive activity in Christ into account rather than the specifics of his argument, may we not conclude that in Christ this alienation is redeemed as well as that between God and humanity? It is, after all, not Christ's maleness that has priority but Christ's humanness in the comparison that Paul makes, a humanness which of necessity must embrace female as well as male nature.[28] We may thus let the garden-story interact with Romans 5 and see how these two are coherent with one another; furthermore, a close read-

27. Even though Paul uses Greek *anthrōpos* rather than *anēr* in the passage, it is clear that he is referring to the male human being alone when he refers to Adam specifically, as in v. 14, or to "the one," using the male gender. Femaleness is here subsumed by the male as it was in Paul's context, and it is hard to imagine that he could have reasoned otherwise. That he could not escape his context does, however, not mean that we are still bound by the same patriarchal logic.

28. Elizabeth Johnson argues this point cogently in her book, *She Who Is: The Mystery of God in Feminist Theological Discourse* (New York: Crossroad, 1992), when she discusses the nature of Christ in the section "Jesus-Sophia" (150-69): "The early Christian aphorism 'What is not assumed is not redeemed, but what is assumed is saved by union with God' sums up the insight that God's saving solidarity with all of humanity is what is crucial for the birth of the new creation" (153). And further: "It is not Jesus' maleness that is doctrinally important but his humanity in solidarity with the whole suffering human race" (165).

ing of the original myth may advance the interpretation of the argument made in Romans.

What about 1 Timothy 2:11-15? Here something of a different nature is going on than in the Romans passage. The writer, at a time that the Christian community was succumbing to governing itself according to the ideology and structure of the patriarchal household, emphatically closes options that may have been available for women at an earlier stage of the life of the followers of Jesus of Nazareth. In order to make the point stick, theological arguments are brought to bear which arise from a distorted reading of the Old Testament story, albeit one that was common for the understandings of that day. These theological arguments lay a theo-mythical foundation for the subordination of women, a move that is never made in the Old Testament, and they are taken to such an extreme that a woman's *salvation* no longer directly is located in Christ, but rather in *childbearing*. The depiction of God in Romans 5 is thematically consistent with the depiction of God in Genesis. There God acted in everything on behalf of the world and its creatures. Paul claims that in Christ God has engaged in a new act on behalf of the world. This consistency does not pertain to 1 Timothy. So we can no longer claim that these particular words in 1 Timothy 2:11-15 should have relevance or authority today by the principles I outlined above (66-69). This text is judged wanting by the biblical word itself.[29]

29. I do not mean to say that there is nothing of value or authority in all of Timothy, but it seems to me a painful and unproductive exercise to try to rescue a text which so clearly is subject to misogynist impulses and which has done such incalculable harm to women in the Christian community for centuries and continues to be harmful today.

CONCLUSION

The Prelude and the Bible

The first 11 chapters of Genesis do not take up a great deal of space in the whole of the biblical text, but they are of crucial importance for all that follows. It may be fair to say that without insight into these texts the rest of the Bible, including the New Testament, cannot be properly grasped. God's care for and God's engagement with the whole world are told in ways that set the tone for the entire biblical story. The New Testament's declaration that "God so loved the world . . ." is rooted in these chapters. The call to ancient Israel to be God's covenant people as well as the call to the Gentiles to become God's covenant people in Christ is provided with its grounding in Genesis 1–11. Basic responsibilities of humanity to the earth and all its creatures, of human to human and of human to God, are furnished with their theological foundations in these texts. Finally, crucial linkage to the entire world is established for the community that views itself as living in a covenant relationship with God, a linkage that serves as a guard against perceiving this relationship as one of special status rather than special responsibility.

In terms of historical context, the material gathered in Genesis 1–11 represents at least three of the sources of traditional source analysis, J, E, and P. Much of what we find here reflects ancient lore and custom. Stories of creation are shared by many cultures and religions.[1] From the construction and telling of these myths of beginnings the present world derives meaning and form. The biblical writers told a story of profound truths that fit the label "myth" as I described it in Chapter 2. These truths spoke powerfully into the historical context of the times that gave birth to the stories, most likely long before the Babylonian exile, as well as to subsequent times of their reception

---

1. Van Wolde: "Every culture attaches a meaning to the beginning, often in the form of stories"; 1.

in the literary context of the entire Torah. The history of the people of the Bible, from tribal confederation to monarchy to exile, is reflected in the stories of violence, pain, and alienation of the Genesis myths. The motifs embedded in these narratives reflect ancient Israel's experience in its history. On a large scale there is a world which is not exactly marked by care and concern for the neighbor; on a small scale there is kin-strife and family tension, experiences which would mark the people of the Bible over and over again. For the community of the restoration in postexilic Judah, the sense of order, of fittingness, and of the fecundity of God's creation afforded a balance to a sense of chaos and turmoil, of being overwhelmed by the large powers of that day. Large empires too are all a part of God's world. The world is God's covenant world. Human violence, so much an everyday part of the ancient and the modern world, comes to the fore in these narratives as opposed to God's intention for the world. Violence so engulfs the creation that even God is affected by its destructiveness. Yet, destruction of the creation is not God's final word. Through one individual, Noah, a new beginning is made. Noah's agency is a model for future interventions on behalf of the creation, interventions that will often take place through the mediation of an individual or group.

We contemplated the genealogical lists at the point of their narrative implications and the manner in which they give the stories of the first 11 chapters momentum to move toward the tale of the direct ancestors of ancient Israel, who descended through Terah from Shem and Noah and ultimately from Seth, who replaced Abel, the brother who was murdered by Cain. The world of the genealogy, in many ways closed to Westerners, also functions as a rich store of information about the world that surrounded the ancient Israelites. In this varied and diverse world, they were a small and insignificant group, one that yet carried the preference of God for the weak, the *hevels* of the creation.

Finally, a review of the myth of the garden in Genesis 2–3 led to a consideration of two very different interpretations of this story in the New Testament. Bringing these three texts into conversation with each other once again pointed to the richness of the Genesis myth and its potential to enhance also Christian understandings of God's saving activity.

PART IV

The Story of the Torah: The Making of a People
(Genesis 12:1–Deuteronomy 34:12)

Introduction: A People of God's Pasture[1]

The world is made, but it is a marred world. Violence permeates it and, left to themselves, human creatures are not able to live in harmonious partnership with God, the earth, and one another. Time and again, God will engage with the world on behalf of its mending by means of a particular individual or group. The prelude has set the theme of the making of this world; the rest of the Torah will concern itself with the making of a people. A crucial step in this process is the concluding of the covenant at Sinai, an event that sets the seal on the special relationship between people and God and that at the same time sets a new process in motion. Henceforth, the people will conduct their life within the covenant bond, and they receive instructions as to how life should be lived within this relationship. The covenant God has made with the world frames the covenant between God and people, which thus exists within the care God extends to the whole creation. The concern of God for the world is evident in the words to Abram that "all the clans of the earth will be blessed in you" (Gen. 12:3), in the mention of God's blessing extending to those outside of the Abraham/Sarah line of descent (Gen. 21:20), and in the declaration that accompanies the covenant charge, "for mine is all the earth" (Exod. 19:5). The covenant community is to exhibit the extent and the depth of God's love for the world in the way they live their life together. They are "special," as the announcement states in Exodus 19, insofar as what is demanded of them is special. Extensive lists of instruction and law-giving thus form an integral part of the covenant

---

1. Cf. Ps. 95:7; 100:3.

relationship. The Torah takes for granted that without such guidance the group's efforts to live according to God's will for it would fail.

It is, after all, abundantly clear from the beginning of the story that this people-in-the-making is deeply affected by the violence that mars the world. Hostility in one form or another runs like a continuous thread through the fabric of the narratives in the Torah. In the Genesis stories, kinfolk exist and operate in a network of relationships that is also a seedbed of antipathy and potential violence. In Exodus, the descendants of Abraham and Sarah suffer under violent oppression in Egypt, and in the sequel to the liberation from Egypt, as told in Exodus and Numbers, the "children of Israel" are frequently at odds with their leader, Moses, and at times in open rebellion against God. Moses himself is a leader who does not escape the violence that brews around him, and he too is involved in a squabble with his siblings. The involvement of God with the community that is called into covenant does not take place in a fairy-tale context of sweetness and light but in a world that mirrors the world all humans know, the world of ordinary human beings, warts and all. Because of this reality, the people need guidance and instruction *(torah)* toward a way of life that more closely resembles what God has in mind for ancient Israel and for the world.

The people called by God into a covenant relationship are promised a place, a land, where they shall make their existence as God's people a reality. Early on in the story this promise is the lure by which God motivates Abram to trek from Haran to Canaan: "Go now . . . to the land that I will show you" (Gen. 12:1). When they reach Canaan the promise is reiterated (Gen. 12:7) and formalized in a covenant ceremony (15:17-21). This promise, together with that of abundant offspring, is the one that gives the narrative its tension, for both sides of the promise seem to hang by a thread. In the entire Torah the people called by God live continuously as strangers, first in Canaan, then in Egypt, and finally on a journey between Egypt and Canaan. Then the Torah leaves them, not in the land but about to enter it. Eventually, they will hold the land as a gift from God, but as a gift conditioned by their ability to live according to the teachings they have received. The latter view is the one expounded in Deuteronomy. It seems clear that both divine promises, of offspring and land, were necessary for the community to live according to the requirements put upon them. Yet, in the end, the "place" turned out not to be as essential for being God's people as one might think, and perhaps we may see the situation at the end of Deuteronomy as a foreshadowing of this reality.[2]

2. This observation is not intended to undermine the significance of the land of Israel both in the Torah and for the self-understanding of ancient Israel or the Jews. I make it to point

Throughout the story, it is often the unexpected person, the one who is less significant in status, who will become prominent in the narrative. In the Genesis stories it is often not the firstborn who will come to the fore. Not Ishmael but Isaac, not Esau but Jacob will carry on the line that leads to the covenant people. Instead of Reuben, Jacob's firstborn, Judah and Joseph, the fourth and eleventh of Jacob's sons, become the bearers of ancestral traditions. The crowd who is languishing in Egypt at the opening of Exodus has no power, and Moses who arises from this crowd is forced to abandon his status of adoptive princeling at Pharaoh's court so that he comes to his task of liberator from the outside.

In addition, individual women, not particularly visible in the first 11 chapters of Genesis, receive a good deal of attention in the narratives: Sarai/Sarah, Rebekah, Leah, and Rachel have a comparatively large amount of text devoted to them.[3] Besides these, two women from outside the clan circle, Hagar and Tamar, play crucial ancestral roles. Continuing with this stress on women's roles, at the opening of Exodus two midwives in Pharaoh's service, Shiphrah and Puah, act in direct opposition to Pharaoh's command and thereby save the life of Moses. Moses' sister, together with the daughter of the Pharaoh, continues the work begun by the midwives. Miriam plays a liturgical leadership role at the crossing of the Sea of Reeds and appears again in the Numbers narrative, where she contends with her brother, Moses.[4] Zipporah, the wife of Moses, and the daughters of Zelophehad, all named, have a significant presence at important moments in the narratives. This emphasis on those who are not significant because of their status in the family, or because

---

out the fact that in time the survival of the ancient covenant community and eventually of the Jews did not depend on their possession of the land. Gradually, the text of the Torah became the center to which the community oriented itself, and this text became one of the crucial factors that enabled it to preserve its existence with a clear sense of who it was and how it should behave. This movement toward the centrality of the text is discernible already in Ezra and Nehemiah (see esp. Neh. 8–10).

3. It goes without saying that the activities of the foremothers take place within the confines of the patriarchal family and that their main role was the furthering of posterity. Within this restricted environment the portraits of the individual women are nevertheless often striking and individual. Perhaps this feature of the ancestor stories is one argument against a view of the narratives as entirely fictive and late as, e.g., Niels Lemche would have it. As women's roles and activities became more and more restricted in the postexilic and restoration era, it would surely be unlikely that a fictive history was created in which women as Sarah and Hagar and Tamar had as large a part to play as they do in the Genesis narratives.

4. Very likely Miriam had originally a larger place in the traditions of the liberation from Egypt and the trek through the Sinai Peninsula. See Phyllis Trible, "Bringing Miriam Out of the Shadows," *Bible Review* 5/1 (1989): 14-25, 34.

of their sex or their position in the hierarchies of power, testifies to God's penchant for the weak foreshadowed in the story of Cain and Abel and articulated so eloquently in Deuteronomy (see above, 86-87).[5]

From Exodus on, the story is everywhere intermingled with regulations for human conduct, regulations that are directed both to the social and the religious ritual sphere. For the ancient writers, the demarcation between narrative and prescription was not sharply drawn, so that the material comes to us as a mixture of both. Life as it was lived in the presence of the Holy One necessitated guidance, so guidance was made available in both story and law. The weaving of narrative and legal material is of one cloth, alien though this may seem to our modern apprehensions.

Each book in the Torah creates its own tensions to which the narratives respond. In Genesis, uncertainty and tension surround the issue of productivity: will there be offspring, and if so will it be sufficient to continue as a group and eventually a people? In Exodus, tension surrounds the issues of liberation from captivity and what constitutes life lived in the presence of God. An undercurrent of tension is provided by the issue of survival. The existence of the people is under constant threat, This survival concern is carried through in Numbers and is extended by the tension surrounding the issue of entry into the land of the promise. In Deuteronomy, the major issue is how to hold on to the land once they are in it. Leviticus may be seen as springing from uncertainty about the correct ways of worshipping God. What narrative there is in Leviticus testifies to the tension created by this issue (Lev. 10:1-20).

---

5. Naturally, an emphasis on the one who appears least powerful, even foolish, also has great entertainment value in a story. See the story of my father and the haystack in Part II, Chapter 2.

Wandering Arameans My Ancestors
(Genesis 12:1–50:26)[1]

A Family of Strangers

The Genesis stories reflect memories of almost constant movement. Not only do the ancestors travel from Mesopotamia to Egypt via Canaan, but in between is movement in the land of Canaan itself, and a number of travels both to Egypt and Mesopotamia take place within the confines of the book.[2] All this movement testifies to the unsettled existence of the group and the uncertainty as to the place of its belonging. The interest in the larger world, so evident in Genesis 1–11, is represented by the destinations of the journeys and also by the family records which review not only the genealogies of the ancestors of ancient Israel but also those of populations indigenous to Canaan and those surrounding the land.[3] As was true of the prelude, the focus now is not only on people who fulfill the requirements God lays on them, as Abram and Sarai, but also on those who are more indirectly involved with the story of promise and blessing that is carried by the ancestors. Genealogies of descendants of Ishmael (Gen. 25:12-18) and Esau (36:1-43), episodes in which Lot and his family play a

---

1. See Deut. 26:5: "A wandering Aramean my ancestor, who went down to Egypt, and lived there as a stranger with few people, and, there, became a people, great, strong and many."

2. On this spatial framework Mary Douglas remarks: "In Genesis the spatial orientation is clearly marked. The patriarchs circled between the two rivers, the story is contained between the Nile and the Euphrates. . . . For the readers of the Pentateuch in the sixth to fifth centuries, Egypt, where the people of Israel endured their first bondage, would be matched by Babylon, where they endured the second. . . . the paths of Abraham, Isaac and Jacob cycle around the center of the world"; *In the Wilderness: The Doctrine of Defilement in the Book of Numbers.* JSOTSup 158 (Sheffield: JSOT, 1993), 96-97.

3. See Gen. 19:30-38; 25:1-6, 12-18; 36:1-43.

major role (ch. 19, esp. vv. 30-38), the story of Hagar and Ishmael (ch. 16; 21:8-21), and the tale of Tamar and Judah (ch. 38) witness to this capacity of the storyteller to break through the confines of the linear movement of the story.[4] Strangers and outsiders make contributions to the ancient narrative, at times essential ones. The ancestor group itself lives, after all, as a stranger in the land of Canaan, and good neighborly relations are indispensable to its survival.[5]

From the start it is made clear to Abram that God will provide both offspring and a land (Gen. 12:2, 7), a promise which at least in part sounds somewhat ironic in view of the earlier announcement of Sarai's barrenness (11:30).[6] In Genesis it becomes not so much an issue when or how the family will take possession of the land but rather how their numbers will increase in view of the constant threat to their continuity. Sarai is only the first of a series of infertile women which includes Rebekah and Rachel. This difficulty is most often overcome by God's direct intervention. The role of God in the process of conception and childbirth is on a continuum with the part assigned to God by Eve when she gave birth to Cain and Seth (Gen. 4:1, 25). Because of the tentative aspects of fertility, the promise God has made to the ancestor families often threatens to come to nothing, and the continuation of the family line is achieved only with difficulty and risk-taking. Just as the productivity of people is uncertain, the natural world does not render its bounty unquestionably. Sometimes it is described in terms of fertility and prosperity (Gen. 13:10; 26:12-13), but in the next breath one finds groups fighting over wells (26:17-33). Famines strike the land with regularity (Gen. 12:10; 26:1), and the final emigration to Egypt of the Jacob family is occasioned by a famine that has spread to all the regions of the known world (41:56-57). In such a context survival is not guaranteed.

As if in counterpoint to the paucity of offspring, there are many references to an abundance of possessions (e.g., Gen. 12:16; 13:2-6; 20:14; 24:35; 26:12-13; 30:43). In addition, the elaborate mention of numerous offspring representing populations other than those that will issue from the Abraham/Sarah/Isaac/Rebekah/Jacob line sets in relief how much this line is jeopardized time and again.

4. Joseph Blenkinsopp suggests that in the genealogies especially one may discern both an emphasis on "relations with other ethnic groups" and an interest in "a successive narrowing down, leaving the descendants of Abraham in the direct line as sole claimants to the land of Canaan"; *The Pentateuch* (New York: Doubleday, 1992), 109.

5. For references to the ancestors as stranger (Hebrew *ger*) in the Genesis narratives, see 12:10; 15:13; 17:8; 19:9; 20:1; 21:23, 34; 23:4; 26:3; 37:1.

6. That the storytellers intended to emphasize Sarai's lack of productivity is clear from the repetition of the information: "And Sarai was barren/there was for her no child" (Gen. 11:30).

It is in the end Jacob whose numerous offspring guarantees the continuation of the ancestral family. Yet, just when one might think the issue of descendants resolved, the family situation is compromised by constant squabbling, sibling rivalry, and unwise or cruel behavior on the part of Jacob's sons (Gen. 34; 37). Joseph, one of the later born of Jacob's children, thoroughly disliked by his brothers, takes up the greatest part of the story of Jacob's descendants (Gen. 37; 39–50). Yet, it is not Joseph who will rise to tribal prominence in ancient Israel but Judah, Jacob's fourth-born, who with his daughter-in-law Tamar establishes the line of King David. Eventually, forced by widespread famine, the entire family of Jacob, now reconciled, ends up in Egypt, where Joseph has achieved prominence. This ending sets the stage for the sequel in the book of Exodus.[7]

As was true for the prelude, God's promises are backed up by a covenant. Two covenants, initiated by God, receive mention in the Abram/Sarai story. The first, described in Genesis 15:1-21, is accompanied by a ceremony and seals God's promises of offspring and land for Abram, who has succumbed to doubt as to the success of the venture he is engaged in. The second covenant, described in Genesis 17, includes a renaming of the ancestral couple, and it entails the obligation of circumcision of all males in the household. God reiterates the promise of offspring and land, a promise that is not dependent on the ritual of male circumcision. That ritual is described as "a sign of the covenant" between God and Abraham and those who will come after, and maintaining it will constitute a keeping of the covenant for Abraham and his descendants.[8]

---

7. For interesting correspondences between the beginning and the end of Genesis, see Terence E. Fretheim, *The Pentateuch* (Nashville: Abingdon, 1996), 69: "Joseph functions as a new Adam (e.g. 41:38) for not only the Egyptians, but the entire world benefits from his 'dominion' (41:56-57), and the command to be fruitful and multiply is fulfilled in this family (47:27)." The same correspondence governs the opening of Exodus: "And the children of Israel were fruitful/ they spread out and multiplied and became very many/so the land was filled with them" (Exod. 1:7 and Masoretic note).

8. Traditionally, Gen. 17 is assigned to the P source while Gen. 15 exhibits a mixture of J and E. Contemporary scholars as John van Seters, Niels Peter Lemche, Thomas L. Thompson, who conceive of the Torah as a work of fiction composed well after the Babylonian exile, view these texts as late theological inventions and constructions. See John van Seters, *The Life of Moses* (Louisville: Westminster John Knox, 1994); *The Pentateuch* (Sheffield: Sheffield Academic, 1999); Niels Peter Lemche, *The Canaanites and Their Land: The Tradition of the Canaanites.* JSOTSup 110 (Sheffield: JSOT, 1991); Thomas L. Thompson, *The Origin Tradition of Ancient Israel.* 1: *The Literary Formation of Genesis and Exodus 1–23.* JSOTSup 55 (Sheffield: JSOT, 1987). Variations of this perspective can be found in Blenkinsopp, who assigns Gen. 15 to D and 17 to P based on his conclusion that the final edition of the Torah was "organized around the Priestly work" and that "This edition incorporated a Deuteronomic-Deuteronomistic strand with its own understanding of promise and covenant and a marked emphasis on possession of the land"; 125. There is in itself

These covenants may be seen as guarantees of the blessing God promises to provide, and they are coherent with the covenant described in Genesis 9. In the sequence of the narratives of Genesis and Exodus they are the precursors to the covenant between God and the people concluded at Sinai. It is not the human world that will guarantee the blessing, since it is shot through with weakness and shortcoming, with frailty and a propensity to violence. God is the one who guarantees the blessing. The future of the world and the future of the ancestral families alike are anchored in the promises of God.

The Presence of the Other (Genesis 16 and 38)

The ancestor narratives are family stories in line with the interest in the family as a focal unit in the biblical world. There is tension in the stories as to who will carry on the family line, who is chosen, and who falls outside the circle. The ancestors live in their context as strangers/*gerim,* and at times it is clear that they want to keep their identity intact. Abraham would have his son marry inside the kindred, eschewing the "daughters of the Canaanites" (Gen. 24:3-4). Similarly, Jacob is constrained by his father to seek a bride among his mother's kinfolk (Gen. 28:1-5). Other times, marriage to women outside the family clan causes negative comment (Gen. 26:34-35). There are, however, also occasions when the lines seem to be less sharply drawn and God's blessing does not remain confined to one group alone.

Genesis 16:1-16

Genesis 16:1-2
1. And Sarai, Abram's woman,
   did not give birth for him;
   and she had a maid, an Egyptian,

---

nothing new in the understanding of the covenant of God with the ancestors and ancient Israel as a late interpretive concept in the development of the religion of ancient Israel. In the 19th century this view was represented especially by Julius Wellhausen and Richard Kraetzschmar. In the 20th century major representatives of this point of view include Alfred Jepsen and Lothar Perlitt and, to a degree, Ernst Kutsch. See Kraetzschmar, *Die Bundesvorstellung im Alten Testament in ihrer geschichtlichen Entwicklung untersucht und dargestellt* (Marburg: Elwert, 1896); Wellhausen, *Grundrisse zum Alten Testament* (Münich: Kaiser, 1965); *Prolegomena to the History of Israel* (Atlanta: Scholars, 1994); Jepsen, "Berith: Ein Beitrag zur Theologie der Exilszeit," in *Verbannung und Heimkehr,* ed. Arnulf Kuschke (Tübingen: Mohr [Siebeck], 1961), 161-79; Kutsch, *Verheissung und Gesetz: Untersuchungen zum sogenannten Bund im Alten Testament.* BZAW 131 (Berlin: de Gruyter, 1973); Perlitt, *Bundestheologie im Alten Testament.* WMANT 36 (Neukirchen: Neukirchener, 1969).

whose name was Hagar.
2. Then Sarai said to Abram:
Look here, the Holy One has denied me birthgiving;
go in now to my maid,
perhaps I will be built from her.
And Abram listened to the voice of Sarai.

Thus begins an episode in the ancestral family with Sarai, the wife who until this point in the narratives has been passive and silent, acting as the protagonist. The importance of Sarai's childlessness has already been pointed out by the double notation of her lack of children when she first appeared on the scene (Gen. 11:30; see above, 108, 134). This episode opens with the same announcement, but emphasizing that it is as Abram's partner that she is failing: "Sarai, Abram's woman, did not give birth *for him*." By this opening line, the story is set in stark contrast to the extravagant promises made by God to Abram in chapter 15.

Sarai is not interested in the promises of God. At least she does not speak of them, and the narrator leaves it an open question as to whether she even knew of them, since each time God has spoken to Abram alone. For Sarai, her life without a son is not viable. Her husband could set her aside for this reason, and she comes up with a plan that will be to her benefit: "Perhaps I will be built from her" (v. 2). The events described here may strike us as peculiar but were probably not unusual in terms of family arrangements of that time and place.[9] Concubinage and polygyny were common enough, certainly for the well-to-do.[10] Sarai is not fulfilling the essential role required of her,

---

9. This episode in the life of Abram and Sarai has received a good deal of attention in recent decades. For extensive treatments of the text, see Phyllis Trible, *Texts of Terror: Literary-Feminist Readings of Biblical Narratives*. Overtures to Biblical Theology 13 (Philadelphia: Fortress, 1984); Renita J. Weems, *Just a Sister Away: A Womanist Vision of Women's Relationships in the Bible* (San Diego: LuraMedia, 1988); Savina J. Teubal, *Hagar the Egyptian: The Lost Tradition of the Matriarchs* (New York: Harper & Row, 1990); Danna Nolan Fewell and David M. Gunn, *Gender, Power and Promise: The Subject of the Bible's First Story* (Nashville: Abingdon, 1993), 44-54; Sharon Pace Jeansonne, *The Women of Genesis: From Sarah to Potiphar's Wife* (Minneapolis: Fortress, 1990); Kathryn Pfisterer Darr, *Far More Precious than Jewels: Perspectives on Biblical Women* (Louisville: Westminster John Knox, 1991); Alice Ogden Bellis, *Helpmates, Harlots, and Heroes: Women's Stories in the Hebrew Bible* (Louisville: Westminster John Knox, 1994), 74-76; Jon L. Berquist, *Reclaiming Her Story: The Witness of Women in the Old Testament* (St. Louis: Chalice, 1992); Trevor Dennis, *Sarah Laughed* (Nashville: Abingdon, 1994); Delores S. Williams, *Sisters in the Wilderness: The Challenge of Womanist God-Talk* (Maryknoll: Orbis, 1993); Naomi Steinberg, *Kinship and Marriage in Genesis* (Minneapolis: Fortress, 1993).

10. That the custom was not unusual does not make the practice a good one, of course. Con-

that of son-bearing, and she herself suggests a substitute or surrogate to fill her own lack. While it may be difficult for those who live in an overpopulated world to imagine the threat to life and well-being that marked the life of a childless woman in biblical times, it is still true that even today a lack of children may be a cause of shame and a sense of diminishment.

So far in the text of Genesis Sarai has not been heard from. Silently, she accompanied her family to a strange land (Gen. 12:1ff.). Silently, she was handed to another man to save her husband's skin (Gen. 12:10-20). She was not a part of the lavish promises made to Abram in terms of offspring. Finally, she gives voice and takes charge. How much she is in charge is indicated by the number of verbs of which she is the subject in the first six verses of chapter 16: "did not give birth"/"had a maid"/"said"/"took"/"gave"/"said"/ "afflicted." Her lack of something, children, together with her possession of someone, a maid, leads to her speech and action. The outcome of the action is such that she renews speech, and the resolution comes not in the redemption of her childless state but in her "afflicting" the earlier positive presence of a maid in her life (v. 6). In addition, Sarai occurs in the first person as verbal subject: "I will be built"/"I gave"/"I became of no account." In this verbal sequence, which turns on the words "I gave," the last phrase stands in sad contrast to the hopeful first. Twice, Sarai refers to God: the first time she lays the blame for her condition on God, and the second time she calls on God to witness to her situation of humiliation. Like Eve, Sarai assigns God a role in the processes of life, and she dares to take a hand in the process. While she has no child, she has a maid.[11] And as she once was "the woman" who was "taken" to

---

cubinage and polygyny point up the vulnerable situation of women in patriarchal societies, where they are economically and socially dependent on a husband and cannot make it on their own.

11. It is not clear what exactly the status of Hagar was in the household. She is called a "servant/maid" (Hebrew *shiphhah*). Some designate her as a slave, others as a maidservant — not in slavery, albeit inferior in the household. Some scholars assign to her a more elevated role. In Teubal's analysis, Hagar represents the Egyptian matriarch who bears a child for the priestess, Sarah. Hagar was "Sarah's companion," rather than her antagonist. According to Teubal (53-62), it is due to the androcentric writing and reading of the story that the two women have been turned into superior and inferior in positions of hostility,. Others view Hagar's position as equal to that of a slave; so Williams, *passim.* Renita Weems, "A Mistress, a Maid and No Mercy," in *Just a Sister Away,* paints Hagar's position as entirely powerless. In the story itself it is at least clear that Hagar, whatever her position may have been, attains the level of wife, since that is the word used in v. 3 instead of the word for concubine *(pilegesh).* In this position, Sarai maintained some power over her, albeit power allotted to her by Abram. It should also be noted that in the Islamic tradition Hagar is the ancestor of the Islamic nations and is revered as a strong and faithful woman.

Pharaoh (12:15), Sarai now "takes" her maid and "gives" her to her "man/husband" to be his "woman/wife" (16:3).[12]

The plan, laid by Sarai, executed by Abram, works. Hagar conceives. From then on, however, it backfires. Hagar has gained power in the household and uses it to make clear the diminished status of her mistress. Twice the text uses the expression "to be of no account," literally, "to be light" (from the Hebrew root *qalal*), in regard to Sarai (vv. 4, 5). Sarai appeals to Abram, who gives Sarai leave to treat Hagar badly (v. 6).[13]

From there on, Hagar is in the center of the story. She was initially identified as "Egyptian" (v. 1). She is thus clearly not only inferior in status but also an outsider. Egypt plays an ambiguous role in the Torah. On the one hand, Egypt is identified with suffering and slavery; it is the "house of servitude" from which God liberates the descendants of Jacob/Israel (e.g., Exod. 19:4; 20:2). On the other hand, it is a land of plenty, a land where the ancestors go when famine strikes their own environs, a land where Joseph and his family find a home and establish themselves with the cooperation of the reigning powers. Even after the exodus from this land, Egypt exerts a powerful lure as a land of abundant food (Num. 11:1-15). Certainly, in the Genesis stories Egypt does not have a negative connotation.[14] In the household, "Hagar the Egyptian's" position is that of an inferior, but it is not clear what kind of inferior, since the Hebrew term *shiphhah* is of necessity vague. Also, her position is not stable, since from servant she goes to becoming a pregnant wife, Sarai having given her as a "woman/wife" to Abram. It would not do to paint a rosy picture of her position, but neither is she entirely a victim of her circumstances.[15]

As Hagar flees the abusive situation in which she now finds herself, a messenger from God meets her on the way and engages her in conversation:

12. The episodes in which a wife in the household is passed off as a sister occur three times in the ancestor narratives, twice with Sarai/Sarah and once with Rebekah (Gen. 12:10-20; 20:1-17; 26:6-11). Each time, it is clear that the patriarch is afraid for his skin and uses his wife as a shield, and in none of the episodes does the woman receive a voice or play an active role.

13. The verb used for Sarai's action toward Hagar, *anah*, has strong connotations of physical violence. It is elsewhere used of physical maltreatment (e.g., Exod. 1:11; 22:23; Deut. 26:6).

14. Fretheim points out that the "primary outsiders" in the Joseph story are the Egyptians. "Generally, the Egyptians treat the chosen family in such a way that their lives are preserved and they are able to develop as a community (47:27); they even deeply grieve the passing of Jacob (50:7-11). . . . God has been at work among the *Egyptians* for good"; *The Pentateuch*, 91.

15. It is not clear how race may enter into the story. It is very likely that Hagar was black, but then Sarai and Abram would hardly have been "white." For a discussion on the importance of race in the story, see Bellis, 75.

Genesis 16:7-10

7. And a messenger of the Holy One found her
   by the spring of water in the wilderness,
   by the spring on the road to Sur.
8. And he said: Hagar, maid of Sarai,
   from where do you come and where are you going?
   She said: Away from Sarai, my mistress, I am running.
9. And the messenger of the Holy One said to her:
   Return to your mistress
   and humble yourself under her hand.
10. And the messenger of the Holy One said to her:
    I will multiply, yes multiply your offspring
    so it cannot be counted for multitude.

The reality of Hagar's position is that without the protection of the household it is not viable, and the messenger thus sends her back.[16] This may seem unkind and perhaps even cruel counsel, but it may have been Hagar's only option for survival.[17] This point is, however, not where the episode ends. In a stunning turn, Hagar receives a promise of multiple offspring in terms that echo the promises of God to Abram/Abraham: "I will multiply, yes multiply your offspring/so it cannot be counted for multitude" (v. 10; cf. 17:2, 5-6). Three times the root for "multiply" is used. Hagar and her offspring too are in the line of those who follow the primordial command to "multiply." The name she will give her son will reflect the fact that the Holy God has "heard" her affliction (v. 11). This is the same terminology that is used for God's hearing of the "affliction" of the oppressed people in Egypt (Exod. 3:7; Deut. 26:7) and in general of God's attention to the abuse of all weak and vulnerable people (Exod. 22:23).

God's messenger clearly signals God's presence, so that in the next breath, it is not the "messenger" but "the Holy God" who speaks with Hagar (v. 13). The name-giving that now takes place on Hagar's part is a unique event in these stories.

Genesis 6:13-14

13. Then she called the name of the Holy One who spoke with her:
    You are the God of seeing.

16. The expression "humble yourself" derives from the same root as the verb used earlier for Sarai's abuse of Hagar.

17. It is worth noting that in the other version of Hagar's expulsion, Gen. 21:8-21, Hagar does indeed remain on her own, or at least no mention is made of her returning to Abraham and Sarah's household.

> For, she said, here have I seen after being seen.[18]
>
> 14. Therefore one calls the well
>   Beer-lahai-roi [the Well of the Living-One-Who-Sees-Me];
>   it is between Kadesh and Bared.

Places and people receive names but not God. Yet, here a *woman* who is an outsider among outsiders, a stranger among strangers, takes it upon herself to name God. Whatever the meaning is of the difficult phrase in verse 13, it is connected with the verb "to see." Hagar connects the God who speaks with her and makes her promises with a God who "sees," a God who pays attention. God's eyes were open to her, and her eyes have beheld God. This statement was a bold one for the biblical writers, perhaps to such an extent that the phrase became garbled in the transmission; but its power shines undiminished. Hagar has named the Holy God correctly as the God of the *hevels*, the nobodies, who "hears" the affliction of the wounded ones of the world and "sees" their oppression.[19] Clearly, this is not a God of insiders only. Nor is this the only mention of God's promises to Hagar and her offspring. Ishmael too receives God's blessing (Gen. 17:20; 21:13-19, 20).

The narrators hasten to retreat from their boldness of venturing into a territory where a foreign woman takes on such an important role, and put Hagar back in her place. The closing verses of the episode make clear that her importance resides mostly in childbearing by reciting three times that "Hagar bore," two of these times with the addition "to Abram" (vv. 15-16). If the effect of this emphasis is to bring Hagar back to a more traditional activity than that of conversing with God and naming God, it also puts Hagar in direct relation to Abram rather than to her mistress. Finally, in contrast to the opening lines, Sarai is eclipsed at the closing of the episode, and her lack of children stands in sad counterpoint to Hagar's fertility.

In many interpretations of this story, it is customary to highlight the traditional hostility between the Arab peoples, descendants of Ishmael, and the offspring of Jacob/Israel, a hostility in part explained by this story of the origin of the Ishmaelites. Such a perspective is true enough, but this narrow focus on one issue causes Hagar to be lost from view. In that case the reader does not "see" her, in contrast to God. The story of Hagar, both in Genesis 16 and 21, is one example of the importance assigned to outsiders in these narratives.

18. The phrase is extremely problematic and could also be translated "for, she said, yes, here have I seen after seeing." See the variants in *BHS*. Very likely, a phrase that at least implied the possibility of seeing the Godhead became confused in the transmission.

19. "Seeing" (Hebrew *ra'ah*) and "hearing" *(shama)* are used interchangeably in the texts cited from Exodus and Deuteronomy to underline God's attention to vulnerable groups.

Genesis 38

Another narrative that likewise centers on anxiety concerning reproduction and the guarantee of proper descendancy is that of Judah and Tamar in Genesis 38. Jacob's family, though numerous enough to provide some assurance for the future, is marked by kin-strife and discord. After the disgraceful behavior of Jacob's sons toward the native inhabitants of the land (Genesis 34), instigated by the second and third oldest, Simeon and Levi, and the attempts of the brothers to do away with their youngest sibling Joseph, Judah, the fourth in line, who has shown at least a modicum of responsibility toward Joseph (37:25-28), is ready to settle down and raise a family.[20] He does this with great success (38:1-6), and not until his first two sons are grown and ready to raise families of their own do problems arise.

It is worth noting that Judah's wife is explicitly referred to as "Canaanite" (v. 2), and that quite likely Tamar, the wife of Er his firstborn, is Canaanite also. This issue is apparently not worthy of comment and shows the degree to which intermarriage with the local inhabitants may at one point have been an ordinary if not a customary occurrence. There is certainly no question of hatred between the different groups here.[21]

Inexplicably, God, the one who promised abundance of offspring to the

---

20. Many commentators have remarked on the odd fit of Genesis 38, since it represents an abrupt switch in focus, and the surrounding chapters all center on Joseph. The case for its fitting into its literary context has, however, been ably made by Robert Alter, who demonstrates the many ways in which Gen. 38 is linked to the surrounding material; *The Art of Biblical Narrative* (New York: Basic Books, 1981), 5-10. Also Johanna W. H. Van Wijk-Bos, "Out of the Shadows: Genesis 38; Judges 4:17-22; Ruth 3," in *Reasoning With the Foxes: Female Wit in a World of Male Power*, ed. J. Cheryl Exum and Johanna W. H. Bos. Semeia 42 (Atlanta: Scholars, 1988), 37-67; *Reformed and Feminist* (Louisville: Westminster John Knox, 1991), 50-62.

21. Nor is there any sign of the narrator considering Tamar "dangerous and unpredictable" or of a supposed negative impact of a story that contains a "warning against mingling with foreign women," as Lemche would have it (117). This perspective is the one initially taken on by father Judah in the story rather than that of the narrator, who has no word of condemnation for Tamar and indirectly commends her through the positive words about her by Judah at the story's denouement (Gen. 38:26). Nor is there any evidence that Tamar was remembered negatively in subsequent literary and religious traditions; from Ruth 4:12 the opposite would seem to be the case. There Tamar appears as an outsider ancestress, similar to Ruth, who benefited the ancestral family lines. Lemche, inexplicably, interprets Genesis 38 as "an exemplary narrative used to support the prohibition against mixed marriages between Israelites and Canaanites, and a warning to every Israelite to avoid intercourse with Canaanite women"; *The Canaanites and Their Land*, 118. Lemche seems driven in this reading by his conviction that ancient Israel was a "closed society" imbued with a "hatred of all foreigners."

first ancestors and guaranteed its continuance by a covenant, here dispatches two of the ancestral offspring. God causes both Er and Onan "to die." One (Er) dies because of an unspecified wickedness, the other (Onan) because he refuses to act responsibly toward both his deceased brother and his sister-in-law by providing them with an heir. Judah, unaware of God's role in these events, sends Tamar back to her parental home, her *bet av*, making her a false promise, for he thinks that she is the one to blame for the death of two of his sons and he will not risk the only remaining one!

Genesis 38:11

11. Then Judah said to Tamar,
    his daughter-in-law:
    Live as a widow in your father's house
    until my son Shelah has grown up.
    For he thought that this one might also die
    like his brothers.
    So Tamar went and lived in her father's house.

Events continue to deteriorate for Judah. After some time his wife also dies, so that he is left with Shelah, his now grown-up son, without fulfilling his promise. After the period of mourning over his wife's death, Judah makes ready to go to a sheep-shearing, an occasion of celebration, together with his friend Chirah. On the way he finds his daughter-in-law Tamar on the side of the road to Timnah, the place where he is bound. Considering her to be a prostitute, he has sexual intercourse with her. Tamar, who has noticed time going by and Judah's promise of uniting her with Shelah not being fulfilled, has placed herself at a strategic point, wrapped in a veil, thus advertising herself as a prostitute. She who was heretofore passive and silent goes into rapid action on hearing of her father-in-law's intended route: "she put aside . . . covered herself . . . wrapping herself . . . and sat" (v. 14). Where she sits is called the "Enayim gate," in Hebrew the *petah enayim*, literally meaning "opening of the eyes." The narrator is playing in this episode with words for observing. Tamar has "noticed" that Judah has not lived up to his promise. Judah "notices" Tamar and "thinks her" to be a prostitute (v. 15) and he does not "know" (v. 16) that she is his daughter-in-law. Throughout the interaction, Tamar's eyes are wide open so that she exacts a high-stakes pledge from Judah in exchange for her favors (vv. 17-18). Judah, on the other hand, is blind to the real situation and stays in his self-deception until his eyes are forcibly opened when Tamar, at the point of her being executed, faces him with the truth:

Genesis 38:24-26

24. After three months
    the report came to Judah:
    Tamar, your daughter-in-law,
    has played the whore
    and now here she is pregnant
    through her whoring.
    Judah said: Bring her out,
    she shall be burned.

25. When she was being brought out,
    she sent the following message
    to her father-in-law:
    By the man to whom these belong
    I am pregnant.
    Look well, as to whose ring,
    cord and staff these are.

26. Judah took a close look and said:
    She is more righteous than I
    because I did not give her to Shelah, my son.
    And he did not know her again.

Tamar, now reduced to the greatest passivity, "when she was being brought out," has waited until the last possible moment to make an attempt to reveal the truth to Judah. Although she takes enormous risks in delaying her revelation, she also chooses her moment well. As her execution will take place in public, her message to Judah is also public and so his declaration of her righteousness is also a public vindication. Her ploy is effective, as Judah's eyes finally open to her worth and his own delinquency, and he declares her to be "more righteous than I." Then Judah steps back so that the final episode of the chapter is devoted to the birth-giving.

An interesting story. Ostensibly, it is a tale that has one of the patriarchal sons at the center, and ostensibly it is about this son going about his task of reproducing faithfully. Gradually the focus changes and the spotlight falls on Tamar, an unexpected character to take a lead role, both an outsider and a failed wife. In the final episode, Judah and his friend Chirah are gone and we see only Tamar, the midwife and the two baby boys that are born. The final word of the entire story is *Zerah*, in Hebrew, the rising sun (v. 30). An interesting story, in which God is said to kill two of the patriarchal sons, and in which a Canaanite woman outwits male authority and escapes male control. The narrator utters no negative judgment about any of the steps taken in the process of Tamar guaranteeing survival and dignity for herself, and the last words spoken about Tamar are that she is declared "more righteous" than the patriarch.[22] Tamar, who began as passive pawn in the patriarchal household, takes the threads of her life in her own hands to make a weaving out of which the male authorities of the story ultimately disappear.

For the audience of a later time, Tamar's worth was crystal clear: she became the foremother of King David through Perez and eventually Ruth. It is her presence and her actions that rehabilitate Judah as an ancestor with important progeny. She does this as a woman, a childless woman, who is therefore one of little value and an outsider.

Whose Memories Are These?

Memory is always problematic, usually deceptive, sometimes treacherous.[23]

If biblical storytelling took place in a context dominated by a mythological worldview, a perspective that demands a greater interest in meaning than in a sequential relating of fact, it must also be said that the historical setting of a story may not be ignored, for it provides important information while at the same time setting appropriate boundaries around the interpretation of a story (see above, 66-67). What do we know then about the historical context of the narratives in Genesis? Let us begin at the end, the period at which the stories were finalized and put in their present context, roughly 500 B.C.E. and afterwards, the era of the reconstruction of Judah as a province of the Persian Empire. In this period a mood of anxiety about identity and survival prevailed in the community, and it went together with a posture toward outsiders that was frequently marked by hostility. The biblical books of Ezra and Nehemiah testify to all these concerns.

Clearly, the material in Genesis reviewed in the preceding pages gains in meaning when read from this context. All the narratives are permeated by an emphasis on the identity of the ancestor group as one that is called by God and taken into covenant with God, as well as by a concern about survival in view of scarcity of offspring. Such concerns which may strike us today as un-

---

22. Such absence of negative judgment is all the more remarkable in view of the recorded prohibition against sexual relations between a man and his daughter-in-law in Lev. 18:15.

23. Yosef Hayim Yerushalmi, *Zakhor: Jewish History and Jewish Memory* (Seattle: University of Washington Press, 1982), 5.

necessarily narrow-minded or unwarranted because of the state of the population of our world become understandable in view of the struggles of a small group aiming to survive with its religious and ethnic identity intact within a world of dominating large cultures and religions. Nor were the Jews the only group so intent on maintaining its identity and way of life. Can we say more than that the memories of the 5th century B.C.E. in Judah are preserved in these stories? If we give up the notion that there were four sources for the Torah, each with its own more or less precise historical context, is it possible to retrieve any historical era in which the material may have originated?

One clue may be found in the two tales I examined more closely, both of which have at the center an outsider to the ancestors of ancient Israel and the Jews of 5th-century Judah — outsiders who were, because of their sex, not naturally a part of the family history to be proud of and who, because of their ethnic status, belonged to those toward whom the family circle in Ezra and Nehemiah's day, for example, was firmly closed.[24] We know that this posture cannot have been a part of ancient Israel during the entire time of its existence and that the boundaries between it and its neighbors for a long time were permeable and flexible. Laws against intermarrying with indigenous and neighboring peoples, for example, are rather rare in the Torah and are clustered in specific material. The stories of Genesis seem to reflect precisely a context in which there is a great deal of ambiguity about who is "in" and who is "out," rather than a great deal of certainty about the identity and the place of outsiders in a context in which the community circle is drawn very closely. Nor are these stories the only examples of a great degree of flexibility in terms of relationships between different ethnic groups, and I used them to illustrate what I believe to be the general tenor of the narratives. Concern for and converse with the stranger, the *ger*, so prevalent in the lawgiving sections of the Torah, are prevalent in the stories also. This concern was one that took a backseat in the period of the restoration of Judah, although it shines through in some prophetic material of the period.[25] The interest in the outsiders and

24. The story of the sending away of the "foreign women" in Ezra 9 and 10 is the most blatant example of the attitude of hostility to outsiders in the period of the reconstruction. Even if this incident never happened exactly as it is told — and it is hard to see how it could have happened — the posture that underlies it was probably indicative enough for this period. Both Ezra and Nehemiah are permeated by a hostile attitude toward outsiders. Cf. Johanna W. H. van Wijk-Bos, *Ezra, Nehemiah and Esther* (Louisville: Westminster John Knox, 1998), 27: "The community in Jerusalem draws a tight line around its circle. The returned exiles are not interested in converts, in those who are outside the covenant community; rather, they are fearful of mixing with them."

25. See. e.g., Isa. 56:3-7 with its clear statements of inclusion of the "foreigner" and the "eunuch" within the family of faith, statements which are in direct contradiction to those made

the importance of the roles they play in the stories of the ancestral families make it highly unlikely that these tales were created as a fictive history at the time of the Persian Empire.[26] It is more reasonable to assume that the material in Genesis preserves authentic memories of a time when the world outside ancient Israel was considered to be of concern to the God who created the world and therefore of concern for the covenant people. Not only are outsiders in the Genesis narratives viewed from this perspective, but they are also seen as filled with possibility and promise for active cooperation in the mending of the world and the creation of God's people. It is remarkable that these memories were preserved and cast in their present form at a time when outsiders were more likely to be seen as a threat. The preservation of these materials may also serve as a warning against viewing the restoration community as too uniformly exclusive and closed.

Can we say more than that? Do the ancestor narratives contain references to a time before the coalescing of the clans into a people? Here we must tread carefully without succumbing to anxiety about the factual existence of a historical Abraham or Sarah or any other figure in the text. The meaning of the material does not depend on such facts, after all. If it is unlikely that the interest in and concern for outsiders in Genesis arose from an invented history, in order to legitimate the existence of Judah and its unique relationship to God, it must also be said that fictive history could have invented more appealing characters with fewer flaws than the ones portrayed here. In addition, religious and social practices that gradually disappeared or were censured here are part of the landscape without a word of disapproval or censure. Concubinage, polygyny, and incest appear on the scene as if they were all a normal part of everyday life. Who would invent a story in which the most important ancestor creates offspring through an incestuous sexual encounter with a despised foreigner at the side of the road? It seems more logical to assume that the ancestor narratives preserve at least a core of tribal memories that go back to a time when a group of pastoralists roamed the land and that the burden of

---

by the prophet Ezekiel and in the Priestly and Deuteronomic literature (see Ezek. 44:7; Deut. 23:1-3; Lev. 21:18-20).

26. So Lemche, Thompson, and Keith Whitelam among others. Lemche, *The Canaanites and Their Land: The Traditions of the Canaanites* (Sheffield: JSOT, 1991); I.d., *Prelude to Israel's Past: Background and Beginnings of Israelite History and Identity* (Peabody: Hendrickson, 1998); Keith H. Whitelam, *The Invention of Ancient Israel: The Silencing of Palestinian History* (London: Routledge, 1996); Van Seters, *The Life of Moses: The Yahwist as Historian in Exodus-Numbers* (Louisville: Westminster John Knox, 1994); *The Pentateuch: A Social Science Commentary* (Sheffield: Sheffield Academic, 1999); Thomas L. Thompson, *The Origin Tradition of Early Israel: The Literary Formation of Genesis and Exodus 1–23* (Sheffield: Sheffield Academic, 1987).

proof is on the side of those who maintain that they are late fiction invented for the purpose of providing a community with its identity and history.[27] In addition, it is at least possible that narratives such as those related in Genesis 16 and 38 may have come from circles that highlighted the roles and importance of the ancestor women, perhaps originating with female storytellers.[28]

These are stories with a mythological cast that grew and that were embellished in the telling, passed on from generation to generation, perhaps orally, perhaps in writing, or both, and at a late date woven together by one writer or a group of writers. This view does not make Abraham and Sarah into historical figures, but it keeps intact the notion that a historical context gave birth to the narratives before the formation of ancient Israel as a people.

27. Thus Stanley N. Rosenbaum: "My assumption is that there are real nuggets of historical memory in the patriarchal narratives, though one may have to dig deep to find them, and even then not be sure of what one has found"; *Understanding Biblical Israel: A Reexamination of the Origins of Monotheism* (Macon: Mercer University Press, 2002).

28. Consider the absence of Sarah's concern for the fulfillment of God's promises and the prominence of Hagar, a lowly foreigner, in Gen. 16, as well as the unlikely view that God would summarily dispatch *two* of the male patriarchal offspring, and the way Judah is slyly ridiculed in Gen. 38. Some scholars have suggested that Gen. 38 originates from a different source than the surrounding stories which center on Joseph. Is it not at least possible that a cluster of narratives were woven around the matriarchs and that these were primarily preserved in women's circles as a way to honor and remember their own ancestors? At a late date then the stories were skillfully inserted into the present material. Both Gen. 16 and Gen. 38 can be read and understood entirely on their own as distinct episodes without reference to the surrounding material.

And, There, Became a People
(Exodus 1:1–24:18)[1]

*The focus of interest is not so much on Moses himself as on the broad
theme of the creation of a people with a special relationship to a God
(YHWH) who nurtures it into viable existence, preserves it, and pre-
pares it to play its preordained role among the nations of the world.*[2]

Getting Out and Getting On (Exodus 1:1–18:27)

The story goes on. The Egyptian context, first so benevolent and filled with
promise, has become one of extreme oppression, and the initial issue in Exodus revolves around the difficulty of getting the descendants of Jacob out of
Egypt on the road back to the land of the promise. The opening of Exodus
emphasizes the growth of the Jacob/Israel group in spite of the odds and,
with its use of verbs, indicates that the family now conforms to the creation
command of Genesis 1[3] as well as to the promise of God to Abram in Genesis
15 and 17: "And the children of Israel were *fruitful,* they *spread out* and *multiplied;* they became so big that the land *was full of them*" (Exod. 1:7; cf. Gen.
1:26-28). The once so tentative outcome of sufficient offspring now seems as-
sured, yet a new threat has arisen with the demise of the old regime and the
rise of a new ruler who introduces extreme oppression:

1. See Deut. 26:5.
2. Joseph Blenkinsopp, *The Pentateuch,* 135.
3. Thus the Masoretic note to v. 7.

Exodus 1:8-13

8. Then arose a new king over Egypt
    who had not known Joseph.

    . . . .

11. So they put over it taskmasters to oppress it with burdens.

    . . . .

13. Then the Egyptians subjugated the children of Israel violently.
14. They made their life bitter
    with harsh labor at mortar and bricks,
    and every kind of field labor;
    all the labor they exacted from them with violence.

In this context of oppression the narratives zero in on a few characters that come to the aid of the people. These characters, on a continuum with the surprising role of some outsiders in Genesis, are all women. The first two receive names, Shifrah and Puah, while their ethnic group is ambiguous. If one translates that they were "midwives of the Hebrews" (Exod. 1:15), there is at least the possibility that the two were Egyptian, and in that case they would conform to the motif of the powerless outsider whose presence in the story is positive and life-giving.[4] If they are considered to be members of the oppressed group, the efforts of making them collaborate in the destruction of their own people ring true as a common tactic to make victims of oppression cooperate with the destruction of their own group, while their disobedience would be no less courageous. In either case, the two are outsiders to the circles of power by virtue of the fact that they are women. Yet, they openly rebel against the Pharaoh and his orders and somehow walk away from this situation with their lives intact. God is said to "deal well" with them and to provide for them (Exod. 1:20-21). The act of the midwives in defiance of Pharaoh is one of startling courage.[5]

4. Thus, Josephus assumed that the midwives were Egyptians (*Jewish Antiquities* 2:207); James L. Kugel, *Traditions of the Bible* (Cambridge, MA: Harvard University Press, 1998), 522.

5. For an analysis of this chapter, see J. Cheryl Exum, "'You Shall Let Every Daughter Live': A Study of Exodus 1:8–2:10," in *The Bible and Feminist Hermeneutics,* ed. Mary Ann Tolbert. Semeia 28 (Chico, CA: Scholars, 1983), 63-82. It is true that the role of the women is in service to the birth and raising of Moses, but in my opinion Alice Ogden Bellis observes correctly that "the most important story in the Hebrew Bible begins with women determining events. It begins with God using the weak and the lowly to overcome the strong. It begins with women who act courageously, defying oppression. . . . Without these women, there would be no Moses to liberate the Hebrews from bondage"; *Helpmates, Harlots, and Heroes,* 101. The disobedience engaged in by the women and the risk they take in view of their oppressive context are often ignored by commentators, who hasten to focus on Moses and his appearance as an adult

Shifrah and Puah, together with the mother and the sister of Moses, and Pharaoh's daughter are portrayed as undermining the destructive plans of the Egyptian overlord as they prepare the ground for the birth and rearing of Moses, the one who will be the main agent in the subsequent stories — the one through whom God will effect the escape from Egypt and who will lead the people on their journey to Canaan. Moses will be their teacher, their priest, and their political leader. Everything in the Exodus narrative presses on to set Moses on the scene, and the attention paid in the text to the role played by these women is therefore all the more remarkable.[6]

It is worth noting that God enters the story at the point of the introduction of the midwives, who are said to "fear God" (Exod. 1:17), rather than in the context of the oppression of the descendants of Jacob in the opening chapters of Exodus, and that God's first intervention in Exodus is on behalf of midwives who may have been Egyptian.[7] Only at the end of chapter 2 is God said to notice the situation of oppression in Egypt: "God saw the children of Israel and God knew" (2:25). This statement provides the springboard for the discussion between God and Moses at the burning bush, where God reveals both divine attention and intention to Moses, who will be the one to get the people out of the situation they are in:

Exodus 3:7-10

7. The Holy One said:
   I have seen, yes seen,
   the misery of my people
   who are in Egypt.
   And their cries I have heard
   from before their slave drivers

---

in the story. We ignore the wisdom embedded in the text of Exod. 1:1–2:10 to our loss, for the picture that emerges of the women is both inspiring and instructive for those who are interested in thwarting the oppressive powers of the world.

6. Cf. Terence E. Fretheim: "The creative disobedience of these women preserves a future for Israel and enables the emergence of a leader in the person of Moses"; *The Pentateuch*, 103. Furthermore, the story of the midwives and the rescue of Moses has the humorous overtones of the story/myth that is created out of a context of oppression: *two* midwives outsmart the powerful oppressive Pharaoh; the same Pharaoh ends up fostering at his court the very one who will undo his plans of mayhem and murder for the enslaved descendants of Jacob, with the help of his own daughter!

7. Cf. Exod. 1:21: "Because the midwives feared God, he made for them houses." The translation "families" for "houses" (so e.g. NRSV) is not wrong as the house represents the family (see above, Part II, chapter 1), but it obscures the concreteness of God's action which foreshadows God's intervention in human affairs at many points in this part of the Torah.

for I know their pain.
. . . .
9. And now, see, the cry of the children of Israel
   has come to me;
   also have I seen the oppression
   with which Egypt oppresses them.
10. And now, come, I will send you to Pharaoh.

Chapters 5–15 concern themselves with efforts to free the people from Egyptian oppression, by means of God's miraculous intervention through the person of Moses, and the final defeat of Pharaoh's armies at the Red or Reed Sea, ending with the victory shout of Exodus 15:

Exodus 15:21
Sing to the Holy One
for God is highly exalted;
horse and its rider
God has thrown into the sea.

As in Genesis, the people portrayed in these texts are far from ideal. Moses is at the same time impetuous and somewhat timid. The people want to go along with God's plans only as long as it suits them, in turn compliant (Exod. 4:31; 12:27; 14:31) or rebellious (5:21; 6:9; 14:11). No sooner are they at large, free from the besetting power of oppressive Pharaoh, than the people turn against Moses and God, complaining and quarreling (Exod. 15:24; 16:2-12; 17:2). This is not an attractive crowd on the face of it, yet everything hastens to get them to the place where they will be taken into covenant by their liberator God, the *midbar Sinai,* the wilderness of Sinai (Exod. 19:1). There they will come to a halt to be engaged in the momentous events that are to take place, of which the description extends to the 10th chapter of Numbers. Although a good deal of attention is paid to Moses, to his miraculous survival, his departure from Egypt necessitated by the defense of one of the beaten-down slaves, to his marriage, his intervention for the people before Pharaoh, and later before God, Moses tends to disappear behind the "children of Israel." No longer concerned primarily with individuals, the text now relates the ups and downs of the descendants who were promised to Abraham and Sarah, their defeats and triumphs. Moses is less important as a person in his own right than as the bridge between the people and God. God speaks and acts through Moses. The moment is coming when this crowd of runaway slaves will be constituted as a people.

The Exodus in History

The dating of texts is a nightmare from which biblical history will never awake.[8]

Was there an exodus of ancient Israelite ancestors from slavery in Egypt, and if so when did it take place? To begin with, we accept that exaggeration of certain features marks the story and that this does not undermine its potential veracity.[9] We recall once more that ancient storytellers were not primarily concerned with factual and objective reporting, and that yet the setting in history of texts has the potential to illumine the meaning of the text and may prevent an "anything goes" approach to interpretation. It goes without saying that those who view the Torah as a fictive account, constructed during the time that Judah was a province of the Persian realm, deny any historical veracity to the events described in Exodus: no "real" exodus, no "real" Moses.[10] It may be helpful to ask whether any of this history *could* have happened, even if the details of the description are unlikely because they belong to the realm of the mythical story. With J. Maxwell Miller and John H. Hayes, I hold that some of the ancestors of Israel and Judah may have been "counted among the disaffected Habiru known from the Amarna correspondence. Some may have been escaped slaves from Egypt or migrating Arameans who settled in the land."[11]

As with the ancestor stories, I suggest that the material of Exodus contains at least some authentic memories of an audacious escape from serious oppression on the part of a group of slaves some time in the 13th century B.C.E., perhaps helped along by natural phenomena of a cataclysmic sort. In Martin

8. Jack Miles in his review of James Kugel, *The God of Old* (New York: Free Press, 2003); *New York Times Book Review*, 12 May 2003, 12.

9. Thus J. Maxwell Miller and John H. Hayes point out that the figure of 600,000 males of fighting age that are recorded to have left Egypt in Exod. 12:37-39 is an impossibility. For one thing, the line formed by such a number would have been 150 miles long; *A History of Ancient Israel and Modern Judah* (Philadelphia: Westminster, 1986), 60.

10. This line of Christian scholarship deprives the Jewish people of a great part of its history. Small wonder then that, as Stanley N. Rosenbaum points out, scholars divide generally along religious lines on the issue of the historicity of the biblical text, with Gentiles deconstructing and Jews defending the tradition; *Understanding Biblical Israel*, 15.

11. Miller and Hayes, 78-79. Jonathan N. Tubb cites the appearance of the *Hapiru* in the Egyptian papyrus Leiden 384 as those who were "employed in dragging stones for the construction of the gateway pylons of one of Ramses II's monumental buildings." He concludes that the coincidence of *Hebrews* and *Hapiru* appearing together in large-scale building programs of Ramses II cannot be dismissed, and "it may well be that the Hebrews of the exodus were indeed drawn from the Hapiru"; *Canaanites* (Norman: University of Oklahoma Press, 1998), 81.

Buber's words, we "feel the breath of some distant event of which there is no longer any clearcut recollection."[12] These memories go to the heart of the identity of the people who were later to settle Canaan, be taken into exile, and return for an existence of dependence as a province of Judah. Interestingly, the memories are not invoked in a spirit of aggrandizing the glorious deeds of leaders and people; the size of the escaped group is the only feature that receives exaggeration.[13] Otherwise, the portrayal of the glorious past is a far from glorious recital of petty behavior, backsliding, and apostasy. "Signs" and "wonders" are ascribed neither to the people nor to its leaders but rather to God.

It is especially important in regard to the covenant whether one understands a historical event to underlie and inspire the texts of Exodus 19–24 or whether one assumes covenant to be an interpretive tool that later writers used to explain the relationship between ancient Israel and its God. We turn now to a consideration of these texts.

Covenant (Exodus 19–24)

What takes place here is the meeting between two fires, the earthly and the heavenly.[14]

This section of Exodus, which mostly consists of a miscellany of regulations and laws, is caught in the framework of the covenant, for which the announcement occurs in chapter 19, discussed in some detail earlier in this book (see above, 15-19), with the execution taking place in chapter 24. The announcement tells the people what they may expect of themselves and their future as it is placed within the covenant bond. The execution forms the bond by solemn ritual and recital. The covenant between God and people as it is described in these chapters does not establish a relationship. A relationship between God and people existed already, one of protective and guiding care on God's part. As covenant partners, however, the maintenance of the relationship will also fall on the shoulders of those who become partners in covenant with God. In some way, the covenant is unbreakable, since it is nowhere assumed or stated in the Bible that God could break the covenant. The people, however, can fail to uphold their side of it, can fail to "listen and do" ac-

---

12. Martin Buber, *Moses* (New York: Harper, 1958), 61.

13. William G. Dever observes that the choice is not between reliable history and propaganda, since all literature is "fundamentally" propaganda, and that "propaganda characteristically and deliberately exaggerates and distorts; but it does not freely invent"; *What Did the Biblical Writers Know and When Did They Know It?* (Grand Rapids: Eerdmans, 2001), 47.

14. Buber, *Moses*, 110.

cording to the "words of the covenant," and in that case will need reaffirmation that God has not broken the covenant nor abandoned the relationship.[15] It can thus in no way be said that the covenant concluded between God and people at Sinai is conditional. Yet it must be said that the people are enjoined to uphold the covenant bond and that the likelihood is that they will fail to do so, perhaps many times over. The covenant at Sinai, as the covenant with the ancestors, is anchored in the promises of God. Within this context of promise, requirements are put upon the human partner, requirements that constitute the human side of living out of the promises made by God. Once the covenant is made, it awaits its unfolding in the manner in which divine and human partner will relate to one another inside the covenanted relationship.

Three texts are crucial for a proper apprehension of the implications of both promise and requirement as they are embedded in the Sinai covenant: Exodus 19:3-6, the announcement of the covenant; 20:1-17, the Ten Words of the covenant; and 24:3-8, the execution of the covenant.

The Announcement of the Covenant (Exodus 19:3-6)

I recapitulate the following points from the earlier discussion on this text (see above, 15-19): in this announcement, which contains both a review of the past and a promise for the future, the people to be taken into the covenant bond with God are charged with maturing from a crowd that accepts God's gracious liberating activity into a people that accepts its responsibility as covenant partner. This possibility for an "active and adult partaking in the covenant relationship is created by attentiveness to God's voice" (p. 18). I argued there also that the primary expression of God's voice is *torah*/instruction, without which the covenant relationship would be meaningless, for the community is not able to construct for itself a way to live inside the covenant. In the marred world of which the "children of Israel" are a part, such knowledge does not come automatically. Rules and requirements are not simply there for their own sake but because they are, in the words of the psalm, "a lamp to their feet and a light to their path" (Ps. 119:105). It is, on the other hand, the promise of God's ongoing presence given with the covenant that grounds torah in hope. By the covenant bond the people know themselves to be "God's own people"; thus, their response to God's voice and to specific regulations and requirements arises out of that awareness rather than out of a sense of human inadequacy and potential for failure.

---

15. Such affirmations take place occasionally in the biblical text, e.g., in Exod. 32 and Jer. 31:31-34.

In addition, the phrase "For mine is all the earth" at the end of Exod. 19:5 bears some elaboration in our present review. The short phrase, only three words in Hebrew, is placed in the middle of the promises for the community's participation in the covenant relationship. The "children of Israel's" status as "treasure," and their task of becoming a "royal realm of priests and a holy nation," are set in the large context of the entire world as belonging to God. In this way it is made clear that both the status and the task of ancient Israel are not created for the sake of Israel alone but rather for the sake of the entire creation.[16] God's words to Abram that "all the clans of the earth will be blessed" in him find renewed expression here. It is telling that these words are spoken just at this point when the descendants of Abram will be drawn into the closest possible bond with God, with its focus on an exclusive relationship with God. Here the scope of God's interest widens when we would perhaps least expect it.[17]

Finally, the word I have translated "realm" (Hebrew *mamlakhah*, literally, "king's rule") highlights that the people will constitute a realm under God's rule. The covenant between God and people concluded at Sinai has a political character, in that it constitutes the "children of Israel" as nation with God as its ruler.[18] The political character does not mean that the relation of the nation to its God and vice versa is not deeply personal. There could hardly be an expression of more profound personal attachment and relationship than the one described in this announcement of the covenant where God speaks of the divine self as the liberator, protector, parent, and educator of the people with the metaphor of the eagle (v. 4). Furthermore, the endpoint of the journey so far has not so much been a place, Mount Sinai, but rather the self of God: "and brought you to myself" (v. 4). It is the presence of God to

16. In this context, it is important to note the absence of a qualifying conjunction in the second phrase of Exod. 19:5-6. "For mine is all the earth" is not followed by "*but* you shall be . . . " Rather, the conjunction in Hebrew is "and" *(we)*, thus "*and* you shall be . . . ," emphasizing the connection of God's people to the rest of the earth rather than the distinction from it. Most translations fail to recognize the importance of maintaining the Hebrew "and," translating *we* with "but."

17. Cf. Fretheim: "The divine calling to be a kingdom of priests and a holy nation is a commission to a task on behalf of God's earth. God's initially exclusive move is for the sake of a maximally inclusive end"; *The Pentateuch*, 118.

18. Cf. Buber: "YHVH and Israel enter into a new relation to one another by making the Covenant, a relation which had not previously been in existence; and further could not have been in existence, because Israel as a nation . . . had been constituted only in that hour"; *Moses*, 104. Cf. Daniel J. Elazar: "[Sinai] is the classic example of covenanting as a theo-political act, which established the basis for subsequent constitution making"; *Covenant and Polity in Biblical Israel* (New Brunswick: Transaction, 1995), 163. Elazar also notes that the regime imposed by the covenant may be of different types and that "no single political regime is imposed by the covenant"; 180.

which they have been brought, and in this presence they will live. God's presence is implicitly promised for the future by the requirement to "listen" to God's voice (v. 5). This is the way God will be present to them, by voice rather than image. Such a divine presence represented a radical departure from religious life elsewhere in the Mediterranean world, and living by this reality will present a constant challenge to the ancient community.

Wording and phrasing of this text is in some ways reminiscent of Deuteronomic and prophetic material. As a speech from God that Moses is commissioned to convey to the people who are called "Jacob's house/Israel's children," the text is reminiscent of much prophetic speech (for example, Isa. 2:6; 8:17; Amos 3:13; Mic. 2:7; 3:9). The expression "Now, listen, yes listen to my voice and keep my covenant," even when translated conditionally with "*if* you listen," is not truly Deuteronomic, since in Deuteronomy conditional sentences like these are always followed by actions on God's part rather than the human partner (see Deut. 11:13-15; 15:4-5; 28:1-2). The term "treasure" to indicate the people occurs in Deuteronomy (7:6; 14:2; 26:18) as well as in some poetic material. It is, however, combined with a different word for people in those passages, Hebrew *am* rather than the *goy* of Exodus 19. The expression "a realm of priests" has no direct parallels, although it is reminiscent of expressions in Isaiah 61:6 and Psalm 114:1, 2. The expression "keep my covenant" is not found in Deuteronomy, where the verb "remember" (Hebrew *zakhar*) occurs instead of *shamar,* but the same combination does occur elsewhere (cf. Gen. 17:9, 10; 1 Kgs. 11:11; Ps. 78:10; 103:18; 132:12). The expression "for mine is all the earth" has no exact parallels, although there are statements elsewhere that declare the earth to be God's (Exod. 9:29; Josh. 3:11; 1 Chr. 29:11; Ps. 24:1; 89:11; Isa. 54:5; Mic. 4:13; Zech. 4:14; 6:5). The closest parallel can be found in Ps. 50:12, where the word is "world" (Hebrew *tevel*) rather than "earth" *(erets).*

The Ten Words of the Covenant (Exodus 20:1-17)[19]

Exodus 20:1-17
1. And God spoke all these words:
2. I am the Holy One your God

---

19. Although ordinarily referred to as the Ten Commandments, in the Bible the list is called the Ten Words (see Exod. 34:28; Deut. 4:13; 10:4). Strictly speaking, the Decalogue belongs to the legal material which I will review separately. I take it up here because the text is integral to the pericopes that center on the Sinai covenant. For an extensive and detailed review of the Decalogue with numerous bibliographical references, see Cornelis Houtman, *Exodus* 3 (Kampen: Kok, 2000), chs. 20–40. An alternative formulation of the Ten Words may be found in Deut. 5:6-21.

who brought you out from the land of Egypt,
from the house of servitude.

3. There will be for you no other gods before my face.
4. You shall not make for yourself an idol,
   or any likeness of that which is in the sky above
   or in the earth below,
   or in the waters under the earth.
5. You shall not bow to them or serve them,
   For I am the Holy One your God,[20]
   a jealous God,
   visiting the sins of the ancestors on the children
   until the third and fourth generation
   of those who hate me,
6. And doing devotion to thousands
   of those who love me
   and who keep my commandments.[21]
7. You shall not apply the Name
   of the Holy One your God
   to an illusion,[22]
   for the Holy God will not hold innocent
   the one who applies God's Name to an illusion.

8. Remember the day of Shabbat
   to hallow it.
9. Six days you shall serve
   and do all your work,
10. and the seventh day
    is Shabbat for the Holy One your God.
    You shall not do any work;
    not you, nor your son, daughter,
    male or female servant,

20. This is the first of three commandments that receive motivational clauses beginning with "for" (*ki* in Hebrew). It is possible that these clauses, occurring in vv. 5, 7, and 11, are later elaborations added to originally more terse articulations.

21. "Love" and "hate" are strong opposites, standing for loyalty and disloyalty.

22. Cf. Fox's translation of these lines: "You are not to take up/the name of YHWH your God for emptiness"; *The Five Books of Moses* (New York: Schocken, 1995), 371; and Martin Buber: "You are not to take up the name of HIM your God to a delusion" ("delusion" here for the original German "Wahnhaft"); "On Translating the Praising," in Buber and Franz Rosenzweig, *Scripture and Translation* (Bloomington: Indiana University Press, 1994), 94 (see *Die Fünf Bücher der Weisung*, 205). For a discussion of the meaning of this requirement, see below.

your cattle,
nor your stranger who is in your gates.

11. For in six days the Holy One made
the sky and the earth
and the sea and all that is in them,
and God rested on the seventh day.
Therefore the Holy God blessed the seventh day
and hallowed it.

12. Honor your father and your mother
so you may lengthen your days
on the ground[23]
which the Holy One your God is giving you.

13. You shall not murder.

14. You shall not commit adultery.

15. You shall not steal.

16. You shall not answer to your neighbor
as a false witness.

17. You shall not desire[24] the house of your neighbor;
you shall not desire the wife of your neighbor,
nor his male or female servant,
nor his ox nor his ass,
nor anything that is your neighbor's.

The entire set of requirements opens with a first-person statement by God that establishes God as the one who liberated the people from bondage in Egypt, from "the house of servitude." In line with the declaration of Exodus 19:4, God is defined as the one who set the people free and "brought them out," the emphasis here being on the liberating activity of God on behalf of the oppressed slaves. The opening words "I am the Holy One your God" are reminis-

---

23. The word in Hebrew is *adamah*, "ground," rather than *erets*, meaning "earth" or "land," a noun more generally used in statements about God's *gift* of the land. The word "ground" connotes the concrete soil, the arable land, and it is the word from which the word for "human" is derived. The intention of the promised consequence, "so you may lengthen your days," is not entirely clear. Richard Elliott Friedman, e.g., understands this to mean that "the people of Israel . . . will endure in their land"; *A Commentary on the Torah* (San Francisco: HarperSanFrancisco, 2001), 238. See also W. Gunther Plaut, *The Torah: A Modern Commentary* (New York: Union of American Hebrew Congregations, 1981), 556.

24. I follow Fox (372) in translating "desire" for the traditional "covet." The last commandment emphasizes a mental state rather than one of action, but action and inclination were seen as closely related.

cent of similar self-revealing declarations on God's part in Genesis (e.g., Gen. 15:1; 26:24; 31:13) and Exodus 3:6. There are also clear similarities between this self-identification on God's part and the preambles of ancient Hittite vassal treaties, which may begin as follows: "These are the words of ———, the great king, . . ."[25] Covenants were a part of the political scene into which ancient Israel was born, and the articulation of contracts between overlords and their vassals followed a tightly structured format, different only in historical particulars, in the introduction often stressing both the power and the liberality of the overlord. For its expression of the bond between itself and God, ancient Israel naturally drew on available models, and such parallels are therefore not surprising. The comparison also helps to highlight the political character of the covenant concluded at Sinai. In a way, the Ten Words, or Decalogue, may be seen as the charter that accompanied the covenant, the act that constituted the group at Sinai as a people.[26]

The list may be divided into three distinct parts: (1) Verses 1-7 focus on God and the manner in which the community should relate to God. (1) Verses 8-12 move the focus to time as it is divided by days as well as by succeeding generations. These verses form the bridge to the last section, (3) verses 13-17, with its focus on relationships of neighbor to neighbor. In my view, the most insightful articulation of this structure remains that of Buber: "If the first part deals with the *God* of the Community and the second with *time*, the one-after-the-other of the Community, the third is devoted to *space*, the with-one-another of the Community in so far as it establishes a norm for the mutual relations between its members."[27] In a way, the Ten Words are a commentary on what constitutes loving God and the neighbor.

The first seven verses provide one instruction in three parts flowing from the introductory statement about God's liberating activity. In Jewish tradition, verse 2 which contains the introduction, constitutes the first of the commandments. Others may count differently, but no matter how one identifies verse 2, we must keep it in view as an essential statement of God's self-disclosure. Buber remarks that "the soul of the Decalogue is to be found in the word

---

25. For a detailed analysis of these treaties which date back to the 15th and 14th centuries B.C.E., see Delbert R. Hillers, *Covenant: The History of a Biblical Idea* (Baltimore: Johns Hopkins University Press, 1969). The citation from the Hittite Treaty can be found on p. 29. There are also analogies with other written testimony from the ancient Near East. See *ANET,* 164 and 320, as cited in Fox, 539.

26. Cf. Buber: "Here YHVH tells the tribes united in 'Israel' what has to be done and what left undone by them as Israel and by each individual person in Israel . . . in order that a people, the people of YHVH which has to come into being, should come into being"; *Moses,* 138.

27. Buber, *Moses,* 133.

"Thou."[28] It is the initial emphatic "I" which sets up the requirements of the ten covenant words as a direct address from God, from an "I" to a "you." The entire list of requirements that follows must be seen as grounded in the opening statement that declares God's activity. God requires these things of the community at Sinai because God is the God who freed it from oppression and slavery.

A three-part requirement stipulates exclusive loyalty toward God. "No other gods before my face" directs the attention and the adoration of the people toward the God of Israel alone. "You shall not make for yourselves an idol" forbids physical representation for purposes of worship. Finally, "you shall not apply the Name . . . to an illusion" bans applying God's name to a fictitious godhead.[29] The community is to pay attention to this God alone, the one who delivered them from Egypt, not to other deities. They are not to pretend that the infinite Holy God can be contained in or represented by finite human handiwork. They are not to give God's name to that which is not God but something cooked up by human minds to give it the illusion of godhead. The radical nature of this requirement and the manner in which it set the community apart from all folk in whose midst they existed is today hard to fathom.[30]

Two instructions follow, the two that are concerned with the community in time, in the one-after-the-other — the keeping of Shabbat and the honoring of parents. (On the significance of the Sabbath, see above, Part III, Chapter 1.) The commandment is provided with a theological underpinning in verse 11. However, the subject of worship, overtly addressed in the first three instructions, is here present implicitly, in that the Sabbath was the foundational religious feast day, rather than explicitly, in that no specific religious regulations are attached to this commandment. The Sabbath law emphatically creates rest for the entire community in an egalitarian manner and therefore spells out who is to cease working (rather than *what* it means to rest), a list that includes "the stranger who is in your gates." In the command to honor parents, the explicit mention of the mother is worth noting.[31] The

---

28. Buber, *Moses*, 130.

29. Cf Isa. 41:29, where the idols are identified as "delusion" and "empty wind." According to Buber, the Hebrew word *shaw* "is 'the fictitious' — and unlike, for example, *hevel*, 'vapor' or 'trifle,' *shaw'* means in particular the fictitious thing that is credited with reality, which accordingly can become a counter-reality or counter-divinity"; *Scripture and Translation*, 94.

30. For Mary Douglas, ancient Israel's anti-iconic bias marks its religion as unique in its context and also contains a rejection of polytheism, magic, divination, and occultism. "Anti-magic, anti-ghosts, anti-icons, pro-purity, pro-monotheism, the tendencies go together as a bundle"; *In the Wilderness*, 32.

31. Houtman (51-52) insists that father and mother denote aged parents. Nothing is said here of age, and the instruction seems to be more inclusive than highlighting just the care of the

Sabbath commandment looks back to the first set (vv. 1-7) with its emphasis on the relationship with God and anticipates the last set (vv. 13-17) by its emphasis on the entire community. The law to honor parents connects the life of the people to the "ground" from which they came as human beings and to which they are going as part of God's promise. The fifth law thus sets its time-related regulation also in space, naturally leading up to the third set of rules. In this way, the fourth and fifth commandments form a bridge between the first set of laws and the third.

Five brief commandments follow in verses 13-17, stipulating the requirements for the with-one-another of the community, in the forbidding style of the negative command: "you shall not. . . ." Only the last, the proscription against desiring what belongs to someone else, receives an elaboration. The others are put forward in the briefest possible way, two words in Hebrew for verses 13-15, five words for verse 16.

Structurally, it is clear that the first five instructions take up three-fourths of the space of the entire text, with the two commandments in the middle portion, the instructions regarding Sabbath and parents, being almost equivalent in length to the first three. Eight of the Ten Words are put in the starkly forbidding style of the "you shall not . . . ." Only two are cast in a positive style. Three of the Words receive a motivational clause, "for . . ." (vv. 5 and 11) and "so that" (v. 12), the first two with the implication of punishment, the third with that of blessing. Otherwise, no consequences or motivations are provided for any of the commandments, no punishments threatened, no blessings promised.[32] In terms of content, these instructions tie together the relationship of people to God and to neighbor into an indissoluble bond.

The Ten Covenant Words lack specificity. While the introductory self-disclosing statement on God's part anchors the commandments in a historical event and specific human experience, and the precepts that follow clearly demand a singular devotion to this God who liberated the people, individual requirements also raise questions and leave openings that need a response. The specific laws following the Decalogue in Exodus 20:22–23:33 may be viewed as one way the Ten Words were given specific shape in the ancient

---

aged, especially in view of the short life expectancy of the time. Yet, it is likely that the instruction is intended especially for adults who might be tempted to forgo the inclusion of their parents in their concerns when the exigencies of life drive them to focus more narrowly on care for their young dependents. What age indicated both adulthood and old age is naturally hard to tell from a contemporary Western perspective. It seems clear that the commandment includes a general respect for those who are older, a respect that is still the norm in many non-Western societies.

32. We will consider motivational clauses as a part of legal material more closely in the next section of this chapter.

faith community. At the same time, a certain indeterminacy allows for the list of Ten to find new specificity and articulation according to the requirements of different times and context.

In the Netherlands Reformed Church of my youth, the reading of the Ten Commandments was a normal part of the Sunday liturgy. Occasionally, our minister would preach a sermon based on the commandments as they are explicated in the Heidelberg Catechism. Certainly, the Decalogue needed interpretation for our day, but it was also applicable for our day. I was reminded recently, while on a visit to the Netherlands, of the possibilities present in the Decalogue for a contemporary sermon. There, in a small town with its huge and beautiful ancient sanctuary, the minister preached on the Ten Words of Exodus 20:1-17. I was impressed by his gentle insistence on the validity of the commandments for our lives today and how necessary they are as "roadsigns to help the community to find its way toward the promised land with each other." The responsorial singing that accompanied the reading of the Ten Words highlighted the importance of the notion that the community is "on the way," a way which is being cleared for them by a God who is implored to "show the way." In his sermon the preacher made clear how important the commandments and the torah are for the "life of the community, a life which is marked by liberation from bondage."[33]

My experience on this occasion once again gave evidence of the timeless quality and universal nature of the Decalogue, a feature that facilitates application for the faithful of any time and place. In light of this aspect of the Ten Words, it is important to recall the introductory phrase declaring these to be the words of the God who liberated the people from their forced service to Pharaoh to put them into new service, the service to the Holy God of Israel. The Ten Words are anchored in the statement about the God who liberated "the children of Israel." In this way, the entire Decalogue is rooted in ancient Israel's history and in the way God went with them, as well as in their remembrance of the demands that were laid on them in this historical context.[34]

---

33. In grateful recognition to Ds. Haasnoot of the Reformed Congregation in Zutphen, the Netherlands, who preached the sermon on 25 May 2003 and was kind enough to lend me a copy. In the impressive and beautiful Walburgiskerk of Zutphen, the Commandments were also strikingly displayed on a large panel, hung from pillars between the choir and the aisle surrounding it.

34. This recognition is important in view of the universalizing of the Exodus events, including the Decalogue, that happens frequently in Christian liberation theologies. Such a universalizing contributes to a renewed erasure of the significance of ancient Israel and its beliefs, with a consequent devaluation of the Jewish religion as direct inheritor of these traditions. The meaning and importance of the exodus, the covenant, and the lawgiving need careful examination in Christian circles.

This recognition may prevent an all too easy universalizing and adaptation of the Covenant Words. Insofar as Christians believe themselves to be adopted into God's covenant bond through Jesus the Christ, they acknowledge the first covenant concluded between the same God and ancient Israel, a covenant that was never abrogated. They acknowledge their indebtedness to the ancient covenant people and to their descendants, the Jews, for keeping faith, for preserving the ancient memories embedded in these texts, for recognizing the importance of torah as a necessary ingredient to the covenant relationship. Finally, Christians acknowledge also their own need for guidance as they seek to be instructed through the Decalogue.[35]

The Ten Words are addressed to the masculine singular "you" throughout.[36] We call to mind Buber's remark that the Decalogue is the address from an "I" to a "you." It is clear enough that the entire community is being addressed, rather than individual males only. But what about the responsibility of women toward the law? We should probably understand the masculine singular verb form to include everyone in the community. Women are subsumed under the masculine singular category, much as they were for centuries in the English language where it used "man" to indicate all of humanity. Such usage does not oblige us to continue the practice of subsuming the category of female under that of the male and to leave the presence of women unrecognized as responsible agents in the community of faith. In our contemporary Western languages, this problem is solved by the absence of an inflected verb form and of a pronoun to indicate the masculine singular alone. In other languages, translations must be found that include women. The very adaptability of the Ten Words itself demands such an adjustment.

The Execution of the Covenant (Exodus 24:3-8)

Exodus 24:3-8

3. And Moses came and told the people
   all the words of the Holy One
   and all the regulations,
   and all the people answered in one voice:
   All that the Holy One has spoken we will do.
4. And Moses wrote all the words of the Holy One

---

35. Naturally, I do not have in mind here the posting of the Commandments in public buildings as is done in places in the U.S. The Decalogue is a document that belongs in the community of faith rather than the public arena of the body politic.

36. The Hebrew verb forms make clear what the English "you" obscures.

and arose early in the morning
and built an altar at the foot of the mountain
and twelve stones for the twelve tribes of Israel.

5. And he sent for boys from the children of Israel,
and they sent up burnt offerings
and sacrificed as peace offerings to the Holy One oxen.

6. And Moses took half of the blood
and put it in basins
and half of the blood he scattered on the altar.

7. And he took the scroll of the covenant
and read it in the hearing of the people,
and they said: All that the Holy One has spoken
we will do and we will listen.

8. And Moses took the blood
and scattered it on the people,
and he said: See, the blood of the covenant
that the Holy One cuts with you
by all these words.

A brief narrative recounts a series of actions by which the covenant bond between God and people is concluded. The spoken words in the story represent the declaration of the covenant by Moses (v. 8) and the repeated promise of the people (vv. 3, 7). Fourteen verbs with Moses as subject constitute seven stages of activity by which the covenant is concluded.[37] The framework for these actions is formed by four verbs related to words and text, which surround three verbs of ritual activity. The one action of scattering the blood on altar and people takes place in two movements separated by reading and response from the people (vv. 6-8). The people respond, and then they are taken into the covenant, which is formally declared by Moses.

The ritual to be executed is in need of holy space created for the purpose by Moses, who constructs an altar and appoints stand-in priests in the boys who perform the sacrifices.[38] A priestly place and a priestly apparatus

---

37. The actions consist of Moses' "telling," "writing," "building," "sending," "scattering," "reading," and "declaring."

38. At this stage an established priesthood not being available, the boys may have been chosen because of their lack of sexual experience, or they may have been the firstborn who fulfill the claim God had on them. Yet another possibility is that the youth were by this action taken up into the community as full members. See Walter Beyerlin, *Origins and History of the Oldest Sinaitic Traditions* (Oxford: Blackwell, 1966), 39ff.; also Herbert Schmid, *Mose: Überlieferung und Geschichte.* BZAW 110 (Berlin: Töpelmann, 1968), 69.

are created for the purpose of the covenant-making. Moses acts in a priestly function by the scattering of the blood on altar and people. Sacrifices were a common part of covenant making in biblical times, and they are an integral part of the proceedings here, standing at the center of the activities recorded on the part of Moses.

The centrality of the "words" of God (vv. 3, 4, 8) is underscored by the repeated mention of Moses' "telling" (v. 3), "writing" (v. 4), and "reading" (v. 7), the repeated response on the part of the people, and by the framing of the episode within the expression "all the words" (vv. 3, 8). Twice the people say they will "do," and the second time they add that they will "listen." They state thereby the recognition that the words of God need their active partici- pation and response, but perhaps more important, they voice the recognition of their need for continued listening. The common translation "we will be obedient" for "we will listen," though not wrong as such, loses the accent on the need for continued listening as a requirement laid on the people. Natu- rally, acting on the requirements involves obedience, but more difficult be- cause less tangible is the demand to continue to be attentive to God's presence as it has come to them and will continue to come to them by word rather than image.

Although elements of the account of the Sinai covenant as it is related here may be found elsewhere, as the reading of the scroll, the sacrificing, and the declaration, as well as the response, a number of features must be recog- nized as unique. Nowhere else in the Bible does a leader undertake the im- promptu priestly role in this context. Although covenant declarations are made elsewhere, the particular wording used here, "the blood of the covenant that the Holy One cuts with you," is singular. Above all, the action of scatter- ing the sacrificial blood on both altar, symbolizing God, and people stands out as a feature peculiar to this passage.[39]

Structurally, the unit is embedded in another story that tells of the en- counter of a group of elders together with their leaders with the Holy God (Exod. 24:1-2 + 9-11) Most likely there are at least two traditions or more that underlie the entire chapter as it now stands, each with their own characteris- tics.[40] The reasons for and the process of combining these traditions now elude us. As it is, verses 3-8 enter like an interruption into what appears to be in part a tale of a small group chosen to have a meal in the presence of the de-

---

39. The words "blood of the covenant" occur only in one other place in the Hebrew Bible, Zech. 9:11, where the reference is most likely to the blood of the circumcision.

40. This chapter is an example of different traditions that were added together to make a whole, resulting in a final text where the seams are clearly showing.

ity and to be granted a vision of the Godhead. What begins as an encounter between the chosen few and God then turns into a description of the bonding of God with the entire people. We note the emphatic "all the people" in the opening lines of our story. It is "all" the people who listen to "all the words" that God has spoken to them. It is almost as if the writer halted the tale that was already begun to pick up another more important thread and unfolds the story of the covenant-making between God and people before continuing with the tale of the elect "eating" and "seeing." Yet, this story too must be preserved to memory, and so it was added, coming now in second place: "Telling" and "speaking" before "eating" and "seeing"; "all the people" before the "seventy elders."[41]

What we have in Exodus 24:3-8 in its singular wording is a unique account and, of course, one of the utmost significance. This passage furnishes a description of the foundational act by which ancient Israel understood itself and its relationship to God. Henceforth, the community was bound into covenant, an indissoluble bond, one that the human partner could choose to ignore or violate by not acting on the demands laid on them by the divine partner, but one they could not dissolve.

Historical Context of the Covenant Texts

It is now some time ago that covenant as a concept deemed crucial for the understanding of the Old Testament was at the center of much Christian scholarship. Ever since Wellhausen's claim that the covenant between God and ancient Israel was a late concept used in postexilic times to explain and articulate preexilic history and identity, debates went back and forth between scholars as to the antiquity of the Sinai covenant.[42] It is not possible here to recap all the arguments. In summary fashion, I make the following observations:

1. The Sinai covenant as presented in Exodus 19–24 is tightly bound up

---

41. The repeated mention of the elders' vision of God is striking: "they saw God" and "they beheld God" (vv. 10, 11).

42. Wellhausen regarded covenant between God and people as belonging to the beginnings of legalism because the *berit* depends on conditions; *Prolegomena to the History of Ancient Israel,* 417ff. According to Wellhausen, the original understanding of the relationship between God and people was as that of father and son, a natural one, not limited by the conditions of a covenant; *Grundrisse zum Alten Testament,* 44. George E. Mendenhall's essay, *Law and Covenant in Israel and the Ancient Near East* (Pittsburgh: Biblical Colloquium, 1955), provided new life for the notion that the covenant went much farther back into Israel's history. This essay presents a study based on comparisons of the covenant formulae as found in the Bible with Hittite treaties of 1450-1200 B.C.E. See also Hillers, who represents this position in his *Covenant: The History of a Biblical Idea.*

with *torah,* instruction and lawgiving, perceived as originating directly from God. The human partner is obligated to live as God's covenant partner and to bring its participation in the covenant into being. To split these two aspects of the tradition, in a literary and/or theological sense, is to do violence to a basic tenet of ancient Israel's faith, that instruction is essential for the human partnership in the covenant bond.[43]

2. The bond between God and ancient Israel is not conditional on God's part.[44] When the children of Israel prove themselves almost immediately incapable of living up to the aniconic demands of the Decalogue, a restatement of the covenant promises is provided by God (Exod. 34:10).

3. The covenant traditions as we have found them in these passages of Exodus are not essentially Deuteronomic, even if a Deuteronomic hand may have worked on them. At their core, unique formulations mark the speeches and narrative, features that seem unexplainable from a postexilic context.

4. There is no reason to assume that these traditions may not go back to the very roots of ancient Israel's existence, possibly before the settlement period.

43. The separation of the traditions of God's revelation at Sinai and the legal traditions was classically posed by Wellhausen and subsequently adhered to by many Christian scholars. A renewed impetus was given to this position by Lothar Perlitt in *Bundestheologie im Alten Testament* (1969) and, more recently, by Erhard Blum and Frank Crüsemann. For a discussion of the development of this separation of Sinai and legal tradition, see Erich Zenger, "Wie und Wozu die Tora zum Sinai kam: Literarische und theologische Beobachtungen zu Exodus 19–34," in *Studies in the Book of Exodus: Redaction, Reception, Interpretation,* ed. Marc Vervenne. BETL 126 (Leuven: Peeters, 1996), 265-88.

44. Even in Deuteronomy this remains so. There, God presents the people with conditions for their keeping of the land, but not for God's maintaining the covenant relationship (e.g., Deut. 11:13; 15:5; 28:1).

CHAPTER 3

"And Brought Us to This Place"
(Numbers 11:1-15; Deuteronomy 34:5-6)[1]

In the Wilderness

The question that permeates the book of Numbers, the continuation of the narrative of the people's journey through the Sinai Peninsula, is whether the goal of reaching the land of the promise will be achieved. Numbers 10 finally records movement away from Mount Sinai, and much of the subsequent 15 chapters is taken up with the tale of the people's trek by stages to the borders of Canaan, until they reach the plains of Moab where they halt. Numbers opens with a long accounting of the organization of the people by tribe, and of the ordering of worship, including the priesthood and the tasks of the Levites (Num. 1:1–10:10). Its final eleven chapters offer a repeated account of the tribes and include a review of the boundaries of the land they will enter, as well as specific provisions for its possession (Num. 26:1–36:13). Whereas the opening and closing chapters are marked by a concern for organization and orderly proceedings, the narratives they enclose are characterized by disorder, rebellion, and disagreement.[2] In Hebrew, Numbers is called "In the

---

1. Cf. Deut. 26:9.

2. In a brilliant analysis of Numbers, Mary Douglas argues for a close interweaving of two strands in this text, that of story and law. Seven narratives alternate with six sections of legal material. Douglas thus counts the opening chapters regarding tribal organization as story. The closing chapters about land partition (33-35) she assigns to "law," while ch. 36 is once again "story"; *In the Wilderness*, 102-26. I suggest that the chapters containing census function much like genealogical material elsewhere, providing an ordered perspective on people and land, where much is troubled and disordered in the narrative. The same might be said of the orderly

Wilderness," and wilderness existence turns out to test the people, Moses, and God to the utmost. All become angry and quarrelsome, and turmoil is the order of the day. Distinct sections of legal material alternate with narratives, continuing the thread of order and regularity in counterpoint to the disorder and tension of the stories.[3] The movement of the narrative proper is toward the land of the promise, with a precise accounting included of the stages traveled from Egypt to Moab (Num. 33:1-49), so that in the end of the book the people are in sight of the land. The last set of regulations is given to the people by Moses "in the plains of Moab, at Jordan-Jericho" (Num. 36:13). In this way, the last line of Numbers connects closely with the first verses of Deuteronomy, a book which purports to be almost entirely a speech to the people by Moses, from the location "across the Jordan, in the land of Moab" (Deut. 1:5).

Together with Leviticus, Numbers may be counted among one of the least favorite books of the Bible for Christians. Its name, Numbers, unlike the Hebrew designation "In The Wilderness," sounds dull, and so a text that is in truth far from dull is assigned to obscurity and neglect. Numbers contains high drama, far more than we can deal with in the span of these pages. It is a disturbing text in many ways because of the constant clamoring of the people against God and their leaders, on the one hand, and the highlighting of God's punitive measures, on the other. Yet, the very dramatic quality of the stories together with the details of the interaction lends them a unique and extraordinarily vivid character. The central issue around which these tales turn is that of trust.[4] After the Sinai covenant, after the demands of holiness laid on the people in Leviticus, they show themselves to be far short of the mark. The people are unable to trust God and their leaders, so they "complain" and are duly punished (Num. 11:1-15; 16–17; 20; 21:4-9; 25). Moses' own family "speak against" him (Num. 12), and Moses, together with Aaron, is accused of mistrusting God's power and severely punished for his offense (20:9-12). Lack of trust constantly erodes the relationships between human agents and between humans and God and creates a kind of wilderness of its own. This agenda item would have served the Priestly editors of Numbers in postexilic times as a warning to the community of the restoration in Judah. More remarkable are the absence of xenophobia and the emphasis on the inclusion of all of Israel

---

recounting of land partition, assignment of cities for certain functions, and the stages of the journey from Egypt to the Jordan.

3. So Everett Fox: "The interruptions also allow each of the memorable rebellion narratives to 'breathe,' giving the audience time to digest the images and the drama presented therein"; *The Five Books of Moses*, 709.

4. On this issue, see Fox, 710.

in this text, as Mary Douglas has pointed out.[5] Both in terms of issues and dramatic character, at least the *narrative material* of Numbers would seem to lend itself quite well to contemporary preaching and teaching.[6]

The Cucumbers and Melons of Egypt (Numbers 11:1-15)

One example must suffice to illustrate some of the points made here.

Numbers 11:1-15[7]

1. The people's mourning was evil[8]
   in the ears of the Holy One;
   the Holy One heard and became angry
   and a fire of the Holy One burned them
   and it devoured the edge of the camp.

2. The people cried to Moses,
   and Moses prayed to the Holy One
   and the fire sank down.

3. And they called the name of that place Taverah
   for it burned them, the fire of the Holy One.

4. The riffraff in their midst
   craved a craving
   and they wept some more,

5. Douglas is convinced that the redactor was, besides a "hierarchist, and a brilliant poet . . . also a person of his times, with strong political concerns, with antixenophobic and anti-government views." The text is also, in her view, anti-Ezra and Nehemiah, a perspective that becomes especially clear in the Balaam cycle, viewed by Douglas as a political satire of the figure of Nehemiah; 159, 216-34.

6. Cf. Peter C. Craigie's remark that Numbers is in some ways "a miserable book . . . because . . . it puts its finger accurately on the pulse of all human perversity"; *The Old Testament: Its Background, Growth, and Content* (Nashville: Abingdon, 1986), 112. The legal material of Numbers will receive review in the next chapter.

7. Clearly, this passage is a section of the entire story told in ch. 11 which involves a great deal more complaining and bargaining, solutions and punishments. I deal with it here only in part in the interest of space, but also because the passage is quite illustrative of narrative material elsewhere in Numbers.

8. For Hebrew *mit'onenim* I translate "mourning" rather than "complaining," the Hebrew root *lun* used elsewhere in Numbers (e.g., 14:2, 36; 16:11; 17:10[16:41]). I also follow Martin Buber in making the first clause of v. 1 a main rather than a dependent one. It is the sound of "mourning" which displeases God. Cf. Buber's translation of *Totenklager* for the verb here, i.e., "those who bewail the dead."

    also the Israelites,
    and they said: Who will give us to eat meat?

5. We remember the fish
    that we ate in Egypt for nothing,
    the cucumbers and the melons,
    the leeks, the onions and the garlic.

6. And now our throats are dry;[9]
    there is nothing but manna before us.

7. And manna was like the seed of coriander
    and its appearance the appearance of gum resin.

8. The people roamed about
    and they picked it up and ground it with handmills
    or pounded it with mortar
    and boiled it in a pot,
    and they made it into cakes
    and its taste was like the taste of an oily dainty.

9. And when the dew fell on the camp at night
    the manna fell on it.

10. And Moses heard the people weeping in their clans,
    each at the opening of their tent;
    and the anger of the Holy One burned hot
    and in the eyes of Moses it was evil.

11. Then Moses said to the Holy One:
    Why have you done evil to your servant,
    and why have I not found favor in your eyes?
    Why lay the burden
    of this entire people on me?

12. Was it I who became pregnant with this people?
    Or I who gave birth to them?
    That you say to me:
    Lift them in your arms
    as lifts the nurse the suckling babe
    to the land that you swore to (give to) their ancestors?

13. From where do I get meat
    to give to all this people?

---

9. It is clear that at this point the Hebrew word *nefesh* should be translated with its most literal meaning, "throat." Cf. Fox, 713.

For they weep at me and say:
Give to us meat so we may eat.

14. I cannot, I by myself alone,
lift all this people
for it is too heavy for me.
15. And if thus you act,
slay, yes slay me,
if I have found favor in your eyes
so I will not look on your evil [i.e., the evil you do].[10]

The introductory verses (1-3) recount in summary fashion an incident of grieving on the people's part, retaliating anger from God's side, and intercessory prayer from Moses, a pattern that will be repeated in the stories of rebellion. The anger of God literally burns the people, and not until Moses prays does God call a halt to it. There is perhaps a touch of humor here which will be continued in the elaborate food descriptions to follow, The people are said to "mourn" instead of complain. Their emotions are grief, as is also made clear by the sequel where they are said to "weep," a root that is three times repeated. Weeping over dull food? Surely, that is a bit much! Grumbling perhaps, or whining, but "mourning"? Martin Buber translates the verb with "weeping for the dead." It is interesting to note that, in both these first verses and the subsequent episode, the people arouse the anger of both God and Moses because of their *attitude*. At this point, they are not committing an overt sin of mistrust, as making an image of God, or challenging Moses' authority, or worshipping other gods. They have an attitude of being victimized and deprived that is so deeply offensive to God that it is called "evil in God's ears." Later, Moses is equally offended and, echoing God's displeasure, the writer records "in the eyes of Moses it was evil" (vv. 1, 10).

Then follows an episode where the people's lamenting as well as their situation are told in great detail, almost absurdly so. It is as if verses 4-9 attempt to fill in the blanks left by the introductory sentences. The issue of "grieving" or "mourning" in the opening lines of this chapter arises rather abruptly after the final lines of chapter 10, which recount the accompanying presence of the Holy God of Israel with the people, and does not reveal the focus of their unhappiness. What exactly did the people have to mourn? Verses 4ff. fill in the

---

10. In the translation "your evil," I follow what I consider to be the original reading before scribal scruples changed it to "my evil." Moses is here connecting a deed of wickedness with God which in later times would be seen as little less than blasphemy on his part; hence the change. The reading "your evil," i.e., the evil that God is planning to do to the people, has also the advantage that it includes the evil which Moses will experience if God eradicates the people.

blanks in a way: "Well, for example . . . take the matter of food." The subsequent lines recount under what circumstances the people grieved and what was the essence of their lament. As if they were people on a pleasure cruise rather than on a difficult life-threatening trek through the wilderness, they whine about the food. The text does not state specifically that they addressed Moses, but Moses clearly *feels* addressed and takes the matter up with God.

Much of the episode consists of speech. Only God does not speak, but that lack will be made up for in the subsequent section (vv. 16-20). This feature lends the story some of its dramatic character. Almost all of verses 4-6 and of verses 10-15 consists of speech. First the people weep; then they explain why they weep. The mention of "riffraff," the wonderful Hebrew word *asafsuf*, in verse 4 is somewhat curious. Are these malcontents that hang around in any community, stirring up strife and dissension? Are they a part of the "multitude" that followed the children of Israel on their way out of Egypt (cf. Exod. 12:38), and thus a category of outsider? Or is this the typical human way of telling a story that does not reflect well on the home group: "Well, you know, it started with those no-goods from out of town"? There is perhaps a hint here of a lack of homogeneity, a glimpse one receives also wherever the "stranger," the *ger*, is mentioned in Numbers. In any case, quite soon the entire community falls to lamenting about the food they want, the food they used to get "back in good old Egypt," and the food they are now receiving to their dissatisfaction.

The recital of fish and vegetables in verse 5 is again humorous but also indicative of the issue at hand. The list consists of flavorful and moisture-rich items: leeks, onions, and garlic on the one hand and cucumbers and melons on the other would certainly enhance the consumption of fish. Now all they have is this dry as dust manna which has them going around with parched throats. The narrator follows this recital with a detailed picture of what manna was actually like. Although the descriptions may not exactly help the contemporary reader, it is clear that manna could be processed and, however one envisions an "oily dainty," turned out not quite as dull and dry as the people describe it. In other words, the complaint is more about monotony than about essentials for survival. They really do not trust Moses or God to provide for them, so they are in despair and, as will happen again, yearn to be back in Egypt. Things may have been bad then, but at least the food was good! There is not much to admire here, but on the other hand there is much to recognize and connect with.

The subsequent verses imply that the grumbling was not addressed directly to Moses, unlike the earlier episode when they "cried to Moses" (v. 2). Here he "heard them weeping" (v. 10), but Moses will take the issue up with God in such a way as to make clear he himself feels like the injured party. The anger of God "burns" once again, but before more specifics can be provided, the text interrupts God's potential action by stating Moses' reaction, "and in the eyes of Moses it was evil" (v. 10). On the surface, it is the people's weeping that displeases Moses. In addition, this declaration follows immediately on the statement about God's anger, which creates an ambiguity as to what exactly Moses finds evil. Perhaps the intention of the writer is to indicate both the people's attitude and God's intended action as sources of Moses' annoyance. From his first words, it is clear that Moses sees himself as the one victimized by God. Once more the word "evil" appears in the phrase "why have you done evil to your servant?" The evil that God has done to Moses is to make him responsible for the people, and so Moses points out in no uncertain words that it is not he, Moses, who is responsible, but rather God.

In a striking turn of phrase, Moses compares God to a pregnant woman and a birth mother whose responsibility it is to "lift" the babe and care for it.[11] It is not Moses who has given birth to this crowd, and Moses alone is not capable of "lifting" them. If God is planning to leave the entire business to Moses, then he would rather be dead. For the last time in the section, the word "evil" sounds when Moses demands to be slain so "I will not look on your evil." The scribe found this language too strong and changed the wording to "my evil," but by restoring the pronoun "your" the issue becomes more clear. The word "evil" is used four times in the section. The first time, it is God's word as a perspective on the people's attitude ("the people's mourning was evil," v. 1). The second time, it is Moses' word as a reaction to his awareness of the people's weeping ("and in the eyes of Moses it was evil," v. 10). The third time, the word applies to Moses' perspective on God's treatment of him ("why have you done evil to your servant?" v. 11). The fourth time, the word comes to a resolution by planting the responsibility for the well and woe of the people squarely in God's hands ("your evil," v. 15). Boldly, Moses holds God accountable, for the ill done to him and for the ill God is planning to do to the people.[12]

Moses' speech to God is far from gentle. It is bold and confronts God directly. It is more angry and less placatory than the intercessions he made during the incident of the Golden Calf. It is also a speech rich in implications because of the unusual comparison of God to a pregnant woman and a mother.

---

11. On the importance of these images and their implications, see Johanna Van Wijk-Bos, *Reimagining God* (Louisville: Westminster John Knox, 1995), 58-59.

12. Standard translations such as the NRSV obscure the emphatic use of the root for "evil" by using a variety of words, including "misfortunes," "displeased," "treated badly," and "my misery." Fox uses some form of "ill" throughout: "ill-fortune," "ill," and "dealt-ill"; 713-14. Although "evil" is a strong word, it seems the writer chose such a word deliberately and let it resound in the passage.

Here too, we may perhaps detect some humorous undertones. "Hah!" shouts Moses. "Did I carry them in my belly? Did I carry them in my arms? Was I their nurse? Am I responsible for feeding them? No, but you are." This baby has become too big for Moses to carry. Moses' scathing tone toward the people is clear from his constant referring to them with the words "this people," an echo perhaps of the people's disdainful reference to him as "this Moses" (Exod. 32:1).

In the next section, God will provide for both Moses and the people, but so far God has been silent and is present only in anger. It is a difficult picture of God that emerges from some of these episodes, one to which I will return in a subsequent chapter. Here, I observe that Moses is not reproached for the boldness of his speech to which a divine response is forthcoming. There is a rawness to the episode, even as there is to Moses' speech. The people have had it with God and Moses, God has had it with the people, and Moses has had it with people and with God. Yet the story goes on. The Priestly editors who compiled Numbers certainly did not portray the desert experiences as romantic. Those were times of testing, and the people failed the test most of the time. Yet they survived. They will eventually reach the land and fail again in time and lose it, but the community will survive. God's anger which seems to burst forth here in an unwarranted fashion is not forever, but God's sustaining presence is lasting in spite of their shortcomings.

The End of the Story (Deuteronomy 34:5-6)

As is Leviticus, Deuteronomy is distinctive in its style, one often called exhortatory, or sermonic. Almost the entire book is cast as a speech by Moses to the covenanted community as it is on the verge of entering the land of the promise. Deuteronomy is also distinctive in its theological outlook, making the possession of the land contingent on the faithfulness of the people and their ability to follow God's directives. These directives are, in the opinion of the writer of this book, within the grasp of the community to follow. In other words, it is not some outrageous demand and expectation that God lays on them (cf. Deut. 30:11-20). The consequences of their failures in this regard will be grave, for they stand to lose the possession that they are just about to inherit. The book was written and edited in view of exactly this loss, of course.[13]

13. The most attractive dating of at least the core of Deuteronomy (Deut. 12–26) is, to my understanding, still its traditional placement in the north shortly before the fall of the northern kingdom, mid-8th century B.C.E., with later editing and expansion, first in Judah during Josiah's

While the conditional casting of some of the covenant promises is not always easy to understand or to reconcile with other perspectives on the covenant between God and the ancient Israelites, the virtue of Deuteronomic theology is to emphasize human responsibility in the enterprise upon which the God of Israel is embarked with the creation, the seriousness of this responsibility, and the consequences of the community's failure to live up to it. Of this failure there are plentiful examples. Over and over again, the people exhibit lack of trust. On the other hand, there is no question but that God's presence with the people does not depend on their following through on their loyalty to God. The land may be lost, but the promise of divine presence is never endangered, and it does not depend on the possession of the land. At the end of the book of Numbers, the community can envision existence in the land on the borders of which they are finally encamped (Num. 32–33). The possession of this land is not yet theirs, and for generations of initial recipients of the story the land was theirs no more. The teaching of Deuteronomy hence is placed in the biblical text at the point of anticipation, the not-yet, and for generations to come was received at the point of reflection on loss, the no-longer.[14] The hope and anxiety created by both perspectives lend to the book a note of greatest urgency. In Hebrew Deuteronomy is called "Words" (Hebrew *devarim*). Emphatically and repeatedly these "words" are addressed to the community *today*.[15] More directly than any other book of the Torah, Deuteronomy demands from the listener a decision to interpret and apply its teaching to the contemporary situation.

The story of the Torah proper closes with the death of Moses recounted in the book of Deuteronomy: "And Moses died there, the servant of the Holy One, in the land of Moab, by the mouth of the Holy One. He buried him in a valley in the land of Moab, opposite Beth Peor, and no one knows his grave to this day" (Deut. 34:5-6).

---

reform (622), and later by the Priestly editors in postexilic Jerusalem. For a different view, see Richard Elliott Friedman, *Who Wrote the Bible?* (Englewood Cliffs: Prentice Hall, 1987), 107-10, who follows Frank Moore Cross in positing authorship during the reign of King Josiah. See also Bernard M. Levinson in *The Jewish Study Bible*, ed. Adele Berlin and Marc Zvi Brettler (Oxford: Oxford University Press, 2004), 357-59.

14. Levinson observes that the Torah concludes "with a panorama that symbolizes dislocation and loss, as Moses looks out over Canaan from the heights of Mount Pisgah." Furthermore: "Ancient editors have deliberately defined the Torah as a literary unit so as, first, to accommodate the addition of Deuteronomy and, second, to sever it from its logically expected fulfillment.... So profound a reconfiguration both of the patriarchal promise and of the overall plot is conceivable only in light of the historical experience of exile, which profoundly called the possession of the land into question"; 359.

15. For a good example of this word use, see Deut. 4 *passim*.

The turbulent saga of the people's deliverance from oppression, their trek through the first part of the wilderness until Sinai, their becoming a people in partnership with God, and their departure from Sinai as a covenant people on the way to the land of the promise comes to an end at the border on the other side of the Jordan. The ending opens into a new beginning, for the land still has to become theirs, and they have much to learn in terms of living with one another and with God. The story is intended as a teaching. It teaches about the people's identity as God's people, that in the first instance this identity does not reside in their own faithfulness but in God's promise to be present to them and to guide them. God is the God who freed them from the slavehouse and who will continue to show them what it means to live as a freed people. The story teaches the people where they come from and where they are going. The restlessness of the trek through the Sinai Peninsula belongs to the heart of the story's teaching, for this is always a people on the way and their God is a God who is on the way with them. It is from the story abundantly clear that on their own they can not find the way, that they need guidance, road signs set up by God to show them the way.

CHAPTER 4

Instructions for the Covenant Life

The obedience demanded of Israel toward the law . . . is the response to the love with which God first loved it. It does not effect salvation, but it moves God to save Israel in God's mercy.[1]

Story and law go together and together form the teaching that is essential to the covenant community, whether before or after the Babylonian exile, whether before or after the time of Christ. Once taken into covenant partnership, the community is in need of instruction as to how it should conduct its life. Hence, texts that deal with specific prescriptions and regulations, whether in the social or the religious sphere, make up the greatest part of the Torah. Large sections of Exodus and Numbers, as well as almost all of Leviticus and Deuteronomy, are devoted to regulating the life of the community. In spite of this preponderance, legal texts are often underrepresented in Christian scholarship, teaching, and preaching.[2] Apart from a common Christian aversion to the "legalism" of the Old Testament, there may be several additional reasons for this absence of attention. First, at many points the subject of the regulations is alien, and a sense of disconnection predominates between the ancient and the modern world. Second, the rules are complex and

---

1. Otto Kaiser, *Der Gott des Alten Testaments: Theologie des AT* 1: *Grundlegung* (Göttingen: Vandenhoeck & Ruprecht, 1993), 351; quoted by Erich Zenger in Zenger, George Braulik, and Heinz-Josef Fabry, *Einleitung in das Alte Testament*, 78.

2. It is, e.g., remarkable that John Van Seters in his elaborate work on the Torah, while acknowledging the importance of the legal material, devotes almost no space to these texts, nor does an evaluation of them enter into his radical revision of ancient Israel's history; *The Pentateuch.* In his work *The Life of Moses,* the covenant pericopes are discussed solely from a source-critical point of view, with no attention spent on clues that may reside in the content of the various laws.

are not organized according to a principle immediately discernible to modern perception, so that the collection may come across as a hodgepodge. Third, it is even for the expert not easy to determine how much of the material we should consider "law" as we understand it today. Do words such as "law," "legal," "legal code" not conjure up a context of judges, lawyers, and codes to be consulted, a context that was alien to the ancient world?

Of these problems, the first one will receive special attention in this discussion since it is my concern to highlight the importance of the Torah for modern Christianity including its directly prescriptive material. In terms of organization, I assume that organizing principles existed with which the modern reader is no longer familiar; it is our task to discern guiding principles for certain sets of instructions wherever possible. As to the third problem, I do not propose a decision on the exact nature of these texts; whether they were a reflection of actual legal practice, or whether they are of a more didactic origin, or whether they provide an idealized and therefore unrealistic picture of the ancient world. I will review the instructions selectively, based on the assumption that the specific prescriptions of the Torah of necessity connect with actual practices in the biblical world, and they reflect this world in some way.[3]

The Book of the Covenant:
Organization and Content of Exodus 20:22–23:19

I observed earlier that the Ten Words of the Covenant lack specificity and that the material of Exodus 20–23 gives shape and specificity to the instructions of the Decalogue for their time and place (see above, 163-64). This section of Exodus is traditionally termed the Book of the Covenant and contains a miscellany of instructions, directed both to the worship of God and to relations among neighbors, although the latter predominate. From the

---

3. In contrast to the arguments brought forward by Anne Fitzpatrick-McKinley, who argues that the legal material of the Torah originally was the creation and the property of a literate elite, the scribes, and that "lawcodes may originate through processes which are independent of, and often unconcerned with, society's everyday legal needs"; *The Transformation of Torah from Scribal Advice to Law.* JSOTSup 287 (Sheffield: Sheffield Academic, 1999), 78. For a different opinion, see Michael Fishbane, *Biblical Interpretation in Ancient Israel* (Oxford: Oxford University Press, 1985), 96: "Despite the fact that the biblical legal corpora are formulated as prototypical expressions of legal wisdom, *the internal traditions of the Hebrew Bible present and regard the covenantal laws as legislative texts.*" Houtman contends that the rules in the Book of the Covenant, e.g., "are not law as practiced but law as *ideal*"; 88.

Ten Words it is clear that relationship to God and relationship to the neighbor are all of a piece. Hence, regulations for worship are presented here together with directions for how to live the common life of the community in such a way that it fosters the well-being of the community. The opening and closing sections concern the issue of worship (Exod. 20:22-26; 23:14-19) and shape a framework around the various directives for the social life of the community.[4]

The organization of the different regulations may be outlined as follows:

1. **Regulations for Worship (20:22-26)**
This section contains the curious directive to build an altar of earth or of uncut stone without steps, whenever and wherever appropriate, a rule that contradicts the actual practice of temple worship and the Deuteronomic regulation of worshipping God at only one place (Deut. 12:5ff.).[5] The verses function as a preamble to the laws, the *mishpatim*, that follow and together with Exodus 23:10-13 provide a framework for them.

2. **Regulations for and Protection of Slaves (21:1-11)**
Slavery was common in the entire ancient world, including the early period of Christianity, and was also a part of the social and economic structures of ancient Israel, though perhaps not a significant factor until the period of the monarchy.[6] The laws presented here set limits around the practice of slavery and afford a certain protection to persons held in bondage. This group is certainly one of the most vulnerable of the society.[7] There is in the entire Bible not a word uttered against the principle of slavery as an institution, and on this point we experience deeply the divide between our own world and that of the Bible. Yet, we note the significance of the primary place of this particular set of laws,

---

4. For a detailed and interesting discussion of the various laws of the Book of the Covenant, see Walter Brueggemann, "The Book of Exodus," in *The New Interpreter's Bible* 1 (Nashville: Abingdon, 1994), 860-78.

5. For a discussion about the different prescriptions regarding the altar, see Houtman, 100-3.

6. So Frank Crüsemann, who maintains that "Slavery only gained currency and significance under the monarchy"; *The Torah: Theology and Social History of Old Testament Law* (Minneapolis: Fortress, 1996), 152. For a discussion of slavery, see Houtman, 113.

7. According to Crüsemann, "the slave laws of the Mishpatim mediated between the interests of the ones who purchased or owned the slave and those of the slaves and their families. They placed boundaries on both sides of the law"; 158.

extending at least a measure of protection to this vulnerable group and mitigating the evil effects of the practice.[8]

3. **Protection against Violence of Persons, Both Intended and Unintended, Extended to Both Free and Slave (21:12-27)**
This set of laws is designed to set boundaries around the exercise of vengeance by exacting restitutions extended in a fairly egalitarian manner.[9] Concern is thus extended both to the victims, that they receive compensation, and to the perpetrator, who compensates the victim directly.

4. **Protection against Violence of Animals (21:28-36)**
These laws protect against violence in domestic animal behavior, including negligence, and show a degree of concern for both animal and owner. Rules of this kind could only belong in an agricultural setting where people keep livestock, the ox being the "paradigm of the domestic animal."[10]

5. **Protection against Violence toward Property and Restitution (22:1-15)**
These laws protect the victim of theft by laying down clear rules of restitution and responsibility.

6. **Protection of the Weak and Vulnerable (22:16-27)**
In its entirety, this section may be seen as aimed at protection of those without the power to defend themselves or take care of themselves. An initial set of rules (vv. 16-20) offers a miscellany by which young unmarried women, victims of magic and sorcery, animals, and God may exact a price for abuse and wrongful manipulation of power.[11] These initial lines thus lead naturally to the next cluster (vv. 21-27) with its interest in

---

8. The extent of the practice of slavery in ancient Israel is not well known, partly because there is no special word for the person who is not free to distinguish her or him from the servant. The Hebrew word *eved* "can mean anything from chattel slave to household hand" and "was also used as an expression of modesty and submission"; Plaut, *The Torah*, 570.

9. The harsh-sounding law of talion ("an eye for an eye") in vv. 23-24 may be seen in this light. In addition, it is most unlikely that these laws were executed literally, for there is "no case of physical talion recorded in the Bible"; Plaut, 571. Plaut argues that the intention was always to compensate for the value of an eye, a hand, etc.

10. Everett Fox, *The Five Books of Moses*, 377.

11. V. 18 is interpreted by Houtman as relating to a seductive woman rather than a sorceress, and he translates: "A woman who seduces to immorality you shall not allow to live"; 210. This inventive, albeit somewhat strained interpretation, yet points out that the concern here is with abuse of power.

poor and unprotected categories of people. I return to this section for a more detailed discussion below.

7. **Protection of the Relationship to God (22:28-31)**
This section which follows on the heels of the regulations regarding the position of the powerless once again shows the unbreakable linkage between the community's posture toward God and the exercise of human relations. It is not in the detail of the particular rules but rather in this required posture that the significance of the section is located.

8. **Protection of the Weak (23:1-9)**
The text returns to the subject of justice as it is extended to marginal groups in the community — the poor, the minority, and the innocent. A part of this text already came to our attention by means of verse 9 (see above, 29-32). Together with 22:21-27 I will review this entire section in greater detail below.

9. **Protection of the Weakest (including Animals) through Sabbath Rest (23:10-13)**
These verses repeat the law of Shabbat, with a remarkable shift in emphasis compared to Exodus 20:8-11. Here the focus is not on the imitation of divine behavior which dictates rest, but rather on the rest that the land, the poor, as well as wild and domestic animals, slave and stranger may enjoy by means of having this break.[12]

10. **Regulations for Worship through Annual Feasts (23:14-19)**
Perhaps the subject of rest naturally flowed into that of keeping holy feasts, so that the final set of rules concerns itself with the three annual festivals that were prescribed for the covenant community. The emphasis on *giving* to God, whether of first fruits or sacrifice, is worth noting here. The series of laws contained in the Book of the Covenant ends as it began with an emphasis on the orientation of the community to its God. As Walter Brueggemann observes in regard to ancient Israel and its gifts brought to God: "It cannot do so . . . until it has been reconciled to brother and sister. . . . The commands of Moses never permit the separation of God and neighbor, or of worship and human justice."[13]

---

12. The wording in v. 12 is worth noting: "so that your ox and your donkey may rest/and your servant and the stranger may take breath."

13. Brueggemann, "The Book of Exodus," 875.

As a whole the sets of injunctions are intended to protect the vulnerable from abuse and hold responsible those who deliberately injure others or their property, in the context of the ancient biblical world. It is well known that these laws share much in subject matter and manner of presentation with legal material elsewhere from the ancient Near East. In form there is a mixture here of case and absolute law, of which the former is especially familiar from legal codes outside of ancient Israel.[14] Overall, the orientation to God frames the orientation of neighbor to neighbor and to the environment. Although the categories are perhaps not as neatly divided into distinctive subject matter as our Western modern minds could wish, they do not lack cohesion in their subsets, and as a total unit they are marked by a movement toward greater emphasis on protection of vulnerable groups of people, an emphasis that predominates in the later sections of the regulations.

While the distance between ourselves and the specific laws is enormous, there are several places where we may seek connections and where the regulations may drive us to scrutinize our own posture and behavior in our common life. While, for example, slavery as a practice has disappeared from our communities, we may want to look for discriminatory patterns that persist in our society and religions. Do these patterns reflect underlying ideologies of discrimination and prejudice that cause attitudes and practices that hold some groups permanently in inferior and deprived positions? Furthermore, while vengeance and retaliation are not a part of our legal system, how much are sounds of vengeance a part of the background chorus from the victim's side in a criminal trial? Does the desire for vengeance, for example, enter into capital punishment cases and, if they do, how far removed are we actually from the age in which the biblical law was articulated? At least in biblical times a limit was set to vengeance and personal retaliation.

Rules that pertain to women as if they were property may sound particularly off-putting to modern ears (e.g., Exod. 22:16-17). Turning away from such laws may help us to reflect on how much or how little we have advanced in our contemporary world, away from the notion of women as property and toward a true equality of women and men in our society, our homes, and our churches. In general, it may be useful to reflect on how great the distance actually is be-

---

14. The sharp distinction between case law and absolute law, or casuistic and apodictic law, goes back to Albrecht Alt, who delineated the two types in his essay "The Origins of Israelite Law," *Essays on Old Testament History and Religion* (Garden City: Doubleday, 1967), 101-71. Alt also argued that absolute law was unique to Israel. Common sense would argue that absolute law, even if no literary parallels have been found in ancient Near Eastern literature, is a basic type of legal formula, common to human legislation. In the Bible, moreover, the two types are found mixed as, e.g., in Exod. 22:21-27.

tween ourselves and the biblical text and to address issues for which the gulf between the world of "now" and "then" is not as wide as we might have assumed.

More important, we must search for an ethos that inspires the entire set of covenant rules. I have cast many of the subsets of laws under the heading "protection" and pointed out that the entire Book of the Covenant exhibits a movement toward greater emphasis on the protection of the weak and vulnerable. I believe that here lies a key to finding a core teaching, one that is moreover not isolated in the biblical text or the Torah. Two sections of laws will bring us closer to this idea.

The Ones Who Cry to God (Exodus 22:21-27)

Exodus 22:21-27[15]

21. And a stranger you must not wrong or oppress
     for strangers you were in the land of Egypt.
22. Any widow or orphan you must not abuse.
23. If you abuse, yes abuse, them,[16]
     when they cry, yes cry, out to me,
     I will listen, yes listen, to their cry.
24. And my wrath will burn
     and I will slay you with the sword,
     and your women will become widows,
     your children orphans.

25. If money you lend my people,
     the poor with you,
     you must not be to them as a creditor,
     you must not exact interest from them.
26. If you take in pledge, yes pledge,
     the cloak of your neighbor,
     at sunset return it to him.
27. For it is his only covering,
     his cloak for his skin;
     in what shall he lie down?
     And when he cries to me,
     I will listen, for compassionate am I.

15. Hebrew text 22:20-26.
16. The use of the plural pronoun for the first part of the unit is warranted by the sense of the passage and supported by certain versions and manuscripts.

Two subsections address a topic in two ways. The first (vv. 21-24) begins by categorically forbidding the "abuse" and "oppression" of three groups of people, "strangers," "orphans," and "widows." The verb "to oppress" we have considered already as a word that connotes physical and psychological violence (see above, 29). The verb "abuse" (Hebrew *yanah*) is a general word for violence, perhaps with the connotation of extortion, which would fit this context. About the already discussed term "stranger" (see above, 26-28), I reiterate here that this word indicates the person who is not by circumstances part of the "in" group, who exists on the margins of the society.[17] The motivation provided for refraining from abusive and oppressive practices toward this group is the standard one of the people's own experience of being "strangers in the land of Egypt," and I have already explored the significance of this phrase (see above, 29-30).

The "stranger" occurs here in conjunction with two other categories of vulnerable people, "widows" and "orphans," a combination which is most commonly found in the book of Deuteronomy. In the context of the ancient world of the Bible, widows (single women living without the protection of a male), together with orphans ("fatherless" children), led lives on the brink of destitution and even extinction. Life without protection of a male figure was extremely tenuous. Protection of widows and orphans is also common in ancient Near Eastern lawgiving outside of ancient Israel. Protection of the stranger, certainly to the extent that it is provided in the Torah, was not known elsewhere in ancient Near Eastern laws, even though a common cultural feature would be expansive hospitality toward guests, also outside of Israel.[18] Strangers are not precisely guests, although they may fall into this category. We take note that the word "stranger" in the Hebrew sentence stands in first place, lending emphasis to the issue.

17. For the full discussion of the category, see above, 26-28 and notes. Cf. also the following definition from Koehler-Baumgartner: "גֵּר is a man who (alone or with his family) leaves village and tribe because of war (2S 4:3, Is 16:4), famine (Ru 1:1), epidemic, blood guilt etc. and seeks shelter and residence at another place, where his right of landed property, marriage and taking part in jurisdiction, cult and war has been curtailed; *HAL*, 1:201.

18. Fitzpatrick-McKinley claims that "care for the גֵּר" was "commonly advised" in Mesopotamia and bases herself on observations made on the subject by Karel van der Toorn; 122. Van der Toorn's actual comments on this subject are more tentative than we are led to believe by Fitzpatrick-McKinley, and neither one of these scholars is able to cite textual evidence for their opinion. See Karel van der Toorn, *Sin and Sanction in Israel and Mesopotamia* (Assen: Van Gorcum, 1985), 16. See also Joe M. Sprinkle, *The Book of the Covenant: A Literary Approach.* JSOTSup 174 (Sheffield: JSOT, 1994), 172: "The regulation on the sojourner shows an enlightened attitude towards non-Israelites for which there is no parallel in Mesopotamian law." Also Christiana van Houten, *The Alien in Israelite Law* (Sheffield: JSOT, 1991), 34.

Throughout the passage the demands are directly addressed to the second person, "you," an unusual feature for the style of the Book of the Covenant. After the introductory lines, prohibiting oppression and abuse of certain categories of people, the text changes in tone and increases in intensity. Verbs are repeated for emphasis: "abuse, yes abuse"; "they cry, yes cry"; "I will listen, yes listen." More surprising, God appears in this text in the first person, which is, outside of the regulations concerning worship, highly unusual for the Book of the Covenant. As in the Ten Covenant Words, God here addresses the community directly; it is once again a case of "I" addressing "You."

Beside the standard motivation cited for not oppressing strangers, "for strangers you were in the land of Egypt," a new motivation for refraining from such behavior toward widows and orphans is introduced. God, speaking in the first person, announces: "when they cry, yes cry, out to me, I will listen, yes, listen to their cry. And my wrath will burn and I will slay you. . . ." Here the motivation to avoid abusive behavior is a threat from Godself. It does not sound attractive to those who would rather not face a punitive God, but in ignoring this idea we miss something vital about the nature of the God of the Bible. The abused cry directly to God, and God hears their cry and acts on it.[19] By the mistreatment of the disadvantaged and by their crying out the passion of God is kindled to such a degree that perpetrators of injustice will become victims themselves. The text represents a passionate outburst and brings home the uncomfortable truth that God's passion for justice for the weak ones has consequences for those who abuse power. The unit opens with a potential victim, the "stranger," and a "you," and it ends with an "I," God. This is between God and the community. "You," as covenant partner, are not to victimize those who are already weak and vulnerable because of their position in the society. It is in "my," God's, character to pay attention to the cry of the oppressed. As I once heard "your" cry, children of Israel, when you were abused in Egypt, and held the Egyptians accountable, so you will be held accountable if you mete out similar treatment to the disadvantaged among you.

It is of the utmost significance that precisely at this juncture, where groups appear that are weak by their social position and therefore potentially victims of abuse, God enters the picture, not only in the first person, but with a statement about God's inclination toward the ones who cry out to God. This point is further elaborated, now in a positive way, in the next subunit,

---

19. As James L. Kugel observes, it is the cry of the victims that unleashes the events that will result in the punishment of the community: "I am powerless *not* to react God seems to say, once the abused party cries out to Me"; *The God of Old*, 110.

Exodus 22:25-27. Here it concerns those who are called "the poor." No interest shall be exacted from those who have nothing to give, and a pledge necessary for their physical protection must be returned at the point when they need it, at sundown. The phrasing, "my people, the poor with you" (v. 25), is of interest. It could be that we should read this as the poor who are members of the community (i.e., "my people"). At the same time, "the poor with you" may be understood as an elaboration of "my people." That is to say, the poor in the community constitute in a special way God's people. Subsequently, the idea is reiterated that God listens to the cry of the victim ("I will listen" [v. 27]), this time with a different ending than in verse 24. Here the text reads, "for compassionate am I." The entire unit ends with a statement about God's nature as compassionate (Hebrew *hannun*).

As in the Ten Covenant Words, the regulations in this section lay down a general demand. It is not specified what refraining from oppression and abuse toward stranger, widow, and orphan might entail. Other texts in the Torah will fill in some of these specifics. Unlike the Ten Covenant Words, the consequences of violating the demand *are* spelled out, with God exacting the price of experiencing equal deprivation on the part of the community that metes out such treatment to the most vulnerable. God's speaking in the first person throughout the section lends the text great weight. Here it concerns not the human cost that is required for violating neighbor relations in the community. Here, God in person threatens to intervene if this law is not followed. The ending of the unit, with its emphasis on God's "compassion," turns the threat in a positive direction. As James L. Kugel has pointed out in his discussion of these verses, the adjective used here, together with its partner "merciful," is reserved for God alone and is never used of human beings in the Hebrew Bible. God is "axiomatically compassionate."[20]

The Heart of the Stranger (Exodus 23:1-9)

Of all the social regulations found in the Book of the Covenant, there is only one that is stated twice, and that is the law regarding the stranger. In addition, the stranger is included in those who benefit from Shabbat rest. This repeated appearance of the stranger on the scene testifies to an ongoing concern for this category of people and to ongoing issues presented by the presence of

---

20. Hebrew *rahum* and *hannun* occur together in one of the best-known texts describing God's nature, Exod. 34:6: "Then the Holy One passed by in front of him and called out: Holy One, Holy One, a God merciful and compassionate, slow to anger and full of devotion and truth." For a discussion of these texts, see Kugel, *The God of Old*, 129-36.

strangers. We have already briefly considered the statement regarding the stranger in Exod. 23:9, and I here present the entire section for our reflection.

Exodus 23:1-9

1. You must not spread baseless rumors.
   You must not join hands with the wicked,
   to act as a malicious witness.
2. You must neither side with the majority to do wrong
   — you must not give perverse testimony in a dispute
   so as to pervert it in favor of the majority —
3. You must not privilege the great[21] in their disputes.

4. When you encounter your enemy's ox or donkey wandering,
   you must return it to him.
5. If you see the donkey of one who hates you
   lying down under its burden,
   and would refrain from raising it,
   you must nevertheless raise it
   together with the one who hates you.

6. You must not pervert the justice
   due to your poor in their disputes.
7. From a false charge you must keep far.
   The innocent and the righteous
   you must not kill,
   for I will not acquit the wicked.
8. A bribe you must not take,
   for a bribe blinds open eyes,
   and perverts the cause of the righteous.
9. A stranger you must not oppress.
   You yourselves know the heart of the stranger,
   for strangers you were in the land of Egypt.

As in Exodus 22:21-27, the regulations are addressed to the second person and are framed in the negative form "you must not," except for the ones in the middle section (vv. 4-5). The "majority," the "wicked," and the "powerful" are not to prevail because of their might. The "poor" are due justice, and the innocent need protection to preserve their life. Gradually in the text, the

---

21. Reading *gadol* for *dal.* For the identical phrase *tehdar gadol,* see Lev. 19:15. It is very unlikely that the Torah would express a demand for not favoring the poor.

dictums are enlarged by motive clauses, "for. . . ." Three such clauses appear in the final section (vv. 6-9). Providing a motivation for following a law is thought to have been unique to ancient Israel, and it is always of interest to consider the specific motivation offered. Here there are not only three motive clauses, but they each represent a different variety of motive. First is the fact of God's interest in the "innocent and the righteous" (v. 7) so that God will personally hold accountable those who do them violence, a motivation reminiscent of Exod. 22:24. Second is the fact that bribes damage impartiality and thus "pervert the cause of the righteous" (v. 8). This type of motive is a logical one: if you do this, then this and that happens. The third motive clause is the one of the community's own experience (v. 9). *Because* they themselves have experienced humiliation, oppression, and abuse in the land of bondage, they themselves must not mete out such treatment to those who are vulnerable in their midst. This motivation, often stated in connection with the prohibition against oppressing the stranger, we found also in 22:21-27. In 23:9, however, we find in addition the most peculiar and unique motivation, that the community "knows the heart of the stranger." As stated earlier, this text not only declares that the children of Israel had "intimate acquaintance with the *self* or the *being* of the stranger," but it also by implication "calls the community to *become* strangers in the land of Egypt" and "to gain intimate knowledge of the stranger's existence" (see above, 31).

The construction of the passage is worth comment. A series of absolute proscriptions is interrupted by two positive laws having to do with an animal that is lost or overburdened (vv. 4-5). Stylistically, these two create an interesting space between sets of rules that are in the terse, somewhat brusque mode of the absolute regulations (vv. 1-3 and 6-7). Verses 4-5 open up breathing room by describing possible incidents that may happen in an agricultural environment and how one should behave in the face of them. The change in style goes together with a sharpening of focus. Here the recipients of the action are not a general group, "the majority," "the wicked," "the poor," "the innocent and righteous," but an animal and its owner, more specifically, "your enemy" and "one who hates you." In addition, these two regulations are put in positive form, "you must," "you must," in counterpoint to the series of "you must not" in the surrounding verses.

The incidents described in an almost leisurely style in verses 4 and 5 are common enough occurrences in their context, and providing for some type of appropriate behavior in the face of them should be equally common. What is uncommon here is that in both cases of the provisions, the owner is said to be not "a neighbor" but "your enemy" and "one who hates you." The two parties that are to receive protective care from members of the community are thus unlikely candidates, enemies and animals. The phrase "together with the one who hates you" (v. 5) is especially telling and speaks to the degree of co-operation that is demanded from individuals as well as the loyalty they are to extend one another in spite of feuds, dislikes, and all that occurs among humans in their social context.[22] The intended beneficiary of the action is no doubt the human being, but it is undeniable that the animal benefits also.

As in Exodus 22:21-27, God appears in this text in person, addressing the community directly, a feature which lends the words added force. Verse 9 comes at the end of a list of those who should not suffer from abusive treatment. All the categories have now been paraded before the ears of the listener, and they may all be embodied in the *ger*, who could easily be "poor," "innocent," "righteous," whose life may be forfeit, and who may also be considered an "enemy."

For the second time, the Book of the Covenant turns toward the subject of the stranger as an obvious recipient of protection. Both in Exodus 22 and here, the laws are stated negatively. But this is not the last word that has been said about the stranger in the Book of the Covenant or the Torah. Indeed, there are more regulations in the Torah concerning appropriate behavior to the stranger, and they range over a wider area than is the case for any other law. Immediately following the passage under discussion here, the Sabbath regulations specify the "stranger" as one of the categories to benefit from the rest provided by the seventh day, together with "ox," "donkey," and "servant." Protection demanded for the stranger, from the very specific to the very general, is a requirement in all the law codes of the Torah.[23]

If there is an ethos that inspires the entire Book of the Covenant, it is that the God of ancient Israel, to whom the people owe exclusive loyalty, requires of the people who live within the divine-human covenant relationship to protect those who are most vulnerable in the society and to refrain from pushing them further to the margins and exploiting their weakness. The two passages we have considered in some detail are typical for the attention paid to this issue in the Book of the Covenant, a text I would place in an early period of the history of ancient Israel before the arrival of the monarchy, perhaps in the era of early settlement.

---

22. Although this text does not speak of "loving one's enemy," it appears to come very close to that notion, "love" in the Bible always being a matter of an orientation toward and acting upon it, rather than one of feeling.

23. According to Diether Kellerman, the noun *ger* occurs 92 times in the Bible, with more than half of the occurrences in the Torah, of which the great majority concern themselves with regulations addressing appropriate behavior toward the stranger; "gur," *Theological Dictionary of the Old Testament,* ed. G. Johannes Botterweck and Helmer Ringgren (Grand Rapids: Wm. B. Eerdmans, 1977), 2:439-49.

The Life of Holiness (Leviticus 19)

The esteem for and love of the stranger is a reflection of our love of God. In the alien we are first and foremost bidden to discover the presence of the redeeming God and thereby to reinforce our bonds with all humanity.[24]

To most scholars the book of Leviticus is a composite text consisting of different laws dating from different times in ancient Israel's history.[25] The text is traditionally assigned to the Priestly school of writers or editors, those who had a great interest in matters of religious rites and their orderly execution, and is dated to the Babylonian exilic or postexilic period. Most scholars also assume that much of the material in Leviticus predates that period. Our focus here is on chapter 19, at the beginning of the Holiness Code, so called because in these chapters the community is reminded to imitate the *holiness* of God: "Holy you shall be/for I the Holy One your God am holy" (Lev. 19:2; 20:26). In rough outline, the first half of Leviticus consists of texts that relate specifically to the priesthood, different sacrifices and the correct way of executing them, ordination rites, etc. (chs. 1–10), followed by food and purity laws (chs. 11–15). These regulations may be summarized as dealing with what and who is acceptable to approach God and how this approach should take place. This section, which may be typified as *instructions for the priests*, culminates in Leviticus 16, with its detailed description of the special feast day of Atonement. Then follow instructions that are directed to the entire people (chs. 17–27), *the instructions of the priests*, often called the Holiness Code.[26] This latter half includes regulations for human behavior in all aspects of life, with chapter 19 providing an overview and a reformulation of many of the laws of the Book of the Covenant.

Because of its focus on ritual and manner of sacrifice, this is not a favorite Bible book for the Christian community, and certainly its usefulness is not everywhere immediately apparent. In the Torah the central place of this text serves as a pointer to its importance. Its name in Hebrew, *Wayyiqra*, "He (God) Called," directs attention to the divine origin of this instruction. Today still, also for Christians, Leviticus may at least serve to remind the community

24. Plaut, 1410.

25. See, e.g., Rolf Rendtorff, *The Old Testament* (Philadelphia: Fortress, 1986), 144-46. But compare Mary Douglas's view of this text as an elegant and profound unity; *Leviticus as Literature* (Oxford: Oxford University Press, 1999).

26. For an illuminating review of the content of Leviticus, see Baruch A. Levine, *Leviticus* (Philadelphia: Jewish Publication Society, 1989), xvi-xvii.

of believers that a faithful life consists in an orientation to both God and neighbor and that the approach to God needs to be studied and practiced. Moreover, some parts of the book, as chapter 19, are concerned with all aspects of life, social as well as religious.

The requirement for holiness is remarkable, in that it is addressed to the entire people rather than to a group of specialists who occupy themselves with "holy" things. Leviticus 19 is addressed through the agency of Moses to the "entire congregation of the children of Israel" (v. 2). The entire set of regulations contained in the chapter is punctuated by the phrase "I am the Holy One," six times with the words "your God" added.[27] The holiness of the people as expressed in their conduct toward God and neighbor is in this way closely tied to the nature of God.

Chapter 19 opens with reverence for parents and the importance of Sabbath, then continues with appropriate ways of making a specific sacrifice, and from verse 9 on reviews various requirements of a social nature, interspersed with obligations related to religious matters (vv. 21-22, 26-28). Here, one encounters reformulations of each of the Ten Words of the Covenant and many subjects that occur elsewhere in the Book of the Covenant.

The Surplus of the Harvest

The following formulations bearing on human relations in the community deserve closer attention within the context of this discussion:

Leviticus 19:9-10, 15-16
9. When reaping the harvest of your land,
    you shall not finish to the edge of your field for harvest
    and the gleanings of your harvest you shall not glean.
10. And your vineyard you shall not pick bare
    or glean the fallen fruit of your vineyard.
    For the poor and the stranger you shall leave it;
    I am the Holy One your God.
    . . . .
15. You shall not do evil in judgment:
    you shall not disadvantage the poor,[28]

---

27. Vv. 3, 4, 10, 12, 14, 16, 18, 25, 28, 30, 31, 32, 34, 37.
28. "To lift the face of the poor" is generally understood to mean partiality in favor of, but it can also mean to pay attention out of negative prejudice. The translation I present here is cogently argued by Günther Schwarz in his note on this verse; "Begünstige nicht . . . ?" *Biblische*

nor shall you privilege the great;
with righteousness you shall judge a co-citizen.
16. You shall not go around slandering your people;
you shall not profit by the blood of your neighbor —
I am the Holy One.

The list concerns itself with the protection of and provision for those who are not in a position to protect themselves or adequately provide for themselves, here named as "the poor" (twice), "the stranger," "a co-citizen," "your people," "your neighbor." "The poor" appear twice in these verses, and they are joined by "the stranger" as a class of people in need of special protection and provision (v. 10). Verses 11-14 focus on the "neighbor" as a potential victim of wrongdoing, and the natural sequence from "poor/stranger" to "neighbor" testifies to the understanding that the neighbor to be protected and provided for is especially the neighbor in need.[29]

Love for the Neighbor

The subject of appropriate concern for and care of the neighbor is taken up once again in verses 17-18:

Zeitschrift 19 (1975): 100. Schwarz argues that the expression *nasa panim* may be understood both in a positive or negative sense and that a translation should be decided case by case. Since *dal* and *gadol* are antithetical, the verbs may also be antithetical. He also points out that the problem with the treatment of the poor is not that they are favored but that they are always and everywhere disadvantaged. In terms of content, similar arguments may be brought to bear on the reading of *gadol* for *dal* in Exod. 23:3 (see above, 189 and note). In terms of the phrasing, see also Deut. 10:17 (200). I was also made aware by my students during a stay in France that the negative practice of "lifting the face" in order to identify a person's ethnic identity and put him under suspicion of a crime committed still occurs.

29. The New Testament gives witness to the same understanding of this *torah* when it provides the parable of the Good Samaritan (Luke 10:25-37). This parable arises out of conversation that centers on how the commandments to love God and neighbor should be interpreted and lived out. The lawyer who comes to Jesus with his questions is concerned with what he must "do," and Jesus asks him how he "reads" what is "written in the Torah" (Luke 10:26). When the lawyer responds with the directives to love God and the neighbor, Jesus proceeds to unfold the story of the victimized Jew who is aided by a Samaritan. These two were at the time "strangers" to one another, and hostile strangers at that. Thus in Jesus' reading of the Torah, the love of God and neighbor is transposed into *doing* the work of justice and compassion to the one most in need in one's location. Here Jesus articulates for a recognizable situation of his day the same principles as those expressed in Exod. 23:4-5 and Lev. 19. See further 268-75.

Leviticus 19:17-18

17. You shall not hate your brother in your heart;
    reprove, yes reprove a member of your community
    and do not bear guilt on his account.
18. You shall not avenge or bear a grudge
    against the children of your people;
    you shall love your neighbor as yourself.
    I am the Holy One.

In these lines, two negative requirements of "hate"/"revenge"/"bear a grudge" are balanced by positive mandates, "reprove, yes reprove," and "you shall love." The negatives center on the wrongful nurture of hatred and resentment. The positives begin with the admonition to give voice to reproach rather than foster animosity in silence, and they end with the demand for "love" for the neighbor. Seen in the light of the earlier mandates of care for and defense of the destitute, it is clear that love of the neighbor finds its fullest expression in extending the self especially to those who are most in need. In the Gospels, Jesus' illustration of the love for God and the neighbor in the parable of the Good Samaritan (Luke 10:25-37) gives evidence of the thematic consistence on this all-important theme of the Old and the New Testament.

Love for the Stranger

There is yet more to be said about what constitutes the emulation of God's holiness:

Leviticus 19:33-34

33. When a stranger lives with you
    as a stranger in the land,
    you must not wrong him.
34. As a native among you,
    so shall the stranger be,
    who lives as a stranger with you;
    and you shall love him as yourself,
    for you were strangers in the land of Egypt.
    I am the Holy One, your God.

Here, as in Exodus 22:21 and 23:9, one encounters the prohibition of oppressing the stranger, followed by the appeal to the past experience of the community. But, in this passage the *torah* provides further specification, turning the negative command in a positive direction by requiring first equal treatment of these people, "as a native among you/so shall the stranger be." Finally, the prescriptions culminate in the mandate "to love" the stranger as "yourself." The stranger must be treated the same as the neighbor. These two, the prohibition "to oppress" and the mandate "to love" constitute the two outer markers of the requirements pertaining to the behavior and attitude toward the stranger. Not to oppress, as it is found in Exodus 23:9, includes an avoidance of certain behaviors, physical and psychological abuse among them. It includes not further depriving strangers of the rights to which they have no automatic access. In Leviticus 19, the avoidance of certain treatments is turned then toward the most positive expression of neighborly relations possible, that of love. It is not sufficient to avoid certain kinds of treatment. The members of the congregation of the children of Israel must dedicate themselves to the well-being of the stranger, to the upholding and restoration of these people that do not naturally benefit from being members of the covenant people. Leviticus 19:34 contains a new way to express the extent of what it means "to know the heart of the stranger" (Exod. 23:9).

The holiness of the community consists in living out of the commandment to love, to love the neighbor, to love the stranger, to love the self.[30] In Leviticus we find a progression from the category neighbor to that of stranger. In Jesus' parable of the Good Samaritan there is a conflation of neighbor with stranger.[31] In between the outer markers, the prohibition of "oppression" and the mandate to "love," specific provisions occur as the directive to make available surplus from the harvest stated earlier in Leviticus 19 (vv. 9-10; see above, 193). The specifics of making possible the sustenance and survival of the stranger provide examples of how the mandates not to oppress on the one hand and to love on the other hand may be put into effect. The book of Deuteronomy furnishes many such examples, as we shall see. While the one marker, that of prohibiting oppression, sets boundaries, the other marker, of

---

30. Walter Kaiser, in commenting on Leviticus, pauses at Lev. 19:18 with lengthy remarks on the importance of the injunction of neighborly love but pays scant intention to the love for the stranger required in v. 34; "The Book of Leviticus," *The New Interpreter's Bible* 1 (Nashville: Abingdon, 1994), 1133-34.

31. As observed by A. David Bos: "One of the ethical guidelines that may be inferred from these texts is that of hospitality to the stranger — the stranger being anyone from whom we feel separated because of his or her 'otherness.' That otherness may be based on poverty or disability as much as on cultural or physical difference. The love that humanity owes God binds humanity together by virtue of God's compassionate covenant with all of creation including humanity. That promise makes every stranger a neighbor in and with our common home, the earth"; *Bound Together: A Theology for Ecumenical Community Ministry* (Cleveland: Pilgrim, 2005), 138.

loving the stranger, removes all boundaries and pushes the requirements of appropriate treatment to an extreme of dedication. *How* the outer markers are put into effect will change over time. The outer markers themselves are determinative as continuous ethical requirements that remain constant for religious communities that view themselves as inheritors of both the promises and the directives laid down in the Torah.

Priestly Regulation in Historical Context

Besides Leviticus 19, the stranger occurs elsewhere in priestly legislation to specify that the same laws apply to the *ger* as those that apply to the member of the community of the "children of Israel." Both in Leviticus and in Numbers the stranger is regularly included in the requirements for ritual and worship. Numbers 15:14-16 provides a characteristic example:

Numbers 15:14-16
14. When a stranger lives with you as a stranger,
    or one who is among you in your generations,
    and makes a fire offering,
    a pleasant odor to the Holy One,
    as you do, so shall he do.
15. Assembly![32] One law for you,
    and for the stranger who lives as a stranger;
    a law forever for your generations;
    like you, like the stranger it will be before the Holy One.
16. One instruction and one regulation
    will serve for you
    and for the stranger who lives as a stranger with you.

Four times the text states in four different ways that the *ger* is included in the rules for bringing sacrifice. It could hardly be stated more emphatically that this instruction is directed to everyone who lives in the community. The outsider to the tribes is thus not excluded from participation in worship, or from rules that govern purity and impurity.[33] In terms of the latter, it is especially important to note that purity and impurity do not depend on the *class* or the *category* of people to which someone belongs but rather

---

32. In retaining the word *qahal* and in the translation, I follow the example of Fox, 732.
33. See also Num. 9:14; 15:29; Lev. 17:15; 24:16; 24:22; 25:35.

on the *condition* of the person, regardless of his or her antecedents or status in the community.

If the Priestly material can indeed be dated to the postexilic period, this was not a time that stands out for its welcome to outsiders. Both Ezra and Nehemiah furnish abundant examples of hostile attitudes and practices to those that were considered not to belong to the community that reconstituted itself in Judah. Even those who claim allegiance to the same God are warded off and kept away from the work of rebuilding and participation in reconstruction (e.g., Ezra 4:1-4). If the tale told in Ezra 9–10 is taken at face value, vulnerable members of the community, women outside of the tribal descendance and their children, were actually banished from the community.[34] The Priestly documents in Leviticus and Numbers offer a strong counterpoint to this theme of exclusion. Strangers are welcomed in the worship practices of the children of Israel and are subject to the same regulations. In social and community life, they are to be provided for and protected and they are to be loved. As Mary Douglas observes, "The same laws which make the Jews safe, make the stranger safe, very important in a community about to divide itself on the basis of pure descent, and possibly about to exclude Samarians."[35] In Douglas's perspective, the Priestly redactor is a person with "strong political concerns, with anti-xenophobic and anti-government views."[36] The setting of these laws in the period of Moses and the Sinai covenant makes the Priestly perspective on the position strangers together with the practices toward them required of the community all the more authoritative.

The Company of Strangers: Deuteronomy

The Deuteronomic material reflects concern with just treatment of the stranger throughout. Moreover, in Deuteronomy the entire scope of attitudes and practices required in the Torah may be found, from the prohibition to oppress to the requirement to love, with directives for the inclusion of the stranger in worship and other religious practices of the community, as well as specific provisions for the welfare of the stranger in between these two poles.[37] Often, the stranger is accompanied by the "orphan and the widow" as

---

34. See also Ezra 3:1-3; Neh. 13:3, 25; Ezek. 44:7. For a discussion of the attitudes reflected in the Ezra/Nehemiah material, see Johanna W. H. van Wijk-Bos, *Ezra, Nehemiah, and Esther*, 26-28, 33-48.

35. Mary Douglas, *In the Wilderness*, 152.

36. Douglas, *In the Wilderness*, 159.

37. See, e.g., Deut. 1:16; 5:14; 16:11, 14; 26:11; 29:11; 31:12.

a category of folk needing special protection and provision. The more general requirements toward strangers occur in chapter 24:

> **Deuteronomy 24:17-19**
> 17. You shall not bend the justice of stranger and fatherless;
>   you shall not take in pawn the clothing of a widow.
> 18. And you shall remember that you were a servant in Egypt,
>   and the Holy One your God ransomed you from there;
>   therefore I myself am commanding you to do this thing.

This quite general prohibition is then followed by very specific instructions of provision somewhat akin to the ones found in Leviticus 19:

> 19. When you harvest your harvest in your field,
>   and forget a sheaf standing in the field,
>   do not return to take it;
>   for the stranger, the fatherless, and the widow it shall be,
>   in order that the Holy One your God may bless you in
>   all the work of your hands.

Subsequently, similar provisions are made for the olive grove and the vineyard (vv. 20-22), concluding with a motivation in verse 22, the remembrance of servitude in Egypt that is identical to that of verse 18. Verse 17 finds its negative counterpart in Deuteronomy 27:19, where the one who perverts the justice of the stranger, fatherless, and widow is cursed.

A comprehensive and foundational statement regarding the stranger may be found in Deuteronomy 10:12-22. This section begins in verse 12 with a rhetorical question about the requirements God has laid on the people, with the typical Deuteronomic response following that they should "revere" God, "walk in God's ways," "love" and "serve" God "with heart and soul," and "follow God's commandments" (vv. 12-13). God has, after all, chosen this community out of love. The unit ends with the same theme, evoking again the service, reverence, and closeness to God demanded of those who have so benefited from God's favor (vv. 20-22). The middle section (vv. 17-19), which at first continues the theme of God's praise, takes an unexpected turn:

> **Deuteronomy 10:17-19**
> 17. For the Holy One your God,
>   is God of gods, and Lord of lords;

> the great God, mighty and awesome,
> who does not lift the face[38]
> and does not take a bribe,
> 18. doing justice for the fatherless and the widow,
> and loving the stranger by giving him food and a cloak.
> 19. And you shall love the stranger
> for you were strangers in the land of Egypt.

All the directives of verses 12-22 are oriented to the people's relationship to God, a favorite theme of Deuteronomy. These directives alternate with descriptions of God's love and care for the community in a context of praise for God's greatness. The emphasis on God's love set in the framework of God's greatness strikes a familiar note for this material. It serves to emphasize the exclusive loyalty owed to God by the people of God's favor. In continuity with this theme, the beginning of verse 17 opens with a paean of praise for the might and the awesomeness of this God. But then the verse takes a turn. Rather than continuing with a mention of God's great and awesome deeds (see v. 21), or with the obligations this puts on the people, what follows is an illustration of God's greatness and awesomeness as evident from God's dealings with people in the sphere of justice. This may strike our ears as incongruous, but the text pursues the imagery to make its point.

The first example consists of a set of two phrases, of which the second one is entirely clear. The phrase "who does not take a bribe" indicates that God is not influenced by those who have the power brought by material goods, since bribes are offered by those who can afford it. The first phrase, "who does not lift the face," is less clear. It is possible that the most common translation here is correct and that it indicates God's lack of partiality in general.[39] It is also possible that "to lift the face of someone" is not meant positively at all but negatively: to lift the face of those regularly disenfranchised in order to discriminate and treat badly.[40] I understand the phrase in this way in this verse. God does not discriminate against the poor and is not blinded by the power of the rich. Rather, as the text goes on to say, God's protective care goes out to the "fatherless," "the widow," and "the stranger," taking care of them concretely and substantively by providing for their sustenance and shel-

38. For a discussion of this expression, see above, 193-94 and note.

39. So NRSV: "who is not partial." Cf. Fox, 898: "he who lifts up no face (in favor)." See also Lev. 19:15 (above, 193-94 and note 28).

40. Such a practice is apparently not uncommon in contemporary France, as students told me during my sojourn there.

ter.[41] The latter constitutes God's "doing justice." In fact, "doing justice" and "loving" are the equivalent terms in the parallel construction of verse 18. God's doing of justice is the equivalent of God's love for the needy, the orphan, the widow, and the stranger, which means God's providing for them. Logically, for the human community their love for the stranger demands of them the same providing for and taking care of. As Mark Biddle observes: "To do justice for them means to provide for them in an 'extra-' or 'supra-legal' fashion, to protect them when the law does not or cannot. In this context, the criteria for 'justice' are not legal matters of rights and privileges, but the ethical and humanitarian values of decency, fairness, and compassion."[42]

The Identity of the Stranger

We have reviewed the major requirements in regard to the stranger as they came to ancient Israel in different historical periods, from its earliest establishment as a covenant community, through its history in the land of the promise, until the era following the Babylonian exile. It is clear that concern for the well-being of the stranger was a permanent one throughout biblical history. There is no regulation in terms of the common life of the community that is as frequently mentioned, nor is there one that embraces as many provisions or the depth and scope of its demands. We may at this point, however, raise the question once more regarding the identity of the stranger. When this subject arose at an earlier point, I stated that "the *ger* has come from outside the family, the clan, the tribe, or the entire people to stay with the community" (see above, 26-27). As time went on, the stranger may have coincided with the resident from elsewhere who had become an adherent of worship practices and basic beliefs of the community where he resided, hence the Greek term *prosēlytos*, the "proselyte" or "convert," in the Septuagint. This presence may be reflected in regulations that specify participation of "strangers" in worship and with those who are in need of instruction. There is no warrant, however, provided by the texts pertaining to the stranger in the Torah to limit the category of stranger to that of convert.[43]

---

41. It would, after all, be curious and incongruous to record God's impartiality just before a statement about God's partiality for the poor. In terms of biblical depictions of God, impartiality does not come to the fore elsewhere as a divine quality and sounds more like a stereotypical Anglo-Saxon virtue than one that should be assigned to the God of the Bible.

42. Mark E. Biddle, *Deuteronomy* (Macon: Smyth & Helwys, 2003), 183.

43. See Karl Georg Kuhn, προσήλυτος, *TDNT*, ed. Gerhard Kittel and Gerhard Friedrich (Grand Rapids: Wm. B. Eerdmans, 1968), 6:727-44.

Of the three categories of "strangers," the *ger*, the *toshav*, and the *nokhri*, the *ger* is most loosely defined and therefore best rendered "stranger" in English, a word that likewise may be understood within a broad range of possibilities, from the resident alien to the person from the next county or state.

CHAPTER 5

Instructions for Life with God

The differentiation between the common life of the community and its relationship to God as it expressed itself in formal worship is a somewhat artificial one. In the Ten Covenant Words, these two aspects belong to the same set of regulations. Yet even there, in the Decalogue, the directives are grouped together, and in the Torah as a whole there are some large clusters of text that are relevant particularly to the regulations of formal worship. Here again, we encounter texts that are rarely, if ever, dealt with in a Christian context. As we consider them across the vast gulf of distance, time, and culture that separates us, we may yet find instruction for our day from this material. I take it up here in order to explore the possible relevance of cultic regulations that relied in the main on animal sacrifice, notions of purity and impurity, and other modes of worship that seem exceedingly foreign.

In regard to worship, we may again locate the development of a motif from the introductory chapters of Genesis. There, we encountered a world that was made and subsequently marred and thus needed mending. One of the ways to restore the relationship between people and God, between the creation and God, is through direct approaches such as sacrifice, prayer, and celebration of holy times (see above, 90-95). The main texts I take up in this section are from the books of Exodus and Leviticus, as we find in this material the regulations concerning the formal apparatus of worship, including the place assigned to it. Formal prayer is not common in the Torah, and the word "to pray," or "to call on the name of God," is rarely used. We will take into consideration, however, textual units in which Moses makes intercession on behalf of the people. Finally, we turn once more to the significance of special holy days, in particular the Day of Atonement.

A Place of Meeting (Exodus 25:1–31:11; 35:1–40:38)

The God who gives the pattern chooses to dwell in the very pattern created.[1]

I have stated in these pages that in the context of the covenant which assumes an initially broken relation, a relation that needs repair, human beings in these stories reach out to God. Worship is the main form this reaching out takes. Like covenant, it assumes a degree of alienation between God and creature. In the material leading up to the covenant-making at Sinai, such reaching out on the part of human beings may be done at any place since presumably God may be found at any place, although some places may be perceived as holier than others. During the covenant ceremony at Sinai, an altar is constructed specifically for the purpose of making appropriate sacrifice. The regulations in the Book of the Covenant regarding sacrifice include the ad hoc construction of altars (Exod. 20:22-26; see above, 181). The notion that there is only one place appropriate for approaching God through formal worship (Deut. 12:2-14) is confined only to certain texts in the Torah.

Almost the entire concluding section of Exodus is devoted to a detailed description of a sanctuary, seven chapters of instruction (Exod. 25–31) followed by six of execution (chs. 35–40). The repeated "you/they will make" of the instructions finds both echo and resolution in the "they made" of the final chapters. Many commentators have observed the parallels between this account and the Priestly account of the creation in Genesis 1:1–2:4a, so that the human "making" of the sanctuary corresponds to God's "making" of the world.[2]

The purpose of the sanctuary is stated early on in the account as follows:

Exodus 25:8-9

8. They will make me a sanctuary
   and I will dwell in their midst.
9. Just as I will show you,

---

1. Terence E. Fretheim, *Exodus*. Interpretation (Louisville: John Knox, 1991), 272.

2. See, e.g., Joseph Blenkinsopp, *The Pentateuch*, 217-19; Fretheim, *Exodus*, 268-272; Jon D. Levenson notes, "The function of these correspondences is to underscore the depiction of the sanctuary as a world, that is, an ordered, supportive, and obedient environment, and the depiction of the world as a sanctuary, that is, a place in which the reign of God is visible and unchallenged, and his holiness is palpable, unthreatened and pervasive"; *Creation and the Persistence of Evil: The Jewish Drama of Divine Omnipotence* (San Francisco: Harper and Row, 1988), 86. So also W. Gunther Plaut, *The Torah*, 598.

the pattern of the dwelling[3]
and the pattern of all the vessels,
so you shall make it.

The most significant visible symbol of God's presence will be the ark containing the stones with the ten words of the covenant in the most holy section of the dwelling. After departure from Sinai, the place where the encounter between God and people had taken place and where the relationship between them had been sealed by the covenant ceremony, the question of God's presence would naturally arise with renewed urgency. The construction of the sanctuary serves to reassure the community of God's abiding presence. It is, however, a *portable* sanctuary, God's presence not being locatable in one specific place but rather with a people as they are on the move. Tangible symbols of ark and altar are allowed, but no visible representations of the Godhead exist in the dwelling, in accordance with the aniconic demands laid upon the people. How difficult to sustain this restriction proved to be is borne out by the story of the golden calf made by Aaron (Exod. 32–34), a story that serves both as bridge between and counterpoint to the sections concerning the sanctuary, God's tent.

Because the dwelling represents God's presence, it is also the place where God's presence is sought in the standard religious ritual of sacrifice (Exod. 29:10-42), handled by the appropriate personnel. Detailed descriptions are devoted to priestly matters, the construction of the altars, priestly clothing, the consecration of the priests, and the correct manner of making sacrifice (chs. 27–29).

The reasons for including a description of a sanctuary in the story of liberation from oppression and subsequent covenant-making are then not difficult to grasp. First, regulated formal worship was and remained of crucial importance throughout ancient Israel's history until the exile and beyond. Second, the sacred tent functioned as a symbol and guarantee of God's "elusive" presence.[4] Third, a special housing is provided by the sanctuary for the

---

3. The Hebrew word translated here as "dwelling" is *mishkan,* most often rendered as "tabernacle" in translations, from the Latin *tabernaculum,* which is how the word is read in the Vulgate. Everett Fox capitalizes the word "Dwelling"; *The Five Books of Moses,* 397; cf. Martin Buber: *"Wohnung"; Die Fünf Bücher der Weisung* (Cologne: Jakob Hegner, 1968), 219. See also Richard Elliott Friedman, who chooses "Tabernacle" and "tent" for the verb "dwell" (Hebrew *shakan*) to indicate the temporary rather than stationary character of the presence of God in the portable sanctuary; *A Commentary on the Torah,* 255.

4. It is very likely that a number of different traditions are combined to describe the making of the portable sanctuary: the tradition of the ark, which may have originally been in-

deposition of the tables with the Ten Covenant Words, the core of the *torah* given for the covenant life.

What remains baffling is the abundance and repetition of detail in the account, creating a "dry as dust recital of everything necessary to build a model house."[5] It is as if the narrator could not get enough of describing and describing yet again all that went into the "making" of the holy dwelling. For the modern reader, whether Jew or Christian, such a text is at best sleep-inducing, and few of us will have the fortitude to read through it from beginning to end.[6] How is one to gather meaning from lists that stipulate coverings and moldings, lampstands and utensils of gold, cloth and hangings of blue, purple and crimson yarn? What is one to make of long lists of measurements and the dizzying array of precious woods, stone, and metals?

This part of Exodus is usually ascribed to the Priestly source and thus would derive from the exilic and postexilic periods, even though the tradition of a sacred tent may long predate that context. The manner of its telling may be intentionally aimed at re-creating a vision of the glory of past worship, of its structures and its patterns. It is almost as if the text paints a word picture, one that is intended to leave one breathless with awe at its richness and opulence, reminding the community perhaps both of what was lost and of the mandate to reconstruct as best as possible a new place where the presence of God could be sought. At the same time, the fact that this particular sanctuary is portable might serve to remind listeners of the inherent tensions between the nature of the free uncontainable presence of God and human desires to locate this presence in a particular *place*.

---

tended as a footstool or a throne of the deity; the tradition of the "tent of meeting," a place where leaders went to receive divine oracles; and, finally, the tradition of a portable sanctuary. Samuel Terrien, who takes a dim view of the religious development in ancient Israel that eventually located the presence of God in a place, holds that "originally both the ark and the tent pointed to an intermittent and elusive presence of the Godhead. They reflected a theology which respected the freedom of Y•hw•h and preserved it from sacerdotal manipulation"; *The Elusive Presence* (San Francisco: Harper & Row, 1978), 186.

It is impossible to say what historical reality may underlie the traditions about the tent/sanctuary/dwelling. Friedman, against the dominant view of biblical scholarship, argues for an actual existence of the structure described in Exod. 25–31; 35–40 and its preservation in the First Temple in Jerusalem; *A Commentary on the Torah*, 263. In my opinion, the opulence and lavishness of the structure are hard to imagine in wilderness times, but it is not unlikely that one tent would be especially set aside for oracular activity, as a depository for the Tables of the Law and as a place for sacrifice.

5. Maarten den Dulk, *Vijf kansen: Een theologie die begint bij Moses* (Zoetermeer: Meinema, 1999), 103 (my translation).

6. Of course, the ancient reader or listener might not have found the recital any more entertaining than do the modern ones. Cf. Fretheim, *Exodus*, 263.

The sanctuaries of my native land, impressive as they are for their beauty, their age, and purity of architectural lines, are not notable for their opulence. Very few churches in the Netherlands made use of stained glass, and such decorations as were originally present were often destroyed during the iconoclasm of the Reformation period. When I read the listings of Exodus 25ff., I am reminded of a visit I once made to a sanctuary in France, the Sainte Chapelle in Paris. It was during a time when few tourists were present, a weekday in the late fall, that I found myself virtually alone in this small ancient space, glowing with the blues, purple, and crimson depictions of biblical tales on its windows, and it literally took my breath. There the holiness of the place was conveyed by its splendor. So perhaps we may consider the word paintings of the Exodus texts about the sacred tent. "The language," observes Terence E. Fretheim, "creates a tabernacle in the minds of those who have none. A sanctuary begins to take shape within, where it can be considered in all of its grandeur and beauty, living once again in memory."[7]

This Is Your God, Israel (Exodus 32–34)

The sole firm and unshakable fact was, in the last resort, that the God could not be seen; and all said and done you cannot actually follow something which you cannot see.[8]

First, it seems as if the newly-minted covenant people are not going anywhere. They linger long at the foot of Mount Sinai — too long perhaps, for they get into trouble almost right away. Eventually, they will trek on toward the land of the promise. But, while the text records no movement until Numbers 10:11ff., when the people finally leave the Mountain, the landscape of the text changes from Exodus 19 on, with regulations for the social and religious life closely interwoven with the narrative. In fact, the greater part of the text is devoted to laws and regulations, while much of the story relates the shortcomings of the people and their failure to preserve their trust in God's promises.

During the pause at Mount Sinai, while Moses lingers in the proximity of God, the people lose sight of the restrictions against physical representation of the Divine and, with the collaboration of Aaron, fashion visible and tangible symbols of the Godhead. In truth, they have lost sight of Moses, their leader, to whom they refer slightingly as "this Moses, the man who brought us

7. Fretheim, *Exodus*, 264.
8. Martin Buber, *Moses*, 151.

up from Egypt" (Exod. 32:1).[9] Naturally, the people clamor for a sign of God's presence. Only through the fervent and repeated intercession of Moses are they saved from utter destruction (32:1–34:35). It is worth noting that the construction of the ark takes place *after* this incident, as if it were a concession to the human desire for visible symbols of God's presence with the people. In Buber's words: "It was necessary to give the people legitimately, that is, in a fashion corresponding to the character of YHVH, that which they had wished to fashion illegitimately; that is, after a fashion running counter to the character of YHVH."[10]

Multiple sources have gone into the creation of these chapters, which give evidence of inconsistencies, episodes that seem out of place, and redundancies. It is not possible within the span of this discussion to unpack this rich and evocative narration in full. I focus therefore on two sections: the making of the calf (32:1-6) and the request for God's presence on the part of Moses (33:12-17). The sacred tent represented God's design, God's pattern for making the approach to God possible and for enabling an encounter with God's presence. The calf represents human efforts to force the issue of God's presence into a recognizable, familiar mold, the bull-calf being a common representation of deities in Canaanite and neighboring regions. The prohibition violated in Exod. 32:1-6 is not in the first place that of making idols but rather of making an image to which deity is assigned, and thus assigning the name of God to an "illusion," which is the foundation for idol worship (see Exod. 20:7 and above, 158, 161).

The story of the request for visible representation, the execution of its making, and the declaration over the calf is told succinctly, without any of the elaboration and repetitions that occurred in the instructions for the making of the sacred tent. The brevity of the story stands in counterpoint to the longwinded leisurely descriptions that precede and follow it, while at the same time word usage and repetitions create echoes that highlight the contrast between the two. There, God instructed the people via Moses' agency to "make" a sanctuary, and God promised to "dwell in their midst." Here, the people instruct Aaron to "make" a deity, an enterprise which will endanger the promise of God's presence with them (Exod. 32:3). The precious metals for the purpose of "making" are gathered by Aaron in this episode, rather than voluntarily offered by the people, and religious ritual follows with an altar and sac-

9. As Buber observed: "All said and done, it is only the man who is followed, and they can all see how often he is uncertain. . . . What kind of guidance is this, after all? And does it not mean that there must be something not quite in order between him and the God, if he cannot produce the God?" *Moses*, 151.

10. Buber, *Moses*, 156-57.

the specifics of God's presence. Thus in the first section, verses 12-13, Moses asks for more *knowledge* from the God who claims to "know" him, Moses. More knowledge is needed about God's plans, "whom you will send," "your ways," and in fact about God, "so I may know you."

God's response to the question of presence in verse 14 is directed to Moses' well-being, as if it is his anxiety at this point that stands in the center. The phrasing, however, leaves ambiguous as to whom God will accompany, since any pronoun as indirect object is lacking in the phrase "my face will go." Not surprisingly, this reply does not provide clarity for Moses as to where God stands with the people, so he renews his plea for God's presence "with us." Moses' "favor" in God's eyes is clearly bound up in the text with the people's "favor," and Moses' fate is not only bound up with God but also with God's people, here called "your people" three times (vv. 13, 16).

The matter of God's presence is between Moses and God but especially and also between God and God's people. It is about the *self* of God, indicated by the emphatic usage of the pronoun "you" in verse 12, and the "face" of God as it represents God's presence and whether it will "go with" the people (vv. 14, 15, 16). The word for people in this passage is worth noting. Referred to by Moses as "this people" in verse 12, the term used thereafter by Moses is "your people," twice coupled with the first person pronoun to indicate Moses. During the first interchange between God and Moses in chapter 32 (32:7-14), the narrator has God referring to the community as "your" (i.e., Moses') "people" (32:7), with Moses turning this around when addressing God and speaking of "your" people (32:11, 12), with a temporary resolution in the wording "his people" of verse 14. Subsequent wording in the second interchange (32:31-34) is "this people" and "the people." In the third interchange the matter of whose people these are has yet to be settled and is moved forward by Moses' words, "see, this nation is your people" (v. 13), and thereafter by linking Moses closely to the people so that each time he speaks of "I and your people" (v. 16).

God consents to Moses' request for divine presence with the people on the basis of the "favor" Moses has in God's "eyes" (33:17). In what follows, the word "favor" (Hebrew *hen*) is echoed in God's self-proclamation in reply to Moses when he asks to "see God's glory"(33:18): "and I will show favor *(hen)* on whom I will show favor" (v. 19). Moses who asked to "see" something gets to "hear" something instead, something that is essential for an understanding of God's nature as one of bestowing "favor/grace" (from the Hebrew root *hanan*) and "mercy" (from Hebrew *rahum*) according to God's freedom. Although Moses will be granted a vision of some kind (33:23; 34:5-9), essentially the vision of God's glory will consist in hearing of God's favor and mercy, the same characteristics to which Moses has appealed in his intercession.

Intercessory prayer is held of great value in the New Testament and in the Christian community today. If there is a model to be found in the text of Exodus 32–34, it may be in the characterization of the beneficiaries of this type of prayer. Moses is himself very angry with the people who have made a mockery of their covenant promises (32:19-22), and yet he prays for them with eloquence, energy, and perseverance. It is not, after all, because of their niceness that the people need Moses' intercession. Although we may be aware of the New Testament admonition to pray for one's "enemies" (Matt. 5:44; cf. Luke 6:28), few congregations today reflect this directive in their liturgical practice.[12] Prayer for others lifts up those we know and love, for whose well-being we are concerned, rather than those who have done us harm, who have caused pain and inflicted hurt. There may a *torah* embedded in the narrative, one thematically consistent with the New Testament admonition to pray for one's enemies, that might help us to reflect on a needed shift in our prayer practices.

At the same time, there is a uniqueness to the account of Moses' intercession in Exodus 32–34 because of the stature of Moses. In this regard Moses' prayers may be compared to those of Jesus, who prayed on behalf of those who participated in his execution. Christians too may look with gratitude to the figure of Moses, who interceded on behalf of God's people so that God's forgiving nature might become clear, also to Christians, latecomers to the "favor" of God.

Following Moses' effective intercession, Exodus 34:10-26 recounts a covenant statement which, as it stands now, must be seen as the divine attempt to repair the broken relationship. It constitutes a renewed promise by God on behalf of the people, this time without reference to past liberative activity (34:10), and referring only to what God will work for them. Tellingly, the obligation to worship the Holy God alone and refrain from idolatry comes first and is the most elaborately stated of the stipulations listed here. On the whole, the list of requirements emphasizes the appropriate ways to worship God, including an emphasis on keeping Shabbat and other holy days.

The actual construction of the wilderness sanctuary concludes the book of Exodus in six chapters (35–40). The recital of an orderly execution of the instructions laid down in chapters 25–31 stands in clear counterpoint to the betrayal, failure, and chaos of chapters 32–34. Once again, as in Genesis 1–3, the biblical text puts side by side the ideal and the messy reality of human life. The Place of Meeting now constructed, all is in readiness for the orderly exe-

---

12. Long and detailed lists of illnesses and difficulties of friends and relatives are the usual focus of intercessory prayer during the Sunday morning worship service. There is nothing against lifting up those in our communities who are in special need, but it could be that we need to be redirected in terms of the intended beneficiaries of intercessory prayer and include also those who are either real or perceived enemies.

cution of ritual as prescribed in the instructions God "called out" to Moses, contained in the book Leviticus.[13]

A Way of Meeting (Leviticus)

The religion of Leviticus turns out to be not very different from that
of the prophets who demanded humble and contrite hearts, or from
the psalmists' love for the house of God.[14]

The construction of the sacred dwelling in the wilderness has set the stage for the next set of instructions concerning proper worship, with which most of Leviticus concerns itself. Of the difficulties embedded in this biblical book for contemporary Christian readers I have already spoken. At that point of the discussion, Leviticus 19 afforded an opportunity to uncover a rich vein of concern for the appropriate, holy life of the community in its social dimensions (see above, 192-97). The question remains whether value and meaning of this text can be assigned only to such passages as may be found in chapter 19 or whether other, more strictly liturgical material may also provide guidance in spite of the vast distance of time, culture, and space. Is it possible to claim with Mary Douglas that "the more closely the text is studied, the more clearly Leviticus reveals itself as a modern religion, legislating for justice between persons and persons, between God and his people, and between people and animals."[15]

If we would like to hold open, at least in principle, the possibility that Mary Douglas is correct, then what is the difficulty in our perceiving this to be so? There are a number of obstacles to a productive reading of Leviticus in the vein that Douglas intends. There is, first of all, the intricacy of its language, much of which is not easily accessible to the contemporary reader, filled with technical terms indicating practices with which there is little familiarity in the Christian world. Not only are there technical terms for which it is difficult to find the correct rendering, but, in the effort to achieve clarity, translations mostly abandon the richness and rhythm of the textual repetitions, so that what was once not only orderly but aesthetically satisfying is lost to us.[16]

13. In Hebrew Leviticus is named *wayyiqra*, "He called," from the opening words of the book, "And the Holy One called to Moses" (Lev. 1:1).

14. Mary Douglas, *Leviticus as Literature*, 1.

15. Douglas, *Leviticus as Literature*, 2.

16. Everett Fox (497) points out that the translation difficulties cause either "overemphasis or strangeness." His own choices for the different words indicating offering, while erring on the

Douglas maintains that Leviticus represents both a particular "style of thought" and a "style of writing" that must be recognized and differentiated from other books in the Torah in order to gain access to this literature.[17] The style of writing is concentric, in rings, rather than linear and logical, somewhat like the style of the nursery rhyme "The House that Jack Built" with its concentric incorporation of each former item together with a new one in subsequent lines.[18]

Even if we are willing, however, through diligent and attentive reading of this text to allow for a certain elegance of style and come somewhat closer to its contents, there are still hindrances to a profitable perception of the material, most of which reside in the fact that the specific practices and perspectives represented in Leviticus do not find resonance in a Christian context.[19]

---

side of strangeness, at least keep the repetitions intact. Certainly, Leviticus exhibits poetic rather than prose patterns. See also Douglas, *Leviticus as Literature*, ch. 3: "Two Styles of Writing."

17. Douglas identifies the style of thought as "mytho-poetical," working with analogies rather than logical explanations, a style she contrasts with that of Deuteronomy: "Instead of explaining why an instruction has been given, or even what it means, it adds another similar instruction, and another and another, thus producing its highly schematized effect"; *Leviticus as Literature*, 18.

18. See Douglas, *Leviticus as Literature*, 54. Another example would be the song "The Old Lady Who Swallowed a Fly," with a succession of animals each consuming the previous one, until "the horse," of which "she died, of course." The fact that the examples are children's rhymes should not lead into thinking of the style of Leviticus as "childish."

In addition, the series of sacrificial offerings are tightly constructed around threes or multiples of three. For example, the first seven chapters are concerned with the proper bringing of various sacrifices, all of them recapitulated in 7:37. Each offering is discussed in clusters of three; thus under the category of offering that is called "a lifting up" (traditionally, "burnt offering") the possibilities are a bull, a sheep or goat, and a bird, each described with its particular mode of sacrifice and closed by the action of turning the offering "into smoke" (1:9, 13 and 17) with the words "it is a lifting up, a firegift of restful aroma for the Holy One" repeated each time. Under the category of "food offering," there are three possibilities of its being offered: raw, prepared, or as first fruits from grain (2:1, 4, 14), with the prepared category again divided into three possible ways of preparation: in the oven, on a griddle, or in a pan. The offering of *shalom* comes in the same three categories as the burnt offering (ch. 3; cf. ch. 1). The "sin offerings," or more appropriately "de-sin offerings," are described in terms of three categories of offenders: "the entire people" (including the "high priest"), "the ruler," and "ordinary citizen" (4:2, 13, 22, 27). Three more "de-sin offerings" are listed, a general one (5:6) covering a list of offenses committed by negligence or unawareness (vv. 1-4), with two variations for those who have not the means to bring the required sacrifice (vv. 7-10, 11-13). Then follow three offerings in the context of reparation, again for sins committed unwittingly (5:14-16, 17-19; 6:1-7). The remainder of ch. 6, together with ch. 7, recapitulates the entire list of offerings, two times three, brought in their appropriate manner, handled by the appropriate personnel, the priests. The text requires close and repeated reading in order to convey its structured elegance.

19. Naturally, the matter of connection with Leviticus lies differently for the world of Ju-

Without claiming an exhaustive treatment of these chapters, I address here three issues that are significant barriers to a contemporary appropriation of Leviticus, at least for Christian readers.

The Acceptable Sacrifice[20]

The issue of bloody sacrifice, ritual slaughter, the main subject of the opening chapters of Leviticus, is certainly a roadblock for many.[21] Seven chapters describing the cutting up of sacrificial animals, the dashing of blood, the consumption of their flesh thus provide no easy access to the rest of the text. In the words of Douglas: "Many consider animal sacrifice strongly repulsive, a barbaric custom, only one step away from human sacrifice."[22]

A few observations may be helpful in regard to this practice: ritual slaughter, of the type prescribed in Leviticus, is an act of piety of the past, and no community is expected to model its liturgical practice literally on the ones reflected in Leviticus 1–7. The practice of ritual slaughter may help us to examine our own practices, not so much of ritual, but of slaughter for consumption of meat. Unless we are ready to critique the violence of our abattoirs, we may not want to be so quick to condemn a consecrated death in which the animal has value and dignity.[23] In some way it is a moot point to condemn the ancient practice, since it no longer exists in the two faiths that are the inheritors of biblical religion, Judaism and Christianity. Rather, a contemplation of the ancient practice may invite us to take a critical look at contemporary practices of execution and consumption of animals.[24]

---

daism for a great part of which regulations present in this book are still in effect today, as the *kashrut* prescriptions and the significance of *Yom Kippur,* even if the specifics of the rituals may have changed.

20. Cf. Ps. 51:17 NRSV (Hebrew 18).

21. Den Dulk (123) observes that the opening chapters of Leviticus "reek of ritual slaughter."

22. Douglas, *Leviticus as Literature,* 66.

23. In discussing this issue, Douglas cites Jean-Louis Durand, according to whom contemporary practices deprive "animals of the dying with meaning and integrity"; *Leviticus as Literature,* 67, citing Durand, "La Bête Grèque, Propositions pour une Topologie des Corps à manger," in *La Cuisine du Sacrifice en Pays Grec,* ed. Marcel Detienne and Jean-Pierre Vernant (Paris: Gallinard, 1979), 133-81.

24. Although there is dispute about this, Douglas holds that Leviticus does not allow profane slaughter: "The extreme sensitivity to bloodshed and loss of life, human or animal, shown throughout the book, is consistent with the prohibition of profane slaughter"; *Leviticus as Literature.* 68. See also the commentary on Lev. 17:3-7 by Baruch J. Schwartz: "The Israelites may not simply slaughter domestic livestock for food; they are required to offer them as a sacrifice of well-being . . . after which they may partake of the offerers' share of the flesh"; "Leviticus," in *The Jewish Study Bible,* 248.

I assume that it is not the notion of sacrifice itself but the mode of its execution that modern readers find offensive. The common word used in these chapters for sacrifice is that of offering (Hebrew *qorban*), the "bringing near," or as Everett Fox would have it, "near-offering."[25] We too bring offerings during our regular worship, of prayer and finances, and Christians celebrate the offering up of the person of Jesus when they gather around the Communion table, an act which points to the connection between *offering* and *communion*. Maarten den Dulk is certainly on the right track when he urges readers to understand Leviticus as the book that practices the "art of communication" and that together with the festivals, the offerings are the means to communication.[26] Worship arises out of a perceived alienation between the divine and the human and aims to set up a bridge to cross the distance. It is not by coincidence that the offerings related to shortcomings are the most elaborately described in these chapters (chs. 4; 5; 6:1-7) and are aimed to achieve restoration of fractured relations between God and human and between human beings themselves. Nor is it coincidental that the Day of Atonement is the most elaborately described liturgical holy day in the book. The ethical prescriptions we reviewed in Leviticus 19 are thus closely bound to the ritual prescriptions of earlier Levitical material. The care one exercises for the proper manner of the offering is linked to the care with which one relates to the neighbor/poor/stranger. All is part of the life of holiness.

Sacrifice, appropriately brought, is of course no guarantee of a restored relationship with God. Naturally, the Levitical material is not the place where such a perspective is made explicit. It would, after all, be an odd and ineffective way to prescribe ritual with the explicit caution that it might or might not bring about the desirable result. The insertion in Leviticus of ethical prescriptions, however, indirectly makes clear that the life of correct ritual must be accompanied by the life of just relations among neighbors in the community. Otherwise, we must look for a critique of a mechanical understanding of sacrifice elsewhere in the Bible.[27]

Is there anything to be gained in this material beyond the common no-

25. Pp. 511ff.

26. Den Dulk, 121-22.

27. The preexilic prophetic material is especially vocal on this point. In fact, for prophets such as Amos, Isaiah, Micah, and Jeremiah correct ritual without the practice of justice and love in the community is not acceptable to God. See for extended examples, Amos 4 and 5; Isa. 1; Mic. 6:6-8; Jer. 7:1-11 (cf. also 1 Sam. 15:22; Prov. 21:3). This requirement is never turned around in the sense that the practice of justice in the community without correct ritual would be acceptable to God. See also Pss. 50 and 51 for a reflection on the connections between moral requirements and sacrifice, on the one hand, and penitence and sacrifice, on the other.

tion of sacrifice with its attendant advantages as well as complications? Mary Douglas has studied the particulars of the parts of the sacrificed body of the animal in detail.[28] She argues that the *body* of the animal is analogous to the tabernacle, which in turn is analogous to Mount Sinai.[29] In Douglas's view, the body of the slaughtered animal carries great significance and its symbolical value is seriously heightened. It is not surprising then that, in her opinion, Leviticus is concerned with all creaturely relations, also those between human and animal. Once again, this material may urge modern-day consumers of animal flesh to contemplate how much dignity and significance are accorded the animal who neither lives a happy life nor dies a dignified death in any sense of that word. Douglas is convinced that Leviticus allows no "profane slaughter." In other words, the only meat that may be consumed is that offered up in sacrifice, and it certainly looks as if Leviticus 17:3-4 takes that position.[30] Extreme respect for all life and prohibition of bloodshed outside of the sacred sphere is thus typical for this literature. We will revisit this issue when we turn to the so-called "purity" laws.

28. See Douglas, *Leviticus as Literature*, 66ff.

29. "The summit of the mountain is the abode of God; below is the cloudy region which only Moses was allowed to enter; and lastly the vast lower slopes where the priests and congregation waited. The order of placing the parts of the animal on the altar marks out three zones on the carcass, the suet set around and below the diaphragm corresponding to the cloud girdling the middle of the mountain"; Douglas, *Leviticus as Literature*, 86.

30. Douglas, *Leviticus as Literature*, 68. She allows that her view is contrary to "many established Leviticus scholars," but defends her point strongly that "the only shedding of animal blood it (i.e. Leviticus) permits is in the consecrated killing of sacrifice." Baruch Schwartz in commenting on these chapters agrees with Douglas: "According to P, the 'shelamim' offering is the one occasion on which lay people would have eaten the flesh of domestic livestock" (211); and "In Priestly law . . . domestic livestock may only be eaten as sacrificial meat" whereas "Deuteronomic law disagrees with P, permitting the non-sacrificial slaughter of cattle" (229). See further his comment on Lev. 17:3-4. For a different point of view, see Baruch Levine, who views 17:3-4 as being in basic agreement with Deut. 12:15ff. because of the technical meaning of the Hebrew verb "to slaughter" used in Lev. 17. Levine reviews the arguments in some detail and allows that "a large body of scholars . . . continues to regard Leviticus 17 as representing a . . . stage . . . when all slaughter of animals for food had to be of a sacral character"; *Leviticus,* 113. The most attractive argument on the side of Leviticus not permitting profane slaughter is, in my view, presented by Bernard Bamberger, who views Leviticus 17 as a postexilic effort to repeal the earlier Deuteronomic law for a "small remnant huddled around what was left of Jerusalem"; in Plaut, *The Torah,* 872-74.

Purity and Impurity

The common denominators of the varied sources of ritual defilement are death and sex.[31]

More serious than objections to the sacrificial system may be a distaste for and even hostility toward the purity regulations contained for the most part in Leviticus 11–22. The so-called purity laws, about "pure" and "impure" foods, persons, and other beings, are difficult to access because in the Christian context such prohibitions do not function any longer overtly while at the same time some others have continued to function with great exclusionary force. Preceding this material is a more descriptive section about matters relating to the priesthood. Here is told of ordination rites and properly executed ritual as well as of the severity with which a seemingly minor transgression on the part of Aaron's sons is judged by God (chs. 8–10). Both the narrative style and the intrusion of a threatening episode work as a balance and contrast to the preceding and following legislative chapters with their orderly listings and protocols.

Foods

Recently, a Christian preacher related an occasion of an interfaith dinner at which he had been present. It had been a complicated meal to construct, he said, because the Hindu partners would not eat beef, the Buddhists could not eat any meat, and the Muslim and Jewish participants avoided pork. It was only easy for the Christians, who, our preacher said, would eat anything. Put like that, it sounded almost rude and barbaric. All these groups had set boundaries around their food habits, except the Christians!

Food avoidance and taboos are not peculiar to ancient Israel and current Judaism, of course, although it seems that the detailed rules of Leviticus 11 are somewhat singular and certainly not known from comparable ancient literature. Christianity, even in its early stages, most likely because of its strong evangelistic impulse, abandoned the distinctions between pure and impure food.[32] In Judaism, historically and today, food laws are strictly observed in certain sectors of the community but not in others. It would be easy to become lost in looking for an incentive for the avoidance of certain foods

---

31. Jonathan Klawans, "Concepts of Purity in the Bible," in *The Jewish Study Bible*, 2044.

32. See, e.g., Rom. 14:14; 1 Cor. 8:8; 10:31. It would seem obvious that evangelization among non-Jews to the extent that it took place among the followers of Jesus of Nazareth could not go accompanied by long lists of rules about eating, slaughter, and how to keep foods separate. Naturally then, once the food regulations were relaxed religious sanction followed. See further below, 279-81.

about which many theories exist, or in the detail of the types of animals that could be eaten versus those that should be avoided.[33] Perhaps it should suffice to observe here, in the words of Mary Douglas, that "unclean animals are safe from the secular as also from the sacred kitchen."[34]

In other words, the avoidance of certain animals for consumption as well as the taboo on the contact with a carcass worked as an advantage for the survival of certain species!

At this point in our reading, we may want to question a Christian sense of superiority in terms of its approach to the consumption of food. For example, interpretations of Acts 10, the narrative concerning Peter and Cornelius, which provides the religious sanction for evangelization of the Gentiles without the burdensome Jewish food laws, often take a turn to Christian arrogance and superiority over Judaism.[35] Rather than taking a stance in this posture, we should press the question whether the Christian approach toward food was and is an improvement over that of religious groups with food taboos, and whether it has been used to improve the relationships between creature and creation. Once again the pertinent question arises whether it is "right to kill any living thing for food."[36]

Reprehensible Fluidity: Menstruation

Nothing is more filthy, unclean than a menstruant; whatever she will have touched, she makes it unclean, and still its filth is cleansed by the baptism of Christ, through the cleansing of sins.[37]

In terms of matters of impurity relating to human beings, the regulations for the menstruating woman have had the strongest life and are still overtly or covertly operating in large sectors of both Judaism and Christianity. I take

33. For pertinent discussions, see Douglas, *Leviticus as Literature*, 134-75; Levine, 63-72, 243-48; Bamberger, 808-23; Klawans.

34. Douglas, *Leviticus as Literature*, 141.

35. The narrative in Acts 10 contains some very problematic statements such as the words put in Peter's mouth that it would be "unlawful for a Jew to associate with or to visit a Gentile" (v. 28). It could, of course, under certain circumstances be awkward or even impossible for a Jew to visit or eat with a Gentile, but the ambiguous truth of this statement comes close to a total falsehood and certainly flies in the face of the concern for the stranger that predominates in the Torah.

36. Bamberger, 813.

37. Jerome, *Commentarii in Prophetam Zachariam* as cited in Jennifer Schultz, "Doctors, Philosophers, and Christian Fathers on Menstrual Blood," in *Wholly Woman, Holy Blood*, ed. Kristin De Troyer (Harrisburg: Trinity Press International, 2002), 97.

them up here insofar as I understand the taboo surrounding menstruation to persist in a damaging way in the Christian context. The long-lasting effects of these rules may, however, not coincide with their original intention or scope. First, then, the regulations in Leviticus 15.

Leviticus operates in a realm where clear boundaries must be set if the community it addresses is going to achieve and maintain "holiness," that which enables them to approach God who is above all holy. What and who is not able to be in a state of holiness, therefore, must be elaborately defined, so that the state can be either avoided or be redeemed, "atoned for," if it is unavoidable, as is the case with certain bodily emissions.[38] Thus both male and female genital discharge make the individual impure and necessitate a cleansing with water (Lev. 15:16-18, 19-30). Sexual intercourse with a menstruating woman makes the male impure for the duration of the female period of impurity (15:24), while elsewhere severe penalties are exacted for such behavior (18:19, 29).[39] The regulations are recapitulated in the last verses of chapter 15:

Leviticus 15:31-33

31. And you shall separate the children of Israel from their impurity,
    and they will not die in their impurity
    while making impure my dwelling in their midst.
32. Such is the instruction for the man who has a discharge,
    a discharge of semen that makes him impure.
33. And for her who is weak through menstruation
    and for one with a discharge, male or female,
    and for the man who lies down with an impure woman.

Earlier in chapter 15, the stipulation is that the woman shall remain impure for seven days as of the onset of her menstrual flow.[40] Most contempo-

---

38. The purity concerns move from the subject of animals, to certain diseases, to genital discharges. All of these cause *impermanent* states, during which the individual is barred from approach to the holy God. Such impermanence is not the case for moral impurity, which is followed by punishment and is far graver in its impact on individual and community (see Lev. 19–21). For the distinctions, see Klawans, 2045.

39. The regulations in ch. 15 mention no penalty beyond that of cleansing and could thus be seen to be in contradiction to 18:19, 29 (so Schwartz, 242). Others see the penalty mentioned in ch. 18 and 20:18 as filling in a lacuna left in ch. 15 (see Bamberger, 850). The severity of the prohibition is certainly what remained the norm in rabbinic explanations of these regulations, but for Leviticus it looks as if different sources lie at the root of the differences between Lev. 15, on the one hand, and chs. 18 and 20, on the other. What in ch. 15 is a matter of *ritual purity* becomes a matter of *moral purity* in subsequent material.

40. The suggestion made by Kathleen O'Grady that the word *niddah,* rendered in most

rary scholarship on this issue has abandoned the view that such boundary setting around the menstruating woman would be inherently primitive and even disgusting. As Jonathan Klawans puts it, scholars now "focus on how the avoidance rules of any single culture work together to form a coherent conception of things permitted and prohibited, of things sacred and defiled."[41] It is not in the rules themselves that a pejorative view of the female body is maintained but rather in later interpretations and applications of the biblical mandate.[42] What could be more indicting than Jerome's statement cited above? In a review of church traditions of both East and West, Jennifer Schultz concludes that "the pathologized, unclean body of woman, constructed by medicine, dangerous in popular ideology, and impure in ritual, stands opposed to the pure body of Christ, the church, and thus must remain outside. The female body is stigmatized."[43] If we could only ascribe such a perception to a dim past, we might assign it to a problem of our tradition alone. But the real problem is that, even for our day, the female body is still "stigmatized." "Although in contemporary Western Christian religious practices the idea of cultic impurity of persons, based upon their physical state or condition, has almost completely faded, women's impurity as menstruants and parturients has been one of the most persistent ritual issues and still marks religious practice and reflection."[44]

A strong taboo on menstrual blood has thus endured until today and is still covertly or overtly present in the rationale of barring women from ordination in large sectors of the Christian church. More subtle is the double-sidedness with which menstruation is approached in our culture, at the same time revealing and hiding the event so that today we exist in a curious cultural environment where the fact that women have a monthly flow of what at least looks like blood is both hidden and open. There are, on the one hand, the

---

translations of 15:19 as "impurity," would be more correctly translated with "(period of) separation" is very attractive; "The Semantics of Taboo: Menstrual Prohibitions in the Hebrew Bible," in De Troyer et al., *Wholly Woman, Holy Blood,* 16. O'Grady draws a strong connection both etymologically and conceptually between the *niddah* and the *nazir,* arguing that avoiding what is impure is essential for maintaining the sanctified order: "A careful reading of Lev 15, rather, makes clear that the underlying motive for the prohibitions . . . is to emphasize the need for separation between the sanctified order and these phenomena [i.e., those that cause impurity] in order to establish and perpetuate the sanctified order itself"; 27.

41. Klawans, 2041.

42. I confine myself here to a critique of concepts of the female body in the Christian family.

43. Schultz, 116.

44. Anne Marie Korte, "Female Blood Rituals: Cultural-Anthropological Findings and Feminist-Theological Reflections," in De Troyer et al., *Wholly Woman, Holy Blood,* 179.

ubiquitous advertisements for "feminine hygiene" products, but, on the other hand, the urgency to make the entire matter go by without noticing, a "spotless" event without causing interference in sports or any other day-to-day activities.[45] In this context, it is interesting to note the avoidance of the subject of the experience of menstruation by even contemporary writers who discuss biblical texts and prejudices in the tradition. In fact, not one of the essays contained in the volume *Wholly Woman, Holy Blood,* all written by women, contains a reflection on the experience of menstruation, as if the taboo were still exercising great cultural force. It is, ironically, a male scholar who reflects on the biblical regulations in light of the actual female experience. Bernard Bamberger, in his comments on Leviticus 15, observes that the provisions found here are "rational . . . in view of the physical difficulties many women suffer during menstruation, ranging from sleepiness to intense pain — to say nothing of the emotional tensions that often appear just before the start of the period. The law protects women from the importunities of their husbands at a time when they are not physically and emotionally ready for coitus."[46] Apart from the merits of these remarks, it is certainly interesting that Bamberger pays attention to the text in the context of the actual experience of women.

Kune Biezeveld asks: "What could be objectionable to specific attention for the phase of menstruation? . . . Is it not possible that behind these ancient laws . . . something may be understood of attention and care for the body with everything belonging to it?"[47] If we see and hear only the exclusionary voice emphasized and reinforced by the faith traditions that built on these texts, we may reinscribe these traditions while bypassing a strand of positive interpretation that may also lie embedded in the text.[48]

Cultural taboos reinforced by religious sanctions are very difficult to root out. The reality of the menstrual experience is that for many girls and women this can be a difficult and painful time, repeated every month for the duration of their premenopausal life. The denial of this reality is not helpful,

45. With gratitude to Kune Biezeveld for making available to me her observations published in the Dutch feminist periodical *Mara (Tijdschrift voor feminisme en theologie)* 10 (1996): 5. Biezeveld in turn leans on an essay by Gerburgis Feld, "Wie es eben Frauen ergeht," in *Von der Wurzel getragen: Christlich-feministische Exegese in Auseinandersetzung mit Antijudaismus,* ed. Luise Schottroff and Marie-Theres Wacker (Leiden: Brill, 1996), 29-42.

46. Bamberger, 850.

47. Biezeveld, 5 (translation J. Bos).

48. Needless to say, pointing in the direction of the Markan text in which Jesus would have broken the menstruation taboo and thus the "primitivism" of the rules that governed Judaism is not a direction for a solution, since it assumes authority of the New Testament text over that of the Old and depicts a negative and restrictive Judaism over against a liberating early Christianity (see Mark 5:25-34).

and recognizing it does not necessarily constitute a pathologizing. Shame, misunderstanding, and secrecy all too often still surround the topic between women and men, and women among themselves.[49] A serious consideration of the posture, if not the actual practice, of the Levitical text might actually be helpful, with its centeredness on the significance of the body as the vehicle of the approach to God and the reflection of God and God's holiness in the world. The application of these texts in a literal sense is, for the Christian context, out of the question. But, as was the case for the consideration of sacrifice, the text may serve to urge us to consider our physical existence and take it more seriously as a vehicle for holiness.[50]

Intimate Relations

Leviticus 18–20 form a type of unit in which the required holiness of the people modeled on the holiness of God is frequently repeated and of which opening and closing sections recapitulate the importance of keeping God's laws *(mishpatim)* and rules *(hukot),* rather than those of the peoples around them (18:1-5; cf. 20:22-27). "Doing," "keeping," and "walking" are central to the meaning of the opening verses of chapter 18. It is by these actions as they respond to God's *torah* that the ancient Israelites shall differentiate themselves from their neighbors.

> ### Leviticus 18:1-5
> 1. The Holy One spoke to Moses:
> 2. Say to the children of Israel
>   and speak to them:
>   I am the Holy One your God.

49. The disparity among women themselves may not be helpful here. For myself, menstruation, although it initially conferred a hidden sense of pride and preadulthood, was always an experience of extreme discomfort, pain, often excruciating, eventually threatening to my health. Psychologically and emotionally, it was during marriage a repeated experience of severe disappointment, since it signaled the failure of conception. The need to hide the event itself, combined with fear of "pathologizing" the experience, prevalent in our Western culture and supported by many modern women, has stood in the way of open acknowledgment of the debilitating effects menstruation can have and therefore finding ways to combat the problem. For a more elaborate description and analysis of my experience, see Johanna W. H. van Wijk-Bos, *Reformed and Feminist* (Louisville: Westminster John Knox, 1991), 55-56.

50. The distracting and sometimes dangerous contemporary emphasis on so-called "spirituality," also in a feminist Christian context, may especially need this counterforce of the consideration of our "physicality." Cf. John Dominic Crossan: "Purity is not holiness or righteousness or justice. It is the appropriate preparation and necessary condition for contact with the God of justice. And purity's emphasis on bodily flesh permanently reminds us that justice is about bodily flesh"; *The Birth of Christianity* (San Francisco: HarperCollins, 1998), 582.

3. Like the deeds of the land of Egypt,
   where you lived,
   you shall not do;
   and like the deeds of the land of Canaan,
   where I am bringing you,
   you shall not do
   and by their rules you shall not walk.

4. My laws you shall do
   and my rules you shall keep
   to walk by them.
   I am the Holy One your God.
5. By the keeping of my rules
   and the doing of my laws
   a human being shall live.
   I am the Holy One.

Leviticus 20 in many ways is a repetition of chapter 18, this time with penalties listed for the different offenses.[51] Regulations pertaining to sexual intercourse (chs. 18; 20) thus form a frame around regulations that relate to social intercourse (ch. 19). The importance of the issue of "separation" returns in the closing verses of chapter 20.

Leviticus 20:24-26
24. And I said to you:
    You shall inherit their land
    and I will give to you as an inheritance
    a land flowing with milk and honey.
    I am the Holy One your God
    who has *separated* you from the nations.
25. And you shall make *separation*
    between clean and unclean beast,
    unclean bird and clean.
    You shall not contaminate yourself
    with beast or bird
    or any creeping thing of the soil

---

51. Mary Douglas argues that Lev. 18 and 20 are a rearrangement of Deut. 27:15-26 in such a way that the sexual prohibitions form a frame around the righteous dealings in other social arrangements which now are in the middle, "conspicuously in the place of honour"; *Leviticus as Literature*, 235.

which I have *separated* for you as unclean.
26. And you shall be to me holy
for holy am I the Holy God
and I *separated* you from the nations
to be mine.

Anxiety around biological productivity and "separateness" govern the choice of subjects addressed in chapters 18 and 20: adultery, incest, homoerotic activity, and bestiality are proscribed. Some of these activities may have been associated with foreign religious cults, and throughout the chapters one finds a condemnation of communing with the dead through mediums (Lev. 19:26, 31; 20:6, 27). Where such a connection might not be obvious to the modern reader, the practices mentioned in Leviticus 18 and 20 are presented in the context of idolatry. Although its possible roots lie in an earlier time, the formulation of these regulations at the time of the exile and afterwards makes the double concern of productivity and separateness a natural one.

Some of this material as it relates to prohibited behaviors is still close to a modern sensibility, as a number of the rules concerning incest for example. However, other texts no longer connect with the modern world. Human fertility and reproduction is again a cause for anxiety, but for the opposite reason than the one prevalent in the biblical world. Overpopulation and an overburdening and distressing of earth's resources are today a cause for reflection and control of human reproductive powers. In addition, sexuality as it is both described and prescribed in the Bible is not a matter in which women are much portrayed as the subject. It is, rather, reflective of both the exigencies of the economic and biological needs of the culture that gave birth to the text and the patriarchal structures and perspectives that governed its expression.[52] Insofar as these latter are open to severe critique and analysis in the search for true equity between women and men both in cultural and religious structures, the biblical text provides relevant guidance for issues of sexual relations mostly in an indirect rather than a direct way. Just as the directions for the making of the tabernacle in Exodus cannot function as a blueprint for the construction of a Christian sanctuary, so can we not use the directions for the construction of sexual relations in a similar manner.[53] Everywhere we must

---

52. For a more elaborate discussion of homosexuality in the context of sexuality and the Bible, see Johanna W. H. van Wijk-Bos, "How to Read What We Read: Discerning Good News About Sexuality in Scripture," in *Body and Soul: Rethinking Sexuality as Justice-Love*, ed. Marvin M. Ellison and Sylvia Thorson-Smith (Cleveland: Pilgrim, 2003), 61-77.

53. Van Wijk-Bos, "How to Read What We Read."

discern our way carefully with attention to the limits set by the ancient context as well as the urgency of our questions.

Reading these texts as a literal blueprint can do incalculable harm, and it has done so especially in the area of sexual experiences that do not correspond to the norm of heterosexuality. Twice in these chapters, homoerotic activity is condemned as it may take place between men (Lev. 18:22; 20:13). For Christianity, the problem is exacerbated by the condemnation found in Paul's Letter to the Romans (1:26-27, 32) of both female and male homosexual intercourse, and what may seem dismissable as part of the "old" dispensation in Leviticus is not so easily declared invalid in Romans 1.[54] In the context of this discussion, there is, however, no way out of a dilemma by simply letting a provision in the New Testament overrule a provision in the Hebrew Bible (see above, 69-70). Others argue that what is meant in Leviticus is temple prostitution and that Paul did not really understand what we understand today by homosexuality, so neither condemnation applies.[55]

It seems that we must approach the matter more broadly and argue that sexuality itself was not understood in the same way in the ancient world as it is today.[56] Because of the vast difference in understanding and experience, rules for sexual intimacy can hardly apply directly from the ancient world to our lives today. We can, however, still adopt the guidance of modeling ourselves as holy people after the Holy God. God is holy, as I have argued in these pages, in God's loving engagement with the creation, especially with the lowly and disenfranchised, the helpless of the earth. God's people are holy insofar as they emulate God's inclinations and preferences in their lives together and their life with the creation. Today, in view of the overburdening and depleting of earth's resources, partly through explosive population growth, unchecked human reproduction can hardly be viewed as holy behavior. The highest standard for holiness is set in Leviticus 19, a chapter we already discussed and which now takes on renewed significance in the context of the discussion of

54. Arguments for the enduring relevance of Paul's condemnation of both male and female homoerotic relations can be found in most conservative treatments of this issue. See, e.g., Marion L. Soards, *Scripture and Homosexuality* (Louisville: Westminster John Knox, 1995). For an overview of opinions from diverse perspectives, see *Homosexuality and Christian Community*, ed. Choon-Leong Seow (Louisville: Westminster John Knox, 1996). For a thorough review of the biblical material with an intriguing analysis of Romans 1, see George R. Edwards, *Gay/Lesbian Liberation: A Biblical Perspective* (New York: Pilgrim, 1984).

55. See Douglas, *Leviticus as Literature*, 238; see also the intricate arguments of Edwards.

56. For a review of the condemnation of homosexuality in the Christian context within the framework of the construction of gender and sexuality, see Bernadette J. Brooten, *Love Between Women: Early Christian Responses to Female Homoeroticism* (Chicago: University of Chicago Press, 1996).

purity and impurity in intimate relations. Leviticus 19, the pivotal chapter of this section, clearly issues the standard of holiness as being one of love — love of the neighbor, love of the stranger and love of the self.[57]

As I have pointed out in earlier chapters, we may define strangers as those who are somehow different from the dominant group and who are therefore not accorded the same rights and privileges as full members of the community. People who do not participate in the social mores defined by heterosexual and patriarchal dominance may certainly be classified as strangers today. In terms of required behavior toward the stranger, I have called the prohibition to "oppress" and the mandate to "love" the outer markers. These outer markers still prevail today, while the specific provisions that put them into effect may change over time. Specific provisions for life with the stranger today should include the approval of same-sex partners living in the same religiously-sanctioned family structures as heterosexual partners.[58] Mainline Christianity is still sadly lagging behind Reform Judaism in this respect.

Holy Days: Atonement

> *This shall be for you a perpetual rule to wipe away from the children of Israel all their failures once a year. (Leviticus 16:34)*

The sacrificial system, separating the foods, living a life according to God's rules all defined the community that is oriented to God. One more marker, at least, deserves to be discussed: the issue of special times set aside for the community to come into the presence of God. Naturally, holy days receive attention in a text devoted for a great part to the shape of formal ritual. In Leviticus, they are described in chapter 23, beginning with the Sabbath, each including a rest from work — a prescription peculiar to Leviticus. In regard to ancient Israel's most holy occasions, modern Christians experience a sense of distance because Christian festivals are not readily recognizable in these observances, even though most of them represent a "baptized" version of a Jewish feast. I focus here on the one holy day that is unique to Leviticus and

---

57. Mary Douglas considers Lev. 19 to be the "most important chapter of the whole book.... The earlier laws remain cryptic and controversial if read separately; they need chapter 19 to bring them together"; *Leviticus as Literature*, 239.

58. With others in my own denomination, the Presbyterian Church (USA), I believe that the recognition of same-sex partners as fully sanctioned marriage partners must come first, before the question of equal rights and privileges in terms of clerical ordination can be legitimately tackled. By the gradual adoption of legislation that legitimizes same-sex marriage in a number of the states, it looks once more as if social practice will march ahead of religious sanction.

that has not found a counterpart in Christian liturgies, the Day of Atonement, as it is described in chapter 16. This occasion is perhaps the farthest removed from Christian experience, yet a closer look may prove to provide a rich understanding of the possibilities for healing and establishing our own communion with God and neighbor.

For Christians, the concept of atonement has become located almost exclusively in the expiatory death of Jesus Christ. In some way this understanding is celebrated each time the rite of the Last Supper takes place in a congregation. For Judaism, it may be said that "it is impossible to exaggerate the importance of Yom Kippur in the life of the Jewish people."[59] The intent of this day is to "bring each person into harmony with each other and with God."[60] When we contemplate the beginnings of this day as described in Leviticus, the prescribed ritual appears arcane: two goats, one of which is sent into the wilderness, after a strange ritual of confession and putting the committed failures on the head of the second goat. It is, of course, especially the role of the second goat that seems outlandish, set free as it is in the desert with sins poured on to its poor head. It should be noted that this animal is not the one killed, however, but that it takes the failures of the community to a place where presumably they can no longer do any harm.[61] While no faith community that inherited the traditions of ancient Israel has kept these rituals intact literally, the Day of Atonement has lived on in Judaism with great vigor to this day, while it was never adopted in Christianity.

In his discussion of this chapter, Bamberger maintains that the ritual of the atonement in itself accomplished nothing but that the effect of the rites was contingent on the process of repentance, Hebrew *teshuvah*.[62] In other words, atonement, the becoming "at one" with God and neighbor and creation, was not achieved mechanistically or magically by going through the proper motions, but rather by joining a desire for change to the ritual executed. It is the fresh start a person is willing to make that makes the ritual effective. "The sacrifices and the ceremony of the Azazel-goat were, it is true, thought to have genuine atoning power," observes Bamberger; "but the effect of these rites was contingent on the *teshuvah* of the worshipers."[63]

---

59. Bamberger, 858.

60. Bamberger, 858.

61. For pertinent discussions regarding the Day of Atonement, Yom Kippur, see Bamberger, 858-67; Levine, 100-3, 250-53.

62. Bamberger, 861.

63. Furthermore, "according to the Mishnah, an offense against a person cannot be wiped out either by ritual or by simple contrition. The sinner must attempt to rectify the wrong and seek the good will of the injured party"; Bamberger, 861.

From our reading of the Torah, it is clear that according to a biblical perspective fissures have opened up in God's creation, between God and creature, between creature and creature and between creature and creation. The Day of Atonement is a human attempt to participate in the mending of what is broken and the bridging of what is distanced. The Torah recognizes that many times the human creature is aware of having missed the mark but that even more times omissions and failures come about unwittingly. The Torah also recognizes that God is engaged in this healing process and is willing to *wipe away,* Hebrew *kipper,* failures committed both knowingly and unknowingly. To this willingness on God's part, God's graciousness, and to the willingness on humanity's part, humanity's readiness to confess its sins and have a change of heart, the Day of Atonement and its ritual offer strong testimony.

CONCLUSION

A Holy Nation

We have traveled a long way with the Israelites, from oppressive bondage in Egypt, to the creation of the covenant bond at Sinai, until they reached the other side of Jordan, waiting to enter the promised land, and there we must leave them. We have paid close attention to the occasion of the covenant-making, to the significance of this event for ancient Israel's understanding of itself, and to the regulations that accompanied it, the torah that formed an inextricable part of the bond forged between God and people. We have seen that the instructions for its conduct addressed the community in all aspects of its life, the social, the political, as well as the liturgical. While much of that world remains alien to modern perceptions, connections with present-day experience could also be made, sometimes in unexpected ways. In the course of the discussion, it became clear that in all aspects the demands for the covenant life, lived as a response to God's presence, were marked by concern for the ones on the outside, symbolized in the text by the stranger. It is the stranger whose distress must be alleviated, whose needs must be provided for, who must, finally, be loved. The theme of concern for the stranger binds together all the social and liturgical provisions that we encounter in the Torah and marks the covenant community as a holy people. For it is, in the end, in the nature of the Holy God to have an eye and an ear for the needs of those who lack privilege in the community.

The people failed many times, sometimes miserably, to live up to the demands made of them, both in their relation to God and to each other. The world remains a marred world, also the world of covenant. Yet each time, God's everlasting compassion outshone God's wrath, and there was always opportunity for atonement, for *teshuvah*, a turning away from violence and betrayal toward the direction of God's good intentions for Israel, for the world.

PART V

Living with the Torah

Introduction: God and People in Covenant

A great deal has been said in these pages regarding the expectations put on the ancient community that viewed itself as existing in a covenant relationship with its God in terms of the behavior of this community, both in its life as oriented to the neighbor and in its orientation to God. The identity of the community and its self-understanding we have explored at some length. In this context we have also considered the nature of God and God's disposition toward the outcast as it sought reflection in the posture of the covenant community, but more needs to be said about the depiction of God in the Torah. We will highlight the God-talk in these pages within the framework of traditionally held assumptions about the God of the Bible in general and the God of the "Old Testament" in particular. I will be intentional about looking for depictions of God that go against the grain of our expectations in regard to the God of the Bible, rooted as they are in Greco-Christian concepts of deity, as well as in Christian prejudice against the Old Testament. The review will be of necessity highly selective, although everywhere guided by the instruction arising from the text.

Next, we will consider once more the way in which torah and covenant need to be understood as a part of one whole rather than in contradiction to one another. First, we will look at the teachings of Jesus as they are presented in the Gospels, on the point of their continuity with instruction found in the Torah. One text, the parable of the Good Samaritan, together with its framework in Luke 10:25-37, will serve as a paradigm for our understanding of Jesus' teaching. Mistaken Christian understandings of the Torah and of its place in Judaism will come into view in the course of this discussion.

Because the subject of Christ and the law is so central to Paul's writings, we then turn to a review of these issues in the Pauline Letters. Within this context we also take into account specific instructions Paul issued for the congregations he addressed. Finally, I will call our attention to Galatians 3:26-28, eventually bringing these words into conversation with two texts regarding the stranger in the Torah (Exod. 23:9 and Lev. 19:34), in order to illustrate the advantage of an approach that takes seriously the revelatory and instructive character of the entire Bible, especially also the Torah.

CHAPTER 1

God in the Torah

The text is the only thing we have that will allow us to enter that lost world, and, with some effort, restore its way of understanding, of seeing.[1]

Most likely, many of us have some fixed ideas about the God of the Bible and about the way God is depicted there. Most likely, these ideas are not based on scholarship or long study of the nature of God and how God is revealed in Scripture. Rather, they came about because of our formation in the Christian context of family, church, and Sunday school. Very possibly, these ideas are not entirely wrong or unbiblical, but over long periods of time cultural and religious factors were added to the biblical perspective to shape the Christian idea of God, so that the final picture may end up to be quite unlike what appears in the biblical text or true to the text only in part. I address here five views of God in the Torah, of which some may go directly against our well-established understandings of the nature of the God of the Bible. Others may not so much contradict our concepts but tap into a vein of thinking that had not occurred to us to explore.[2]

1. James L. Kugel, *The God of Old* (New York: Free Press, 2003), 1.
2. This review is by no means intended to be exhaustive, and I confine myself to God's portrayal in the Torah.

A God Who Regrets

If the philosophy of ancient Greece failed to become an alternative
and rival to the monotheistic faith of Israel it did contrive to become
at least the handmaid of Christian theology.[3]

One of the foundational understandings of God in Christianity is that God, the creator of heaven and earth, does not change. As one of the historical confessions of the Protestant tradition has it: "There is but one only living and true God, who is . . . , immutable. . . ."[4] The divine and change are seen as incompatible according to this perspective. There is no doubt that this view was held by early framers of Christian theology and that it has prevailed through the ages in one form or another. It is also clear that this contrasting of the divine and change is one of the contributions of Platonic and Neo-Platonic thought, Greek philosophical concepts, which over time fed into biblical understandings of God, favoring some while neglecting others with the effect of solidifying only one stream of biblical views of God. It certainly is not clear in the Torah that God does not change in terms of rethinking a decision, from positive to negative and the other way around. In a number of texts God makes a decision, only to recant it later in terms of its severity, softening or even entirely changing the intended result.[5] In other texts God appears to adjust divine presence according to the changed situation brought about by human decisions.[6] Finally, a key text in the Torah purports to offer insight into the divine nature by making a statement that has direct bearing on the understanding of God's nature as dynamic rather than static.[7] We will take a closer look at some of these texts to highlight a view of God in the Torah that is often more complex and ambiguous than the one presented in our confessions, one that may enrich our own contemporary understanding of the God of the Bible, the God of our faith.

The first eleven chapters of Genesis present a world that is still in flux, a world which is not yet clear exactly what it will be or how it will be. It is a world

---

3. N. H. G. Robinson and D. W. D. Shaw, "God," in *The Westminster Dictionary of Christian Theology,* ed. Alan Richardson and John Bowden (Philadelphia: Westminster, 1983), 232.

4. The entire statement reads: "There is but one only living and true God, who is infinite in being and perfection, a most pure spirit, invisible, without body, parts, or passions, *immutable,* immense, eternal, incomprehensible, almighty"; Westminster Confession, II/1, as cited from *The Constitution of the Presbyterian Church (U.S.A.),* Part I: *The Book of Confessions* (Louisville: Geneva, 1996), 176. Besides God's immutability, this discussion will address also the perception of God as invisible as well as dispassionate.

5. See, e.g., Gen. 4:1-16; Exod. 32:14; 33:17; Num. 11:2; 14:20.

6. Cf. Gen. 3:21; 6:6-7; 9:12-17.

7. Exod. 3:13-14.

that is still in the making. At the same time, God as portrayed especially by one stream of the tradition reflects somewhat of the same fluidity. Two announced sentences, one of death in the garden concerning the fruit of the tree of knowledge (Gen. 2:17), the other of banishment from God's presence (Gen. 4:12), are commuted and ameliorated. Unlike the powerful creator God of Genesis 1 who brings into being by the word, the God of the garden story and its sequel seems not always sure of him/herself, creating a complementary human creature only at second try, uncertain of the whereabouts of humanity after they eat of the fruit and of the murderous deed of Cain. The God of Genesis 2–4 certainly makes pronouncements but also asks a lot of questions, questions that should have obvious answers beginning with "where," "who" and "what."[8] Even if the questions are understood to be rhetorical, the impact of their frequent occurrence in the text is to lend the character of God at least a note of uncertainty and questioning. It is not until chapter 6, when God contemplates what the world will become in view of the state of humanity, that a word is used which in Hebrew indicates regret. I recall a text cited in an earlier chapter:

Genesis 6:5-7

5. And the Holy One saw
   that the evil of humanity was great in the land
   and that all the imagination of the deliberations of their heart
   was only evil, all the day.
6. Then the Holy One rued
   having made humanity on the land
   and God had pain in his heart.
7. The Holy One said:
   I will destroy humanity that I created
   from the face of the ground,
   from human to beast
   to crawling creature and bird of the sky,
   for I rue having made them.

The word I have translated with "rue" has the basic meaning of "regret, being sorry, repent." Frequently this root (Hebrew *niham*) occurs with God as subject. In the Torah, it appears again during the wilderness period following the making of the golden calf, when God intends to destroy the people and

---

8. The questions in Gen. 3 are in order: "Where are you?" "Who told you?" and "What have you done?" (Gen. 3:9-13). Even if these are considered rhetorical questions, their impact in the narrative is to reflect a far from all-powerful decisive God, but rather one who is also waiting for how it will all turn out. The questions continue in ch. 4, to become statements of regret in ch. 6.

upon Moses' intercession is said to "renounce/repent" (Hebrew *wayyin-nahem*) this decision and to come back from the planned punishment (Exod. 32:14).[9] In the Genesis passage God does not see the created world going in the right direction, and the violence and wicked imaginations of the human heart call forth a violent reaction from the "pain" in God's heart. The text clearly states that God "regrets, is sorry" for having made human creatures who are making a mess of things and will continue to make an ever greater mess. So God decides "to destroy" the creature. Yet, almost right away, God comes back on this decision, and decides to keep one human family together with animals intact, because "Noah found favor in the eyes of the Holy One" (Gen. 6:8).[10] Even more important, after the flood has taken place, God makes a self-limiting promise never to engage in this type of action again:

Genesis 8:21-22

21. And the Holy One smelled the pleasant odor
    and said in his heart:
    I will not again account as cursed the ground
    because of humanity,
    for the imagination of its heart
    is evil from its youth;
    and not again will I strike all life
    as I have done.
22. From now on all the days of the land,
    seedtime and harvest,
    cold and heat,
    summer and winter,
    day and night,
    they will not cease.

9. Exod. 32:12, 14: "Turn from your blazing anger, and *repent* of the evil to your people. . . . And the Holy One *repented* of the evil he had said he would do to his people."

10. As J. Gerald Janzen observes, "The divine decision for the flood is accounted for, not by appeal to the inscrutable caprice of God, but by appeal to the state of affairs in the world. . . . The state of affairs has become so incompatible with the divine creative aims and enjoyment, that the indignant pain which it gives leads God to a change of mind concerning the viability of such a world as a means to those aims. . . . Secondly, the fact of Noah's existence in righteousness effects a modification in the changing divine purpose"; "Metaphor and Reality in Hosea 11," in *Old Testament Interpretation from a Process Perspective*, ed. William A. Beardslee and David J. Lull. Semeia 24 (Atlanta: Scholars, 1982), 19. Janzen is here arguing that the depiction of God in the Bible accords more easily with a process theological view than with traditional understandings. See also Jack Miles, *God: A Biography* (New York: Knopf, 1995), in which he argues that God is very much affected by the creation and the human creature: "endlessly and often unpleasantly surprised. God is constant; he is not immutable"; 12.

This promise is subsequently ratified by the covenant God makes with the whole earth through the person of Noah. Preceding this covenant ratification of God's promise, the situation is clearly stated in Genesis 8:21: humanity has not changed, "the imagination of its heart" is still "evil from its youth." It is God who has changed, who promises not to respond again in violent ways to the violence of human children. As Terence E. Fretheim observes: "The images of God developed in this story are striking: a God who expresses sorrow and regret; a God who judges, but doesn't want to, . . . a God open to change and doing things in new ways; a God who promises never to do this again. The story reveals and resolves a fundamental tension within God, emphasizing finally, not a God who decides to destroy, but a God who wills to save, who is committed to change based on experience with the world, and who promises to stand by the creation."[11]

In the Torah God's changes of heart always take place in the context of planned chastisement for human transgression, and they occur after intercessory prayer.[12] It is thus the assumption of the one who intercedes that God may be persuaded to do otherwise than planned. So Abraham assumes that God may be persuaded not to destroy Sodom and Gomorrah (Gen. 18:22-32), and Moses brings to bear all the force of his persuasive powers to convince God not to destroy the people (Exod. 32–34; Num. 11:10-15; 14:13-20). The arguments employed by Moses on the occasion of his intercession in Numbers 14 are of particular interest in the context of this discussion.

Numbers 14:13-20

13. And Moses said to the Holy One:
    The Egyptians will hear —
    for by your power you brought
    this people up from their midst —
14. and they will speak to the inhabitants of this land.
    They have heard that you the Holy One
    are in the midst of this people,
    that you the Holy One are seen eye to eye
    and your cloud stands over them;
    with a column of cloud
    you go before them by day

---

11. Terence E. Fretheim, "The Book of Genesis," *New Interpreter's Bible* 1 (Nashville: Abingdon, 1994), 395.

12. On this point see Patrick D. Miller, *They Cried to the Lord* (Minneapolis: Fortress, 1994), 126: "The mind and heart of God are vulnerable to the pleas *and the arguments* of human creatures."

and with a column of fire by night.

15. If you kill this people as one person,
    the nations will say:
16. Because the Holy One could not bring out this people
    to the land that he swore to them
    God has destroyed them in the wilderness.
17. Now let your power be great,
    as you spoke with these words:
18. The Holy God slow to anger,
    full of devotion,
    bearing failure and wickedness,
    while not holding innocent [the guilty],
    visiting the sin of the ancestors on the children
    to the third and fourth generation — [13]
19. Forgive, please, the failure of this people
    according to the greatness of your devotion
    and because you have borne this people
    from Egypt until now.
20. And the Holy One said:
    I have forgiven on your word.

God has announced the plan to destroy the people and preserve Moses and his descendants to make a new start, and Moses once again pleads with God to renounce the punishment. The passage is not easy to translate into smooth English because Moses takes a long time to get to his point, interjecting phrases and interrupting himself after his initial words.[14] There are a number of references to "hearing" and "speaking." Egypt and the nations have "heard" things and "say" things and "will say" things, and God has also "said" something. What Egypt and the nations know and hear will harm God's reputation: God will be spoken off scornfully by the ones who have witnessed God's power, a similar appeal as the one made by Moses after the episode of the golden calf (Exod. 32:11-12).[15] This time, however, that is not

13. The recitation of God's qualities is not identical to the one found in Exod. 34:7. The omissions could be due to scribal errors or serve to make the larger point of getting Moses more quickly to his real request. See Richard Elliott Friedman, *A Commentary on the Torah* (San Francisco: HarperSanFrancisco, 2001), 474.

14. Standard translations obscure this feature of the intercession in their attempts to make the sentences flow more smoothly in English. I have left the phrases somewhat rough and unfinished for the purpose of conveying the impression of Moses' anxiety.

15. For a discussion of this passage in the context of prayers for help, see Miller, 117-22. As Miller remarks: "God's reputation is at stake in Israel's fate" (121).

where Moses' argument ends; it is only a way to get to his final and real point. Attention is directed to God's power from the first words Moses utters, for it was by "power" that God brought the people out of slavery and by powerful signs that God is seen to accompany the people. At the end of the prelude to Moses' real plea, he brings up once again God's power: "now let your power be great" (v. 17). Surely, it would be a clearly discernible sign of power for God to destroy the people God created as a covenant community, but daringly Moses redirects this kind of power and declares it implicitly to be a sign of impotence: "because the Holy One could not. . . ." Then in an even more startling turn, Moses makes his final appeal on the basis of God, God's character which was once "said" by God and heard by Moses in the self-revelation of God on Mount Sinai (Exod. 34:6-7). The real "power" of God is that God is "full of devotion" and therefore willing to "bear" the wrongdoing of the people, even while holding those who have sinned responsible. The statement about "visiting the sin of the ancestors" does not lead to a request for punishment but rather to a direct plea for forgiveness.

The final arguments to which Moses has built up are then not the reputation of the God of Israel in terms of usual displays of power and intervention, but rather God's reputation in relation to God's people as a God who "bears with" the sins of the people because of God's "devotion" (Hebrew *hesed*) and because of the relationship of the people to God, "because you have borne this people" (v. 19).[16] This intercession is first of all followed by God's words of forgiveness ("I have forgiven," v. 20), and Moses' intervention has therefore brought about a change of mind on the part of God. The punishment announced in the sequel (Num. 14:21-25) is not the total destruction of the people and presents an amelioration of the earlier divine plan. To assert with Patrick D. Miller: "The impassibility of God and the immutability of God were not a part of Israel's understanding of prayer. . . . The prayer for help assumes that God can be moved and that God can be persuaded to act in the situation so that it is changed for good, even if that means that God changes."[17]

The Torah then portrays God as ready to change at the point of God's willingness to bear with humanity. In other words, the changes that take place

16. The play on the Hebrew root *nasa*, used in both vv. 18 and 19, first with the object "sin" and second with "this people," is not easy to render in English. Many English translations provide a variation on the verb "forgive," as do, e.g., the KJV, NRSV, and JPS translations. Friedman and Fox both render with a version of "to bear." There is a play on the root in the text that is lost when translating "forgive," for God "bears with" the sins of the people God "bore" (i.e., carried). The verb is the same as the one used in Exod. 19:4 (see above, 16ff.).

17. Miller, 126.

in God's heart are not arbitrary. It is not a fickle unreliable God that comes into view,[18] but rather a God who is willing to relent, to "rue" the harshness of a decision that was made on the basis of the "evil" of humanity, for this decision may go counter to the "devotion" of God and the relationship God has established with the community.[19]

A text that does not directly testify to the willingness of God to have a change of plan, but rather is a witness to an essential statement about God's nature as dynamic rather than static, may be found in Exodus. Because it is also a statement that is frequently mistranslated and misunderstood, we need to consider it with close attention. It occurs during the well-known episode of the encounter of Moses and the burning bush, after Moses' self-imposed exile from Egypt and before the liberation of the people from slavery, when Moses receives his commissioning directly from God who speaks to him out of the bush (Exod. 3:10). Moses then replies:

Exodus 3:11-14[20]

11. And Moses said to God:
    Who am I
    that I shall go to Pharaoh
    and lead Israel's children from Egypt?

---

18. This contra Miles, who claims that God is "frighteningly unpredictable" in this part of the Bible; *God: A Biography*, 401.

19. The best-known example of a change of plan on God's side may be the story of the Ninevites, whose conversion from their wicked ways causes a reversal of plan for God. There the language of a turn-around is very explicit:

> Jonah 3:9-10
> 9. Who knows, God may turn and repent
>   and turn from his fierce anger
>   and we will not perish.
> 10. When God saw their deeds
>   that they turned from their evil ways,
>   God repented of the evil he had said to do them
>   and did not do it.

For another prophetic statement concerning this issue, see Jer. 18:7-8:

> At one moment I may declare concerning a nation or a kingdom, that I will pluck up and break down and destroy it, but if that nation, concerning which I have spoken, turns from its evil, I will change my mind about the disaster that I intended to bring on it. (NRSV)

20. For a discussion of this text and its larger context in connection with divine naming, see Johanna W. H. van Wijk-Bos, *Reimagining God* (Louisville: Westminster John Knox, 1995), 89-98.

12. God said:
    Because I will be with you.
    And this is the sign for you
    that I am the one who sent you:
    when you have led the people from Egypt,
    you will serve God on this mountain.
13. And Moses said to God:
    Look, I come to the children of Israel
    and say to them:
    The God of your ancestors has sent me to you,
    and they say to me: What is his name?
    What do I say to them?
14. God said to Moses:
    I will be who I will be.
    He said: Thus you must say
    To Israel's children:
    "I will be" has sent me to you.

Moses' opening gambit is more a protest than a question. Nevertheless the phrase "Who am I?" (v. 11) is a real question that revolves around identity, motivated by reluctance and real or pretended humility though it may be. In reply to the question, God promises presence (v. 12). But Moses is not satisfied, and he turns the question of identity to God. His indirect way of stating the matter — "I say . . . they say . . . what do I say?" (v. 13) — does not hide the fact that he, Moses, wants to know God's name, that is, God's identity. God's response (v. 14) contains three Hebrew words, *ehyeh asher ehyeh*. Most of our contemporary translations, directly or indirectly influenced by the Greek translation of this phrase, render it with some version of "I am who I am."[21] Many translators and commentators remark that the syntax of the phrase is difficult, as the verb "to be" rarely occurs in Hebrew in this particular way, without qualification. According to Martin Buber, the verb means "happening, coming into

21. It is interesting to note that Jewish translations do not escape the influence of Greek-philosophical thought in their renderings. But see Everett Fox: "I will be-there howsoever I will be-there"; *The Five Books of Moses* (New York: Schocken, 1995), 273. Fox is of course directly influenced by Buber in his translation. For arguments concerning the translation of the phrase and the rendering of the divine name, see Martin Buber, *Moses* (New York: Haprper, 1958), 39-55. See also Franz Rosenzweig, who discusses the translation "The Eternal" for the tetragrammaton in an essay originally published in 1929; "'The Eternal': Mendelssohn and the Name of God," in Martin Buber and Rosenzweig, *Scripture and Translation* (Bloomington: Indiana University Press, 1994), 99-113.

being, being there, being present, being thus and thus; but not being in the abstract sense." He translates the phrase, "I will be there as I will be there,"[22] thus putting the accent on the promise of presence. God is present-with but in God's own way, as God will be present. This promise is stated three times in the passage, first in 3:12, then again in 4:12 and 15. The repetition warrants the emphasis on presence included in the phrase "I will be as I will be," understanding it as a statement both about God's being and God's relating.[23]

The conveying of God's presence is important, but equally important is the dynamic quality of the revelation of God's name and the loss of this dynamism with the rendering "I am who I am." In this passage God is also throughout identified as the God of the ancestors (lit., "the God of your fathers"), an identification that anchors the promises of God for the present in the relationships of the past. The name of God, which in reality is not a name at all, of Exodus 3:14 looks also to the future. God has been there for the ancestors in the past and made them promises, and God will be there in the future, as uncertain as this future may appear. The manner of God's presence, however, will be up to God and is not manipulable by human terms and human images and human concepts: God will be as God will be. This is not a picture of a God who is static, unmoved and unchanging, but one who is dynamic and, while not vulnerable to human control, yet open to change in response to the human situation. The possibility of change is embedded in the self-revelation of God recounted in Exodus 3:14.[24]

A God Who Appears

The spiritual is not something tidy and distinct, another order of being. Instead, it is perfectly capable of intruding into everyday reality, as if part of this world. It is not just "in here"; it is also out there, a presence, looming.[25]

22. My translation of the German "Ich werde dasein als der ich dasein werde"; Martin Buber, *Die fünf Bücher der Weisung* (Cologne: Jakob Hegner, 1968), 158. For a discussion of the phrase, see Buber, *Moses*, 52.

23. For further arguments, see Martin Buber, "On Word Choice in Translating the Bible: In Memoriam Franz Rosenzweig" (first published in 1930), in *Scripture and Translation*, 79-89.

24. From the perspective of the community, this means that "the manner of God's presence with the community and the world is to be named anew, again and again, as the community's experience changes and God's presence needs to be reimagined"; van-Wijk Bos, *Reimagining God*, 98.

25. Kugel, *The God of Old*, 36.

Another traditional assumption about the God of the Bible, the God of Christianity, is that God cannot be seen, is "invisible," as the Westminster Confession testifies (see above, 234, note 4), a viewpoint for which there is indeed some warrant in Holy Scripture. Exodus 33:20 states it as baldly as possible: "for no human being shall see me and live."[26] There are texts that assume being face to face with God is indeed perilous, as characters express amazement at having survived the experience of "seeing God." So Jacob exclaims after his encounter at the Jabbok that he has "seen God face to face" and lived to see the day (Gen. 32:30), in the same manner as Hagar cries out her amazement that the vision of God has not blinded or destroyed her (Gen. 16:13). Both of these texts witness to the awe of the experience, but both also present meeting God face to face within the realm of the possible. It is not the fact that God would have no form but the fact of God's holiness which provides a difficulty, for it is incompatible with imperfect creation and thus presents problems for the contact between God and human (see, e.g., Exod. 19:18-24). Texts that report the encounter with the Holy God more matter-of-factly may still take note of the fact that the occasion passed without incident, as does Exodus 24:9-11, where the leaders of the community are said to "see the God of Israel" (v. 10) without destructive action on the part of the deity. This episode ends with a reaffirming statement of the vision of God: "they beheld God and they ate and drank."[27] In the section of Numbers 14 we considered earlier in this chapter, the phrase "you the Holy One are seen eye to eye" sounds almost laconic and conveys no bewilderment at all nor threat to the well-being of the beholder.[28]

Often, the text reports the appearance of God in the form of an "angel" or "messenger."[29] While conversing with this being, the human creature finds herself or himself eventually in the presence of the Holy One. In this way,

26. See also Deut. 4:12: "and an image you did not see, [there was] only a voice."

27. The difficulties posed by the bold statements of this text for biblical interpreters are reflected in Buber's discussion of the passage. Buber holds firmly to the invisibility of God and therefore to the idea that the narrative cannot state what it seems to state, i.e., that God is actually seen. "If it really told of the seeing of a divine form, it would mean that the redactor had not noticed the vast contradiction to be found between this passage and that other one in which Yhvh soon afterwards warns Moses, who wishes to look upon Him, that 'Man' cannot see him and remain alive" (*Moses*, 115). A desire for a more harmonious presentation on the presence of God than can actually be found in the biblical text is clearly driving this interpretation. See also Jeffrey H. Tigay in *The Jewish Study Bible*, 163.

28. Other texts in the Torah with references to Moses' seeing God, with or without the implication of possible danger, include Exod. 3:6; Num. 12:8; Deut. 34:10.

29. The Hebrew word *mal'akh* may be more appropriately translated with the word "messenger" or "divine messenger" in view of the religious freight and possibly mistaken notions that are attached to the word "angel."

Hagar's encounter begins with the mention of a divine messenger (Gen. 16:7). This being, who finds her in the wilderness, converses with her, and makes a pronouncement or a blessing in regard to her progeny (16:7-12), is identified by Hagar as the Holy One in response to her vision (v. 13). Similarly, during the prelude to the narrative of the destruction of Sodom and Gomorrah, Abraham hosts "three men" who evolve into "one," eventually referred to as the Holy One (Gen. 18:1, 2, 9, 10, 13-15, 16, 17). Jacob wrestles with a "man," who is then referred to as "God," both by the being with whom he struggles and by Jacob himself (Gen. 32:24, 28, 30).[30] Moses, who first confronts a burning bush, in the text said to contain a "messenger of the Holy One" (Exod. 3:2), finds himself confronting God, who continues to converse with him (Exod. 3:4). James L. Kugel explains these incidents as examples of human illusion, that is, the messenger does not undergo a metamorphosis into God; God was present in human form all the time, and it remained only for the human partner to gain clarity of sight:[31] "The angel is essentially an illusion, a piece of the supernatural that poses as ordinary reality for a time. The angel — is — God unrecognized, God intruding into ordinary reality."[32] Before the fog lifts, there is a moment of confusion, but finally the human partner recognizes whom he or she confronts. It looks like a human person, but it turns out not to be the case. It is as if at such times the veil between the created world and the reality of the divine is torn and the two intersect and commingle briefly. It should be noted that the moments of such intersecting are many times moments of culmination or climax of the episode.[33]

In the Torah these encounters take place with regularity, contradicting the notion that the God of the Bible is invisible. In addition to the more elaborately described appearances, God is said to "appear before" many times.[34] The verb "to appear" literally means "to be seen," and so the phrase with God as subject could also be translated "God was seen by," underlining this possibility of access to God.[35] Sorting through the various reports on God's direct interaction with

---

30. For an insightful discussion of this episode, see Kugel, *The God of Old,* 27-31.

31. For a New Testament example, one thinks immediately of the companions that meet the resurrected Jesus on the road to Emmaus (Luke 24:13-35, esp. v. 31): "their eyes were opened, and they recognized him" (NRSV). It is due to the blindness of the companions that they have not recognized Jesus.

32. Kugel, *The God of Old,* 34. See also Richard Elliott Friedman, who considers the angel to be a "hypostasis, a concrete expression of the divine presence, which is otherwise inexpressible to human beings"; *The Hidden Face of God* (San Francisco: HarperSanFrancisco, 1996), 13.

33. Kugel, *The God of Old,* 100.

34. Cf. Gen. 12:7; 17:1; 18:1; 26:2, 24; 35:9; 48:3; Exod. 3:16; 4:1; Lev. 9:4.

35. Thus Fox for Gen. 12:7: "YHWH *was seen* by Avram"; 55. In this Fox follows Buber, al-

human beings in the Torah, it seems that God is in some sort of visible contact with any representative of humanity (Gen. 1–11), with individual ancestors (Gen. 12–49), with the community of ancient Israel (Exodus and Numbers), with Moses and other leaders (Exodus, Leviticus, Numbers, Deuteronomy).[36]

While there seems then little holding back when it comes to mentioning divine appearances in the Torah, there arose in the same context the prohibition against making God visible in any form (Exod. 20:3-7). Whereas the experience of encounters with the deity, also in human form, may be counted as shared religious tradition in the ancient Near Eastern world, the anti-iconic posture of ancient Israel was unique for its time and place.[37] We may perhaps understand the proscription more clearly if we consider again the mystery of the divine self-disclosure in Exodus 3:14. In whatever way one interprets the meaning of the phrase "I will be who I will be," it entails among other things the freedom of God to decide on the manner of God's presence. Human-made images could not and should not represent the untrammeled free presence of the Holy One of Israel, because such would too easily be understood as containing the Holy God.[38] The prohibition against seeking and locating the presence of God in anything human-made is thus directly connected to the expression of divine self-disclosure in Exodus 3. Taken to its logical consequence, the ban includes permanently locating God in concepts or metaphors as well as physical representations. The God of the Torah, the God of the Bible is not to be located forever in any one image, be it physical or verbal, for then the Holy Name may be applied to what is in reality an "illusion" (Exod. 20:7; see above, 158, 161).[39] God may appear in the

---

though Buber maintains God as subject in the rendering "liess ER von Abram sich sehen," which literally translates as "YHWH let himself be seen by Abram"; *Die fünf Bücher der Weisung*, 44.

36. Both Miles and Friedman *(The Hidden Face of God)* argue that there is a gradual diminishment of God's appearing both in the Torah and in the Bible as a whole. At this point I am above all interested in pointing to the frequent sighting of God in the Torah, perhaps contrary to expectation, rather than in discerning a type of evolution of God's appearing. I will return to that possibility at a later juncture.

37. For a discussion of the prohibition in the context of the Decalogue, see above, 161.

38. While the prohibition on images has been far more consistently maintained in Judaism than in most branches of Christianity, it had its influence on the Protestantism of the Reformation and Calvin's understanding of the material not being capable of containing the immaterial, which in part motivated the strong iconoclastic impulse of the Reformation.

39. In connection with considerations on how to render the holy name of God, YHWH, I wrote: "In the end human beings do not have the capacity to name God, . . . in speaking of God and writing of God we always write on the water as it were: we write and 'tis gone, 'tis erased. . . . All our speaking and writing of God is inaccurate as well as accurate, . . . we always have it wrong as well as right"; Johanna W. H. van Wijk-Bos, "Writing on the Water," in *Jews, Chris-*

Torah numerous times, but in what shape or form remained for God to decide.[40]

A number of biblical scholars have argued that the manner of God's presence undergoes change in the biblical text, that gradually the direct interchange between God and humans disappears and "God cedes . . . more and more of the visible control of events to human beings themselves."[41] This point has been most forcefully argued in recent years by Richard Elliott Friedman and Jack Miles, who in their respective books, *The Hidden Face of God* and *God: A Biography,* explore the transition of the God of the Bible from activity to passivity and from speech to silence, from visible appearance to hiddenness. Although we are in this discussion more directly concerned with the way God is revealed in the Torah, the point is an important one and I will return to it.

A God Who Accompanies

God drove the human out, and made dwell east of the garden of Eden the Cherubs and the flaming sword turning back and forth to guard the road to the tree of life. (Genesis 3:24)

The fact that God is intimately engaged with human history is firmly established in the Torah, first on the large screen of the entire created world, subsequently through the involvement with the ancestors of ancient Israel, and eventually through the relationship with the "children of Israel" as a community first freed and then taken into covenant with God. I have argued in these pages that this engagement on God's part effected changes of divine intention and plan, that God does not remain unaffected by the interaction with the creation and the creature, a perception that finds support in the biblical text. In addition, God's involvement often took visible form according to the frequently mentioned divine appearances in the biblical text of the Torah. It is clear from the beginning that whatever the adventure of the created world is going to entail, it will take place in the company of God, for good or ill. A God who is remote from the creation would not likely have a "heartache" at the contemplation of human violence and its corrupting influence on the entire

---

tians, and the Theology of the Hebrew Scriptures, ed. Alice Ogden Bellis and Joel Kaminsky (Atlanta: Scholars, 2000), 55.

40. God's response to the one "request" to be made visible to a human being is telling in both its accommodation to this desire on Moses' part and its warning that what Moses is asking for is too much for a human to sustain (Exod. 33:18-23). See also above, 209, 211.

41. Friedman (1995): 59.

created world (Gen. 6:6), but would rather look on as unmoved and unmovable deity, dispassionately contemplating the mess it had become and would still become. A remote God would not sniff the "pleasing odor" of the sacrifice and announce a change in divine intentions (Gen. 8:21). A remote God would not deign to "come down" to meddle in human affairs and steer the creature away from doing more harm (Gen. 11:7). That God would hardly pin so many hopes on and invest so much energy in an unruly and rebellious crowd such as the "children of Israel." But the God of the Torah does all these things and more. In fact, one could claim that the one essential feature of God in the Torah is God's accompaniment of the experiment God created.

The verse cited at the heading of this section may not be one that first comes to mind when we consider the fact that in the Bible God chose human company, for it is too overwhelmed by the reality of the banishment of humans from the ideal garden that was their first home. The reason for the banishment is spelled out by the text when God ruminates that the presence of the "tree of life" in the garden would be tempting the human beings to eat from it, which would then cause them to live forever within the fraught context of tensions set up by their act of disobedience (Gen. 3:22). So it is easy to overlook the fact that when God closes the door to the garden of Eden, God is outside and not inside the garden. The text does not emphasize this, for it would probably not do to depict God as locked out of anything. But the upshot of the sequel to the human eating of the tree of knowledge of good and bad is that God henceforth is in it with them, accompanies them into the world of broken relation, disparity of power, and violence that has been brought about. That this is indeed the case becomes clear immediately when in the verse following (Gen. 4:1) Eve declares, "I have acquired a male (child) with the Holy One."[42] God is, in the words of the text, directly involved in the nitty gritty of human life, in birth-giving, which by God's own announcement (Gen. 3:16) goes accompanied by pain and labor. In my view, it is not coincidental that these words follow directly on the action of God "driving out" the human beings from the garden and setting a guard on the gate to the Edenic space.[43]

42. Eve's speech contains a play between the name of her firstborn, Cain (Hebrew *qayin*) and the verbal form "I have acquired" *(qaniti)*. Translations render the verb in various ways, as "I have gained" (JPS), "I have produced" (NRSV), "I have gotten" (Fox), and "erworben habe ich" (Buber), which comes closest to "I have gained" or "acquired." In addition, the word "man" *(ish)* is odd used in relation to a child.

43. Although not relying on Gen. 3:24, Terence E. Fretheim argues in a similar vein that the place of the God of the Bible is "in the world": "Since the creation God has taken up residence within the creation, and thus works from within the world, and not on the world from without"; *The Suffering of God.* Overtures to Biblical Theology 14 (Philadelphia: Fortress, 1984), 38.

Assertions about God's presence with the creation and the human creature are not made in a vague or general way. God is *specifically* with someone or a group of people, and the accompanying presence is concretely portrayed in the Torah. This feature naturally gives rise to the question: whose company does God seek? As enigmatic as Eve's words at the birth of Cain may be, they point at the very least to an understanding that the first accompanying act of God after the closing of the gate to the garden takes place at the side of the woman, Eve, not hereafter a main protagonist in the story.[44] At the close of the episode, before the first listing of the generations in Genesis 5, Eve speaks once more, after she gives birth to Seth/Shet: "God has granted me another seed in place of Abel for Cain slew him" (Gen. 4:25). In between the two utterances by Eve, we find the story of Cain and Abel depicting a God who favors Abel/*Hevel*/ "Mist," the one whose name indicates that he does not count (see above, 19 and 156). First in the Torah and then paradigmatically, God is placed on the side of the ones who are least powerful, who have the least voice — the woman and the victim of murder. Although Eve speaks twice in the sequel to the garden story of Genesis 3 and is the subject of verbs indicating birth-giving, she is in the aftermath of the act of disobedience receding fast into the background of a story taken over by male protagonists. Abel/"Mist" never speaks in the narrative and has no voice at all. But it is this voiceless character for whom God "has regard" (Gen. 4:4) and for whose murder God calls Cain to account.

These first perceived preferences of God should not be overlooked, for they speak to a picture of a God in the Torah who prefers the company of those who are, on the face of it, not the most attractive or powerful or rich. These preferences call to mind once again the words of Deuteronomy: "Not because you were more numerous than any other people did the Holy One desire you and choose you but *because you were littler than all nations*" (Deut. 7:7). It is not because of Noah's power that God chooses him to preserve humanity from the destruction of the flood, but because Noah finds favor with God on account of his "righteousness," a quality that counts before God.[45]

---

44. In the narratives of ancient Israel's ancestors, God is often viewed as intimately connected with conception and birth-giving, the ongoing process of life. This connection may be viewed as that of a male God who is in control of female fertility. But viewed from the perspective of God's ongoing presence, there is a telling intimacy of God with precisely that area of women's lives which spelled their survival in a world where progeny could be a matter of life or death.

45. Gen. 6:9: "Noah was a righteous man, blameless in his age — with God walked Noah." Righteousness, as is often pointed out by biblical scholars, is often misunderstood as if it were a mechanical legalistic quality, whereas it is rather in the Bible — whether it is applied to God or human — that quality which upholds the well-being of the community, especially by an ongoing concern for the poor and oppressed. See further below.

When God "comes down" to thwart the plans of the builders of city and tower in Genesis 11, it is to preserve and protect the earth and its role in the ongoing creation. Although Abram is eventually depicted as rich (Gen. 13:2), his wealth is viewed as a result rather than the cause of God's favor. In the confessional statement made in Deuteronomy 26, he is recalled as a "wandering Aramean," and it is not on account of the great numbers and the strength of his descendants that God liberates them, but because they "cried to the Holy One" (Deut. 26:5-7). God in the Torah "goes with" those in trouble and distress. It is this aspect of God's accompanying presence that is key to the understanding of God's nature as it is depicted here by those who wrote and edited the texts that make up the first five books of the Bible.

To understand how essential this understanding of God was to ancient Israel, we look once more at the self-disclosure of God in Exodus 3:1–4:17. Three times God repeats the promise of presence to Moses: "I will be with you" (3:12; 4:12, 15). The revelation contained in the phrase "I will be who I will be" must therefore also be seen in light of this promise. The what and how of the presence remain located in the freedom of a God who will accompany the people that need liberation from bondage, but the promise stands. In the announcement to the covenant at Sinai, it is the *self* of God to whom God has brought the people (Exod. 19:4: "and brought you to myself"; see above, 156-57). The people's trust will have to be in this promise, and it will be put to the test severely before they enter the land of the promise and afterward. Moses will have to rely on this promise. At the start he has a difficult time of it, as his protests during the conversation with God testify (Exod. 3:1–4:17). The temptation for the people will be to make the presence visible and stable somehow, if not in images, then in a sanctuary. But in the end, all that remains for them is the presence in the word, God's *torah*. In view of the people's mistrust, God is hard put to stick to the promise of presence and is tempted at times to reduce it back to the initial promise to Moses. Moses knows the significance of God's presence and therefore pleads repeatedly with God to "go" with the people. I recall here the words of his prayer in Exodus 33:15-16:

15. He said to God:
    If your face does not go,
    do not bring us up from here.
16. How will it be known otherwise,
    that I have found favor in your eyes,
    I and your people,
    if not in your going with us?

And we are distinct,
I and your people,
from all other people
on the face of the earth.

As I pointed out earlier (see above, 211), this prayer is "about the *self* of God, indicated by the emphatic usage of the pronoun 'you' in verse 12, and the 'face' of God as it represents God's presence and whether it will "go with" the people (vv. 14, 15, 16)."

The presence of God with the people of the first covenant is not on account of their size, power, or attractive character traits. In the context of the covenant people themselves, something more may be said about whose company God prefers. God's preference is, by the account of the Torah, for those who are down and out, for the ones who do not share the privilege of full belonging, the ones on the verge of sliding into the abyss of poverty and death. Three texts we have already considered in the context of the community's obligations, neighbor to neighbor, come to mind. First, a passage from the Book of the Covenant with its various laws, Exodus 22:21-27, in the strongest terms declares God's interest in the ones who are most vulnerable: "stranger," "orphan," and "widow," and God's ear for the cry of the "poor." It belongs to the essence of the God of Israel to have the divine attention turned especially to these who are powerless to take care of themselves, congruent with the first observations about God's presence after the closing of the gate to paradise. In Leviticus, the regulations for the life of the community lay down that it is incumbent on God's people to love and care for the poor, the neighbor in need, and the stranger (Lev. 19:9-10, 15-18, 33-34; see above, 192-97). These prescriptions stand in the context of the requirement to be "holy" as the God of Israel is "holy" (Lev. 19:2; 20:26). The people exhibit God's holiness when they are so turned to the poor, the neighbor, the stranger, as God is turned to them. This type of holiness represents a true conversion of the human heart. Finally, we considered a text about love for the stranger in Deuteronomy which may well contain one of the most remarkable statements about God and God's penchant for the marginalized in the Bible. After the great hyperbolic statement about who God is, the text turns to describe what God *does:* "doing justice for the fatherless and the widow, and loving the stranger by giving him food and a cloak" (Deut. 10:18). Just in case there was any doubt as to what constitutes God's justice and love, the last words fill in the content with most concrete acts of protection: "giving him food and a cloak." Provision of food and shelter is symbolic for making life possible. From almost the first to the last word in the entire Bible, God accompanies those whose company "decent" folk might want to avoid, and is to be found in their company.[46]

A God Who Is Prejudiced

God, the creator of humanity, having made a covenant with all humanity, then turns to one people and commands it to be different, teaching humanity to make space for difference.[47]

The previous section on the accompanying presence of God already led to a consideration of the particular company God chooses. The understanding that God accompanies a world that is turned away from God by its own inclination is not a vague, nonspecific perception, but it finds expression in choices God makes for particular people and places. God's concern for the whole world is made tangible through association with individuals and groups. This perspective may feel offensive to us if we assume that God must be impartial and not take sides. We have seen already that in the Torah the God of the Bible is portrayed as siding with those who have little power in terms of size or status and those who are unable to take care of themselves — a mother in childbirth (Eve), a victim of murder who even when alive had not amounted to much (Abel), a people in bondage (ancient Israel in Egypt), the stranger, the widow, the orphan. In these instances God's choice, according to textual witness, does not rest on outward appearance, for God "does not lift the face" (Deut. 10:17).[48] Rather, if there is a discernible basis for God's choice it arises out of God's "righteousness." Righteousness (Hebrew *tsedaqah*) is not an easy word to translate because it includes concepts that we hold to be mutually exclusive, such as justice and charity. *Tsedaqah* means justice that has an eye for the inequality and disparity between individuals and groups and aims to redress such differences. In the words of Rabbi Jonathan Sacks: "What *tzedakah* signifies, therefore, is what is often called 'social justice', meaning that no one should be without the basic requirements of existence, and that those who have more than they need must share some of that surplus with those who have less." And further: "God, for the Israelites, was actively concerned in the economic and political order, especially with those

---

46. We may consider Jesus' preference for the company of "tax collectors and sinners" on a continuum with this articulation of God's interest in the Hebrew Bible (e.g., Matt. 9:10-11; 11:19; Mark 2:16; Luke 5:30; 7:34; 15:1-2).

47. Jonathan Sacks, *The Dignity of Difference* (New York: Continuum, 2002), 53.

48. For a discussion of the phrase, see above, 200.

who, because they lacked power, or even a 'voice', became the victims of injustice and inequity."[49] God's *tsedaqah* involves judgment for those who refuse to follow this model of "righteousness." I will return to this difficult issue in the following section, touching closely as it does on perceptions of God as passionate.

So far, so good, and we have not said anything here that of necessity creates an understanding of an inside group and outsiders, an "us" and "them." We must, however, nudge the concept of the particularity of God's choice a bit further and consider also the choice God makes in the Torah for a particular kin-group, the "children of Israel," whom God chose to accomplish God's purposes for the world. Especially when recognizing God's prejudice in favor of the poor and deprived, one needs to not let go of the particularity of God's choice in the kinship group taken into covenant by God. In the words of Jon D. Levenson, we must "take account of the tension between the 'preferential option for the poor' and the chosenness of Israel."[50] We must not only take account of the tension, but we must hold to both insights as being true to the text that reveals to us still today the God of the Bible, the God of both Jews and Christians. What we must recognize then and not lose sight of is that God chose the ancestors of Israel, and then the kinship group of ancient Israel itself, to be in an exclusive relationship with God. At the same time, we must recognize that this relationship confers special responsibilities toward the human society rather than privilege, responsibilities which put the human community in line with God's understanding of *tsedaqah*.[51] Moreover, God's choice of the covenant community represented by the "children of Israel"

---

49. Sacks, *The Dignity of Difference*, 114-15.

50. Jon D. Levenson, "The Perils of Engaged Scholarship: A Rejoinder to Jorge Pixley," in *Jews, Christians, and the Theology of the Hebrew Scriptures*, ed. Alice Ogden Bellis and Joel S. Kaminsky, 240; quoting Levenson, "Liberation Theology and the Exodus, in *The Hebrew Bible, the Old Testament, and Historical Criticism* (Louisville: Westminster John Knox, 1993), 224. It is true that for many Latin American liberation theologians the history of the exodus and liberation from bondage is all too easily universalized, or where the specificity is recognized is seen as a step in a process to which Jesus Christ brings fulfillment. Both perspectives in their own way erase the significance of the history to which the Jews are direct heirs as well as the importance of Judasim as Christianity's sister religion. See, e.g., Gustavo Gutiérrez, *Essential Writings*, ed. James B. Nikoloff (Maryknoll: Orbis, 1996), 83. For Gutiérrez, the covenant made at Sinai is no longer valid and he can thus say: "When the infidelities of the Jewish people rendered the Old Covenant invalid, the Promise was incarnated in the proclamation of a New Covenant" (85). Note in this thinking also the conflation of biblical Israel and "the Jewish people," which renders in one stroke the Jews of today no longer eligible to be part of God's covenant.

51. For a discussion of the importance of the responsibilities of the human partner in the covenant relationship, see Part IV, ch. 4.

must also be seen in the broad context of God's interest in, and God's engagement with, the entire world. The blessings and promises to the ancestors and the people of the Sinai covenant have, after all, a universal frame of reference. The "exclusive moves" on God's part "are for the sake of a maximally inclusive end, including all human families, indeed the entire creation."[52] God is indeed prejudiced, but when all is said and done, God is prejudiced toward the entire creation. It is this prejudice that finds expression through the election of the children of Israel. If it is offensive to us that God exercises prejudice in this way, so be it. The text testifies to a God who is bent toward the creation and its well-being and who puts the human being in service of the same end. The means God uses toward the end include the election of a particular kinship group for a special relationship. We have no reason to assume that this special relationship was ever annulled. Christians who believe themselves also as in special relationship to the God of ancient Israel must hold this faith in light of the fact that someone was there before them and that there is still a sibling at their side who treads a different path of faith. In the meantime, it is as incumbent on them to practice this faith as it was on the children of Israel, as it is on the Jews, to make visible and real God's prejudice toward the powerless and voiceless in our world.

A God Who Is Passionate

Biblical literature leads one to the inevitable and inescapable conclusion that the deity, like humankind, is indeed a "social being," and without the society of humankind the deity would remain . . . pure, absolute, infinite potential.[53]

The God who is actively, often visibly, interacting with the world for the world, with Israel for Israel, as perceived in the Torah is clearly not dispassionate. As distorted as Christian images of a fiery, wrathful God of the "Old Testament" versus a peaceful, loving God of the New may be, the germ of truth in them is that the God of the Bible is not depicted as "cool." At the same time, it must be acknowledged that the depiction of a passionate God is true for the entire Bible. If as Christians we believe in God incarnate in a hu-

---

52. So Terence E. Fretheim, "Which Blessing Does Isaac Give Jacob?" in Bellis and Kaminsky, 283.

53. Murray H. Lichtenstein, "An Interpersonal Theology of the Hebrew Bible," in Bellis and Kaminsky, 79.

man person, God's only child Jesus, who in this incarnation "suffered and was crucified under Pontius Pilate," then the heart of God has to be affected. That a God who is described primarily in God's relation to the creation is affected by this creation has become clear throughout the previous discussion, and in this respect the New Testament is on a continuum with the Hebrew Bible. In the words of Ellen Davis: "If we properly understand the dynamics of covenant relationship, then we are confronted with a God who is vulnerable."[54]

At the moment of God's self-revelation on the mountain after the golden calf episode and Moses' intercession on behalf of the people, the first words are about God's "compassion" and "favor." The entire statement reads:

Exodus 34:6-7
6. And the Holy one passed in front of him
    and called out: The Holy One, the Holy One,
    [is] a God of compassion and favor,
    slow to anger
    and full of devotion and faithfulness.
7. Extending devotion to the thousandth generation,
    bearing with failure, wickedness and sin,
    and *not*[55] holding innocent [the guilty],
    taking account of the failure of ancestors
    toward children and children's children
    until the third and the fourth generation.

This statement, or one like it, is repeated various times in the scriptural text and constitutes as much of a confessional statement about God as we have in the Hebrew Bible.[56] "Compassion," here in its adjectival form *rahum*, is a part of a cluster of words that all connote "tender, loving care," connected to the Hebrew word for "womb" *rehem*. Clearly, a female aspect is present in

54. Davis maintains that God's vulnerability arises directly from the covenantal relationship into which God enters with human partners. "For, as both Testaments maintain, the covenant with God is fundamentally an unbreakable bond of love *(hesed)*. And ordinary experience teaches that love and vulnerability are inextricably linked"; Ellen F. Davis, *Getting Involved with God: Rediscovering the Old Testament* (Cambridge, Mass.: Cowley, 2001), 62. On the issue of God's vulnerability, see also Fretheim, *The Suffering of God*.

55. The verb is used twice in Hebrew which I here choose to render with the italicized "not" because negated verbs are difficult to double in English. For the use of such devices, see Richard Elliott Friedman, *A Commentary on the Torah*, xv.

56. Cf. Num. 14:18; Neh. 9:17; Ps. 86:15; 103:8, 17; 145:8; Jer. 32:18-19; Joel 2:13; Jonah 4:2. A form of the statement may be found in Exod. 20:6; Deut. 5:9-10; 7:9; 1 Kgs. 3:6; 2 Chr. 30:9; Neh. 9:31; Ps. 106:45; 111:4; 112:4; Jer. 30:11; Lam. 3:32; Dan. 9:4.

this word, and some translate it with "motherly compassion."[57] "Favor," also in the adjectival form, may be translated as "gracious," or "merciful,"[58] and is closely related to God's prejudice on behalf of the powerless and on behalf of God's people discussed in the previous section. Certainly, the qualities of "compassion" and "favor" testify to God's nature as engaged with humanity and with ancient Israel in particular, and as affected by this engagement in positive ways. The idea of God's compassion calls to mind once again the passage in Exodus 22:21-27, where it is applied specifically toward the "poor."[59] The admonishment to treat the ones who live on the edge of nonexistence with protective care ends with the statement from God that God will listen to their cries, "for compassionate am I" (Exod. 22:27).

In addition, Exodus 34:6 speaks of God as "full of devotion and faithfulness." The word here translated with "devotion," Hebrew *hesed,* is often rendered in English with "lovingkindness." Like the Hebrew *tsedaqah,* this term is difficult to contain in one English term. Buber has said that *hesed* "is trustworthiness between beings, especially trustworthiness in the covenantal relation between the liege lord and his vassals, above all the covenantal fidelity of the Lord who sustains and protects his servants, and so also that of the servants faithfully committed to their Lord."[60] In line with Buber's observations, translations at times use "covenant loyalty" to translate *hesed.* With "devotion" I intend to highlight a perception of God as entirely turned toward, "devoted" to the well-being of the covenant community.[61] *Hesed* is not just an attitude, however, or a mental state, but always issues in positive action on behalf of. It is the only quality of God that is here mentioned twice, for in the

---

57. To my knowledge, the first scholar to discuss the word in its connection to the womb in a meaningful way was Phyllis Trible, who observed that the verbal root for this word establishes a major metaphor for biblical faith; *God and the Rhetoric of Sexuality* (Philadelphia: Fortress, 1978), 33. For an earlier though more passing observation of the connection between compassion and womb, see Buber, *Moses,* 154.

58. Translating with adjectives while maintaining the word "favor" would end up in the awkward "favoring," and I have therefore substituted nouns in both cases. Fox solves the dilemma by adding a verb: "showing-mercy, showing-favor" (*The Five Books of Moses,* 455), while Buber uses two verbal forms.

59. For discussion, see above, 187-88.

60. Buber, "On Translating the Praisings," in *Scripture and Translation,* 93. For a full discussion of the concept, see Katherine Doob Sakenfeld, *The Meaning of Hesed in the Hebrew Bible.* HSM 17 (Missoula: Scholars, 1978). Fox translates with "loyalty"; 455.

61. In aiming to translate the concept throughout the biblical text with one word, I have difficulty with the translation "grace," which is the English for Buber's German *Huld,* because this word works well only from "the top down," so to speak, and less well in relation to a reciprocal posture on the part of human beings.

sequel to verse 6 God is said to "guard" or "observe devotion" long into the future (v. 7). The term joined to *hesed* is Hebrew *emet*, "faithfulness," a word frequently paired with *hesed*, and it essentially connotes "trustworthiness, fidelity."[62] Taken together, the two concepts indicate that God's devotion may be relied on, may be trusted to endure.

God has "compassion." God is moved on account of the covenant community, the people of God's "favor," and is filled with "enduring devotion" toward them. It is hard to understand the basis for Jack Miles's conclusion that God as portrayed in the Torah is a lot of things but is "not loving."[63] In light of Exodus 34:6-7 and related passages, what else is described here but a dedicated, loving God? In addition, one finds in the Torah a straightforward declaration of God's love such as the following: "Not because you were more numerous than any other people did the Holy One desire you and choose you but because you were littler than all nations. For out of love for you and out of keeping the oath God swore to your ancestors the Holy One brought you out" (Deut. 7:7-8). Lest we miss the point, to love and choice is here added "desire," a word used elsewhere in the Bible of sexual love.

In between these positive declarations occurs a more negative note when God is said to be "slow to anger." If it is not immediately clear why God should be angry at all, we only bring to mind that the entire statement takes place in the context of the golden calf incident, which entailed a loss of trust and devotion from the side of the covenant people. Exodus 34:7 thus states more fully God's position toward human shortcoming within the covenant partnership. As tempting as it may be to overlook the side of God's devotion that holds the covenant partner accountable and thus avoid a discussion of what is here called God's "anger," the only way out of the difficulty may be *through* a consideration of this seemingly negative aspect of God's nature. Ancient Israel as God's covenant partner was called to uphold the covenant by listening to God's voice and acting upon God's instructions, God's *torah*. The negative side of God's "favor," "compassion," and "reliable devotion" is God's judgment on the failure of the

---

62. Buber, "On Translating the Praisings," 93. According to Buber, the three concepts of *hesed*, *tsedeq* and *emet* are central to biblical theology: "They celebrate divine virtues, and portray them for imitation to those who are to go 'in God's ways.'"

63. "He has been wrathful, vengeful, and remorseful. But he has not been loving. It was not for love that he made man (sic!). It was not for love that he made his covenant with Abraham. It was not for love that he brought the Israelites out of Egypt or drove out the Canaanites before them. The 'steadfast love' of the Mosaic covenant was, as we saw, rather a fierce mutual loyalty binding liege and vassal than any other gentler emotion"; *God: A Biography*, 237. And further: "to judge from the entire text of the Bible from Genesis 1 through Isaiah 39, the Lord does not know what love is" (238).

human partner to uphold its side of the deal. Human beings, according to the Bible in full measure partaking of the evil that fills human imagination (Gen. 8:21), face consequences when they refuse the task of living as God's covenant partner.[64] In the Book of the Covenant, God's "anger" comes into play specifically when the community fails in its task of upholding the well-being of those who are in special need, whose rights are not automatically accorded to them. In Exodus 22:21-24, the community is told that abuse toward "stranger," "widow," or "orphan" will result in their "crying out" to God, that God will hear their cry and that God's "wrath will burn" (v. 24). The contradiction embedded in Exodus 34:6-7 is that the God of Israel is a God who both "bears with" the people's failure and at the same time "takes account" of it, "holds them accountable." It will be up to God and the human interaction with God to see which of the two gets greater play. In the meantime, God's favor, compassion, and enduring devotion both outweigh the anger of God's judgment and set limits around it and thus call to mind the words of Psalm 30, that God's wrath is momentary while God's favor is for a lifetime (v. 5).[65]

A last and more unsettling aspect of God's passionate involvement with the creation and with ancient Israel is the mention of God's posture toward those who are hostile to the people that God has chosen. Both Egypt and the peoples that live in the land of the promise are on the receiving end of God's anger, the first in the narratives that look back on the liberation from Egypt, the second in the texts that look forward to the settlement in Canaan. The "signs and wonders" that constitute God's acts on behalf of the slaves to be freed from bondage in Egypt include appalling violence toward the land and its inhabitants (Exod. 7–12). In addition, the preparations for entry into the promised land include encouragement of great violence toward the inhabitants of the land (Exod. 23:23-33; 34:11-16; Num. 33:50-56; Deut. 7:1-26; 20:16, 17), combined with a promise of divine violence. The passion of God for God's people in the Torah provides glimpses of a dark side in which a passionate God is engaged in the struggle against those who stand in the way of the flourishing of the covenant people.

The passages that call for the total annihilation of the inhabitants of Canaan are few. All bear the stamp of the Deuteronomistic editor. Here is a text from Deuteronomy as one example:

64. Here the words of Amos come to mind: "Only you have I known/of all the clans of the earth;/therefore I will take account of/all your failures" (Amos 3:2).

65. For an extensive discussion of the qualities of God cited in Exod. 34:6-7 and specifically of God's anger, see Walter Brueggemann, "The Book of Exodus," *New Interpreter's Bible* 1 (Nashville: Abingdon, 1994), 946-48. According to Brueggemann, the contradiction "makes the God of the Bible, interesting, credible, and dangerous"; 947.

Deuteronomy 7:1-11

1. When the Holy One your God brings you to the land
   that you will enter to possess it
   and will clear away many peoples from before you
      — the Hittite, the Gerushite, the Amorite,
   the Canaanite, the Perizzite, the Hivite, and the Jebusite,
   seven nations greater and stronger than you —
2. and the Holy One your God will deliver them up to you
   and you slay them,
      you must put them under the ban;
   do not make a covenant with them
   and do not have pity on them.
3. Do not intermarry with them;
      your daughters do not give to their sons
   and their daughters do not take for your sons.
4. For that will cause your sons
   to turn aside from me
   and they will serve other gods;
   and the anger of the Holy God will burn against you
   and God will destroy you quickly.
5. But this you will do:
      their altars you will throw down,
   their pillars you will break
   and their asherahs you will hew
   and idols you will burn with fire.
6. For you are a people dedicated to the Holy One your God;
   the Holy One your God chose you to be a people
   treasured by God above all the peoples on the face of the earth.

7. Not because you were more numerous than any other people
   did the Holy One desire you and choose you
   but because you were littler than all nations.
8. For out of love for you and out of keeping the oath
   God swore to your ancestors
   the Holy One brought you out by a strong hand
   and rescued you from the house of slavery
   from the hand of Pharaoh the king of Egypt.
9. And you know that the Holy One your God is God,
   the trustworthy God, keeping covenant devotion
   with those who love God and keep God's instructions

for a thousand generations.
10. God will repay those who hate God personally
and destroy them;
there will be no delay for those who hate God personally;
God will repay them.
11. You must keep the instruction
and the statutes and laws
which I myself instruct you today, to do them.

Deuteronomy, sometimes characterized as a sermon, may be viewed as a long meditation on what it means for the people and for their life together to be in a covenant relation with God and what it means for their continued existence in the land of the promise. The setting the text poses is just before the entry into the land, but it was composed long afterwards, written either in the face of the imminent loss of the land or after looking back on this reality.[66] The material gives witness to great anxiety concerning the place of the land within the framework of God's promises. Possession of the land is conditional in Deuteronomy, dependent on how well the Israelites fulfill the obligations that are laid upon them. In a few texts, specific groups are proscribed for the Israelites in terms of contact and friendship, and their annihilation is commanded.[67] How does one reconcile this requirement with that of love for the stranger, of care for their welfare and protection of their persons?[68]

The crucial passages where total annihilation of inhabitants of the land

66. See above, page 59. There seems to me to be good reason to maintain a traditional northern 8th-century dating for this book of the Torah. Alternatively, it was composed shortly before the exile of Judah, or even after the exile. For a helpful approach to the historical context of Deuteronomy, see Patrick D. Miller, *Deuteronomy*. Interpretation (Louisville: John Knox, 1990), 5-8.

67. See Deut. 7:1-26; 20:16-18; Exod. 23:23-33; 34:11-16; Num. 33:51-66.

68. The violence required by these passages is often ignored in biblical hermeneutics, or it is focused on to the exclusion of anything else. But the contradictions between these regulations and the concern expressed for the stranger elsewhere in the biblical text are rarely of concern. Thus Susan Niditch in her otherwise excellent study, *War in the Hebrew Bible: A Study in the Ethics of Violence* (Oxford: Oxford University Press, 1993), does not raise the question of inner inconsistency. This question is raised by Regina M. Schwartz, who notes: "A moving accountability for the widow, the orphan, and the poor and commitment to liberation from oppression is joined to obliterating the Canaanites"; *The Curse of Cain: The Violent Legacy of Monotheism* (Chicago: University of Chicago Press, 1997), xi. Schwartz finds an answer to the contradiction in the notion of scarcity, a context in which everything must be competed for. In addition, Schwartz is concerned that the biblical myth of scarcity has had a strong hold on "our politics, in our culture, and in our imaginations."

of the promise is demanded may be found in Exodus and Numbers as well as Deuteronomy, and their tenor is identical: if the inhabitants of Canaan are left to survive, the temptation for the ancient Israelites will be to idolatry. Thus these texts emphasize the need to destroy the inhabitants and their idols, for idol worship is tempting and would "become a snare" for the children of Israel (Deut. 7:16). Leaving the nations intact would mean leaving the idols intact and thus provide an opportunity for temptation for the Israelites. In essence, these passages address the dangers of false worship. The main concern of the text is thus with the total dedication of the people to their God. If the words were indeed composed hundreds of years after the events they claim to describe, when loss of land and sanctuary, as well as the endangered covenant bond, were staring people in the face, then a complete reorientation to the God of Israel is demanded, the God who "keeps covenant devotion." Only if the people wholeheartedly, purely, and without compromise dedicate themselves to the covenant God will the blessings follow that will keep them intact as a people: possession of the land, increase in numbers, and abundance in foodstuffs to keep them alive. Mixing with the neighbors would cause straying from the course: "your sons will turn aside . . . will serve other gods. . . . you shall not serve their gods, for that would become a snare for you. . . . do not bring a horror into your house" (Deut. 7:4, 16, 26). The mode of relation must be to God alone and will not extend to the strangers that live with them in the promised land. This insight does not make the violence of the text any more palatable but rather shifts the emphasis of concern.[69]

More importantly, the defeated people who wrote these words or received them had neither the opportunity nor the capability to destroy other peoples. The scenario set out here is artificial. The text is mythological, even to the listing of the seven nations to be destroyed, most of which were no longer in existence to threaten ancient Israel and some of which had never been known as nations at all. This type of wholesale destruction could never have happened, it never did happen. Yet, such mythologies exert power, even when they are not based on historical fact. God, by the mouth of Moses, is commanding the people to do violent acts, and people of violence have excused their deeds by appealing to such biblical texts as these and others to

---

69. The regulations governing the conquest of the land and those governing life with the stranger once settled in the land come from "separate realms." That is to say, the one set of texts demanding annihilation of the inhabitants arises from traditions pertaining to the myth of the "conquest" of Canaan, while texts relating to life with the stranger arise from socio-religious traditions that reflect conditions and realities in the organized life of the community. See Moshe Greenberg, "Some Postulates of Biblical Criminal Law," in *A Song of Power and the Power of Song*, ed. Duane L. Christensen (Winona Lake: Eisenbrauns, 1993), 284.

justify what they do. In the words of Regina M. Schwartz: "This disturbing bit of our cultural inheritance alone has done powerful ideological work, reflecting and spawning a way of thinking about identity, about territory, about the Other, and about violence."[70] In other words, it is not so much the ideology of the text in its own historical circumstance but the life that such a text may have in the religious ideologies of peoples that indeed do conquer that needs to worry us.[71]

In light of the frequency, the intensity, and the scope of the laws regarding life with the stranger in the Torah, I suggest we add to the statement that it could never have happened and that it did never happen the phrase: it *should never happen.* The Bible itself in its entire witness makes a problem of the violence encouraged in Deuteronomy 7. In view of this thematic consistency, we must reject the direction of violence that this text may lead to. As we observed earlier: the concern of the text is with the total dedication of the community to its God, with its holiness. At its core, this dedication to the Holy One resides in the posture and the practice toward the stranger. Without loving the stranger, there cannot exist a dedicated (i.e., a holy) community. Love for the stranger is closest to holiness. The attitudes and practices that govern the behavior toward the stranger both then and now stand in judgment over the texts in Exodus, Numbers, and Deuteronomy that reflect violence toward the stranger and might incite to similar violence. We must firmly set aside the direction of violence that the text might take us in. We must turn our backs on it, as we turn our backs on an outdated piece of an ancient past that was never played out, should not have been played out, and will not be played out by us.[72]

---

70. P. 158. And further: "Oppressed people write utopian myths of conquest. Peoples in exile write fantastic tales of land acquisition. *But conquerors also celebrate their conquests, and empires describe their subject peoples as indeed subjected.* If historical events give rise to narratives in complex ways, the historical afterlife of a given narrative is equally convoluted"; 156 (emphasis mine).

71. Regina M. Schwartz, *passim.*

72. Ultimately, the analysis that the inhabitants of Canaan are "exploiters," whose "system" needs to be destroyed in order for the "covenantal ways" of the ancient Israelites to flourish, is unsatisfactory as a total way of dealing with such texts as Deut. 7 (So Brueggemann, "The Book of Exodus," 878, following Norman K. Gottwald, *The Tribes of [Y•hw•h]*, 591-621). For this is certainly not the emphasis the narratives give. In addition, recovery of the historical facts offers only a partial solution. As Regina M. Schwartz asks (155), "How was the real (historical) story — whatever it was — so completely misremembered in the biblical narrative? . . . If we did uncover the true story of Israel's 'settlement' in Canaan . . . and if we even unveiled the process by which it was distorted into the biblical story we have, how would that discovery alter our thinking?"

Conclusion

It may amount to a truism to say that the Bible, the Torah included, does not offer a systematic treatment of God. We, latecomers to the task, must piece together a picture of the God of ancient Israel as best we can. The God that has come into view here is one who is deeply involved with and affected by the creation and the human creature. While some of the aspects of God's nature described in the Torah may be more obviously close to the core of Christian belief than others, the appearing of God in human form has taken on special significance in the person of Jesus Christ. We believe, after all, that in Christ the overwhelming "devotion" of God for the world took human form. Christians too believe that God's mercy outweighs any destructive impulses God may have toward the creation and that God is affected by prayer. In the Christ, God's accompanying presence and God's favor are become manifest for the world and are extended to those outside the kin-group of the first covenant people. Clearly, the God of the Torah is also the God of Christianity.

Christ and Torah

Judaism was the dominant force in the world of early Christianity.[1]

The Torah's depiction of God, as we reviewed it in the previous chapter, is essentially that of a God who is passionately oriented to the world and its inhabitants, a God who desires the healing of the creation, and to that end enters into a special relationship with a kin-group which finds formal expression as a covenant. This group carries a special obligation to respond to God and God's desires for the life of the community and the world in specific ways for which they receive instruction, *torah*. It is among this group that Jesus was born, lived, and taught. Although divine instructions were eventually codified in a text, *torah*, like God, is not conceived of as static and unchangeable, but rather indicates directives, rules, laws, and stories that are adaptable to different situations. At the time of Jesus, this perception of the capacity of the biblical laws to address situations very different from the time in which the text was originally composed had given rise to elaborate discourse and interpretation. It is evident from the Gospels that Jesus himself engaged constantly with such interpretation, an endeavor that must be placed within the Jewish context of his day.[2] The Gospels

1. John G. Gager, *The Origin of Anti-Semitism: Attitudes Toward Judaism in Pagan and Christian Antiquity* (Oxford: Oxford University Press, 1983), 115.

2. It is not easy to define more closely where and how Jesus fit into his context, because information about the Judaism of that day is not plentiful. In this regard, Lewis John Eron's suggestion is attractive, that Jesus' attitude toward the law may reflect his Galilean background. Such a background might be evident from Gospel perspectives on purity, for example. Lewis John Eron, "Jesus: A Torah-True Jew?" in *Bursting the Bonds? A Jewish-Christian Dialogue on Jesus and Paul,* ed. Leonard Swidler, Eron, Gerard Sloyan, and Lester Dean (Maryknoll: Orbis, 1990), 70-77. For a more detailed and informed overview of the different positions in 1st-century Palestinian Judaism, see Peter J. Tomson, *"If This Be from "Heaven"* (Sheffield: Sheffield Academic, 2001).

portray a Jesus who is indeed oriented to the Torah, whether it be in disagreement, expansion, or agreement. The question is whether Jesus' concept of total dedication to God as depicted in the Gospels is on a continuum with understandings we gleaned from our overview of the Torah, or whether his orientation and teaching take us in a different direction.[3]

Subsequently, I will take up the issue of Torah and Christ, or law and gospel, as the subject appears in Pauline material. When Paul set aside specific Torah regulations as not valid for Gentile Christians, did this movement away from the Torah include an abandonment of Torah ethics? We will look specifically at the context of Paul's letters, at the significance of the Greek word *nomos* for Hebrew *torah,* and at the instructions Paul gave to the nascent Christian churches. While it is impossible to explore the subject of Pauline understandings of the place and significance of the Torah in detail, in view of the extent of the subject, we may yet hope to find some new insight into old problems. For both the Gospels and the Pauline material, the crucial question is whether the opposition of gospel and law is a necessary outcome of Christian interpretation of these texts.

Finally, we will take up the subject of a Christian orientation to the Torah. Since Christians understand themselves to exist in a covenant relationship with God, the God of Israel, the God of the Jews, *torah* as the logical companion piece to the covenant relationship must still be relevant. An initial exploration will lead toward the final chapter of this book, in which we will take a closer look at Galatians 3:26-29. Putting these well-known verses in conversation with passages from the Torah will lead to a reading that produces valid instruction for contemporary Christian faith and practice.

Jesus and the Torah

Jesus was a law-abiding Jew.[4]

Assumptions

Our vision is often more obstructed by what we think we know than by our lack of knowledge.[5]

---

3. Because the Gospel of John raises its own issues and problems in regard to Jesus and the Torah, an exploration of which would lead too far afield, I will concentrate mainly on portions of the Synoptic Gospels.

4. E. P. Sanders, *Jewish Law from Jesus to the Mishnah: Five Studies* (Philadelphia: Trinity International, 1990), 90.

5. Krister Stendahl, *Paul Among Jews and Gentiles* (Philadelphia: Fortress, 1976), 7.

It is probably safe to say that most Christians today assume that the Judaism of Jesus' day was a religion of petty rules, the observance of which governed the lives of the Jews and guaranteed their relationship to God. Judaism in Jesus' time was a "legalistic" religion, according to this view, of which the Pharisees were the primary representatives.[6] This type of religion Jesus opposed, setting the Torah aside and teaching instead a religion of love for God and neighbor. Second, 1st-century Judaism is often portrayed as an exclusivist religion, averse to contact with outsiders and arrogant about its status as the chosen people of God. Contrary to this exclusive and arrogant stance, Jesus offered an inclusive and universalist religion in which all people were embraced by God, regardless of their ethnic origin. The views of Jesus brought him into such conflict with the legalizing Jews of his time that he was eventually executed at the instigation of Jewish religious leaders by the authority of the Roman governor. This view of Judaism and the Jews of the 1st century C.E. is by no means confined to lay persons, but is rather sustained and perpetuated by the mainstream of Christian scholarship on the New Testament of the past 200 years.[7] The negative depiction of Judaism in Jesus' day is moreover preached from our Christian pulpits and taught in our Sunday schools. By extension, such denigration of 1st-century Judaism includes a negative judgment on contemporary Judaism, although this subject is rarely explored, and for the most part Judaism as a living religion is treated not only as a petty "legalistic" religion, inferior to Christianity, but as a *dead* religion by implication.

Let us begin with some different assumptions. First, let us assume that the Judaism of the 1st century of our era is not well known to Christians, who generally and vaguely identify it as something called "Old Testament religion." Our first step then in another direction than negative and derogatory judgments must be an admission of our lack of knowledge.[8] There must also be recognition that taking information about 1st-century Judaism from the New Testament at face value is a bit like assuming acquaintance with a person

6. How this view of Judaism was developed and made the norm in influential Christian scholarship has been effectively argued in the landmark article by George Foot Moore, "Christian Writers on Judaism," *HTR* 14 (1921): 197-254.

7. For a good overview of such scholarship, with the names of famous scholars such as Günther Bornkamm and Rudolf Bultmann in a prominent place, see the works of E. P. Sanders: *Jesus and Judaism* (Philadelphia: Fortress, 1985), esp. the Introduction; *Paul and Palestinian Judaism* (Minneapolis: Fortress, 1977); *Paul, the Law and the Jewish People* (Minneapolis: Fortress, 1983); *The Historical Figure of Jesus* (London: Penguin, 1993); "Jesus and the Kingdom: The Restoration of Israel and the New People of God," in *Jesus, the Gospels and the Church*, ed. Sanders (Macon: Mercer, 1987), 225-39.

8. For a detailed overview of Palestinian Judaism from a Christian perspective with a thorough referencing of sources, see Sanders, *Paul and Palestinian Judaism*.

solely on the basis of character descriptions from a hostile divorcing partner. Second, let us assume, as people of good will, that 1st-century Judaism was a valid religion that deserves our respect.[9] Let us assume that this religion had its problems and aberrations, as do all religions, and that it expressed itself in a variety of perspectives, among which Jesus took his place, and that it was no more "petty," "legalistic," or "exclusivist" than any other religion that lays claim to the truth about itself and God. In addition, let us be clear that *contemporary* Judaism in its manifold expressions, as it took shape at approximately the same time as Christianity and in distinction to it, is a valid religion that deserves Christian respect, and about which Christians do not know much unless they make an effort to study Talmud, engage in cross-religious conversation, and in other ways set themselves to learn about concepts, customs, and practices that are alien to their own.[10] Furthermore, we recognize that Judaism in past and present has an equal or even greater claim to the heritage of biblical Israel and the promises of God than does Christianity. Finally, we acknowledge that a Christian posture toward Judaism and the Jews must take distance from any hostility that may be present in the Gospel narratives, not only because it does not provide an accurate picture of religion and people, but because of a long history during which Christianity as the dominant partner perpetuated this hostility in ways that we must abhor.

It is not here our task to delineate a picture of 1st-century Judaism. This work has been undertaken and is carried on by a number of scholars, and excellent discussions have appeared on this subject. It is clear from the Gospels that Jesus had a number of disputes in his time with religious leaders and that

---

9. In this context, Katharina von Kellenbach's observation is helpful, that it is "critical to move beyond mere rejection of antisemitism." Instead, we must *replace* the teaching of contempt with a "teaching of respect"; *Anti-Judaism in Feminist Religious Writings* (Atlanta: Scholars, 1994), 137. Von Kellenbach bases the phrase on Clark Williamson's argument in his book *A Guest in the House of Israel: Post-Holocaust Church Theology* (Louisville: Westminster John Knox, 1993), 245.

10. Both the Palestinian and the Babylonian Talmud can be found in English translations, but to master this vast literature is a daunting task even for the serious student. The Jewish scholar Jacob Neusner has made an enormous contribution with works that interpret Judaism and Judaic Literature. In addition, and especially in the United States, a lively Jewish-Christian conversation as well as an exploration of historic Christian hostility toward Judaism and the Jews has taken place during the past few decades. An impetus for these explorations was provided by Rosemary Ruether's work, *Faith and Fratricide* (New York: Seabury, 1974), followed by *Antisemitism and the Foundations of Christianity*, ed. Alan T. Davies (New York: Paulist, 1975). For an excellent exploration of early Christian-Jewish relations, see Gager. Earlier works include the significant contributions of George Foot Moore, *Judaism in the First Centuries of the Christian Era: The Age of the Tannaim*, 3 vols. (Cambridge, Mass.: Harvard University Press, 1927-1930); *HTR* 14 (1921): 197-254. See also the works by E. P. Sanders.

the arguments centered chiefly on Sabbath and purity regulations.[11] It is also clear that the Gospel writers, composing their narratives a relatively long time after Jesus' death, highlighted these disputes for their own reasons. What interests us here is not so much whether Jesus took his own position in terms of applying Torah rules on purity and Sabbath or how he departed from what may have been mainstream traditions within Judaism. Rather, we seek to place the Jesus of the Synoptic Gospels in relation to the covenant responsibilities laid on the human community, especially as they are expressed in the concern for the outcast and the stranger in the Torah.

The Teachings of Jesus

Of all the things that we can say about the short career of Jesus of Nazareth as it is described in all the Gospels, it is evident that he taught. Words for teaching abound in the literature, and one of the early titles of Jesus was certainly that of "teacher," Aramaic *rav* or *rabbi*.[12] Mark 6:34 expresses Jesus' calling as teacher in a particularly strong image: "And on debarking he saw a great crowd. And he was moved on their account for they were like sheep without a shepherd and he began to teach them many things." Not only by words but also by actions, whether through healings or other miraculous manifestations, Jesus' aim seems consistently to be instruction about the way faithful members of the community should relate to God and neighbor. In combining the two laws from the Torah regarding the love for God and the neighbor, from Deuteronomy 6:5 and Leviticus 19:18, either by Jesus himself (Matt. 22:37-39; Mark 12:30-31) or by a questioner with whom Jesus agrees (Luke 10:27), no new perspective on a faithful life is offered but one that exists already in the Torah and that was affirmed among Jews of Jesus' day.[13] The so-called Golden Rule found in Luke 6:31 (cf. Matt. 7:12) can be found in identical form in rabbinical literature.[14] The uniqueness of Jesus resides in that Christians believe he not only taught these Torah convictions but embodied them to the utmost, and that in his person the devotion of God for the world became uniquely manifest. It is the person rather than the teaching that is distinctive.

---

11. E.g., Matt. 12:1-8; 15:1-20; Mark 2:23-28; 3:1-6; 7:1-23; Luke 6:1-11.

12. For the Greek *didaskalos*, see Matt. 8:19; 12:38; 19:16; 22:16, 24, 36; Mark 4:38; 9:17, 38; 10:17, 20, 35; 12:14, 19, 32; 13:1; Luke 7:40; 9:38; For the Aramaic *rabbi*, see Matt. 26:25, 49; Mark 9:5; 10:51; 11:21; 14:45; John 1:49; 4:31; 6:25; 9:2; 11:8.

13. See Leonard J. Swidler, "Yeshua: a Torah-true Jew?" in Swidler et al., 58-59.

14. See Tractate *Shabbat* 31:a, where the quotation is put in the mouth of Rabbi Hillel who lived at the time of Jesus.

The Good Samaritan

In line with the Torah, Jesus applied his teaching specifically to those in need. The sick, the disabled, the outcast, those without social or religious privilege were those who drew his attention. By this preference, Jesus embodied the quality of righteousness *(tsedaqah)* that is a crucial aspect of a God who is prejudiced toward the outcast. While many texts could be cited to illustrate Jesus' teaching, we explore here in greater detail one passage that speaks to this issue. While the witness of one text may not seem sufficient in view of the variety of witness of the Gospels, a close-up look may go a long way toward a deeper insight into old and new ways of understanding Scripture.

Luke 10:25-37

25. And, look, a certain expert in the Torah stood up to test him and said: Teacher, what shall I do to obtain eternal life? 26. And he said to him: What is written in the Torah? How do you read? 27. He answered: You shall love the Holy One your God with your entire heart and with all your soul and all your strength and your whole mind, and your neighbor as yourself. 28. He said to him: You answered correctly. Do this and live. 29. He, wanting to justify himself, said to Jesus: And who is my neighbor?

30. In reply Jesus said: A certain person went down from Jerusalem to Jericho, and fell in the hands of bandits who robbed him, beat him, and left him lying half-dead. 31. By chance a priest went down that road, saw him, and passed by on the other side. 32. The same with a Levite who came by the place and passed by on the other side. 33. And a Samaritan who was traveling came near him and seeing him was moved to pity. 34. And he went to him, bound up his wounds, pouring on oil and wine; he put him on his own animal, brought him to an inn, and took care of him. 35. And the next day he took two pieces of money and gave them to the innkeeper and said: Take care of him and if you have other costs I will reimburse them on my return.

36. Which of these three in your opinion was the neighbor of the one who fell in the hands of bandits? 37. He said: The one who treated him with compassion. Jesus said to him: Go and do the same.

The Frame

Approximately half of the passage is devoted to the story, while the other half presents an exchange between Jesus and a questioner. The exchange is presented in such a way that it both opens and concludes the unit, thus forming a frame around the story. In the Gospels of Matthew and Mark, the combination of the love commandments are set in different contexts, so it is of some interest that Luke chooses to introduce and conclude a story that is found only in this Gospel, in this particular way: as an illustration of neighborly love.[15] In respect to the question-and-response exchange, it is apparent that the conclusion does not quite fit the opening part. The question of verse 29, "Who is my neighbor?" presents the neighbor as the potentially passive recipient of love, as does the Torah commandment. The question posed by Jesus at the end concerns the neighbor as the active giver of love.[16] The discrepancy may well have come about through redactional activity as John Dominic Crossan suggests, but as it now stands in the passage, Jesus reframes the question.[17] Let us look more closely at the details of the frame.

Luke sets up an exchange between Jesus and an expert in the law (the Torah), and without adding specifics of time and place creates a context of controversy by the words "to test him," an expression used most frequently in the Gospels of Jesus' opponents, who somehow try to trip him up.[18] The comment elicits the suspicion that the questioner is not entirely sincere in his purpose. Furthermore, his second question is uttered in order "to justify himself," a comment which puts the questioner in a no more positive light.[19] Without these qualifications, the questions could be read as sincere and unprovocative. For the first question, Jesus sends the expert directly back to his own religious resources, the Torah itself, and in response to the second question, Jesus tells the story. The opening question asks about a way of action

15. In Matthew and Mark, the two commandments are combined by Jesus, in Matthew in response to a hostile question from one of the Pharisees (Matt. 22:34-40), in Mark in response to a neutral question from a scribe (Mark 12:28-34). Both Mark and Matthew place the utterance much later in Jesus' ministry than does Luke, after the entry into Jerusalem, and neither offers a story to illustrate the requirements to love God and neighbor.

16. Although many comment on the discrepancy, the issue is most clearly put by New Testament scholar John Dominic Crossan, who observes that "the prefixing of x.27,29 would indicate that the neighbour in the parable is the wounded man by the roadside; but the suffixing of x.36 would mean that the neighbour is the Good Samaritan"; "Parable and Example in the Teaching of Jesus," *NTS* 18 (1972): 288.

17. "A single controversy dialogue in Luke x.25-8 has been very carefully and skillfully expanded into a double controversy by taking the parable of x.30-6 and framing it with x.29 and x.37"; *NTS* 18 (1972): 291.

18. A form of the verb used here occurs in the context of controversy, e.g., in Matt. 16:1; 19:3; 22:18; Mark 8:11; 10:2; 12:15; Luke 11:16; John 8:6.

19. Cf. Luke 16:15. "The legist, therefore, is one of those Torah-observant Jews, associated with the Pharisees, who seek to justify *themselves* — that is, who seek to manage their own salvation, by following a certain *halakah*"; Jack T. Sanders, *The Jews in Luke-Acts* (Philadelphia: Fortress, 1987), 183.

that will help the believer "to obtain eternal life." That is, he asks what he should do in order to be saved. Interestingly enough, Jesus does not say: "All you need to do is believe in God!" Or: "Don't you know that you are saved by God not by works?" Or: "All you need to do is believe in me!" Rather, Jesus asks "what is written in the law (the Torah)" and how the expert "reads." What should be done by the believer to live faithfully is written in the Torah, to be read and interpreted by those who hold to the Sacred Text. "How do you read?" may be understood both literally and figuratively. That is, "What are the words you read and how do you understand them?" The expert indeed knows what the Torah says and gives the answer that combines two directives, one from Deuteronomy on the love of God and one from Leviticus on love for the neighbor. Jesus agrees and counsels him to act on these. But the expert is not content, either for his own purposes or for the purpose of creating trouble for Jesus, and asks his second question: "Who is my neighbor?"

Jesus tells his story in reply, quickly and dramatically. When it is over, it is his turn to ask a question: Who do you think acted "like a neighbor"? The expert has no trouble in answering with the obvious truth. Jesus then has the final word on counseling him once more to act in the same manner as the Samaritan in the story. Jesus has reframed the question so that the issue becomes a matter of acting in an appropriate neighborly manner, "with compassion," across major dividing lines of orientation and outlook, of ethnic and religious allegiance. This may put those performing the loving act at physical and psychological risk and involve them in expenditure of energy and resources. With this directive Jesus has said no more and no less than that a compassionate God requires of the human partner similar compassionate behavior. In Sharon H. Ringe's words: "The question 'who is my neighbor?' is changed into 'Who am I in this relationship of neighboring?' . . . Neighboring is a two-way street."[20]

The Story
On one level, the story is a clear example of what Jesus intends to teach. A violent incident on the road from Jerusalem to Jericho presents a picture of an environment inhospitable to single travelers that at the same time provides a hideout and place of protection for gangs and outlaws. Even today, the inhospitable aspect of the wilderness of Judah is forbidding. The robbers leave the man for half-dead, and he surely would have died, had not one person come to his rescue. This person is the third passer-by, after a priest and a Levite

---

20. Sharon H. Ringe, *Luke.* Westminster Bible Companion (Louisville: Westminster John Knox, 1995), 160.

"passed by on the other side" (vv. 31 and 32). Those two see no reason to involve themselves and keep their distance. The Samaritan, the third character to provide potential help, on the other hand "came near him" and, on coming near, "was moved to pity." Six verbs of action in the next lines emphasize the thoroughness of his act of mercy, which concludes by his doing everything he can to provide for the victim now and into the future.

On this level, the story involves characters that rouse the interest. Anyone coming by would have a number of reasons to abstain from action for help: helping a victim of crime in a dangerous area is always dangerous to the helper; touching a dead body at that time caused uncleanness, which would necessitate the inconvenience of ritual cleansing, especially inconvenient for those associated with temple service.[21] Beyond these obvious reasons, the passers-by may have a host of reasons of their own for not engaging in help. The point is that we are not told of any, and the listener is left to imagine them. The third character to appear is the one who extends himself. He is an unlikely character to do so, for there was great tension between Samaritans and Jews, and we assume that the victim of the assault was a Jew, even though this is never stated as such in the story. A person who by social and religious allegiance would find himself at odds with the victim, naturally in a hostile rather than an amicable relation, is the one who puts himself out to help. That is what being a neighbor is all about. The story then pushes the commandment to love the neighbor in the same direction as the requirements of Leviticus 19:34. As in Leviticus, the holiness of the community and the individual exhibits itself in loving action toward those who are not naturally inside the circle of concern and may even be in a hostile relation to it. In addition, the story of the Samaritan who helps the roadside victim is an illustration of the requirements of Exodus 23:4-5, which demands actions of cooperation across lines of hostility. There is nothing new here, except that Jesus applies the requirement to love the potentially hostile neighbor to a contemporary setting that makes it acute and unsettling for the audience, as such demands are supposed to do.

The requirements for the community that considers itself to be in a covenant relationship with the Holy One of Israel do not change, although they may take on different shape in differing contexts. It is the holiness of God, a God who is above all "compassionate," that must be emulated in deeds of "compassion." The expert in the law thus responds correctly with his final reply to Jesus' question as to who acted in a neighborly way: "the one who treated him with compassion."

---

21. For Torah rules on contact with a dead body, see Num. 19:11-13.

How Do We Read?

Jesus was a Jew who in his time and context engaged with other Jews in disputation and religious argument about the right way to act and believe. A story such as this may well have come from his teachings, or he may in telling it have drawn upon material available to him from his tradition. We are not certain about what constituted mainline Judaism of the time, since it was still in its formative stage, and there were most likely a number of groups in competition for the tradition that would eventually carry the day. We know of Pharisees, of Sadducees, of Samaritans and Essenes, and Jesus must have taken his place somewhere among them. By the time Luke writes his Gospel, the temple in Jerusalem has been destroyed and the ones who follow the way of Jesus of Nazareth have become predominantly Gentile rather than Jewish. All the Gospel writers have a tendency to put the Jewish opponents of Jesus in a bad light, and controversies still rage today as to what according to the Gospels, if any, was the place of the Jews in the promises of God for the world as they became manifest in Jesus. Some scholars see only hostility to Jews and Judaism in Luke, also in the Parable of the Good Samaritan, while others take a more moderate view.[22] The issues are complicated, because the audience for whom Luke is written may consist of Jewish Christians, of Gentile Christians, or of Gentile Christians who intended the full observance of the Mosaic laws, the so-called Judaizers. While the debates about these different audiences and therefore different interpretations of Luke's intentions have gone on and will no doubt continue, is there anything we can say with certainty? How we read is, after all, connected with how the story was read at the time it was composed.

If Luke was written no later than 80 and 90 of our era as seems to be the general opinion, then we may assume that for the followers of Jesus as the Christ "one problem was essentially solved — the salvation of the Gentiles without circumcision."[23] But the problem of what to do about following the Mosaic law was not solved, and a number of different solutions may be found in the New Testament.[24] If Luke wrote for Jewish Christians, is he denouncing

---

22. For an extreme example of the opinion that derogatory opinions of Judaism and the Jews prevail in Luke, including in this parable, see Jack T. Sanders. Also Samuel Sandmel, *Anti-Semitism in the New Testament?* (Philadelphia: Fortress, 1978), views the entire New Testament as "permeated" by anti-Semitism (160). For a more moderate view, see Jacob Jervell, *Luke and the People of God* (Minneapolis: Augsburg, 1972). According to Craig A. Evans, the interpretation of Sanders suffers from misreading; "Faith and Polemic: The New Testament and First-Century Judaism," in *Anti-Semitism and Early Christianity: Issues of Polemic and Faith,* ed. Evans and Donald A. Hagner (Minneapolis: Fortress, 1993), 16-17.

23. Jervell, 135.

24. Jervell, 136.

the Jews as "enemies of Jesus and the Church"? In the parable of the Samaritan, is he setting up the Samaritan as an example of true Christian behavior that is contrasted to the behavior of Jewish leadership who claim to follow the Torah?[25] Would for Luke "the world. . . be much better off when 'the Jews' get what they deserve and the world is rid of them"?[26] Or is Luke, also with this story, laying claim to the Torah and to Jewish Christians as the true followers of the Torah, unlike the Jews who do not follow Jesus? In the words of Jacob Jervell: "Jewish Christians, being the restored Israel, are the foundaton of the church, and so they must be upholders of the law."[27] Is this position any advance on viewing Gentile Christians as the replacement of Israel? And in this perspective is not the only good Jew a converted Jew? It seems we cannot get away from a derogatory and negative judgment of those Jews who chose not to follow Jesus as the Messiah and clung to their own faith and its traditions. Clearly, we must set these disputes within early Christian contexts when the followers of Jesus originally constituted a movement within Judaism. Recognition of this context goes a little way toward mitigating the derogatory posture of the Gospel writers to Judaism and the Jews, for it is not the same as anti-Judaism and anti-Jewishness that has centuries of hatred and persecution on the part of Christians toward Jews behind it. Yet, the derogation and negativity must be recognized and unearthed for Christians to be able to deal with it honestly and put its demons to flight.

As church-going people we have all heard scores of sermons on the parable of the Good Samaritan. If the preacher was a responsible exegete, he or she would make clear that the priest and the Levite in the story stand as examples for any leaders of a religious establishment who live by the rules rather than the law of love, not specifically Jewish religious leaders. Yet, the fact remains that the tension between Samaritans and Jews needs to be explained, for this is no longer a known entity for most Christians. Once this tension is explained as hostility from the Jewish side for Samaritans, the specificity of Jewish "hatred" for the outsider and love for "petty rules" comes into play and cannot help but function in the sermon, at least as a subtext.[28] The surface line may then disavow any disparagement of Jews and their religion. But under the surface we know it is certainly about Jews and their petty reli-

---

25. So Jack T. Sanders, 145.

26. Jack T. Sanders, 317.

27. Jervell, 143.

28. The tension and resulting feelings of antagonism between Samaritans and Jews were, in reality, mutual. For information on the Samaritans as a Jewish sect, see "Samaritans," in *The Dictionary of Judaism in the Biblical Period 450 B.C.E. to 600 C.E.*, ed. Jacob Neusner and William Scott Green (New York: Macmillan, 1996), 2:546-48.

gion, for we all know what they were/are like. During a recent sermon on the parable of the Prodigal Son in Luke 15, a story equal in popularity to that of the Good Samaritan, I heard the preacher refer to the Pharisees and scribes mentioned in the context of this and other parables as "the religious leaders of Jesus' day who have a Santa Claus theology, a simplistic judgmental faith of a God who rewards and punishes." Over against such plainly condemnable beliefs, Christianity is the faith of "everyone is in. Jesus wanted everyone to know that we all belong to God's family." At no point did the preacher refer to the Jews or to Judaism, but it is difficult to avoid making direct connections, connections that may be all the more dangerous because they are made covertly. How do we combat such readings of the text, in recognition that we need to be reoriented once more toward the Torah demands of love for God and the neighbor? How do we read differently in recognition that this neighbor must first of all include Jews victimized by Christians?

In his essay "Catholic Dogma after Auschwitz," Gregory Baum remarks that "Auschwitz. . . is an altogether special sign of the times, in which God empowers the Church to correct its past teaching, *including its central dogma*, to the extent that it distorts God's action in Christ and promotes human destruction."[29] In terms of the "Good Samaritan," a way to start the correction process is by drawing a clear line from the teaching of Jesus in this passage, both in the framing of the story and the story itself, to the teaching of the Torah concerning love for God and neighbor. Neither in the Old Testament texts nor in those of the New Testament is the love for the neighbor presented as something easy. Love for the neighbor in the Leviticus text is ultimately love for the stranger. The stranger as present in the passage from Luke is not a far-off outsider but one close by, akin in outlook perhaps but different in origin, Samaritan to Jew, Jew to Christian. The traditional anti-Judaic and anti-Jewish readings of the passage, whether overt or hidden, must be clearly addressed. Jesus himself points to the Torah as the text that instructs in what is necessary "to live." If we follow the direction pointed by Jesus, our acts of mercy and compassion, of love for the neighbor, must be expressed in full repentance for past crimes.

Parables are tricky stories with more than one surface meaning, usually demanding that the listener make a judgment, a judgment which often turns out to put the listener on trial. The classic example of such a parable is the one the prophet Nathan tells David after his transgression with Bathsheba and the murder of Uriah (2 Sam. 12:1-7). David *thinks* the prophet is pronouncing judgment on someone else, but in fact the pointing finger and the ringing

---

29. In Davies, *Antisemitism and the Foundations of Christianity*, 142.

declaration of the death sentence are turned on himself and his own mis-
deeds. Nathan's words, "You are the man" (verse 7), go straight to the heart of
the matter. Just so with us, when listening to a parable we are tempted to join
in at the point of becoming the judge rather than the judged, in the manner
of David. As Christians reading the parable of the "Good Samaritan" today
after Auschwitz, where do we see ourselves in the story? Perhaps we should
see ourselves as the band of robbers who left their victim for dead on the
roadside or as those who ignored the suffering and "passed by on the other
side." Insofar as Christians participated in the persecution and attempts at
annihilation of the Jews or ignored their plight, the parable indicts us for past
actions and postures, and Jesus' words drive us to consider anew what for us
is the meaning of love for God and neighbor if we do not first of all include
the Jews.

Paul and the Torah

*It is a topic that has been discussed by numerous scholars in great de-
tail, with the result that one pauses before thinking that fresh light
can be shed on it.*[30]

Paul's discussion of the law is complicated and has given rise to seemingly
endless discussions, spanning centuries of Christian thought on the subject.
Our goal here is not to systematize what are often ad hoc, and sometimes
contradictory, declarations in different Pauline letters, addressed to various
audiences, each with their concerns about which we are not always clear, nor
to provide an overview of the varied and often contradictory Christian interpretations of them.[31] We look, rather, for an understanding of Paul's reasoning in light of his own perception of his mission and in light of the concerns
of the recipients of his writings. In addition, it is important to consider the
change that took place with the use of Greek vocabulary for what were originally Hebrew concepts and articulations. What changes took place in terms of
perception when the Hebrew *torah* became the Greek *nomos*?

30. E. P. Sanders, *Paul, the Law, and the Jewish People*, 3.
31. I consider the work of E. P. Sanders in this regard to make one of the most informative
and thorough contributions, taking seriously both the Jewish and the Christian context of
Paul's concerns. See esp. *Paul, the Law, and the Jewish People* and *Paul and Palestinian Judaism*.
An especially clear outline of the various parties in the Judaism of Jesus' day and Paul's position
within these different representations may be found in Peter J. Tomson, *"If This Be from
Heaven."*

Finally, we review briefly the grounding and direction of Pauline teachings concerning appropriate Christian conduct, both in their connections with and in their distinction from Torah guidance.[32]

Torah and Nomos

Over a wide range the rendering of תּוֹרָה *by νόμος is thoroughly misleading, and it is to be regretted that the English versions followed the LXX (via the Vulgate) in so many cases.*[33]

In between the composition of the texts that constitute the Torah and the writing of the books that came to constitute the New Testament, the world of the Bible underwent radical changes. In the centuries after the exile to Babylon, the imperial province of Judaea, the birthplace for both rabbinic Judaism and Christianity, existed first under Persian, then Greek domination, and at the time of Jesus and Paul was under Roman occupation, shortly thereafter to succumb to the destructive military power of Rome. Rome's management of the imperial territory was probably harsher than any regime that had reigned in biblical lands theretofore. Yet we must not forget that a presence of foreigners, including a military presence, with their culture and languages had been woven into the fabric of daily life in the land of the Bible for hundreds of years. Culturally, the world of Hellenism was more dominant than either Persia before it or Rome after it, so that by the time of Jesus and Paul Greek was the language in which people communicated most easily across regional and national borders. The holy texts of Judaism had been translated into Greek from the 3d century B.C.E. and onwards, originally for the Jewish community in Alexandria, Egypt, and eventually functioning as the Bible for the early Christian movement. The writers of the books that would make up the New Testament wrote in Greek. Greek language and concepts were the vehicles for conveying the meaning of Christ and the place of the Torah.

Torah is translated into Greek as *nomos*. These two words do not mean the same thing — translated words rarely do — but in this case the difference

32. I will consider by general scholarly agreement the following letters as authentically Pauline: Romans, 1 and 2 Corinthians, Galatians, Philippians, 1 Thessalonians, and Philemon.

33. C. H. Dodd, *The Bible and the Greeks* (London: Hodder & Stoughton, 1935), 33. It is noteworthy that Dodd, in this entire discussion with its many excellent insights, does not escape the taint of a negative appraisal of Judaism. He judges Hellenistic Judaism and specifically the Jews of Egypt to have read the *nomos* ideas back into those connected with *torah* so that the "prophetic type of religion was obscured, and the Biblical revelation was conceived in a hard legalistic way" (34).

is significant for the formation of perceptions on the Torah within the Christian faith. The depth and richness of the Hebrew word *Torah* was reviewed in the first section of this book (see above, 3-14). First and most obviously, the Greek word *nomos* does not cover the different meanings of *torah* in all their ambiguity and multileveled ramifications. Lexical meanings of the Hebrew noun *torah* list first of all "direction" and "instruction," with only a third meaning provided of "particular instruction, rule," while the word "law" is not listed as a translation.[34] For the Greek word *nomos,* the first listing is "law," and there is no mention of "instruction" or "direction" in the entire listing.[35] Yet, *nomos* is mostly how the Hebrew *torah* is translated in the Septuagint. Generally speaking, *nomos* represents a part of what is *torah.* It indicates in the Gospels and the rest of the New Testament especially the divine legislation in the moral and ritual realm that make up a part of the Torah, for which Hebrew had specific words.[36] Besides this meaning, *nomos* can indicate "custom" or "principle." Overall, the Greek word represents a narrowing of the broad understanding and the flexibility of the Hebrew *torah.*[37] The best way to express the distinction may be that of C. H. Dodd, who observed that "תּוֹרָה in its widest sense means divine teaching or revelation; νόμος in its widest sense means a principle of life or action."[38] Heikki Räisänen has provided a thorough review of *nomos,* and from his observations it is clear that the meaning of the word only at times coincides with the Hebrew *Torah* and that Paul uses it in a number of different ways within one section.[39] As Lloyd Gaston remarks: "It would have been much simpler for everyone if Paul had used a different word than *nomos* when he wanted to speak of the law outside the context of the covenant, but of course he could not."[40]

---

34. *HAL* 4:1710-12.

35. William F. Arndt and F. Wilbur Gingrich, *A Greek-English Lexicon of the New Testament and Other Early Christian Literature* (Chicago: University of Chicago Press, 1957), 544-45.

36. So Dodd (32): "The natural Greek equivalent of תּוֹרָה in the more general sense would have been something like διδαχὴ or διδασκαλία or some other derivative of verbs used to translate תּוֹרָה."

37. At times, *nomos* can indicate also a text, the first five books of the Bible, the Torah.

38. Dodd, 40.

39. Räisänen cites Rom. 7:21-25, where *nomos* is used in at least three different ways; *Jesus, Paul and Torah.* JSNTSup 43 (Sheffield: Sheffield Academic, 1992), 63. Räisänen is also helpful in casting a critical eye on the material in the standard lexicons and the *TDNT,* in which the article on *nomos,* written by Kleinknecht, appeared at the height of the Nazi era in Germany. Generally, Christian scholars writing about *nomos* in Paul seem to have little or no understanding of the Hebrew word it replaced.

40. Lloyd Gaston, *Paul and the Torah* (Vancouver: University of British Columbia Press, 1987), 43. See also the important discussion in the work of Hans-Joachim Schoeps. Schoeps is of

Context

The movement around Jesus began as a group within Judaism, and there are no historical indications that Jesus ever envisioned it otherwise. Jesus himself was, as far as we can tell, a circumcised, Torah-abiding Jew. His disputes with other religious representatives of his time may be considered to fit within the varied expressions of the Judaism of his time. Soon after his death, this situation changed and a strong evangelistic impulse drove the seeking of converts among Gentiles, as well as the Jews. Eventually, the followers of Jesus were called Christian and Christianity became a mainly Gentile movement. This transition happened not without difficulties and tensions, each context providing its own slant on the difficulty experienced by those who converted to belief in the God of Israel, by the mediation of the Jew Jesus, and through the preaching of a Jew, Paul, who had come to believe that in this Jesus the good news of God's love for the world was made available to all, Gentile and Jew alike. The predominant questions were always "who belongs" and "what are the *marks of belonging?*"[41] For Jews, the response to these questions was one connected to the kin-group and to religious tradition. One who "belongs" was a descendant of the "children of Israel," bound to God in covenant, who honored the Torah, and held to certain ways of life, one of which was circumcision for men, another the keeping of the food laws, valid for both male and female, and yet another the Sabbath regulations. In this context, ethnicity is not overriding, so that those who wished to become a member of the covenant people could do so by adopting circumcision, laws of kosher, and Sabbath, the so-called "proselytes." Others would join in certain observances but not in all of them, the so-called "God-fearers" (Luke 7:5; Acts 10:2). "In contrast to what is often thought, it was not unusual for Jews and non-Jews to visit one another socially and partake of refreshments together."[42] At the time of Jesus' life, a number of different groups existed within Judaism, each representing their

---

the opinion that Paul misunderstood both the nature of the law and that of the covenant and bluntly judges Paul to have suffered from a "fateful misunderstanding" which caused him to tear "asunder covenant and law"; *Paul: The Theology of the Apostle in the Light of Jewish Religious History* (Philadelphia: Westminster, 1961), 218. Schoeps lays the blame for Paul's misunderstandings at the door of Hellenistic Judaism, while they might rather be the result of the limitations of the Greek versus the Hebrew language. These two issues, while not unrelated, should not be seen as identical.

41. E. P. Sanders: "The question is not about how many good deeds an individual must present before God to be declared righteous at the judgment, but . . . whether or not Paul's Gentile converts must accept the Jewish law in order to enter the people of God or to be counted truly members"; *Paul, the Law, and the Jewish People*, 20.

42. Tomson, *"If This Be from Heaven,"* 109.

own version of Judaism. We know of the Pharisees, the Sadducees, the Essenes, and the Samaritans. With the arrival of the movement of followers of Jesus, yet another category was created: those Jews who held Jesus to be the Messiah. Very soon Gentile Jesus believers were on the scene as well, and there was dissent among these as to what Jewish customs and ways of life they should follow: should they be circumcised, eat kosher, and keep Shabbat? Or, were they freed from these obligations that were basically a part of Jewish existence? We may imagine that some of these believers were those already attracted to Judaism or attached to it in some way, as God-fearers or proselytes.

Jewish Christians may have been of divided opinions on these matters also, as is evident from the disputes among the apostles. Two main groups that held strong opinions may have resulted in a fourfold division: (1) Jewish Christians who held to the Jewish way of life (Peter and James); (2) Jewish Christians who held that the Jewish way of life was not relevant for Gentile Christians and that each group should abide in its own way (Paul); (3) Gentile Christians who held that the Jewish way of life should be followed by all (the so-called Judaizers, to whom the Galatians may have belonged); (4) Gentile Christians who held that they were not obligated to follow Jewish customs and marks of belonging (eventually the entire Christian community). The disputes about Jewish customs are, above all, centered on circumcision and dietary laws, as is apparent from the frequency of the mention of these subjects in Paul's letters.[43] It is also self-evident that these would be among the most cumbersome of the regulations that determined the life of faithful Jews and that distinguished it from that of the world around them. Paul became by his own definition the "apostle to the Gentiles" in the years 40-60 C.E. Early on he decided that Gentiles who believed in Jesus as their Lord (their *kyrios*), who wanted to enter into the circle of those who believed in the God of Israel, did not need to adopt specifically circumcision and diet laws. Without any cynicism one could see this as an eminently practical move on the part of the missionary Paul, who did not envision much success for his good news if it came accompanied by a scalpel aimed at the genitals of adult males.[44] Nor, so one imagines, would it be an easy task to explain complicated and esoteric food laws that all came with the package of the good news of Jesus Christ. Both circumcision and dietary regulations were, moreover, occasionally cause for ridicule of the Jews by outsiders. Once

---

43. To a lesser extent the controversy involved the keeping of Shabbat and feast days.

44. As Francis Watson points out, Paul himself is quite frank about his motivation for abandoning the law of Moses. It is done so he "might win the more" (1 Cor. 9:19); *Paul, Judaism and the Gentiles: A Sociological Approach*. SNTSMS 56 (Cambridge: Cambridge University Press, 1986), 35. We note also that Paul himself refers at least once to circumcision as "mutilation" (Phil. 3:2).

Gentile male genitals were declared safe by Paul, and food regulations were at least softened, once a part of the law was set aside, he was obligated to explain on the basis of what understandings of the law he could make such a move and what the place of the entire law was in the lives of the believers.[45] Paul did this adroitly, but not always without contradicting himself or while reaching perfect coherence. He made extremely negative statements about the law, on the one hand (Rom. 7:9-13; 2 Cor. 3:6; Gal. 3:23, 25), and positive ones, on the other (Rom. 7:12, 14-16; 9:14; 13:8-10; 1 Cor. 7:19; Gal. 5:14), depending on the argument he brought to bear in the course of his reasoning.[46] All of Paul's arguments, however, need to be seen, first of all, in the context of the struggle between Jewish and Gentile Jesus-believers about what constituted their identity and what the place was of the certain customs and regulations as "the mark of their belonging." Was this movement going to be basically one that would fit inside Judaism as one of the reform movements? Or was it going to be a separate group and eventually form a separate religion?[47]

It could be said that Paul's position won the day. But we need to understand at the same time that a part of his position, that taken regarding Jewish Christians, became eventually irrelevant and dropped out of view as Christianity became a predominantly Gentile religion and no one any longer had a crisis of conscience in regard to circumcision or a kosher kitchen. Paul's context was gone, but his positions were still read and studied and thus found new interpretations within new Christian contexts in which new problems had arisen (as, for example, during the Roman Catholic/Protestant conflict at the time of the Reformation). As Krister Stendahl points out, "The West for centuries has wrongly surmised that the biblical writers were grappling with problems which no doubt are ours, but which never entered their conscience."[48]

In summary: For practical purposes, Paul set aside certain marks of Jewish identity, specifically circumcision and dietary laws, for Gentile believers who through Jesus Christ came to believe in the God of Israel. Theologi-

---

45. It may well have come as a surprise to Paul that there were those among his converts who strongly held to the keeping of all Torah regulations and marks of Jewish identity — hence, his vehement tone in much of the Letter to the Galatians.

46. It is not my intent here to trivialize or ridicule Paul's position toward the law, a position which was also colored by his eschatological outlook. My point of view runs counter, however, to those who believe Paul himself to have experienced the law as a burden.

47. Watson argues that the basic struggle at the time of Paul is that between a sect and a reform movement. "Paul's theoretical discussions of such themes as the law and works, grace and faith, election and promise, are thus to be regarded as an *attempt to legitimate the social reality of sectarian Gentile Christian communities in which the law was not observed*. Paul sought to construct a theoretical rationale for separation"; 178.

48. P. 95.

cally, Paul argued that it was acceptance of Christ as the *kyrios* that enabled Gentiles to enter into the covenant community of the people of God and that everyone belongs to this community *by this acceptance.* Jewish Christians were not required to give up their customs, and Gentile Christians were not required to adopt Jewish customs. It may well have been that Paul viewed it a danger for Gentile Christians to accept circumcision and dietary regulations, because for them it constituted a special temptation to regard these customs as the major characteristic of their identity rather than their faith in God through Christ.[49] Christ is the means by which Gentiles are drawn into the circle of those who belong to the God of Israel. Gentiles, as outsiders at first, might naturally understand the new rituals and customs by which they came into the community as the gateway into the new circle of believers. For Jews, who were already inside, this temptation was nonexistent.

The Teachings of Paul

> *Paul thought that salvation basically depends on membership in the in-group, but that within that context deeds still count.*[50]

While Paul gave priority at times to the issues surrounding entry and identity requirements of Gentile Christian believers, he had to deal also with the question of appropriate Christian behavior. Very early in this book I stated that for the believing community the covenant bond speaks to the understanding of identity, while *torah* responds to the question of how the community should conduct its life. Naturally, then, Paul laid down directives for the different communities he addressed in his letters, directives that depended in their focus on the particular difficulties or questions the congregation was facing. In fact, there is no letter he wrote without a portion of it dedicated to exhortation. Even the letters that focus most strongly on the function and character of the *nomos*/law contain sections with instructions as to appropriate and inappropriate behavior (cf. Rom. 12–14; Gal. 5:13–6:10). In providing his guidance to the early Christian communities, Paul drew from a number of sources, including Scripture, his own rabbinical tradition, and Christian-Jewish or apostolic traditions.[51] General instructions regarding appropriate Christian behav-

---

49. So Gaston argues that the issue of winning God's favor by "works of the law" arose as a Gentile problem rather than a Jewish one. "The phrase 'works of the law' . . . refers to the adoption of selected Jewish practices on the part of the Gentiles and their attempt to impose them upon others as means of self-justification"; 25.

50. E. P. Sanders, *Paul, the Law, and the Jewish People,* 111.

51. These connections have been made most cogently by E. P. Sanders in his several works

ior may cite lists of virtues or vices and culminate in repeating the law of love for the neighbor.[52] We note, however, that Paul rarely resorts to explicitly citing a commandment from the Torah as the authority for his regulations. Nor does he invoke Scriptural authority often to support his argument.

The Law of Love (Romans 12:9-13; 13:8-10; Galatians 5:1, 13-14)

Because the needs of the different communities were diverse, the guidance provided by Paul ranges rather widely, sometimes so specific that it connects only with difficulty to current concerns, and sometimes so broadly conceived that it has a more obvious permanent validity. In terms of general ethics, Paul's teachings contain the commandment of love from neighbor to neighbor in two key places, Romans 13:8-10 and Galatians 5:14, both of them letters that deal in general with the place and function of the *nomos*/law in Paul's thought. In Romans, Paul has been arguing his views of God, of the *nomos*/law and of the God-human relationship at length. In chapter 12 he turns to the subject of what it means to live as a member of the new community, first appealing to the idea of the community as the body of Christ as the authority for his admonishment (Rom. 12:3-8), followed by a general list of virtues headed by the requirement to "love":

Romans 12:9-13

9. Let love be without hypocrisy. Abhor evil, cling to the good. 10. In familial love be devoted to each other,[53] in showing honor to each other be exemplary, 11. in zeal unflagging, in the spirit ardent. Serve the Holy One.[54] 12. In hope be glad, in suffering patient, in prayer persevering. 13. To the needs of the saints contribute; love/kindness/hospitality to the stranger pursue.

---

and especially by Peter J. Tomson in his book, *Paul and the Jewish Law: Halakha in the Letters of the Apostle to the Gentiles* (Minneapolis: Fortress, 1990).

52. For such lists see, e.g., Rom. 13:8-10; 1 Cor. 5:11-13; Gal. 5:19-23; 1 Thess. 4:1-12; 5:12-22.

53. The Greek term used for "love" in v. 10 is *philadelphia*, lit., "brotherly love." I have chosen the more inclusive term "familial love" (Gaston, 181), but note that the language used in the passage addresses the congregation as "brothers" and that all the forms of the reflexive pronouns are masculine. Translating *philadelphia* with "love" as does the NRSV, e.g., obscures the difference between this word and the more general *agapē*.

54. Because the Greek word *kyrios* is used both for Jesus Christ and God in this material, it is not always easy to distinguish between them. Romans 12 seems to urge service of God (see vv. 1-2; another reference to God in v. 19) and is clear when referring specifically to Christ. I read this verse on a continuum with vv. 1-2, and it seems therefore preferable to opt for my customary rendering of the Tetragrammaton, "the Holy One."

The list goes on, working out with greater specificity what it means to "love sincerely/without hypocrisy" (vv. 14-21). On the whole, this exhortation urges loving behavior for the inner circle and thus refers to love as "familial love" (Greek *philadelphia*). Yet, a more general word for "love," *agapē* (v. 9), opens the short list, and it closes with a reference to "love/hospitality" (v. 13). The Greek word for "hospitality" used here is *philoxenia,* which contains within it the words for "love" (*philia*) and "stranger" *(xenos)*. This is the only time that Paul uses this word, and it is rare elsewhere in the New Testament. "Hospitality" is a rather pale word for what underlies the notion of a demand to provide for the outside guest, the "stranger," a demand that was both cultural and religious. It is only here that Paul approaches the Torah concern for the stranger. In the following section, where he addresses love more emphatically, it is missing.[55]

After a section on proper relationship to authorities, Paul returns to his subject of love and declares the following:

Romans 13:8-10

8. Owe no one anything but to love one another; for one who loves the other has fulfilled the law. 9. For "you shall not commit adultery, you shall not kill, you shall not steal and you shall not covet," and whatever other commandment, are encapsulated in this word: you shall love your neighbor as yourself. 10. Love does not do harm to the neighbor; thus the fulfillment of the law is love.

In this brief list, the "fulfillment" or "fullness" of the law is mentioned twice and in such a manner that it brackets the brief list of specifics, all citations from the Decalogue. Apparently, after all the arguments for setting aside the law for the believer in God's new act in Jesus, the "fulfillment" of the *nomos* — here more clearly denoting *torah* — remained a key issue for the communal life of those who followed Jesus. The word "love," each time with a form of the word *agapē,* occurs five times in the span of these few lines and also encloses the unit, placed both at the opening and at the end, thus echoing through the lines with great emphasis.[56]

In a similar way, the Letter to the Galatians, which emphatically declares Gentile believers free, especially of the obligation to adopt the Jewish law/cus-

---

55. It is particularly difficult to render *philoxenia* appropriately, and most lexical listings provide "hospitality." Its opposite is *xenophobia,* "fear" or "hatred of the stranger."

56. The commandment to "love the neighbor as the self" occurs only here and in Gal. 5. Other references to neighborly love occur in 1 Cor. 14:1; 16:14; Eph. 4:2; 1 Thess. 4:9.

tom *(nomos)* of circumcision, returns to the law of love toward the end of the letter.

Galatians 5:1

For freedom Christ has set us free; stand fast then and no longer to the yoke of slavery be subjected.

In the following verses, Paul once more declares vehement opposition to circumcision of Gentile believers (vv. 2-12), thus making clear to what the "yoke of slavery" refers, then to resume:

> 13. For you were called to freedom, brothers. Only not freedom as an opportunity for indulgence, but through love serve one another. 14. For the entire law is fulfilled in this word: love your neighbor as yourself.

As in Romans, once freedom from the law is declared the writer comes back to speak of the "fulfillment of the law" *(torah)*, which is said to be "fulfilled" by "love" of the neighbor as the self. Paul goes on to elaborate what this love entails and what its absence portends in the familiar recital of the opposition of the "fruits of the Spirit" versus the "desires/works of the flesh" (vv. 16-26). In Galatians, Paul does not push neighborly love in less comfortable directions, toward either the enemy or the stranger. On the whole, with the one exception of Romans 12:13, the broadly conceived moral exhortation of Paul stops short of the depth and extent of neighbor love required by the Torah and the Gospels. It could be that Paul counted on an acquaintance with these prescriptions, so that he felt no need for a further spelling out of what may have seemed obvious. On the other hand, it is clear that the law of love as prescribed for Christian communities by Paul would benefit from the illustrations and amplifications provided in the Torah, as well as the Gospels.

Gender Relations (1 Corinthians 7:1-7; 11:1-16; 14:33-36; Romans 1:26-27)

In the more specific and practical guidelines of his letters, Paul spends a great deal of attention on matters that relate to sexuality and gender relations, either within the family structure or outside of them.[57] Partly for this reason and partly because Pauline statements have exercised and continue to exercise great authority in Christian traditions, I lift them out for special attention.

---

57. So-called vice lists, e.g., always include references to sexual transgressions (e.g., Rom. 1:29-31; 1 Cor. 6:9-10; 2 Cor. 12:20; Gal. 5:19-21).

The subject is taken up most elaborately in 1 Corinthians, perhaps on account of specific problems in the Corinthian community. Paul's exhortations in this letter will serve as typical examples of this type of material within the Pauline corpus.[58] Guidelines for appropriate and inappropriate sexual relations take up all of chapter 5 and a major portion of chapter 6. Next, Paul takes up marriage, the desirability of it, sexual relations within it, if or when it may be ended by one of the partners, or whether one should avoid it altogether (1 Cor. 7). Three subsequent chapters focus on the question of permission to eat food left from sacrifices made to other gods (1 Cor. 8–10).[59] From the emphasis on these concerns, it is clear that it was deemed urgent by Paul to lay down rules for normative behavior that would not make the fledgling communities objects of ridicule or draw accusations to them of following behavioral codes that were not observed elsewhere. He returns to the subject of gender relations in chapter 11 and once more in chapter 14. It is instructive to pause at the content and the tone of some of these guidelines, especially as they relate to women's lives and acceptable behavior.

I briefly recall earlier remarks about the lives of women during the centuries that produced the Hebrew Bible. Regulations that governed sexual relations in the biblical world were primarily intended to further biological productivity in all biblical periods, in view of the scarcity of population, demands created by the agricultural lifestyle, and the high mortality rate of women and children (see above, 41, 45, 225). Boundaries around sexual relations arose generally from concerns about orderly family relations and the greatest biological productivity possible. Intimacies that threatened order and procuring of progeny, as adultery, incest, prostitution, and homosexual relations were forbidden. The Torah, however, offers no arguments that lay a theological or mythical foundation for these arrangements. This is significant, for it meant that male and female relations in their hierarchical/patriarchal ordering were not viewed as founded in the God-created order.[60]

Three regulatory passages come to our attention in relation to the subject of male-female relations: 1 Cor. 7:1-7; 11:1-16; 14:33-36. Each of these contributes to a view of the position of women, the first in relation to sexual ac-

58. See, e.g., 1 Cor. 5:1-13; 6:15-20; 7:1-16, 25-40; For regulations that pertain only to women: 1 Cor. 7:25-40; 11:2-16; 14:33-36.

59. In this discussion it is worth noting that the issues of idol worship and sexual immorality are closely related for Paul, as he easily moves from the one topic to the other in 1 Cor. 10:6-8. Cf. also Rom. 1:18-32.

60. This did not mean that people did not *experience* gender divisions and super/subordination as divinely ordained but that such views were never given theological/mythical support in the text.

tivity within marriage, "for the woman does not have rights over her own body but the man does; likewise, the man does not have rights over his own body but the woman does" (7:4). To go by the phrase that introduces this section (7:1), there was "concern" about abstention from all sexual relations in Corinth, and Paul recommends here that sexual relations within marriage, mutually agreed on, are appropriate. How freeing this recommendation might be in a patriarchal society is somewhat doubtful, but at least in theory a kind of mutuality is achieved here.

In chapter 11, the picture becomes more traditional, with prescriptions regarding hair and head covering during public worship, short and no hats for men, long and veils for women. The section opens with the following words:

1 Corinthians 11:2-3

2. I praise you because you remember me in everything and hold fast to the traditions just as I delivered them to you. 3. I want you to know, though, that Christ is the head of every man, the head of the woman is the man, and the head of Christ is God.

Having established the accepted hierarchies, Paul moves to lay down the rules for hair and head covering. In the middle of this discourse, he observes:

7. For a man is not obligated to cover his head, being as he is the image and the glory of God. But the woman is the glory of the man. 8. For a man is not out of a woman but a woman out of a man; 9. and neither was a man created because of the woman but a woman because of the man.

This, then, is the reason why a woman should wear a veil. Only the man is said to be "the image of God," in contradiction to Genesis 1:27, where both male and female are declared to be created in God's image. Here, the woman reflects, "is the glory of," the man and thus only secondarily God's image. The references echo traditional understandings of Genesis 2:18-25, common enough in Paul's time. To bring the point home, the traditional interpretation of the second Creation story is emphasized by the explanation in verse 9. Then Paul seems to have second thoughts:

11. And yet, the woman is not (anything) apart from the man or the man apart from the woman in the Holy One. 12. Just as the woman is from the man, so the man is through the woman, but everything is from God. 13. Judge for yourselves: is it proper for a woman to pray

to God with a bare head? 14. Does nature not teach you that if a man has long hair this dishonors him, but if a woman has long hair this is her glory? For the hair is given to her for a covering.

A reconsideration of the two, male and female in relation to God, which first looks as if it may move once again to greater mutuality, ends in a renewed prescription for women to "cover" themselves, this time with an argument from "nature" (Greek *physis*).[61] Here not God or the text, but "nature" is the teacher.

In 1 Corinthians 14, a short paragraph prescribes behavior of women in public worship:

1 Corinthians 14:33-35

33. As in all the churches of the saints, the women in the churches should be silent; 34. for they are not permitted to speak, but they should be subordinate just as the law reads. 35. But if they want to learn something, let them ask their husbands at home. For it is disgraceful for a woman to speak in church.[62]

This passage is a forerunner of 1 Timothy 2:11-12 (cf. Tit. 2:5), where the argument is given a more elaborate theological foundation. From the preceding verses, it becomes clear that the Corinthian congregations are having trouble conducting their worship in an orderly way and that they need some clear directions as to how to conduct themselves so that everything will go "decently and in order." The voices and speech of women are seen as contributing to disorder and chaos.

Apparently, issues of distinctions between male and female are a cause of considerable concern and even anxiety for Paul. There are at least two convictions that struggle against each other in the Pauline literature in terms of gender relations. There is first the understanding voiced by Paul in several places that traditional distinctions are abolished by the new life of faith "in Christ Jesus." In Galatians 3:28, these distinctions include male and female.

---

61. It is not clear whether Paul has abandoned the issue of the veil and whether long hair is intended as a substitute for a veil or whether both are required. Many commentators remark on the confusion that typifies the arguments used here. It is, however, very clear that outward appearance and behavior serve as markers for gender boundaries in Paul's reasoning.

62. Although the text sounds somewhat severe for Paul and some interpreters assume it to be secondary, I am taking the passage at face value as fitting in well with the rest of Paul's argument regarding female roles in 1 Corinthians. The ascription of these verses to a later interpolation seems to be driven by a desire to read a more "liberated" Paul than the one found in this letter, rather than on the basis of text-critical evidence.

He argues the same point in 1 Corinthians 12:13 but leaves out the male/female pair. Yet, also in 1 Corinthians Paul makes an effort to articulate a degree of mutuality between male and female in regard to sexual relations. In addition, procreation, such a prevalent concern underlying the texts that determine gender distinctions in the Torah, is of no concern to Paul, who was unmarried and in some way viewed marriage as a possible distraction from more serious faith matters (1 Cor. 7:8ff.).[63] An apparent understanding of the disappearance of traditional distinctions, including those that have bearing on gender relations, "in Christ," combined with an absence of preoccupation with biological productivity, may have provided the framework within which the reality of female leadership in the early church communities took place. By all accounts, women took on positions of considerable authority early on in the movement of those who followed Jesus.[64]

On the other hand, Paul had strong and traditional religious and cultural understandings of the distinctions between male and female that come to the fore in the regulations cited above from 1 Corinthians.[65] Whereas Paul held, on the one hand, that such distinctions were no longer valid, as testified to by his declaration in Galatians 3:28, on the other, when it came to practice he apparently held that they needed to be maintained. In the words of Bernadette Brooten: "Paul envisions a social order in which Jew and gentile are no longer relevant categories and attempts to break down the boundaries distinguishing them (e.g., circumcision and dietary laws). In contrast, within this same social order Paul deems necessary a natural, and therefore immutable, gender

63. Although a number of commentators view Paul's advocacy of the single state as freeing for women in itself, it seems doubtful how liberated a single woman in 1st-century Roman society would be. A patriarchal household in some way would always define women's existence, whether married or not.

64. Of the many excellent studies on this topic, I mention here Elisabeth Schüssler Fiorenza, *In Memory of Her: A Feminist Theological Reconstruction of Christian Origins* (New York: Crossroad, 1983); Antoinette Clark Wire, *The Corinthian Women Prophets: A Reconstruction through Paul's Rhetoric* (Minneapolis: Fortress, 1990); *Women and Christian Origins*, ed. Ross Shepard Kraemer and Mary Rose D'Angelo (New York: Oxford University Press, 1999); and Judith Lieu, *Neither Jew nor Greek? Constructing Early Christianity* (London: T & T Clark, 2002). Of these, Wire reconstructs a lively and authoritative female leadership in the Corinthian church from the very arguments used by Paul to restrict women. Lieu and Bernadette Brooten are especially careful not to contrast women's leadership in early Christian circles with that in the Jewish community. See Brooten, *Women Leaders in the Ancient Synagogue*. Brown Judaic Studies 36 (Chico: Scholars, 1982); and von Kellenbach, esp. ch. III: "Judaism as Antithesis of Early Christianity."

65. That Paul in his view of male and female nature and gender boundaries was thoroughly a child of his culture and religion is most persuasively argued by Bernadette Brooten in *Love Between Women* (Chicago: University of Chicago Press, 1996), esp. chs. 8, 9, and 10.

boundary."[66] Brooten bases her statement on a close analysis of Romans 1:18-32, a section which contains the strongest condemnation of same-sex relations between both women and men found anywhere in the Bible. I include here a brief review of this text unit because it will help to set Paul's statements about gender relations in 1 Corinthians within a broader framework.

Paul's introductory chapter to Romans lays out the arguments for general human knowledge of God's laws that govern all existence and human transgression of these laws. This line of thought sets the stage for the claim he makes eventually that, while "all are under the power of sin" (Rom. 3:9), all need to be justified in Christ. It is within this prelude that Paul highlights transgressions of natural gender boundaries as an illustration of godless behavior, deserving of death. The most pertinent verses read as follows:

Romans 1:26-27

26. Therefore, God gave them up to degrading passions. Their females exchanged natural use for that which is against nature. 27. In the same way also the males, giving up the natural use of the female, burned with lust for one another, males with males committing shameful acts and receiving in themselves due recompense for their error.[67]

The word often, and justifiably, rendered with "intercourse" I have translated with the more literal word "use" (Greek *chrēsis*) to highlight the thought that underlies this expression. In the ordinary course of male-female relations, the "natural" course of things, men "use" women and women "are used" by men. Women are the passive, men the active partner. Anything else goes against nature. And it is precisely this "use" that both women and men have abandoned. Further, a form of the word "nature" (Greek *physis*) is employed three times in these lines, making clear that it is the "natural order" that is transgressed. We are reminded that in 1 Corinthians 11:14 Paul similarly bases his defense of long hair for women on "nature." While the concept of nature and natural law is a complex one, Romans 1 places nature within that which God has created (v. 20). Logically then, what is contrary to nature is contrary to God.[68] Hence, sexual relations that transgress ordinary "use," that cross the gender boundaries, are contrary to God.

The interdiction against same-sex "use" in Romans 1, the regulations for

---

66. Brooten, *Love Between Women*, 264.

67. For a verse by verse analysis of the section in which these verses are embedded, Rom. 1:18-32, see Brooten, *Love Between Women*, ch. 9.

68. So Brooten, *Love Between Women*, 267-80.

male-female relations in 1 Corinthians, together with the prescriptions for appropriate female behavior may be viewed together as arising from Paul's concern for maintaining appropriate, God-ordered, "natural" distinctions and boundaries.[69] In 1 Corinthians, these boundaries are signaled by outward appearance. In this reasoning Paul thought and spoke as a child of his religion and culture.[70] Postbiblical Jewish traditions, Greek as well as Roman writings, testify to convictions regarding gender relations and boundaries similar to the convictions present in Romans and 1 Corinthians.[71] It would, however, be a mistake to ascribe the setting of gender boundaries to a particularly Jewish environment. Paul was not a "Christian" in his statement in Galatians and a "Jew" in his exhortations in 1 Corinthians. Of course, Paul's thinking was influenced by rabbinic thought, but the gender boundaries outlined in the texts we reviewed are no more Jewish than they are Greek or Roman. Such boundaries were also a part of the culture and the writings of the time. The impetus provided by the conviction that life in Christ did not sustain such boundaries lost out to beliefs and anxieties that urged to maintain the traditional distinctions. I will return to the formula of Galatians 3:28 as well as to the issue of the authority Christians today should ascribe to Pauline regulations regarding male-female relations and conduct. First, a brief consideration of other New Testament material on this issue.

Post-Pauline Codification of Gender Relations

Relations between male and female and gender boundaries remained quite traditional in Paul, in spite of and contrary to the formula he articulated in Galatians 3. Yet to some extent, a struggle is discernible in the Pauline exhortations, at least in 1 Corinthians, to bring what he perceives as the "natural"

---

69. Another connection between the Romans and Corinthians texts may reside in the possibility that men with long hair were considered to be homosexual. So Markus Bockmuehl, in *Jewish Law in Gentile Churches: Halakha and the Beginning of Christian Public Ethics* (Edinburgh: T. & T. Clark, 2000), 134: "The particular argument of this passage [i.e., 1 Cor. 11:14], however, derives from the fact that in this context the perversion of hairstyles denoted a perversion of sexual identity."

70. Brooten, *Love Between Women*, ch. 10: "Intertextual Echoes in Romans 1:18-32."

71. Brooten discerns lines of connection between Paul's reasoning in Rom. 1:18-32 and "Jewish anti-idolatry polemics, as exemplified in the Wisdom of Solomon." Furthermore, "we can recognize 'natural' and 'unnatural' as categories born of controversy" about social order and socially ordained gender roles. Paul's condemnation of homoeroticism relates to the discussion around Levitical concepts in the Roman world, and there is overlap between his views and those of "Philo of Alexandria, for whom males in same-sex relationships either lose their masculinity or teach others effeminacy." In his condemnation of sexual love between women, Paul's links to the Roman world are strongest, according to Brooten (*Love Between Women*, 301).

order more in line with the vision of how relationships between the sexes could be worked out. Two convictions struggled against each other and one prevailed, so that it did not become clear how the statement that in Christ there is no "male and female" could be worked out in the social and religious structures of Paul's day. Five passages in post-Pauline material testify to the inability of the early Christian movement to maintain the vision of Galatians 3:28 alive. Ephesians 5:21-33; Colossians 3:18-19; 1 Timothy 2:8-15; Titus 2:5; and 1 Peter 3:1-7 codify the subordination of women to their husbands. Women should, in the words of 1 Peter 3:1, "accept the authority of their husbands in the same way" as slaves should obey the authority of their masters. I recall here the words of 1 Timothy:

1 Timothy 2:11-15

11. Let a woman learn in silence in full submission. 12. Teaching for a woman I do not permit, nor to have authority over a man, but to be in silence. 13. For Adam was first formed, then Eve. 14. And Adam was not deceived but the woman fell into transgression by being deceived. 15. But she will be saved through childbearing; provided they remain in faith, love and holiness, with modesty.

Words that in Galatians evoked a vision of freedom and abolishing of oppressive boundaries are silenced here. Woman's subordination has received its definitive theological grounding, and her salvation no longer resides "in Christ" but in her procreative abilities, an issue that never arose with Paul. I wrote earlier that these words from 1 Timothy should no longer have relevance or authority, judged wanting as they are by the biblical text itself (see above, 125). Now that we have looked at a more extensive network of such pronouncements, it cannot fail to strike us how frequently the gender codes occur in this New Testament material. Most likely, the codes reflect on actual situations in which women took roles of leadership and authority, which was felt to be unnatural and went counter to established cultural and religious custom. With some difficulty we may be able to reconstruct these realities, but in effect the voices of women leaders are mostly silent, and we are left with the voice of prescription, a voice that gained rather than lost authority in time.

In summary: In his writing Paul was restricted by the Greek word *nomos* which, depending on the context in which it is used, at times refers to a specific commandment, at times to the entire Torah, and in other places only to the prescriptions regarding circumcision and diet. While Paul abolished the necessity for circumcision and dietary laws for Gentiles who followed Jesus, he also made clear that such communities were expected to conduct themselves in appropriate ways. While different contexts of congregations determined the focus of Paul's writing, he emphasized the rule of love in a number of places and twice referred to the love of neighbor as the self. In terms of specific issues addressed in the different communities, it is striking how much attention Paul spent on matters of sexuality and on gender boundaries.

In terms of the rule of love, while in line with demands made in the Torah, it became apparent that the Pauline articulation lacks the depth and richness of the Torah expressions. In terms of specific directives, Pauline and post-Pauline material prescribe gender arrangements that exhibit a preoccupation with gender boundaries and express a gradually more and more narrow and restrictive code for female behavior and appearance, while providing a theological basis for such restrictions that is absent from the Torah. Here the Torah speaks to a greater opening for possible equality of women and men as they lived their daily lives. The boundaries that are set up and maintained in Leviticus, for example, are not so much gender boundaries as boundaries that apply to the entire community (see above, 219-27). Although there is an impetus in Paul to lift the hierarchical divisions between male and female, this vision did not express itself in specific guidance for male and female relations in the community.

The Gospel of God

A Jew's righteousness does not come from observance of the Torah; it comes from being a part of God's covenant people.[72]

In the opening lines of his Letter to the Romans, Paul identifies himself as "an apostle set apart for the gospel of God" (Rom. 1:1). What is this gospel/good news for the announcing of which Paul saw himself set apart? Briefly, the good news Paul came to bring to the Gentiles is that they are included in God's love and God's loving design for the creation. They are, in the words of the writer to the Ephesians, "no longer strangers and guests but . . . members of the household of God" (Eph. 2:19). The means of their inclusion is God's act on behalf of the world in Jesus Christ. The entrance requirement for belonging in this household is acceptance of and faith in the redemptive action of God in Christ. Through Christ the God of Israel establishes a covenant with Gentiles, a covenant Christians call to mind each time they celebrate the

---

72. Lester Dean, "Paul's 'Erroneous' Description of Judaism," in Swidler et al., 138.

supper of Christ.[73] The "gospel of God" is then, first of all, the good news of God's redemptive action. The New Testament begins with this creative act of God, parallel to the creative activity of God's covenant making as described in Exodus. Through this creative act, Christians understand themselves as a people in covenant with God, a covenant based on God's grace.

Perhaps because they came to the household initially as outsiders, Gentiles were tempted to assume that some special act should be performed on their part in order for them to become members of God's people. Circumcision and dietary requirements were obvious candidates for entrance requirements. Once these were abolished by Paul, he was obligated to involve himself in complicated discussions of the place and meaning of the entire law. Later Christian communities and interpreters, for whom the idea of entrance requirements into what was originally a Jewish movement was no longer a valid one, kept struggling with the notion of the place of God's commandments and requirements, veering either in one direction, viewing human deeds as a way to God, or its opposite, considering them worthless and of no account compared to faith. It seems, then, that the perceived opposition of gospel and law is a peculiarly Christian one. The self-understanding of Christianity as a faith that defined itself over against Judaism sharpened also the presumed opposition of gospel and law, with Christianity understanding itself as a religion of the gospel while identifying Judaism as the religion of the law.

Partly arising from subsequent interpretations, and partly because the seedbed for such interpretation lies embedded in the Pauline material of the New Testament, Christians have constructed distorted views of the Judaism of past and present. From the arguments adduced in Romans and Galatians, it is possible to derive a picture of Judaism as a religion that tried to earn its way into heaven by the "works of the law." As Jewish interpreters observe: this is not a Judaism they recognize. In the words of Lester Dean: "A Jew's relationship to God is based upon God's covenant established with the Israelites and their descendants. Jews believe this covenant is a covenant of grace, just as Christians believe the covenant of the 'New Testament' is a covenant of grace."[74] What Paul argues against is a distorted view of Judaism, one to which Gentile converts of the early Christian movement may have been prone.[75] As Hans-Joachim Schoeps observes: "It must ever remain thought-provoking that the Christian church has received a completely distorted view of the Jewish law at the hands of a Diaspora Jew who had become alienated

73. For the eucharistic formula, see 1 Cor. 11:25.
74. Dean, 138.
75. Dean, 137.

from the faith-ideas of the fathers. . . . And still more astounding is the fact that church theology throughout Christian history has imputed Paul's inacceptability to the Jews to Jewish insensitivity, and has never asked itself whether it might not be due to the fact that Paul could gain no audience with the Jews because from the start he misunderstood Jewish theology."[76]

In line with Paul's reasoning, once Christians are counted as "members of the household of God," they are as much as the Jews were, as the ancient Israelites were, in need of instruction as to how to conduct themselves within the household. He does not hesitate to provide instructions for their life together, for their worship, and for their relating as male and female, among other issues, going so far as to assert that certain sins cut perpetrators off from the realm of God (Gal. 5:21; cf. 1 Cor. 5:13). Although the Torah then did not and could not take up the same significance in the lives of Christians as it did and does for Jews, *torah* in the more general sense was a strong part of Paul's evangelizing efforts, as we have seen above. He would probably not have disagreed with the words of James: "So it is with faith by itself; when it has no works it is dead" (Jas. 2:17). Being taken into covenant always asks for a human response, a response that works itself out within the context of human reality. The Gospel accounts of Jesus' teaching testify to the same understanding of life lived within the grace of God. Human beings always need to "listen and learn," for without instruction they are not going to get far. Setting Christ and the law in opposition creates a false dichotomy that has kept Christianity alienated from a crucial part of its heritage. Jesus' teaching shows that his application of the law of neighbor love is on a direct continuum with Torah teaching. The Pauline law of love needs everywhere the depth and richness and the expansion of the Torah commandments to become a lived reality that sets the believing community apart from other people of good will and that reflects the holiness of God.

Instruction that addresses specific situations and questions shows in Paul a marked focus on male-female relations and gender boundaries. In the Pauline and post-Pauline material, the prescriptions for gender arrangements exhibit increasing restriction of the place and function of women inside the patriarchal household and the fledgling church. Such arrangements are provided with a theological foundation. Thus, Pauline and post-Pauline texts are in need of the reminders, not only about the oneness of male and female in

76. Schoeps, 261-62. It is rather remarkable that Schoeps, who generally treats Judaism with respect and appreciation and who wrote his book in Germany 14 years after the Second World War ended, nowhere in his book refers to the destruction of European Jewry under the Nazi regime, and hence does not make the crucial connection between these Christian "misunderstandings" and active hostility and persecution.

Christ, but about the oneness of male and female in God's image, about the twoness of humanity as it was created, so both are set free to be equally human in the redemption offered in Jesus Christ. Restrictive gender roles do not exhibit the life of freedom in Christ. Patterns of domination and their repetition across the ages on the basis of God-created orders are not a mark of healed creation. Christians, as people with a biblical text that is held to be both revelatory and instructive, are blessed to have the Old Testament, especially the Torah, to reveal to them the nature of the God of Israel whom both Jews and Christians together confess as the Holy One, and to instruct them in the way they should live together as Christians and Jews, as men and women, members of the household of God.

CHAPTER 3

How Then Shall We Live?

Exodus 23:9
A stranger you must not oppress;
you yourselves know the heart of the stranger,
for strangers you were in the land of Egypt.

Leviticus 19:34
As a native among you,
so shall the stranger be,
who lives as a stranger with you;
and you shall love him as yourself,
for you were strangers in the land of Egypt.
I am the Holy One, your God.

Galatians 3:28
There is neither Jew nor Greek, neither slave nor free, there is no male and
female, for you are all one in Christ Jesus.

Two of the texts cited here have been discussed at length in the preceding pages. The third I have mentioned in passing while reviewing Paul's notions of gender boundaries, especially in 1 Corinthians and Romans 1. It deserves closer examination, setting it in the context of its surrounding verses.

Galatians 3:26-29
26. For you are all children of God, through the faith, in Christ Jesus. 27. For as many of you as were baptized in Christ, have put on Christ. 28. There is neither Jew nor Greek, neither slave nor free, there is no male and female, for you are all one in Christ Jesus. 29. If

you are Christ's, then you are Abraham's seed, heirs according to the promise.

In its immediate context these lines are preceded by a review of the relationship of "faith," the "law," and "righteousness," and they are followed by a discussion of what it means to be "heirs." The congregations in Galatia who may have received this letter in the late 40s or early 50s C.E. were clearly under pressure to be circumcised, and it is this issue together with that of the place of the law/*nomos* and the role of faith that is the focus of the letter.[1] We concentrate here not so much on Paul's discussion of faith, law, and righteousness as on his words in chapter 3 on the meaning of being "in Christ." Verse 26 opens the unit by declaring the oneness of all who are "in Christ," a statement that is repeated in verse 28. "In Christ" occurs emphatically in each phrase until verse 29. "Baptism" signals the faith and the putting on of a new existence, the "putting on Christ." Verse 28 then elaborates on the consequences of this new existence: the abolishing of distinctive ways of being.[2] The three pairs, Jew/Greek, slave/free, male/female, bear closer scrutiny.

The "Jew/Greek" pairing occurs elsewhere in Pauline material and points to Paul's view of a religious prerogative assumed by one group over against another.[3] "Greek" here equals "Gentile" or even "sinner," while "the Jew" stands in Paul's perception for the one who has benefited from God's gracious action, "the Greek" being on the outside of this action.[4] Ritually, the set-apartness of the Jews was symbolized by circumcision. This symbol of separateness is not necessary for the Gentile follower of Jesus, as Paul argues in this letter. The separation between "Jews" and "Greeks" was in reality also ethnic and cultural, but I believe that Paul in this verse mainly addresses religious differences with the word pair "Jew/Greek," as in general Paul's dis-

1. While it is evident from Galatians that this pressure existed, one cannot be sure *where* it came from, whether Jewish or Gentile Christ followers.

2. The foundation for the statement in Gal. 3:28 may be a baptismal or other liturgical formula here used by Paul either in its original or a revised form: Hans Dieter Betz, *Galatians*. Hermeneia (Philadelphia: Fortress, 1979); Daniel C. Arichea and Eugene Nida, *A Translator's Handbook on Paul's Letter to the Galatians* (Stuttgart: United Bible Societies, 1976). Others see close connections mostly with gnostic formulations: Dennis Ronald MacDonald, *There Is No Male and Female: The Fate of a Dominical Saying in Paul and Gnosticism* (Philadelphia: Fortress, 1987).

3. Cf. Rom. 1:16; 2:9ff.; 3:9; 1 Cor. 1:24; 10:32; 12:13.

4. I understand the term "Greek" to refer broadly to Gentiles rather than specifically to Greeks. This contra Christopher D. Stanley, who argues that the term is specific rather than general; "'Neither Jew nor Greek': Ethnic Conflict in Graeco-Roman Society," *JSNT* 64 (1996): 101-24.

course uses this pairing to indicate one's relationship to God. Here and elsewhere Paul is much engaged with the topic of religious privilege, or "righteousness." Of the three pairs, the first is the one that occupies him most thoroughly in his other epistles. Clearly, the state of being "in Christ" is not meant to be utopian or ideal existence, but is meant to be lived out in actual human relating. In other words, the declaration of Galatians 3:28 does not only speak to the inadequacy of human difference and distinction but is also speech that calls for changes in lived reality.

The "slave/free" wordpair indicates social, economic, and psychological inequality. With this saying the old oppressive systems of class and race privilege are swept away. How much this became for Paul and his followers a lived reality is not clear. As Hans Dieter Betz observes, the statement regarding this pair could be seen as either "a declaration of the abolishment of the social institution of slavery" or "a declaration of the irrelevancy of that institution, which would include the possibility of its retainment."[5] He goes on to say that in other letters Paul does not give evidence of encouraging abolition of slavery (cf. 1 Cor 7:21-24 and Philemon) and that he may have been hesitant to support social rebellion. Slaves, however, if they were aware of the formula, may have experienced the saying very much as having direct application to their situation and may have taken the occasion of their baptism as an opportunity to grasp their freedom.[6] Slavery, while not directly condemned in biblical texts, went not unopposed in ancient times, and there was "a long tradition of social criticism against the institution of slavery in the Hellenistic world."[7] There were Jewish sects that had no slaves, and Philo disapproved of it. In other words, the cultural milieu was not entirely unreceptive to the notion of slavery as inhumane. Yet, Christianity did not take up this cause for perhaps obvious reasons, as not wanting to be viewed as a hotbed of social upheaval and rebellion, which surely would not have furthered its good standing with the Roman authorities. We may, however, rue the inability of Christianity to take up the radical statement of Galatians 3:28 regarding slave and free with more seriousness, for much grief and harm might have been avoided in the religious as well as the social and political realm if the consequences of the vision for human existence had been more clearly drawn out at an earlier time.

The "male-female" pair recalls the creation in the image of God of both

---

5. Betz, 193.

6. "There can be no doubt that the slaves themselves never ceased to regard freedom as their first priority and that they sought to attain freedom by whatever means they could"; Betz, 194.

7. Betz cites Sophists, Cynics, and Jewish sects as opposing slavery; 193.

men and women in Genesis 1:27 and points to the relations between the sexes. Patriarchal as the world of the Bible was, these relations were manifestly unequal throughout the period that the texts of the Bible were composed, with the male the dominating and the female the subordinate party. We have already looked at the care with which Paul delineated gender boundaries in other contexts and have observed how after his time such boundaries solidified and were given theological foundations. As with the category "slave/free," an inability to draw the consequences of the statement combined with opposing cultural and religious pressures hardened patriarchal modes of relating in the household, the church, and society. When finally women's equality and dignity was partially attained in the 20th century, Christianity had few tools ready for analysis and support. This declaration too was bound to stay in the realm of the ideal, or as valid only of a Christian's relationship to God.

While the statement of Galatians 3:28 does not intend to do away with difference or present a monochrome picture of human diversity, it makes clear that "in Christ" the new being does not cater to old modes of oppressive attitudes and behavior. Three unequal modes of human relations address the entire spectrum of human existence: as religious/spiritual, as social and political, and as gendered beings. Three possibilities of breaking through barriers and bars of oppression were not lived into fruition in a Christian context. Jews and Christians eventually formed oppositional groups filled with misapprehension of one another, with a gradual gain of dominance on the Christian side. Slavery remained for centuries unopposed and even justified as an oppressive reality in Christian contexts and was only abandoned with great difficulty. Gender relations remained stuck in oppressive patterns that are only at present beginning to unravel. Galatians 3:28 remains in many ways an unfulfilled call to freedom in the Christian household.

CONCLUSION

How Do We Read?

In the Torah we found descriptions of a God who is not only involved with the creation but who is affected by it. This is a God who may have a change of heart, especially in light of planned destructive action on God's part. This is a God who is so close that God is said to be "seen" on numerous occasions. This is a God who has favorites, the poor, and the helpless, and a specific kin-group. This is a God who is "in it" with the creation and who accompanies the kin-group with special presence into a covenant relationship, who confers on them favor and blessing in order to bring about blessing for the earth. In conjunction with this conferral of favor, God calls the group to account for their fulfillment of the life of the covenant partner. Human cooperation with God's design is demanded and spelled out in the Torah.

Like the people who wrote the Torah, Christians *look back* at a time when God appeared in human form and intervened directly in human affairs. Jack Miles and Richard Elliott Friedman have both argued that, in a sense, God "disappears" in the Hebrew Bible, that from depicting direct experiences with the divine, from being in touch with the otherworldly, the biblical text moves gradually away into the everyday world where such experiences are unknown or where they belong to a special realm of visionaries.[1] The text then looks back at a time when things were different, when God took a direct hand in the doings of humanity. One could pose the same situation for the New Testament. The Gospels, written after the events that took place around

---

1. Thus Miles: "From the end of the book of Job to the end of the Tanakh, God never speaks again. . . . Job has reduced the Lord to silence"; *God: A Biography,* 329. Friedman: "Gradually through the course of the Hebrew Bible . . . the deity appears less and less to humans, speaks less and less"; *The Hidden Face of God,* 7. For both arguments one needs to follow the canon and order of the Hebrew Bible, ending with 2 Chronicles, rather than the Christian canon ending as it does with the prophetic book Malachi.

the person of Jesus Christ, look back on a time when Jesus was present, walked among humans, healed and taught, a Jew among Jews. They look back on a time when humanity rejected this God who appeared among them in human form. In the words of Friedman: "In the New Testament account, God has reappeared, angels have been seen, voices have spoken, and miracles have abounded. And humans have rejected it."[2] At the same time, both Jewish and Christian communities look forward to a future when God will in some way once again and finally intervene to bring it all to a grand conclusion, one final "judgment day." In the meantime, believers practice their faith for the in-between time. In spite of the different ways the two religions responded to the hiddenness of God, both had to be concerned with the way believers conduct their lives, practice their faith, and relate to one another as well as to their God. As Friedman and Miles argue, the fading out of God meant a highlighting of human responsibility. While we may not agree that God has in any way "faded out" of interaction with human affairs, we may allow that the sacred text functions as an orientation point for the community and as a deposit for instruction and revelation of lasting significance.[3] Human responsibility and orientation to the text have become key features of the life of faith for Christians and Jews.

Throughout this book I have argued that biblical texts need to be understood from within their historical context in order to be interpreted in a meaningful way in settings separated by vast distances from the original place and time in which the texts originated. We have, therefore, carefully considered historical circumstances and concerns in which we place texts from the Torah and the New Testament. In addition, the form of the text received careful attention at every turn of our review. Words and phrases and their translation, the way a story is told or a legal prescription is written provide important insight about meaning. Historical context and language concerns set boundaries around the multiple levels of meaning and at the same time open up new fields of understanding for the reader. Also, as people oriented to a text, we are guided by the thematic consistency of the Bible. In order to gain the point of consistency we may have to make choices and at times turn our back on textual implications that contradict consistent themes of the Bible. In our reading we encountered texts in both the Torah and the New Testament that required such choices (see above, 125, 261). Finally, as Christian believers,

---

2. Friedman, *The Hidden Face of God,* 135.

3. Parts of this process of the significance and the place of text as revealing of God and authoritative instruction for the community become evident from 2 Kgs. 22:8–23:20 and Neh. 8–10.

we interact with the biblical text with contemporary concerns and questions. As people for whom the Bible reveals both the nature of God and of human responsibility, we are obligated to bring to the text our deepest anxieties, our most urgent questions and preoccupations. This interaction is by definition a complex one, since different times will elicit different questions. It is also an interaction that cannot be entirely separated from the endeavor of delineating historical placement, outlining linguistic considerations, and determining consistency of theme. It is not as if we do all our work and then begin to ask questions about how to live with this or that text. Our questions and preoccupations are at work long before that point and interact with the text at every stage. Rather than struggling against this reality, we do better to live with it and within it, recognizing the limitations it provides us as well as the opportunities it offers.

Finally, I have argued throughout that Christian readings of the Bible all too often relegate material from the Hebrew Bible to a position of, at best secondary, at worst negative value in relation to that of the New Testament. I have attempted to show that texts from both parts of the Bible gain in meaning when they enter into conversation with each other. In this conversation, historical context, language considerations, biblical consistency, and contemporary concerns interact to arrive at meaningful reading of the text for our lives today. The exploration of the Torah highlighted the central concern of divine and human interest in the stranger, the outsider who does not share in the privileges of those who belong. The quantity and quality of statements and prescriptions concerning the stranger testify to the consistency of the biblical interest in this category of people. Crucial declarations relating to God's passion for this group clarify how human posture and action toward the stranger must emulate God's inclination. Instructions regarding the stranger may thus be found throughout the Torah, exhibiting a range and depth of concern unequalled in any other part of Torah regulations. We found that in the New Testament Jesus' interpretation of the law of love went in the same direction as Torah guidance, equating love for the neighbor with love for the stranger.

The declarative statement of Galatians 3:28 is in danger of remaining in the realm of the ideal or of human relating to God only, while keeping social relations in stasis, unless we read these words together with prescriptive formulations from the Torah. If we let the declarative words from Galatians 3 interact with the prescriptive ones from Exodus 23:9 and Leviticus 19:34, we may reach a level of understanding that speaks meaningfully into present-day predicaments. "To know the heart of the stranger" and "to love the stranger as one loves the self" presented to the ancient Israelite covenant community the highest calling in its life as a covenant partner with God. That such high ideals were meant to find concrete expression in people's daily lives was made clear by a multitude of specific provisions to illustrate how the ideal should be put into practice. Many regulations illustrated how the stranger should be provided for: with food, shelter, and clothing, the basic necessities of life. Similarly, the declaration in Galatians 3:28 presents an ideal, one that equally seeks to find expression in the realities of its time. "Who is my neighbor?" asked the expert in the law of Jesus. In other words, "How do I live this law of neighbor love?" Jesus then illustrated to him what it might mean to put this demand into practice in their time. Each new age will need to find its own ways of understanding "how we read."

Returning to the declaration of the pairs of opposites in Galatians and bringing it into conversation with the stranger texts from the Hebrew Bible, let us take once more each pair in turn. If the pair "Jew and Greek" refers primarily to religious boundaries and identities, then the Pauline declaration indicates an erasure of religious inequality. The statement does not erase religious identity but rather the domination of one religion, its view of itself as the only path to God, the only divine truth. Here I call to mind the words of Rabbi Jonathan Sacks: "The idea that we fulfill God's will by waging war against the infidel, or forcing our specific practices on others, so that all humanity shares the same religion is an idea that . . . owes much to the concept of empire and little to the heritage of Abraham, which Jews, Christians and Muslims claim as their own. . . . Fundamentalism, like imperialism, is the attempt to impose a single way of life on a plural world. It is the Tower of Babel of our time."[4] Looking back on centuries of Christian misrepresentation of Judaism and persecution of the Jews, we recognize in the face of our Jewish sisters and brothers the face of the stranger, the face of ourselves, the image of God.

In terms of the second pair, "slave and free," slavery may no longer be operative in our immediate social and cultural context. But the race hatred that gave it birth and perpetuated its structures is still with us and testifies to the fact that, once structures of oppression are dismantled, their ideologies may still be very much alive and do their destructive work. We are reminded of the words of historian Gerda Lerner, that such ideologies may long outlive their institutional abolishment.[5] Slave/free is a dichotomy that speaks to class and race domination, also to the posture that nourishes and perpetuates such hierarchies. Living within this social reality and mindset, we not only ignore

4. Jonathan Sacks, *The Dignity of Difference*, 201.
5. Gerda Lerner, *The Creation of Patriarchy* (Oxford: Oxford University Press, 1986), 240.

the stranger, do not love her or him, and further oppress them, but we actually *make* of the other a stranger, an outsider to privilege. Stranger provisions in the Torah set up this group as having a special claim on justice and compassion/love. In conjunction with Galatians 3:28, the Bible instructs those who believe themselves to be living in covenant with God that neither the structures nor the ideologies of class and race divisions have a legitimate place among them.

The last unequal pair is that of "male and female." Of the three pairs mentioned in Galatians 3:28, it is the one that cuts across all other inequalities. For where equality and dignity within the religious sphere might be acquired, or in the social and racial arena, gender dualisms may still remain intact. Each movement within the Christian community toward racial and social equality or to greater respect toward other religions needs to be always scrutinized, therefore, on the point of the equality and dignity of women. This particular inequality may be the most intransigent of the three and the most difficult to eradicate. If the phrase "in Christ no male and female" is understood as a call to the life of the Christian community, then it may stand also as an indictment of the way Christianity has lived its covenant charge. Within Christian communities, for centuries woman's equal humanity before God went unrecognized, her existence was a subordinated one, her voice only rarely heard. Only now is women's position changing, and in many places it is still vulnerable in the extreme. In Christianity, woman was and still is constructed as the "other," the stranger without equal claims to justice and compassion.

The two markers of the stranger laws, "not to oppress" and "to love," together with the call of Galatians 3:28, still await their being lived into reality in the Christian household. According to that call, constructs of religious imperialism, of class and race hierarchies, and of gender domination have no legitimate place in our midst.

How then shall we live as Christians with a Bible that includes the Torah? I have argued in these pages for a Christian appropriation of the biblical text in its entirety, letting text enter into conversation with text, and thus addressing present-day questions and issues. I do not claim for Christians a Jewish reading and appropriation of Torah, even if this could be done. I do reclaim, however, the Torah as a vibrant, God-revealing word for the Christian household, a word that we can hear if we are willing to "listen and learn." The particulars of this word may be revealed differently in different times, but its timelessness resides in the abiding nature of God who is turned to the creation with grace and devotion. For the One "whose name Moses described as 'I will be what I will be' is in the distinctiveness of God's revelations ever one and the same God, who ever is to the Jews absolutely what God was when once God turned to them in grace and favor, and who ever is and will be to Christians absolutely what God became for them in mediating Godself to them differently."[6]

6. Revised from Hans-Joachim Schoeps, *Paul: The Theology of the Apostle in the Light of Jewish Religious History,* 258.

Bibliography

Books

Albertz, Rainer. *A History of Israelite Religion in the Old Testament Period.* 2 vols. Old Testament Library. Louisville: Westminster John Knox, 1994.

Alt, Albrecht. *Essays on Old Testament History and Religion.* Garden City: Doubleday, 1967.

Alter, Robert. *The Art of Biblical Narrative.* New York: Basic Books, 1981.

Armstrong, Karen. *The Battle for God.* New York: Knopf, 2000.

Balz, Horst and Wolfgang Schrage. *Die "Katholischen" Briefe: Die Briefe des Jakobus, Petrus, Johannes und Judas.* Göttingen, Zürich: Vandenhoeck & Ruprecht, 1993.

Barclay, William. *The Letters of James and Peter.* Rev. ed. Philadelphia: Westminster, 1976.

Barr, James. *The Concept of Biblical Theology: An Old Testament Perspective.* Minneapolis: Fortress, 1999.

————. *History and Ideology in the Old Testament: Biblical Studies at the End of a Millennium.* Oxford: Oxford University Press, 2000.

Bartlett, David L. *The First Letter of Peter: Introduction, Commentary and Reflections.* The New Interpreter's Bible, 12. Nashville: Abingdon, 1998.

Barton, John. *Reading the Old Testament: Method in Biblical Study.* Philadelphia: Westminster, 1984.

Bellis, Alice Ogden. *Helpmates, Harlots, and Heroes: Women's Stories in the Hebrew Bible.* Louisville: Westminster John Knox, 1994.

———— and Joel Kaminsky, eds. *Jews, Christians, and the Theology of the Hebrew Scriptures.* Atlanta: Scholars, 2000.

Berquist, Jon L. *Reclaiming Her Story: The Witness of Women in the Old Testament.* St. Louis: Chalice. 1992.

Betz, Hans Dieter. *Galatians.* Hermeneia. Philadelphia: Fortress, 1979.

Beyerlin, Walter. *Origins and History of the Oldest Sinaitic Traditions.* Oxford: Blackwell, 1966. Trans. from *Herkunft und Geschichte der ältesten Sinaitraditionen.* Tübingen: J. C. B. Mohr, 1961.

Biddle, Mark E. *Deuteronomy.* Macon: Smyth & Helwys, 2003.

Blenkinsopp, Joseph. *The Pentateuch: An Introduction to the First Five Books of the Bible.* New York: Doubleday, 1992.

Bockmuehl, Markus. *Jewish Law in Gentile Churches: Halakha and the Beginning of Christian Public Ethics.* Edinburgh: T. & T. Clark, 2000.

Boersema, Jan J. *The Torah and the Stoics on Humankind and Nature: A Contribution to the Debate on Sustainability and Quality.* Leiden: Brill, 2001.

Boesak, Allan. *Farewell to Innocence: A Socio-Ethical Study on Black Theology and Power.* New York: Orbis, 1977.

Bos, A. David. *Bound Together: A Theology for Ecumenical Community Ministry.* Cleveland: Pilgrim, 2005.

Brenner, Athalya. *The Intercourse of Knowledge: On Gendering Desire and "Sexuality" in the Hebrew Bible.* Leiden: Brill, 1997.

Brooten, Bernadette J. *Love Between Women: Early Christian Responses to Female Homoeroticism.* Chicago: University of Chicago Press, 1996.

———. *Women Leaders in the Ancient Synagogue.* Chico: Scholars, 1982.

Brown, John. *Expository Discourses on the First Epistle of the Apostle Peter.* Evansville: Jay Green, 1868.

Brueggemann, Walter. *Texts Under Negotiation: The Bible and Postmodern Imagination.* Minneapolis: Fortress, 1993.

———. *Theology of the Old Testament: Testimony, Dispute, Advocacy.* Minneapolis: Fortress, 1997.

Buber, Martin. *Die Fünf Bücher der Weisung.* 3rd ed. Cologne: Jakob Hegner, 1968.

———. *Good and Evil: Two Interpretations.* New York: Scribner, 1953.

———. *Moses: The Revelation and the Covenant.* New York: Harper, 1958.

Buber, Martin, and Franz Rosenzweig. *Scripture and Translation.* Trans. Lawrence Rosenwald with Everett Fox. Bloomington: Indiana University Press, 1994. A large part of this work is a translation of the German original written by Martin Buber and Franz Rosenzweig: *Die Schrift und ihre Verdeutschung.* Berlin: Schocken, 1936.

———. *Die fünf Bücher der Weisung-Füf Bücher des Moses: Verdeutscht von Martin Buber Gemainsam mit Franz Rosenzweig.* Cologne: Jakob Hegner, 1968. Original publication: Berlin: Schocken, 1938.

Camp, Claudia. *Wisdom and the Feminine in the Book of Proverbs.* Sheffield: Almond, 1985.

Clines, David J. A. *The Theme of the Pentateuch.* 2nd ed. JSOTSup 10. Sheffield: JSOT, 1997.

Cohen, Norman J. *The Way into Torah.* Woodstock, VT: Jewish Lights, 2000.

Coote, Robert B., and David Robert Ord. *The Bible's First History: From Eden to the Court of David with the Yahwist.* Philadelphia: Fortress, 1989.

Craigie, Peter C. *The Old Testament: Its Background, Growth, and Content.* Nashville: Abingdon, 1986.

Crossan, John Dominic. *The Birth of Christianity: Discovering What Happened in the*

Years Immediately After the Execution of Jesus. San Francisco: HarperCollins, 1998.

Crüsemann, Frank. *The Torah: Theology and Social History of Old Testament Law.* Minneapolis: Fortress, 1996.

Darr, Kathryn Pfisterer. *Far More Precious than Jewels: Perspectives on Biblical Women.* Louisville: Westminster John Knox, 1991.

Davids, Peter H. *The First Epistle of Peter.* New International Commentary on the New Testament. Grand Rapids: Wm. B. Eerdmans, 1990.

Davies, Alan T., ed. *Antisemitism and the Foundations of Christianity.* New York: Paulist, 1979.

Davis, Ellen F. *Getting Involved with God: Rediscovering the Old Testament.* Cambridge, Mass.: Cowley, 2001.

Deist, Ferdinand E. *The Material Culture of the Bible.* Sheffield: Sheffield Academic, 2000.

Den Dulk, Maarten. *Vijf kansen: Een theologie die begint bij Moses* (Zoetermeer: Meinema, 1999.

Dennis, Trevor. *Sarah Laughed.* Nashville: Abingdon, 1994.

De Troyer, Kristin, Judith A. Herbert, Judith Ann Johnson, and Anne Marie Korte, eds. *Wholly Woman, Holy Blood: A Feminist Critique of Purity and Impurity.* Harrisburg: Trinity Press International, 2003.

Dever, William G. *What Did the Biblical Writers Know and When Did They Know It? What Archaeology Can Tell Us about the Reality of Ancient Israel.* Grand Rapids: Wm. B. Eerdmans, 2001.

Dodd, C. H. *The Bible and the Greeks.* London: Hodder & Stoughton, 1935.

Douglas, Mary. *In the Wilderness: The Doctrine of Defilement in the Book of Numbers.* JSOTSup 158. Sheffield: Sheffield Academic, 1993.

———. *Leviticus as Literature.* Oxford: Oxford University Press, 1999.

———, Gerald Barry, J. Bronowski, James Fisher, and Julian Huxley, eds. *Man in Society: Patterns of Human Organization.* Rev. ed. Englewood Cliffs: REC, 1968.

Edwards, George R. *Gay/Lesbian Liberation: A Biblical Perspective.* New York: Pilgrim, 1984.

Elazar, Daniel J. *Covenant and Polity in Biblical Israel: Biblical Foundations and Jewish Expressions.* New Brunswick: Transaction, 1995.

Elliott, John H. *The Elect and the Holy: An Exegetical Examination of 1 Peter 2:4-10 and the Phrase* Basileion Hierateuma. Supplements to Novum Testamentum 12. Leiden: Brill, 1966.

———. *A Home For The Homeless: A Social-Scientific Criticism of 1 Peter, Its Situation And Strategy.* Minneapolis: Fortress, 1990.

Fewell, Danna Nolan, and David M. Gunn. *Gender, Power and Promise: The Subject of the Bible's First Story.* Nashville: Abingdon, 1993.

Fishbane, Michael. *Biblical Interpretation in Ancient Israel.* Oxford: Oxford University Press, 1985.

Fitzpatrick-McKinley, Anne. *The Transformation of Torah from Scribal Advice to Law.* JSOTSup 287. Sheffield: Sheffield Academic, 1985.

Fox, Everett. *The Five Books of Moses: A New Translation with Introductions, Commentary, and Notes.* New York: Schocken, 1995.

Fretheim, Terence E. *Exodus.* Interpretation. Louisville: John Knox, 1991.

———. *The Pentateuch.* Nashville: Abingdon, 1996.

———. *The Suffering of God: An Old Testament Perspective.* Philadelphia: Fortress, 1984.

Friedman, Richard Elliott. *A Commentary on the Torah: With a New English Translation.* San Francisco: HarperSanFrancisco, 2001.

———. *The Hidden Face of God.* HarperSanFrancisco, 1997.

———. *Who Wrote the Bible?* Englewood Cliffs: Prentice Hall, 1987.

Gager, John G. *The Origin of Anti-Semitism: Attitudes Toward Judaism in Pagan and Christian Antiquity.* Oxford: Oxford University Press, 1983.

Gaston, Lloyd. *Paul and the Torah.* Vancouver: University of Columbia Press, 1987.

Gerstenberger, Erhard S. *Theologies in the Old Testament.* Minneapolis, Fortress, 2002.

Gottwald, Norman K. *The Tribes of [Y·hw·h]: A Sociology of the Religion of Liberated Israel, 1250-1050 B.C.E.* Maryknoll: Orbis, 1979.

Hillers, Delbert R. *Covenant: The History of a Biblical Idea.* Baltimore: Johns Hopkins University Press, 1969.

Houtman, Cornelis. *Exodus.* 3 vols. Commentaar op het Oude Testament. Kampen: Kok, 1993-2000.

Isserlin, B. S. J. *The Israelites.* Minneapolis: Fortress, 2001.

Jeansonne, Sharon Pace. *The Women of Genesis: From Sarah to Potiphar's Wife.* Minneapolis: Augsburg Fortress, 1990.

Jervell, Jacob. *Luke and the People of God.* Minneapolis: Augsburg, 1972.

Johnson, Elizabeth A. *She Who Is: The Mystery of God in Feminist Theological Discourse.* New York: Crossroad, 1992.

Kellenbach, Katharina von. *Anti-Judaism in Feminist Religious Writings.* Atlanta: Scholars, 1994.

Kelly, J. N. D. *A Commentary on the Epistles of Peter and Jude.* 1969; repr. Grand Rapids: Baker, 1981.

King, Philip J., and Lawrence E. Stager. *Life in Biblical Israel.* Louisville: Westminster John Knox, 2001.

Kraemer, Ross Shepard, and Mary Rose D'Angelo, eds. *Women and Christian Origins.* New York: Oxford University Press, 1999.

Kraetzschmar, Richard. *Die Bundesvorstellung im Alten Testament in ihrer geschichtlichen Entwicklung untersucht und dargestellt.* Marburg: N. G. Elwert, 1896.

Kugel, James L. *The God of Old: Inside the Lost World of the Bible.* New York: Free Press, 2003.

———. *Traditions of the Bible: A Guide to the Bible As It Was at the Start of the Common Era.* Cambridge, MA; London: Harvard University Press, 1998.

Kutsch, Ernst. *Verheissung und Gesetz: Untersuchungen zum sogenannten Bund im Alten Testament.* Berlin: De Gruyter, 1973.

Lemche, Niels Peter. *The Canaanites and Their Land: The Tradition of the Canaanites.* JSOTSup 110. Sheffield: JSOT, 1991.

―――. *Prelude to Israel's Past: Background and Beginnings of Israelite History and Identity.* Peabody: Hendrickson, 1998.

Lerner, Gerda. *The Creation of Patriarchy.* New York: Oxford University Press, 1986.

Levenson, Jon. *Creation and the Persistence of Evil: The Jewish Drama of Divine Omnipotence.* San Francisco: Harper & Row, 1988.

Levine, Baruch A. *Leviticus* ויקרא. JPS Torah Commentary. Philadelphia: Jewish Publication Society, 5749/1989.

Lieu, Judith. *Neither Jew nor Greek? Constructing Early Christianity.* London: T. & T. Clark, 2002.

Lillie, John. *Lectures on the First and Second Epistles of Peter.* New York: Scribner, 1869.

Lohfink, Norbert, and Erich Zenger. *The God of Israel and the Nations: Studies in Isaiah and the Psalms.* Collegeville: Liturgical, 2000.

MacDonald, Dennis Ronald. *There Is No Male and Female: The Fate of a Dominical Saying in Paul and Gnosticism.* Philadelphia: Fortress, 1987.

McKenzie, Steven L., and Stephen R. Haynes, eds. *To Each Their Own Meaning: An Introduction to Biblical Criticisms and Their Application.* Rev. ed. Louisville: Westminster John Knox, 1999.

Mann, Thomas W. *The Book of the Torah: The Narrative Integrity of the Pentateuch.* Atlanta: John Knox, 1988.

Meyers, Carol. *Discovering Eve: Ancient Israelite Women in Context.* New York: Oxford University Press, 1988.

Miles, Jack. *God: A Biography.* New York: Knopf, 1995.

Miller, J. Maxwell, and John H. Hayes. *A History of Ancient Israel and Modern Judah.* Philadelphia: Westminster, 1986.

Miller, Patrick D. *Deuteronomy.* Interpretation. Louisville: John Knox, 1990.

―――. *They Cried to the Lord: The Form and Theology of Biblical Prayer.* Minneapolis: Fortress, 1994.

Moore, George Foote. *Judaism in the First Centuries of the Christian Era: The Age of the Tannaim.* 3 vols. 1927-1930; repr. New York: Schocken, 1971.

Neusner, Jacob. *Fortress Introduction to American Judaism: What the Books Say, What the People Do.* Minneapolis: Fortress, 1994.

―――. *Torah: From Scroll to Symbol in Formative Judaism.* Philadelphia: Fortress, 1985.

Niditch, Susan. *War in the Hebrew Bible: A Study in the Ethics of Violence.* Oxford: Oxford University Press, 1993.

Oden, Thomas C. *First and Second Timothy and Titus.* Interpretation. Louisville: John Knox, 1989.

Ogletree, Thomas W. *Hospitality to the Stranger: Dimensions of Moral Understanding.* 1985; repr. Louisville: Westminster John Knox, 2003.

Peck, Abraham J., ed. *Jews and Christians After the Holocaust.* Philadelphia: Fortress, 1982.

Pedersen, Johannes. *Israel, Its Life and Culture.* 2 vols. London: Oxford University Press, 1926.

Perkins, Pheme. *First and Second Peter, James, and Jude.* Interpretation. Louisville: Westminster John Knox, 1995.

Perlitt, Lothar. *Bundestheologie im Alten Testament.* WMANT 36. Neukirchen: Neukirchener, 1969.

Plaut, W. Gunther, ed. *The Torah: A Modern Commentary.* New York: Union of American Hebrew Congregations, 1981.

Presser, Jacob. *The Destruction of the Dutch Jews.* New York: Dutton, 1969.

Presser, J. *Ondergang: De Vervolging en Verdelging van het Nederlandse Jodendom 1940-1945.* Dutch Institute for War Documentation (Rijksinstituut voor Oorlogs-documentatie), 1965. Trans. by Arnold Pomerans into an abridged English version, *The Destruction of the Dutch Jews.* New York: Dutton, 1969.

Räisänen, Heikki. *Jesus, Paul and Torah.* JSNTSup 43. Sheffield: Sheffield Academic, 1992.

Rendtorff, Rolf. *The Old Testament: An Introduction.* Philadelphia: Fortress, 1986.

Ringe, Sharon H. *Luke.* Westminster Bible Companion. Louisville: Westminster John Knox, 1995.

Rosenbaum, Stanley N. *Understanding Biblical Israel: A Reexamination of the Origins of Monotheism.* Macon: Mercer, 2002.

Ruether, Rosemary Radford. *Faith and Fratricide: The Theological Roots of Anti-Semitism.* New York: Seabury, 1974.

Sacks, Jonathan. *The Dignity of Difference: How to Avoid the Clash of Civilizations.* New York: Continuum, 2002.

Sakenfeld, Katherine Doob. *The Meaning of Ḥesed in the Hebrew Bible.* HSM 17. Missoula: Scholars, 1978.

Sanders, E. P. *The Historical Figure of Jesus.* London: Penguin, 1993.

————. *Jesus and Judaism.* Philadelphia: Fortress, 1985.

————. *Jewish Law from Jesus to the Mishnah: Five Studies.* Philadelphia: Trinity Press International, 1990.

————. *Paul and Palestinian Judaism: A Comparison of Patterns of Religion.* Minneapolis: Fortress, 1977.

————. *Paul, the Law, and the Jewish People.* Minneapolis: Fortress, 1983.

————, ed. *Jesus, the Gospels, and the Church.* Macon: Mercer, 1987.

Sanders, Jack T. *The Jews in Luke-Acts.* Philadelphia: Fortress, 1987.

Sanders, James A. *Canon and Community: A Guide to Canonical Criticism.* Philadelphia: Fortress, 1984.

————. *Torah and Canon.* Philadelphia: Fortress, 1972.

Sandmel, Samuel. *Anti-Semitism in the New Testament?* Philadelphia: Fortress, 1978.

Schmid, Herbert. *Mose.* Berlin: Töpelmann, 1968.

Schoeps, Hans Joachim. *Paul: The Theology of the Apostle in the Light of Jewish Religious History*. Philadelphia: Westminster, 1961.

Schüssler Fiorenza, Elizabeth. *In Memory of Her: A Feminist Theological Reconstruction of Christian Origins*. New York: Crossroads, 1983.

———. *Searching the Scriptures*. 2 vols. New York: Crossroad, 1993-94.

Schwartz, Regina M. *The Curse of Cain: The Violent Legacy of Monotheism*. Chicago: University of Chicago Press, 1997.

Seow, Choon-Leong, ed. *Homosexuality and Christian Community*. Louisville: Westminster John Knox, 1996.

Sprinkle, Joe M. *The Book of the Covenant: A Literary Approach*. JSOTSup 174. Sheffield: JSOT, 1994.

Steinberg, Naomi *Kinship and Marriage in Genesis: A Household Economics Perspective*. Minneapolis: Fortress, 1993.

Stendahl, Krister. *Paul Among Jews and Gentiles*. Philadelphia: Fortress, 1976.

Swidler, Leonard J., Lewis John Eron, Gerard Sloyan, and Lester Dean, eds. *Bursting the Bonds? A Jewish-Christian Dialogue on Jesus and Paul*. Maryknoll: Orbis, 1990.

Terrien, Samuel. *The Elusive Presence: Toward a New Biblical Theology*. San Francisco: Harper & Row, 1978.

Teubal, Savina J. *Hagar the Egyptian: The Lost Tradition of the Matriarchs*. 1990; repr. Athens: Ohio University Press, 1997.

Thompson, Thomas L. *The Origin Tradition of Ancient Israel: The Literary Formation of Genesis and Exodus 1–23*. JSOTSup 55. Sheffield: JSOT, 1987.

Tomson, Peter J. *"If This Be from Heaven": Jesus and the New Testament Authors in Their Relationship to Judaism*. Sheffield: Sheffield Academic, 2001.

———. *Paul and the Jewish Law: Halakha in the Letters of the Apostle to the Gentiles*. Minneapolis: Fortress, 1990.

Trible, Phyllis. *God and the Rhetoric of Sexuality*. Overtures to Biblical Theology. Philadelphia: Fortress, 1978.

———. *Texts of Terror: Literary-Feminist Readings of Biblical Narratives*. Overtures to Biblical Theology. Philadelphia: Fortress, 1984.

van der Toorn, Karel. *From Her Cradle to Her Grave: The Role of Religion in the Life of the Israelite and the Babylonian Woman*. Sheffield: Sheffield Academic, 1994.

———. *Sin and Sanction in Israel and Mesopotamia: A Comparative Study*. Assen: van Gorcum, 1985.

van Houten, Christiana. *The Alien in Israelite Law*. JSOTSup 107. Sheffield: JSOT, 1991.

Van Seters, John. *The Life of Moses: The Yahwist as Historian in Exodus-Numbers*. Louisville: Westminster John Knox, 1994.

———. *The Pentateuch: A Social Science Commentary*. Sheffield: Sheffield Academic, 1999.

Van Wijk-Bos, Johanna W. H. *Ezra, Nehemiah and Esther*. Westminster Bible Companion. Louisville: Westminster John Knox, 1998.

———. *Reformed and Feminist: A Challenge to the Church*. Louisville: Westminster John Knox, 1991.

————. *Reimagining God: The Case for Scriptural Diversity.* Louisville: Westminster John Knox, 1995.

Vaux, Roland de. *Ancient Israel: Its Life and Institutions.* 1961; repr. Grand Rapids: Wm. B. Eerdmans, and Livonia: Dove, 1997.

Venema, G. J. *Reading Scripture in the Old Testament.* Leiden: Brill, 2003.

Watson, Francis. *Paul, Judaism and the Gentiles.* SNTSMS 56. Cambridge: Cambridge University Press, 1986.

Weems, Renita J. *Just a Sister Away: A Womanist Vision of Women's Relationships in the Bible.* San Diego: LuraMedia, 1988.

Wellhausen, Julius. *Prolegomena to the History of Ancient Israel: With a Reprint of the Article "Israel" from the Encyclopaedia Britannica.* Cleveland: World, 1957.

————. *Prolegomena of the History of Israel.* New York: Meridian, 1957.

————. *Grundrisse zum Alten Testament.* Ed. Rudolf Smend. Munich: Kaiser, 1965.

Whitelam, Keith H. *The Invention of Ancient Israel: The Silencing of Palestinian History.* London: Routledge, 1996.

Whybray, R. N. *The Making of the Pentateuch: A Methodological Study.* Sheffield: Sheffield Academic, 1987.

Williams, Delores S. *Sisters in the Wilderness: The Challenge of Womanist God-Talk.* Maryknoll: Orbis, 1993.

Williams, Lukyn. *Adversus Judaeos: A Bird's-Eye View of Christian Apologiae Until the Renaissance.* Cambridge: Cambridge University Press, 1935.

Williamson, Clark. *A Guest in the House of Israel: Post-Holocaust Church Theology.* Louisville: Westminster John Knox, 1993.

Wire, Antoinette Clark. *The Corinthian Women Prophets: A Reconstruction through Paul's Rhetoric.* Minneapolis: Fortess, 1990.

van Wolde, Ellen. *Stories of the Beginning: Genesis 1–11 and Other Creation Stories.* London: SCM, 1996.

Yerushalmi, Yosef Hayim. *Zakhor: Jewish History and Jewish Memory.* Seattle: University of Washington Press, 1982.

Zenger, Erich, et al., eds. *Einleitung in das Alte Testament.* Stuttgart: Kohlhammer, 1998.

Chapters and Articles

Bartlett, David L. "The First Letter of Peter: Introduction, Commentary and Reflections." *The New Interpreter's Bible* 12. Nashville: Abingdon, 1998, 227-319.

Baum, Gregory. "Catholic Dogma After Auschwitz." In *Antisemitism and the Foundations of Christianity,* ed. Alan T. Davies. New York: Paulist, 1979, 137-50.

Bird, Phyllis. "Images of Women in the Old Testament." In *Religion and Sexism: Images of Woman in the Jewish and Christian Traditions,* ed. Rosemary Radford Ruether. New York: Simon and Schuster, 1974, 41-88.

————. "The Place of Women in the Israelite Cultus." In *Community, Identity, and*

Ideology: Social Science Approaches to the Hebrew Bible, ed. Charles E. Carter and Carol L. Meyers. Winona Lake: Eisenbrauns, 1996, 515-36.

Brueggemann, Walter. "The Book of Exodus: Introduction, Commentary and Reflections." *The New Interpreter's Bible* 1. Nashville: Abingdon, 1994, 675-981.

Crossan, John Dominic. "Parable and Example in the Teaching of Jesus." *New Testament Studies* 18 (1972): 285-307.

Davis, Ellen F. "Losing a Friend: The Loss of the Old Testament to the Church." In Alice Ogden Bellis and Joel Kaminsky, *Jews, Christians, and the Theology of the Hebrew Scriptures.* Atlanta: Scholars, 2000, 83-94.

Dean, Lester. "Paul's "Erroneous" Description of Judaism." In Leonard J. Swidler et al., *Bursting the Bonds?* Maryknoll: Orbis, 1990, 136-42.

Eron, Lewis John. "Jesus: A Torah-True Jew?" In Leonard J. Swidler et al., *Bursting the Bonds?* Maryknoll: Orbis, 1990, 70-77.

Exum, J. Cheryl. "'You Shall Let Every Daughter Live': A Study of Exodus 1:8–2:10." In *The Bible and Feminist Hermeneutics,* ed. Mary Ann Tolbert. Semeia 28. Chico: Scholars, 1983, 63-82.

Fretheim, Terence E. "The Book of Genesis: Introduction, Commentary and Reflections." *The New Interpreter's Bible* 1. Nashville: Abingdon, 1994, 319-674.

———. "Which Blessing Does Isaac Give Jacob?" In Alice Ogden Bellis and Joel Kaminsky, *Jews, Christians, and the Theology of the Hebrew Scriptures.* Atlanta: Scholars, 2000, 279-91.

Greenberg, Moshe. "Some Postulates of Biblical Criminal Law." In *A Song of Power and the Power of Song,* ed. Duane L. Christensen. Winona Lake: Eisenbrauns, 1993, 283-300.

Howard, Richard. "Esther — Apart: Hearing Secret Harmonies," In *Congregation: Contemporary Writers Read the Jewish Bible,* ed. David Rosenberg. San Diego: Harcourt Brace Jovanovich, 1987, 406-17.

Janzen, J. Gerald. "Metaphor and Reality in Hosea 11." In *Old Testament Interpretation from a Process Perspective,* ed. William A. Beardslee and David J. Lull. Semeia 24. Atlanta: Scholars, 1982, 7-44.

Jepsen, Alfred. "Berith: Ein Beitrag zur Theologie der Exilszeit." In *Verbannung und Heimkehr,* ed. Arnulf Kuschke. Tübingen: J.C.B. Mohr, 1961, 161-79.

Kaiser, Walter C., Jr. "Leviticus: Introduction, Commentary and Reflections." *The New Interpreter's Bible* 1. Nashville: Abingdon, 1994, 983-1191.

Klawans, Jonathan. "Concepts of Purity in the Bible." In *The Jewish Study Bible,* ed. Adele Berlin and Marc Zvi Brettler. Oxford: Oxford University Press, 2002, 2041-47.

Levenson, Jon D. "The Perils of Engaged Scholarship: A Rejoinder to Jorge Pixley." In Alice Ogden Bellis and Joel Kaminsky, *Jews, Christians, and the Theology of the Hebrew Scriptures.* Atlanta: Scholars, 2000, 239-46.

Lichtenstein, Murray H. "An Interpersonal Theology of the Hebrew Bible." In Alice Ogden Bellis and Joel Kaminsky, *Jews, Christians, and the Theology of the Hebrew Scriptures.* Atlanta: Scholars, 2000, 61-82.

Marks, Herbert. "Biblical Naming and Poetic Etymology." *JBL* 114 (1995): 21-42.

Meyers, Carol. "Everyday Life: Women in the Period of the Hebrew Bible." In *The Women's Bible Commentary,* ed. Carol A. Newsom and Sharon H. Ringe. Rev. ed. Louisville: Westminster John Knox, 1998, 251-59.

———. "The Roots of Restriction: Women in Early Israel." In *The Bible and Liberation: Political and Social Hermeneutics,* ed. Norman K. Gottwald. Maryknoll: Orbis, 1983, 289-304.

Moore, George Foot. "Christian Writers on Judaism." *HTR* 14 (1921): 197-254.

O'Grady, Kathleen. "The Semantics of Taboo: Menstrual Prohibitions in the Hebrew Bible." In Kristin de Troyer et al., *Wholly Woman, Holy Blood.* Harrisburg: Trinity Press International, 2003, 1-28.

Rosen, Jonathan. "The Uncomfortable Question of Anti-Semitism." *New York Times,* 4 November 2001.

Sanders, E. P. "Jesus and the Kingdom: The Restoration of Israel and the New People of God." In Sanders, *Jesus, the Gospels and the Church.* Macon: Mercer, 1987, 225-39.

———. "When Is a Law a Law? The Case of Jesus and Paul." In *Religion and Law: Biblical-Judaic and Islamic Perspectives,* ed. Edwin Brown Firmage, Bernard G. Weiss, and John Woodland Welch. Winona Lake: Eisenbrauns, 1990, 139-58.

Sanders, James A. "Canon and Calendar: An Alternative Lectionary Proposal." In *Social Themes of the Christian Year: A Commentary on the Lectionary,* ed. Dieter T. Hessel. Philadelphia: Geneva, 1983, 257-63.

Schultz, Jennifer. "Doctors, Philosophers, and Christian Fathers on Menstrual Blood." In Kristin de Troyer et al., *Wholly Woman, Holy Blood.* Harrisburg: Trinity Press International, 2003, 97-116.

Stanley, Christopher D. "'Neither Jew nor Greek': Ethnic Conflict in Graeco-Roman Society." *JSNT* 64 (1996): 101-24.

Trible, Phyllis. "Bringing Miriam Out of the Shadows." *Bible Review* 5/1 (1989): 14-25, 34.

Van Wijk-Bos, Johanna W. H. "How to Read What We Read: Discerning Good News about Sexuality in Scripture." In *Body and Soul: Rethinking Sexuality as Justice-Love,* ed. Marvin M. Ellison and Sylvia Thorson-Smith. Cleveland: Pilgrim, 2003, 61-77.

———. "Out of the Shadows: Genesis 38; Judges 4:17-22; Ruth 3." In *Reasoning with the Foxes: Female Wit in a World of Male Power,* ed. J. Cheryl Exum and Bos. Semeia 42. Atlanta: Scholars, 1988, 37-67.

———. "Writing on the Water: The Ineffable Name of God." In Alice Ogden Bellis and Joel Kaminsky, *Jews, Christians, and the Theology of the Hebrew Scriptures.* Atlanta: Scholars, 2000, 45-59.

Zenger, Erich. "Wie und Wozu die Tora zum Sinai kam: Literarische und theologische Beobachtungen zu Exodus 19–34." In *Studies in the Book of Exodus: Redaction, Reception, Interpretation,* ed. Marc Vervenne. BETL 126. Leuven: Peeters, 1996, 265-88.

Index of Names and Subjects

Aaron, 38, 45, 83, 170, 205, 207, 208, 209, 218

Abel, 83, 87, 88, 90, 91, 93, 96, 97, 127, 132, 248, 251

Abram/Abraham, 23, 37, 71, 72, 79, 95, 96, 97, 103, 105, 106, 107, 108, 129, 130, 134, 135, 137, 138, 139, 140, 141, 147, 148, 149, 152, 156, 237, 244, 249, 303

Ada, 97

Adam, 93, 95, 96, 97, 98, 117, 119, 120, 121, 122, 291

Agriculture/agricultural, 41, 42, 42n., 43, 45, 46, 47, 52, 54, 55, 56, 76, 105, 182, 190, 285

Altar, 70, 92, 165, 166, 181, 204, 205, 208

Amsterdam, 5, 9

Ancestors, 36, 37, 45, 62, 70, 71, 78, 95, 96, 101, 102, 103, 127, 131, 133, 135, 136, 139, 143, 146, 153, 155, 239, 242, 245, 246, 252, 253

Ancestor lists, 96

Animal, 50, 82, 115, 119, 182, 190, 191, 203, 215, 217, 228

Animals, 36n., 54, 82, 110, 112, 115, 182, 183, 190, 213, 215, 219, 236

Anti-Jewishness, xviii, 273

Anti-Judaism, xv, xviii, 273

Anti-Semitism, xv, xviii, xix, 10

Ark, 5, 49, 205, 208

Armstrong, Karen, 63

Atonement, 56, 192, 203, 216, 228, 229, 230; Augustine on, 7n.15, 122n.25

Auschwitz, xiv, 10, 274, 275

Babel/Babylon, 71-77, 78, 89, 105, 124, 303

Babylonian exile, 3, 7, 15, 46, 48, 50, 55, 56, 75, 88, 126, 179, 201

Bamberger, Bernard, 222, 228

Bathsheba, 274

Baum, Gregory, 274

Betz, Hans Dieter, 298

Biddle, Mark, 201

Biezeveld, Kune, 222

Brooten, Bernadette, 288

Brueggemann, Walter, 31, 32

Buber, Martin, xviii, 74, 154, 160-61, 164, 173, 208, 241-42

Cain, 83, 87, 88, 90, 91, 92, 94, 96, 97, 101, 127, 132, 134, 235, 248

Calvin, John, 7, 23

Canaan, 36, 37, 38, 39, 40, 41, 48, 87, 95, 104, 105, 108, 130, 133, 134, 151, 154, 169, 257, 260

Canaanite(s), 46, 48, 104, 142, 144, 208

Christ, 7, 8, 11, 13, 20, 22, 33, 70, 120, 121, 124, 125, 164, 179, 221, 228, 262, 264, 272, 276, 279, 281, 282, 287, 288, 289, 291, 292, 294, 297, 298, 299, 301, 304

Christians, Gentile, 264, 272, 273, 279, 281, Jewish, 272, 273, 279, 280, 281

316

Circumcision, 120, 135, 272, 278, 279, 280, 281, 284, 288, 291, 293, 297
Clan, 27, 45, 46, 47, 56, 131, 136, 201
Class, 43, 44, 47, 197, 298, 303, 304
Commandment, 53, 85, 161, 196, 269, 271, 282, 291
Compassion: of God, 51, 188, 230, 254, 255, 256, 257; of humanity, 201, 270, 271, 274, 303, 304
Coote, Robert, 118
Covenant: of God with world, 36, 79, 84, 85, 86, 89, 127, 136, 237; of God with God's people, xiv, xvi, 1, 11, 12, 13, 18, 23, 24, 33, 34, 92, 179, 204, 303; of God with ancient Israel, 10, 16, 19, 23, 35, 37, 39, 44, 48, 51, 76, 79, 85, 86, 126, 130, 177, 246, 250, 252, 263; of God with ancestors, 85, 135, 143, 145, made at Sinai, xvi, xvii, 12, 15, 26, 37, 129, 152, 154-68, 198, 204, 230, 253, 256, 293; made through Jesus Christ, 11, 20, 70, 262, 264, 292; as political bond, 156 and nn.; Book of the, 180-85, 187, 188, 191-93, 204, 250, 257; Ten Words of the, 157-64, 180; and Torah, 19, 24
Crossan, John Dominic, 269

David (king), 135, 145, 274-75
Davis, Ellen, 11, 254
Dean, Lester, 293
Decalogue/Ten Words, 48, 49, 52, 53, 54, 94, 157-64, 168, 180, 181, 203, 283
Den Dulk, Maarten, 216
Dodd, C. H., 277
Douglas, Mary, 171, 198, 123, 214, 215, 217, 219

Earth, xvi, 16, 17, 37, 47, 74, 75, 76, 79, 81-90, 98, 109, 112, 116-18, 123, 126, 129, 156, 157, 181, 225, 226, 234, 237, 249, 300
Economy, 42
Ecumenical Lectionary, xiii, 49n., 123n.
Egypt, 15, 16, 28, 30, 31, 37, 40, 41, 46, 50, 62, 63, 74, 76, 78, 87, 130, 133-35, 139, 140, 149-53, 159, 161, 170, 174, 186, 187, 190, 199, 208, 209, 230, 238, 240, 251, 257, 276

Election, 13, 20, 253
Enoch/Hanokh, 101
Enosh, 98
Essenes, 272, 279
Eve, 93, 95, 96-98, 116, 120, 121, 122, 134, 138, 247, 248, 251
Ezra, 3, 59, 131n., 145, 146, 146n. 198

Family, 40-48, 56, 83, 96, 136, 201, 227, 284, 285
Female, 48, 82, 84, 99-101, 109n., 112, 115, 123, 124, 148, 164, 220-22, 226, 254, 278, 285-92, 294, 297, 298-99, 304
Feminism, xv, 109n.
Festival, 52-55, 94, 183, 216, 227
Food/Diet, 82, 85, 86, 117, 118, 120, 123, 139, 173, 174, 192, 218, 219, 219, 250, 278, 279, 280, 281, 288, 291, 293, 303
Fretheim, Terence, 75, 92, 207, 237
Friedman, Richard Elliott, 246, 300

Gaston, Lloyd, 277
Genealogy, 37, 72, 73, 95, 96, 102, 105, 104, 107, 127, 133
Gender boundaries, 121, 122, 124, 284-92, 294, 296, 299
Gentile(s), 11, 70, 120-22, 126, 219n., 264, 272, 273, 278-81, 283, 284, 288, 291-93, 297, 298
Germany, xivn., xviin., 9n., 58, 63, 65, 277n.
God-fearers, 278, 279

Habiru, 153
Hagar, 131, 134, 138n.-41, 148, 244
Ham, 96, 102, 104, 105, 122
Hayes, John, 153
Hellenism, 61n., 276, 278n. 298
Hesed, 239, 254n., 255, 256
Hevel, 87, 97, 127, 141
Holiness, 17, 38, 53, 121, 170, 192-203, 216, 220, 223, 226, 227, 243, 250, 261, 271, 294
Holocaust/Shoah, xiv, xv, xix, 5, 10
Holy days, 52-56, 212, 227-28
Homosexuality, 45, 225, 226, 227, 227n., 285, 289, 290n.
House/hold, 23, 24, 42, 44, 124, 135, 137,

140, 145, 288n., 292, 293, 294, 295, 299, 304

Humanity, xvi, 51, 73-76, 81, 82, 83, 85, 86, 89, 90, 93, 98, 101, 109, 112, 114, 116, 119, 120, 124, 126, 164, 229, 235, 237, 240, 245, 248, 255, 294, 300, 303, 304

Idols, 49, 141n., 208, 260
Idolatry, 48, 212, 225, 260, 290n.
Image of God, 82, 85, 123, 173, 286, 299, 303
Impurity, 59, 197, 203, 218-27
Incest, 45, 147, 225, 285
Ishmael, 83, 131, 133, 134, 141
Israel, State of, xv, xviii

Jacob, 74, 83, 131, 134, 135, 136, 139, 141, 142, 149, 151, 157, 243, 244
Jerusalem, 3, 41, 42, 50, 62, 74, 88, 270
Jervell, Jacob, 273
Jesus, xiii, xvi, 7, 8, 10, 12, 20, 21, 33, 40, 41, 70, 120, 125, 164, 195, 196, 212, 216, 228, 231, 254, 262-80, 283, 287, 288, 291, 292, 294, 295, 298, 301, 304
Jew, 6, 206, 264, 271, 272, 273, 274, 278, 288, 290, 293, 297, 298, 300, 302
Jews, xiv, xv, xix, 5-11, 13, 21-23, 33, 34, 35, 70, 146, 164, 198, 252, 253, 264-67, 271-74, 275, 278-81, 293, 294, 295, 297, 299, 301, 303
Joseph, 66, 83, 131, 135, 139, 142, 148n.
Josiah, 3, 50, 59
Judah, 41, 46, 54, 55, 58, 59, 76, 127, 131, 134, 142-48, 153, 154, 170, 176, 198, 270
Judaism, xiv, xv, xvi, xviii, xix, 6, 7, 8, 10, 23, 57, 58, 60, 68, 70, 120, 215, 218, 219, 222n., 227, 228, 231, 265-67, 272, 273, 274, 276, 278-80, 293, 303
Judaizer, 272, 279
Justice, xiii, 17, 24, 29, 31, 32, 34, 183, 187, 189, 199, 200, 201, 213, 223n., 230, 250, 251, 303, 304

Klawans, Jonathan, 221
Kosher, 278, 279, 280
Kugel, James, 188, 244

Lamech, 92, 97, 100, 101
Land of the promise, 15, 37, 38, 48, 62, 78, 132, 149, 169, 170, 176, 178, 201, 207, 249, 257, 259, 260
Law, xi, xiv, xvii, 4, 6, 7, 8, 15, 19, 28, 29, 31, 52, 54, 120, 129, 132, 161, 162, 164, 179, 180, 183, 184, 188, 190, 191, 201, 222, 231, 264, 269-73, 275, 277, 280-84, 289, 293, 294, 297, 302
Leah, 31
Legalism, 7, 167n., 179
Lerner, Gerda, 303
Levenson, Jon D., 252
Liberation theology, 252n.
Life expectancy/mortality rate, 41n., 44n., 43n., 45, 161n., 285
Love, xiii, xiv, 8, 23, 28, 31, 39, 86, 121, 124, 129, 194-96, 198, 199-201, 212, 227, 250, 256, 259, 261, 265, 267, 269, 270, 271, 273-75, 278, 282, 283, 284, 292, 294, 302, 303, 304

Male, 42, 44, 59, 82, 84, 97, 99, 100, 101, 112, 115, 123, 124, 135, 144, 145, 164, 186, 220, 222, 226, 247, 248, 278, 280, 285, 286-92, 294, 297, 298-99, 304
Marcion, 8n.
Marriage, 45, 136, 152, 227n., 285, 286, 288
Men, xv, 5, 31, 41, 42, 64, 97, 99, 184, 223, 225, 226, 244, 278, 286, 289, 292, 295, 299
Menstruation, 219-23
Mesopotamia, 40, 41, 74, 95, 110n., 133
Messiah, 273, 279
Midwives, 131, 150, 151
Miles, Jack, 246, 300
Miller, Maxwell, 153
Miller, Patrick, 239
Miriam, 38, 83, 131
Moses, 3, 4, 6, 12, 16, 36-39, 45, 51, 58, 61, 83, 130, 131, 151, 152, 153, 157, 165, 166, 170, 173-77, 179, 183, 193, 198, 203, 207, 208-13, 217, 223, 237, 238-45, 249, 254, 260, 304
Myth, 63, 65, 66, 71, 72, 78, 96, 115, 123, 124, 126, 127, 259n., 260n.

Na'amah, 97
Nathan, 274, 275
Nature, 119, 287, 289
Nazi occupation, xiv, 9n., 10, 64n., 277n., 294n.
Nefesh, 30, 152n.
Nehemiah, 3, 62, 131n., 145, 146, 198
The Netherlands, xiv, 9, 63, 163, 207
Neusner, Jacob, 5n.4
Noah, 72, 84-86, 91-93, 95, 96, 100, 101-5, 127, 236, 237, 248

Ord, David, 118
Orphan/fatherless, 44, 68, 87, 186, 188, 198, 199, 201, 250, 251, 257

Patriarchy, 44, 82, 124, 131n., 144, 145, 225, 227, 285, 286, 294, 299
Paul, xvi, 4, 22, 23, 119ff., 124, 156, 226, 231, 264, 275ff.
Persia, 41, 276
Pharaoh, 74, 86, 131, 139, 150, 151, 152, 163
Pharisees, 7, 265, 272, 274, 279
Philo, of Alexandria, 298
Population, 41, 42, 45, 47n., 56, 146, 226, 285
Poor, 29, 43, 47, 66, 68, 183, 188, 189, 190, 191, 194, 200, 201n., 216, 248n., 250, 252, 255, 259n., 300
Prayer, 51, 52, 62, 92-94, 173, 203, 211, 212, 216, 237, 239, 249, 250, 262
Presence (of God), 7, 12, 16, 19, 31, 33, 41, 43, 49, 50n., 93, 117, 132, 155-57, 166, 173, 176, 177, 205, 206, 208, 209-11, 230, 234, 235, 241-43, 245, 246, 247-51, 262, 300
Prescriptions, 19, 38, 48ff., 51, 68, 120, 179, 180, 196, 216, 250, 284, 286, 290, 291, 294, 303
Priests, 16, 17, 23, 59, 62, 156, 157, 165, 192, 205; Priestly, 59, 60, 61, 72, 78, 165, 166, 170, 176, 192, 197ff., 204, 205, 206
Procreation, 82, 99, 102, 288
Productivity, 42-45, 47, 54, 85, 87, 97, 132, 134, 225, 285, 288
Proselytes, 26n., 201, 278, 279
Puah, 131, 150, 151
Purity, 38, 47, 50, 59, 192, 197, 203, 217, 218-27, 267

Race, 139n., 298, 303, 304
Rachel, 131, 134
Räisänen, Heikki, 277
Rebekah, 131, 134
Reformation, Protestant, xviii, 245n.
Regulations, 1, 4, 19, 24, 28, 30, 32, 34, 42, 43, 45, 47, 54, 132, 154, 155, 161, 170, 179, 181, 183, 184, 187-93, 198, 201, 203, 204, 207, 218-20, 222, 224, 225, 230, 250, 264, 267, 278, 279, 280-82, 285, 288, 289, 290, 303
Rest, 52, 54, 81, 102, 161, 183, 188, 191, 227
Righteousness, 144, 248, 251, 252, 268, 297, 298
Ringe, Sharon, 270
Rosen, Jonathan, xv
Rosenzweig, Franz, xvii

Sacks, Jonathan, 77, 251, 303
Sacrifice, 50, 51, 57, 90-93, 183, 192, 193, 197, 203-6, 215-17, 223, 247
Sadducees, 272, 279
Sabbath/Shabbat, 5, 52-54, 57, 78, 81, 94-95, 120, 161, 162, 183, 188, 191, 193, 227, 267, 278, 279
Samaritan (good), 194n., 195, 196, 231, 268-75
Samaritans, 271-73, 279
Sanctuary, 38, 49, 62, 95n., 163, 204, 205-8, 212, 225, 249, 260
Sanders, James A., 19, 49
Sarah/Sarai, 95, 107, 108, 130-34, 136-41, 140n., 147, 148, 152
Schoeps, Hans-Joachim, 293, 294, 305
Schrage, Wolfgang, 22
Schwartz, Regina M., 261
Schultz, Jennifer, 221
Scribes, 7, 59, 274
Second World War, 9, 10, 63, 66, 69, 294n.
Seth/Shet, 93, 96, 98, 100, 134, 248
sexual relations, 42, 45, 225, 226, 284, 285, 286, 288, 289, 292
Shem, 72, 73, 96, 103, 105, 106, 127
Shifrah, 131, 150, 151
Slave, 138n., 182, 183, 296-304
Slavery, 62, 86, 105, 138n., 139, 161, 181, 182, 184, 239, 240, 284, 298, 299, 303

Snake, 113-15, 123

Stendahl, Krister, 280

Synagogue, 5, 6, 9

Talmud, 6, 54, 266

Tamar, 66, 131, 134, 135, 142-45

Temple, 3, 50, 54, 59, 62, 91n., 181, 226, 271, 272

Tent, 51, 205, 206-8

Tree of knowledge, 82, 117, 123, 235, 247

Trible, Phyllis, 119

tribe, 27, 45, 46, 169, 201

Tsedaqah, 251, 252, 255, 268

Van Wolde, Ellen, 75, 82, 87, 99, 105, 117

Violence: of God, 257-61; of humans, xv, 10, 28, 29, 39, 83, 85, 91-93, 97, 98, 118, 127, 129, 130, 136, 182, 186, 190, 215, 230, 236, 237, 246, 247; of animals, 182

war, 9, 41, 65, 259n., 303

Wellhausen, Julius, 8, 58

widow, 68, 87, 186, 188, 198, 199, 201, 250, 251, 257

Wiesel, Elie, xix

Women, xv, 148, 150, 151, 182, 198, 295; and ancestral history, 77, 99, 100, 101, 107, 131; and economy, 42, 87; and gender boundaries, 221, 285-92, 294; and household, 44, 136; and image of God, 299, 303, 304; and law codes, 164, 184; and life expectancy, 42n., 45; and menstruation, 219-23; and procreation, 134, 248n.; and religious practices, 48, 49n.; and sexuality, 225, and sin, 121, 122n.; submission of, 24, 82, 121, 125

worship, 5, 7, 38, 48-52, 56, 69, 75, 90-93, 161, 169, 180, 181, 183, 187, 197, 198, 201, 203-6, 209, 212, 213, 216, 260, 286, 287, 294

Index of Biblical References

OLD TESTAMENT

Genesis

1–11	xvi, 10, 37, 79, 80, 83, 90, 93, 95, 96n., 109, 119, 126, 133, 235, 245
1–3	81, 83, 212
1	82, 112, 235
1:1–2:4a	81, 88, 94n., 123, 139n., 204
1:1–11:32	79-119
1:4	81
1:5	81
1:8	81
1:10	81
1:12	81
1:13	81
1:18	81
1:19	81
1:21	81
1:22	82
1:23	81
1:25	81
1:26	89
1:26-28	82, 94
1:27	286, 299
1:28	75, 85 88, 111, 116
1:31	81
2–4	235

2–3	72, 118, 121, 122, 123, 124, 127, 139n.
2	121
2:1-3	94, 95
2:4b	72, 82, 88
2:4b-14	109
2:4–3:24	109-27
2:7-9	110
2:15	82, 88, 116
2:15-17	85
2:15-25	110
2:17	112, 235
2:18	111
2:18-25	286
2:19-20	111, 112
2:21-25	111
2:23	112
2:24-25	112
2:25	112
3	235, 248
3:1-5	113
3:2	113
3:6-7	114
3:6-13	114
3:9-13	114, 235
3:11	115
3:12-13	115
3:14-15	115
3:14-19	83, 115
3:14-24	115
3:16	115, 247

3:16-17	84, 115
3:17-19	115
3:18-19	88
3:20-24	115
3:21	116, 234n.
3:22	111, 114, 247
3:23	114
3:24	116, 246, 247
4	83, 93, 94, 97, 119, 235
4:1	87, 134, 247
4:1-16	234n.
4:3-5	90
4:4	248
4:4b-5a	87
4:6-7	91
4:7	83, 91n.
4:10-11	88
4:12	235
4:17	93, 101
4:17-22	93n.
4:17-24	107
4:17-26	96, 99
4:17–5:32	96-102
4:19	97
4:22	97
4:23-24	93, 97
4:25-26	93, 98, 134, 248
4:26b	51, 93
5	97, 99, 102, 103, 122, 248

5:1-3	100	11	103, 249	16:15-16	141
5:1-32	93, 96	11:1-9	71-77, 78, 88, 89	17	85, 135, 149
5:18ff.	101	11:6	74	17:1	244n.
5:22-24	101	11:7	89, 247	17:2	140
5:28-29	102	11:10	37n., 103	17:5-6	140
5:32	103	11:10-26	72	17:9	157
6-9	102	11:10-32	105, 106	17:10	157
6:1-4	102	11:24	106	17:17	94
6:5-7	83, 84, 235	11:26	104, 108	18:1	244
6:5-8	85	11:27	37n., 106	18:2	244
6:6	247	11:27-32	106	18:9	244
6:6-7	89, 234n.	11:30	108, 134, 137	18:10	244
6:8	84, 236	11:31	37n., 108	18:13-15	244
6:9	101	11:32	37, 108	18:16	244
6:11-12	89	12	37	18:17	244
6:11-13	84	12:1	130	18:18	79
6:11-22	85	12:1-3	37n.	18:22	51
6:14-16	85	12:1-49:26	133ff., 245	18:22-32	237
8:20-22	91-92	12:3	37, 79, 129	19:9	134
8:21	89, 237, 247, 257,	12:4	108	19:30-38	133n.
	313	12:5	108	20:1-17	139
8:21-22	236	12:7	130, 244n.	20:14	134
9	136	12:8	94n.	21	42
9:1	85	12:10	134	21:8-21	133, 140
9:1-17	84	12:10-20:1	138, 139	21:13-19	141
9:3-4	86	12:15	139	21:20	129
9:6	86	12:16	134	22:18	79
9:7	86	13:2	249	22:20-24	107
9:8-11	104-5	13:2-6	134	24	85
9:8-17	36n.	13:4	94n.	24:1-67	107
9:12-17	234n.	13:10	134	24:3	104n.
9:18-28	102	15	85, 135, 137, 149	24:3-4	136
9:25-27	104	15:1	160	24:35	134
10-11	72	15:1-21	135	24:37	104n.
10	103, 105, 106, 122	15:18-21	37	25:1-6	133n.
10:1	103	16	133, 136ff., 142, 148	25:12-18	133
10:1-5	103	16:1-2	137, 139	26:1	134
10:1-20	96	16:1-6	138	26:2	244n.
10:1-32	72, 102ff.	16:1-16	136ff.	26:4	79
10:5	72	16:4	139	26:5	94n.
10:6	104n., 105	16:6	139	26:6-11	139n.
10:20	72	16:7	244	26:12-13	134
10:21-31	96, 105	16:7-12	140	26:17-33	134
10:22	106	16:10	140	26:24	160, 244n.
10:24-27	106	16:11	140	26:34-35	136
10:31	72	16:13	140, 243	28:1	104n.
10:31-32	103	16:13-14	141	28:1-5	136

28:6	104n.	3:6	160, 243n.	19:5-6	20
28:8	104n.	3:7	140	19:18-24	243
28:14	79	3:7-10	151, 240	20–24	38
30:43	134	3:8	48n.	20:1-17	155, 157-64, 163
31:13	160	3:9	29n.	20:2	15n., 139
31:19-46	49n.	3:10	240	20:3	49
32:24	243, 244	3:11-14	240-42	20:3-7	48n., 245
32:28	243, 244	3:12	249	20:4-6	49
32:30	243, 244	3:13-14	234	20:6	254n.
34	135, 142	3:14	245	20:7	49, 208, 245
35:9	244n.	3:17	48n.	20:8-11	52, 54n., 161, 183
36:1-42	133	3–15	37	20:11	52, 94
37	135	3–4	49	20:13-17	162
37:25-28	142	4:1	244n.	20:22-23	48n.
38	45n., 66, 133, 136,	4:12	249	20:22-26	181, 204
	142ff.	4:15	249	20:22–23:19	180-91
38:1-6	142	4:31	152	20:22–23:33	162, 28n.
38:2	142	5	74	21:1-11	181
38:11-16	143	5:21	152	21:12-27	182
38:17-18	143	6:9	152	21:28-36	182
38:24-26	144	7–12	257	22	191
38:26	142	9:29	157	22:1-15	182
38:30	144	11:10-15	237	22:16-17	184
39–50	135	12:27	152	22:16-27	182
41:56-57	134	12:37-39	153n.	22:21	195, 28n., 30
46:27	102	12:38	174	22:21-23	87n.
48:3	244n.	13:5	48n.	22:21-24	257
50:7-11	139	14:11	152	22:21-27	184n., 185-88, 189,
		14:30-20	237		191, 250, 255
Exodus		14:31	152	22:23	139, 140
1–2	37	15	152	22:24	190
1:1–2:10	151n.	15:21	152	22:25-27	188
1:1–18:27	149-54	15:24	152	22:27	255
1:1–24:18	149ff.	16–17	38	22:28-31	183
1:7	86n., 135n., 149	16:2-12	152	23:1-3	190
1:8-13	150	16:23-29	54n.	23:1-9	183, 188-91
1:11	139	17:2	152	23:4-5	189, 190, 194n.
1:14	74	19–24	37, 49, 154-68	23:5, 9	190, 191
1:15	150	19	20, 103, 124, 129,	23:6-7	190
1:17	151		157, 207	23:7-9	190
1:20-21	150	19:1	20	23:9	26n., 28, 29-34,
1:21	151n.	19:3	45		189, 195, 196, 232,
2:25	151	19:3-6	1, 15-19, 23-24, 155		296, 302
3	245	19:4	16, 139, 159, 239n.,	23:10-11	52
3:1–4:17	94, 249		249	23:10-13	183
3:2	244	19:5	23, 18, 12, 12n., 79,	23:12	28n., 52
3:4	244		129, 156, 156n.	23:14-17	55

23:14-19	183	34:6	188n., 255	16:34	227	
23:17	55	34:6-7	239, 254, 256, 257,	17–27	192	
23:23-33	257, 259n.		257n.	17	217, 217n.	
24	12, 12n.	34:7	238, 256	17:3-4	217, 217n.	
24:1-2	166	34:9	209	17:3-7	215n.	
24:3-8	155, 164-68	34:10	212	17:10-14	86	
24:7	12, 12n., 18	34:10-26	212	17:15	197n.	
24:9-11	166, 243	34:11-16	45n., 257, 259n.	18–20	223-27	
24:10	243	34:28	157n.	18	45n., 220n., 225	
25ff.	207	35–40	49, 204, 212, 206n.	18:1-5	223-24	
25–31	204, 206n.			18:15	145n.	
25–31:11	49, 204-12	**Leviticus**		18:19	220	
25:8-9	204	1–10	169, 192	18:22	226	
26–31	38, 212	1–7	50, 215-17	18:29	220	
27–29	205	1	214n.	19–21	220n.	
29:10-42	205	1:1	213n.	19	192-97, 199, 213,	
31:12-17	52, 54, 54n., 94n.	1:9	214n.		216, 224, 226, 227,	
32–33	38	1:13	214n.		227n.	
32	155n.	1:17	214n.	19:2	17, 192, 193	
32:1	208	2:1	214n.	19:3	193n.	
32:1-6	208	2:4	214n.	19:4	193n.	
32:3	208	2:14	214n.	19:9-10	193-94, 196, 250	
32:4	209	4:2	214n.	19:9ff.	193	
32:10	176	4:13	214n.	19:10	193n.	
32:11	239	4:22	214n.	19:12	193n.	
32:11-12	238	4:27	214n.	19:14	193n.	
32:11-14	209	5	214n.	19:15	189n., 200n.	
32:12	236n., 239	5:1-4	214n.	19:15-16	193-94, 196	
32:14	234, 236, 236n.	5:6	214n.	19:15-18	250	
32:31-34	209	5:14-16	214n.	19:16	193n.	
33–34	205, 207-12, 212,	5:17-19	214n.	19:17-18	195	
	237	6	214n.	19:18	193n., 196n., 267	
33:3	48n.	6:1-7	214n.	19:21-22	193	
33:12	250	7	214n.	19:25	193n.	
33:12-13	211	7:37	214n.	19:26	225	
33:12-17	209-10	9:4	244	19:26-28	193	
33:14	250	10:1-20	132	19:28	193n.	
33:14-16	211	11–22	218-27	19:30	193n.	
33:15	250	11–15	192	19:31	193n., 225	
33:15-16	249	11	218	19:32	193n.	
33:16	250	12–15	44	19:33-34	195-97, 250	
33:18	209	15	220, 220n., 222	19:34	193n., 196, 232,	
33:18-23	246	15:16-18	220		271, 296, 302	
33:19	209	15:19-30	220	19:37	193n.	
33:20	243	15:24	220	20	45n, 20n., 224, 225	
33:23	211	15:31-33	220-23	20:6	225	
34:5-9	211	16	56, 212, 227-28	20:13	226	

20:22-27	223
20:24	48n.
20:24-26	224-25
20:26	192
20:27	225
21:18-20	147n.
23	54, 227
24:16	197n.
24:22	197n.
25:1-7	52
25:2-6	54
25:2b-7	54
25:35	197n.

Numbers

1–10	38
1:2-16	46
9:14	197n.
10	173
11:1	173, 175
11:1-3	173
11:1-15	139, 171-76
11:2	51, 94n., 174, 175, 234n.
11:4-6	174
11:4-9	173
11:5	174
11:10	173, 174, 175
11:10-15	174
11:11	94, 173, 175
11:15	173, 175
11:16-17	170
11:16-20	174
11:20	170
12–14	38
12	170, 45
12:8	243n.
13ff.	38
13:27	48n.
14	243
14:2	171n.
14:8	254n., 48n.
14:13-20	237-39
14:17	239
14:19	239
14:20	234n., 239
14:21-25	239

14:36	171n.
15:14-16	197
15:29	197n.
16:11	171n.
16:13	48
16:14	48
17:10(16:14)	171n.
19:11-13	271n.
20:9-12	170
21:4-9	170
21:7	51, 94n.
21:25	170
22–24	38
22:25	29
25:1-8	45
26:1–36:13	169
27	39, 45
31:9-18	45
32–33	177
33:1-49	170
33:50-56	257
33:51-56	259n.
36	39, 45
36:13	149

Deuteronomy

1:5	170
1:16	198n.
1:39	117n.
4	177n.
4:12	243n.
4:13	157n.
4:15-24	48n.
4:37	20n.
4:39-40	48n.
5:6-21	157n.
5:8-11	48n.
5:9-10	254n.
5:12-15	52, 54, 54n.
5:14	52, 198n.
5:15	30n., 52
6:3	48n.
6:5	39, 267
6:14-15	48n.
7	261, 261n.
7:1-3	104n.
7:1-11	258-61

7:1-26	39, 257, 259n.
7:3-4	45n.
7:4	260
7:6	157
7:6ff.	20n.
7:7	248
7:7-8	87, 256
7:9	254n.
7:16	260
7:25-26	48n.
7:26	260
9:12-21	48n.
9:20	51, 94n.
9:26	51, 94n.
10:4	157n.
10:12	199
10:12-13	199
10:12-22	39, 199, 200
10:15	20n.
10:17	194, 200, 251
10:17-19	199, 199-201
10:18	201, 250
10:19	30n.
10:20-22	199
10:21	200
11:9	48n.
11:13-15	157, 168n.
11:16-17	48n.
12–26	176n.
12:2-14	204
12:5ff.	181
12:15	217n.
12:15-27	86
12:18	20n.
12:26	20n.
12:29-32	48n.
13:1-18	48n.
14:2	157, 20n.
14:25	20n.
15	52
15:4-5	157
15:5	168n.
15:20	20n.
16:7	20n.
16:11	198n.
16:14	198n.
17:8	20n.

17:10	20n.	24:5	15n.	43	20
17:15	20n.	24:6	4n., 15n.	43:5-6	15n.
18:6	20n.			43:20-21	20
20:16-17	257	**Judges**		54:5	157
20:16-18	259n.	4:3	29n.	56:3-7	146n.
20:17	104	5:8	18	61:6	157
23:1-3	147	10:12	29n.		
24:17	30n.	17:5	49n.	**Jeremiah**	
24:17-19	199	18:4	49n.	7:1-11	216n.
26	249	18:17	49n.	7:5	91n.
26:5	133n., 149n.	18:20	49n.	18:7-8	240n.
26:5-7	249	19:16	27	22:13-17	91n.
26:6	139n.			30:11	254n.
26:7	140	**1 Samuel**		31:31-34	155n.
26:8	15n.	1:1–2:10	52	32:18-19	254n.
26:9	48n., 169n.	15:22	216n.		
26:11	198n.	19:13-16	49n.	**Lamentations**	
26:15	48n.			3:32	254n.
26:18	157	**2 Samuel**			
27:3	48n.	6:21	20n.	**Ezekiel**	
27:15-26	224n.	12:1-7	274	44:7	147n.
27:20-23	45	12:7	275		
28–30	48n.	19:36(35)	117n.	**Daniel**	
28:1-2	157, 168n.			9:4	254n.
28:15-68	39	**1 Kings**			
28:61	4	3:6	254n.	**Hosea**	
29:11	44, 198n.	3:8	20n.	1:9	20
30:10	4	11:11	157	2:23	20
30:11-20	176	12:25-33	209n.	11	17
31	12n.			11:9	17
31:6	36n.	**2 Kings**			
31:11	20n.	14:6	4n.	**Joel**	
31:11-13	12-13	22:8	3, 4n.	2:13	254n.
31:12	28, 44, 198n.	22:8–23:20	301n.		
31:16-21	48n.	22:11	3	**Amos**	
31:20	48n.	23	50n.	3:2	257n.
31:26	4	23:2-3	3	3:13	157
32:15-18	48n.			4	216n.
34:5-6	177	**Isaiah**			
34:10	39, 243n.	1	216n.	**Jonah**	
		2:6	157	3:9-10	240n.
Joshua		6:3	17	4:2	254n.
1:8	4n.	6:5	17		
3:11	157	8:17	157	**Micah**	
8:31	4n.	9:1	20	2:7	157
8:34	4n.	19:2	29n.	3:9	157
23:6	4n.	41:29	161n.	4:13	157

6:6-8	91n., 216n.	**Ruth**		22:36	267n.
		4:12	142n.	22:37-39	267
Zechariah				26:25	267n.
4:14	157	**Ezra**		26:49	267n.
6:5	157	3:1-3	198n.		
9:11	166n.	4:1-4	198	**Mark**	
		9–10	146n., 198	2:16	251n.
Psalms				2:23-28	267n.
19:7	xi, xix	**Nehemiah**		3:1-6	267n.
24:1	157	8–10	131n., 301n.	4:38	267n.
30	257	8:1-3	3	5:25-34	222n.
30:5	257	8:9	3	6:34	267
50	216n.	9:3	4n.	7:1-23	267
50:7ff.	91n.	9:17	254n.	8:11	269n.
50:12	157	9:31	254n.	9:5	267n.
51	216n.	9:36	62	9:17	267n.
51:17	215	13:3	198n.	9:38	267n.
78:10	157	13:25	198n.	10:2	269n.
86:15	254n.			10:17	267n.
89:11	157	**2 Esdras**		10:20	267n.
95:7	129n.	3:21	120n.	10:35	267n.
100:3	129n.			10:51	267n.
103:8	254n.	**Sirach**		11:21	267n.
103:17	254n.	25:24	122n.	12:9	21
103:18	157			12:14	267n.
106:45	254n.			12:15	269n.
111:4	254n.	**NEW TESTAMENT**		12:19	267n.
112:4	254n.			12:28-34	269n.
114:1	157	**Matthew**		12:30-31	267
114:2	157	5:17	4	12:32	267n.
119:105	155	5:44	212	14:45	267n.
132:12	157	7:12	267		
137	74	8:19	267n.	**Luke**	
137:8	74	9:10	25n.	5:30	251n.
145:8	254n.	9:11	25n.	6:6-11	267n.
146	68	11:19	251n.	6:28	212
146:9	68	12:1-8	267n.	6:31	267
		12:38	267n.	7:5	278
Proverbs		15:1-20	267n.	7:35	251n.
13:16	113n.	16:1	269n.	7:40	267n.
14:8	113n.	19:3	269n.	9:38	267n.
14:15-18	113n.	19:16	267n.	10:25-37	195, 268-74,
21:3	216n.	21:41	21		194n.
22:3	113n.	22:16	267n.	10:26	194n.
27:12	113n.	22:18	269n.	10:27	267
		22:24	267n.	10:31-32	271
		22:34-40	269n.	11:16	269n.

15:1	251n.	7:21-25	277n.	11:25	293n.
15:2	251n.	9:14	280	12:13	288, 297
16:15	269n.	12–14	281	14:1	283n.
20:16	21	12	282n.	14:33-35	287
24:13-35	244n.	12:1	282n.	14:33-36	285
24:27	4	12:2	282n.	14:34-36	121n.
24:44	4	12:3-8	282	15:21-22	120n.
		12:9	283	16:14	283n.
John		12:9-13	282ff.		
1:49	267n.	12:13	283, 284	**2 Corinthians**	
4:31	267n.	12:14-21	283	3:6	280
6:25	267n.	12:19	282n.	12:20	284n.
8:6	269n.	13:8-10	183, 280, 282n.,		
9:2	267n.		282ff.	**Galatians**	
11:8	267n.	14:14	218n.	3	290
				3:23, 25	280
Acts of the Apostles		**1 Corinthians**		3:26-28	296ff., 232
7:4	108n.	1:24	297	3:26-29	264, 296
10	219	5	285	3:28	287, 288, 290, 291,
10:2	278	5:1-13	282n.		297n., 298
10:28	219n.	5:11-13	282n.	5	283n.
13	4	5:13	294	5:1	282, 284
		6	285	5:2-12	284
Romans		6:9-10	284n.	5:13-14	282, 284
1	226, 226n., 267n.,	6:15-20	285n.	5:13–6:9	281
	296	7	285	5:14	282
1:1	292	7:1	286	5:16-26	284
1:16	297n.	7:1-7	285	5:21	294
1:18-32	285n., 289, 289n.,	7:1-16	285n.	5:19-23	282n., 284n.
	290n.	7:4	286	6:16	21
1:20	289	7:8ff.	288		
1:26-27	226, 289	7:17	284ff.	**Ephesians**	
1:29-31	284n.	7:19	280	2:19	401
1:32	226	7:25-40	285n.	4:2	283n.
2:9ff.	297n.	8–10	285	5:21-33	291
3:9	289, 297n.	8:8	218n.		
3:21	4	9:19	279n.	**Philippians**	
5	120n., 122, 122n.,	10:6-8	285n.	3:2	279
	124, 125	10:31	218n.		
5:12-21	119	10:32	297	**Colossians**	
5:14	119	11:1-16	285, 286-88	3:18-19	291
5:18-19	119-22, 123	11:2-3	286		
6:1ff.	140	11:2-16	285n.	**1 Thessalonians**	
6:3	280	11:7-9	286	4:1-12	282n.
7:9-13	280	11:9	286	4:9	283n.
7:12	280	11:11-14	286-87	5:12-22	282n.
7:14-16	280	11:14	290n.		

Index of Biblical References

1 Timothy

2:8-15	291
2:11-12	287
2:11-15	121ff., 123-25, 291
3:4	122n.

Titus

2:5	287, 291

James

2:17	294

1 Peter

1:1	25
2	23
2:1ff.	33
2:4	20

2:9	22, 23
2:9-10	1, 19ff., 25, 33
2:11	25
2:13	24
2:18	24
3:1	24, 291
3:1-7	291